The Trials of Rasmea Odeh

The Trials of Rasmea Odeh

How a Palestinian Guerrilla Gained and Lost
U.S. Citizenship

Steven Lubet

George Mason University Press

ISBN: 978-1-942695-25-7   hardback
ISBN: 978-1-942695-26-4   PDF
ISBN: 978-1-942695-27-1   ePUB
ISBN: 978-1-942695-28-8   Kindle

Library of Congress Cataloging-in-Publication Data
Lubet, Steven
The Trials of Rasmea Odeh: How a Palestinian Guerrilla Gained and Lost U.S. Citizenship / Steven Lubet.
1. Odeh, Rasmea   2. Citizenship, Loss of – United States   3. Trials
4. Terrorism   5. Palestinian Arabs
KF228.O34 L83 2021
Library of Congress Control Number: 2021938676

The publisher has no responsibility for the persistence or accuracy of URLs for any external or third-party internet websites referred to in this book and does not guarantee that any content on such websites is, or will remain, accurate or appropriate.

Design by Bourchier Ltd

Printed in the United States of America
First edition
Published by George Mason University Press
Fairfax, Virginia
https://publishing.gmu.edu/press/catalog/the-trials-of-rasmea-odeh/

Contents

Acknowledgments

Thanks are due to the following people for their editorial and research contributions to this project, as well as for wise counsel: Arthur Rouner, Aaron McCullough, Melissa Montemayor, Aya Neeman, Raja Anabosi, Edwar Makhoul, Jesse Bowman, Cary Nelson, Yael Sass, Zora O'Neill, Eva Derzic, Andrew Koppelman, Amanda Gvozden, Steven Calabresi, Jide Nzelibe, Jeff Rice, Maria Hawilo, Wendy Muchman, Avi Leitner, Jillian Melchior, Robert Burns, William Jacobson, John Conroy, Gretchen Rachel Hammond, David Schraub, John Conroy, James Schulz, and David Tuller.

I am also grateful to the Robert Childres Memorial Fund and the Northwestern Pritzker School of Law Faculty Research Program for financial support for this project.

Thanks on this page are not nearly enough for Linda, and I am sure she knows that, but life, much less acknowledgments, would not be complete without her.

Author's note

There are no standard English transliterations of many of the Arabic and Hebrew proper names found in this book, and spellings therefore vary in the source materials. I have consistently written "Rasmea Odeh" for the protagonist, which is the spelling used by her defense committee. Citations and quotations, however, may spell her first name Rasmieh, as in the U.S. court records, and elsewhere Rasmiya or Rasmiyeh, and her last name has occasionally been spelled Oudeh. Other examples of alternative spellings include Widad Qumri or Kaimery for one of Odeh's PFLP comrades, Yusuf or Yousuf for her father, and Sgt. Ezra Kalish or Klige for the IDF officer who transcribed her formal confession. The Arabic-speaking Israeli interrogator has been called Abu Anni, abu-Ghani, and Abuhanni, with varying capitalization and hyphenation. I have generally referred to Rasmea Odeh only by her last name, unless the context made it necessary to distinguish her from one of the many other Odehs—Aisha, Yousuf, Khalil, Yakoub—in which case I have used her first name.

Introduction

After enduring nearly four years of relentless prosecution, Rasmea Odeh finally realized it was time to give up the fight. Her case had gone through many stages since she was first indicted, including bewilderment, hope, despair, momentary triumph, and now grim resignation. Although her defense lawyers were the best in the business—experienced, resourceful, and dedicated to the cause of Palestinian liberation—they had to confront her with the hard truth. The government's case had only gotten stronger over the years, and her chances of winning were now vanishingly small. Conviction by a jury would lead to a long prison term, followed by deportation, so she had little choice but to cut her losses while she could.

Fortunately for Odeh, her attorneys had been able to negotiate a tolerable plea agreement. She had to admit lying on her visa application when she emigrated from Jordan in 1996 as well as during her U.S. citizenship examination in 2005, but she did not have to say anything at all about the underlying crime the prosecutors claimed she had intentionally concealed—her conviction and prison sentence in Israel for participating in a 1969 supermarket bombing that killed two university students.

There was only one step remaining, although it was the hardest of all. She had to stand before Judge Gershwin Drain and admit out loud everything she had been denying to her friends and supporters ever since her indictment. In many courts, such a statement would have been perfunctory—accomplished with a nod of the head or perhaps even "stipulated" by the defense attorney—but Judge Drain had never believed Odeh's earlier denials and he now wanted to hear a full acknowledgment of guilt before accepting the plea deal.

On April 25, 2017, in a courtroom packed with her friends and supporters, Odeh could not bring herself to say she was guilty, forcing Judge Drain to repeat the crucial question time and again. Only on the seventh attempt did she acknowledge intentionally concealing her conviction in Israel, and even then she balked. "I think to sign this, it makes me guilty," she said, pointing to the written plea agreement. After a long pause, the judge decided that was close enough. He pronounced Odeh guilty and recessed the hearing. Formal sentencing would come in a few months, although the outcome had already been determined. Odeh would be stripped of U.S. citizenship and deported to Jordan, but she would not have to serve any time in federal prison. In the meantime, she could return to her home in Chicago.

Outside the courthouse, 150 of Odeh's supporters gathered for a rally. The featured speaker was defense attorney Michael Deutsch, who did his best to rationalize copping a plea. Under the newly installed Trump administration, he said, there was no possibility that Odeh would get a fair trial. "A decision was made that the best result was to avoid having this woman go to prison and having to go into immigration custody and to let her leave with her head held high and with her principles and integrity intact."[1]

It was left to Rabbi Brant Rosen, of Jewish Voice for Peace (JVP), to explain how the guilty plea, after years of ardent denial, squared with keeping "her principles and integrity intact." He seized on Odeh's reluctant admission in the courtroom and addressed her directly. "What I take away today is the image of you standing before the judge, who was demanding that you say to him and the world that you are guilty and you refused, because you are not guilty."[2]

To Rosen, Odeh had been falsely accused and wrongly imprisoned in Israel, only to have her new life shattered by a vindictive prosecution in the United States for no reason other than her advocacy of Palestinian rights. She was neither a terrorist nor a perjurer in his eyes but rather a victim—tortured by Israel and persecuted in the United States—who deserved sympathy and admiration. "Your strength and your courage and your kindness and your compassion really teaches all of us how to be in this world," he said.[3]

It was a poignant moment, as the American rabbi declared the innocence of a Palestinian woman, though it was anything but a surprise. Odeh's cause had been enthusiastically embraced across the entire spectrum of the American left, from the broadest possible range of Palestinian and Muslim groups to African American, Native American, Filipino, and other minority organizations. She was one of four leaders of the 2017 Women's Strike and an invited speaker when the Puerto Rican nationalist Oscar López Rivera was released from prison. Fundraisers were held on her behalf in cities across the country, and when a California restaurant displayed her mural-sized portrait, it garnered a favorable review in the Sunday travel section of the *New York Times*. According to a JVP announcement, Odeh had "survived decades of Israeli and US government persecution and oppression" and the accusations against her stemmed "from a context of long-standing anti-Palestinian and anti-Muslim persecution by both the Israeli state and the United States."[4]

Most of Odeh's allies were no doubt sincere, but much of the story was untrue. She had indeed participated in the Jerusalem bombing that took two lives in 1969, and she had lied about it repeatedly in order to obtain U.S. citizenship. Her defense to the charge of immigration fraud, which had drawn many progressives and leftists to her cause, was based on false denials, and ultimately rested on a contrived theory of suppressed memory that had virtually been invented for her benefit.

None of this mattered to Odeh's supporters and contributors, for whom the case was an important political vehicle for "putting Israel on trial," in addition to vindicating Odeh herself.[5] No amount of evidence would convince them that she had committed the underlying offense in Israel or that she had intentionally concealed her background on her visa and citizenship applications. But as I have documented—based on extensive research, including sources that were never discovered by either the prosecution or defense—the evidence against Odeh is clear and powerful.

* * *

Article I, section 8 of the U.S. Constitution grants Congress the authority to enact a "uniform Rule of Naturalization," which implicitly includes the power of denaturalization in appropriate circumstances. Even so, there was no statutory basis for denaturalization until Congress passed the Immigration Act of 1906, which provided for "setting aside and canceling the certificate of citizenship on the ground of fraud or on the ground that such certificate of citizenship was illegally procured."[6] Similar provisions have remained in the law through revisions in 1940 and 1990. The possibility of a criminal penalty, in addition to revocation of citizenship, was added in 1948 and amended in 1994 and 1996. The current maximum for most offenses is ten years' imprisonment (with greater penalties for crimes committed to facilitate international terrorism or drug trafficking). Criminal prosecutions have been relatively uncommon, and denaturalization cases have mostly been pursued only under the civil provision.

The initiation of denaturalization proceedings involved political judgments right from the start, beginning with the case against the prominent anarchist Emma Goldman in 1909. The proceeding was complex, illustrating how far the government would go to remove "Red Emma" from the country. The actual defendant was her ex-husband Jacob Kersner, through whom Goldman had been naturalized upon their marriage many years earlier. When Kersner's citizenship was revoked on a technicality—at a hearing of which Goldman had no official notice, and in which she had no right to participate—Goldman's was invalidated as well. The dubiousness of the proceeding caused some second thoughts in government circles, and Goldman was not actually deported until December 1919, after having spent two years in prison for espionage during World War I.[7]

For over one hundred years, denaturalization proceedings have been instituted in waves, with the numbers rising and falling as the political climate shifted in the United States. The high points occurred in the years of the Red Scare, during and immediately after World War I, again during World War II, this time directed at Nazi sympathizers in the German American Bund, and of course in the McCarthy era. In the peak years, there were as many as a thousand denaturalizations annually.[8]

Over twenty-two thousand Americans were denaturalized in the twentieth century, nearly all of them in civil proceedings, most for reasons that would not be permissible today. In a series of decisions culminating in 1968, the U.S. Supreme Court restricted the allowable bases for denaturalization. These had once included extended return to one's native land, a woman's marriage to a foreign citizen, enlistment in a foreign army or voting in a foreign election, or post-naturalization conduct, including speech, organizational membership, or petition-signing, that was interpreted as proof of disloyalty at the time citizenship was acquired.[9]

Today, denaturalization may be sought only for "illegal procurement," including fraud or misrepresentation, or in the case of individuals who have committed gross violations of human rights.[10] The latter provision has been invoked in the cases of alleged Nazi war criminals, leading to at least eighty-six denaturalizations.[11]

As recently as 2013, a leading authority on citizenship law opined that denaturalization had "largely become a thing of the past," retaining symbolic function while leaving all naturalized citizens "secure in America except those who have committed the very worst crimes against their fellow human beings."[12] He spoke too soon.

In late 2018, the Trump administration announced the creation of a task force—called "Operation Second Look"—to review the applications of as many as seven hundred thousand naturalized citizens, using newly digitized data to locate discrepancies between their naturalization applications and other records.[13] The Justice Department recently sought funding to hire as many as three hundred new attorneys for immigration fraud investigations, including Operation Second Look. In December 2018, the *New York Times* reported that the U.S. Citizenship and Immigration Service had flagged 2,500 "likely targets for denaturalization," of whom 167 had already been referred for the institution of civil proceedings. In toto, annual denaturalization filings doubled from 2016 to 2018.[14]

Operation Second Look reflected the political stance of the Trump administration, embodying the president's campaign promise to pursue a policy of "zero tolerance" regarding immigration offenses, whatever the cost to the affected individuals. It is unlikely to be continued in the same unforgiving form under President Biden, who has taken a much more welcoming approach to immigration. "We have always focused on those who have done something terrible," a former Democratic immigration official explained to the *New York Times.* Under the Trump policy, however, authorities appeared to be "going after people who did nothing of note, or whose wrong caused no harm."[15]

The Odeh case, which was initiated during the Obama administration, stands apart from Operation Second Look's civil cases as an exemplar of an earlier class of criminal prosecutions. It is based on the alleged concealment of serious crimes rather than the "ordinary cases" based on documentary inconsistencies in addresses, names, or marital status.[16] Nonetheless, Odeh's attorneys and supporters claimed that the case against her was also driven by political concerns. Her lead counsel described it as "part of a campaign to suppress the Palestinian people living in the U.S. who want to educate U.S. people about the occupation and the attacks on Gaza, and the attacks on the Palestinian people."[17]

There is no question that the Odeh case, by its very nature, was deeply entangled in the contentious politics of the Middle East. It would be impossible to prosecute an alleged Palestinian terrorist without raising issues of motive and culpability, in addition to innocence or guilt, that will be explored in the following chapters.

*   *   *

Although sentenced to two life terms in prison for her role in the Jerusalem supermarket bombing and another bombing at the British consulate, Odeh was released in a prisoner exchange with the Popular Front for the Liberation of Palestine (PFLP) on March 14, 1979. Three months later she was in Geneva, testifying about her ill-treatment in Israel before a session of the U.N. Special Committee investigating human rights violations in the occupied territories.

Within the first minutes of her testimony, Odeh began lying about her participation in the PFLP's guerrilla operations. She told the committee that she had never had explosives in her home, that she knew nothing about Palestinian commandos or resistance, and that she had no involvement in the Jerusalem bombings or other "military operations."[18] As we will see, all of these assertions were untrue and have been flatly contradicted by Odeh's own words in later interviews as well as by other participants in the bombing.

Shortly after appearing in Geneva, when she was living in Beirut, Odeh was interviewed by the Lebanese journalist Soraya Antonius, to whom she described her involvement with the PFLP and her commitment to "military action," thus contradicting her own sworn testimony. Odeh also admitted her part in the British consulate operation:

> We had placed a bomb there to protest Britain's decision to furnish arms to Israel. Actually we placed two bombs, the first was found before it went off so we placed another.[19]
>
> I didn't do it for money, I was trying to defend my home, and that real honor lay in fighting and rejecting the occupation of our country.[20]

In a 1990 interview with the American academic Amal Kawar, conducted in Amman, Jordan, Odeh acknowledged having been among the women "active first as guerrillas," and she identified herself as a member of the PFLP Central Committee.[21]

In addition, one of Odeh's codefendants has repeatedly named her as among the bombing conspirators. In a 2004 Palestinian documentary titled *Women in Struggle*, Aisha Odeh (no relation to Rasmea) admitted placing the lethal bomb in the Jerusalem supermarket and explained that she had participated in the implementation rather than planning. "Rasmiyeh Oudeh was more involved than I was," she said. "I placed the bombs," but Rasmea "scouted the location and chose the targets." With Rasmea sitting next to her and smiling, Aisha thanked her for "dragging me into military work."[22] Buthina Canaan Khoury, the film maker who conducted the joint interview, recognized that Rasmea had acknowledged her involvement in the bombing, saying, "She was a Palestinian at that time and she acted like the rest of the Palestinians would act."[23] *Women in Struggle* was widely distributed, winning awards at the San Diego Film Festival and the Al Ismailia Film Festival in Egypt.[24]

More recently, in a 2013 interview on Palestine television, Aisha described her "armed activity" as a PFLP operative and named Rasmea as a member of the cell that carried out "an operation in western Jerusalem" in February of 1969, in which "two were killed" and many wounded.[25] Aisha was even more specific in her Arabic-language memoir, published in Amman, Jordan, explaining how she and Rasmea assembled the bombs with the assistance of an "explosives expert" at Rasmea's house in al-Bireh.[26]

Another of the bombing conspirators who appeared in *Women in Struggle*, Rasheida Obeideh, was never apprehended by the Israelis, having successfully crossed into Jordan before she could be arrested. In 1993, Obeideh was interviewed in an Arabic-language video about Palestinian women, in which she described organizing cells and collecting weapons to resist the Israeli occupation. Recognizing that some of their planning had been haphazard, she explained that she and her colleagues "did not have the patience" to delay "military attacks." Regarding "the operation on the super sol in Jerusalem," Obeideh said "me and my friends Aisha and Rasmieh participated in the one operation."[27]

Finally, Odeh's own father, Yousuf Odeh, who was a naturalized American citizen, admitted to a U.S. consular officer that he had been "present when police found explosives" in her bedroom.[28]

For European and American audiences, Rasmea Odeh has presented herself as the innocent victim of an Israeli frame-up, in which a false confession was extracted by torture. There is no doubt that she was fiercely brutalized by her interrogators, leading to a confession that would not be admissible in American courts. But inadmissibility does not change the reality of her participation in the deadly bombing. Confessions may be coerced from the innocent and guilty alike, and Odeh has freely admitted her participation in the supermarket bombing—although only when speaking Arabic.

And why not? In most of the Arab world, armed struggle against Israel is a matter of pride, rather than something to be concealed. As one of the first young women to engage in guerrilla operations against the occupation of her homeland, Odeh is therefore someone to be celebrated, as indeed she has been in the Arabic press. Upon her arrival in Jordan, following deportation from the United States, the Arabic language news site *Arab 48* reported that "the struggler Rasmea Odeh" had conducted an operation "in the heart of Jerusalem" that resulted in killing two Israelis and injuring nine others. A release from the Palestine Information Center also praised Odeh as having resisted the occupation "with all of her power and determination," including participation in "the military resistance" and involvement, with Aisha Odeh, in the Jerusalem bombing.[29]

Odeh's false assertions of innocence served her well as both public relations and legal strategy. Israel's security services could be condemned even more when shown using violent interrogation techniques on innocent civilians chosen at random. Likewise, her defense to the U.S. charges of immigration fraud could be made more convincing, and attract more popular support, when she was portrayed as a torture victim rather than a guerrilla operative. In large part, the stratagems were successful. The U.N. Special Committee members asked Odeh no questions about her role in the bombing, and numerous community organizations rallied to her side during the U.S. prosecution, all of them assuming that her Israeli conviction had been a complete miscarriage of justice. In 2017, Odeh was the keynote speaker at the national membership meeting of JVP, where she was applauded as a symbol of "Palestinian resilience" while her "false confession" was dismissed as purely the result of Israeli coercion.[30]

The full story of Rasmea Odeh, however, requires a greater recognition of the actual facts. Whether regarded as a terrorist or freedom fighter, and despite how cruelly she was treated by her Israeli interrogators, Odeh was undoubtedly a participant in the 1969 bombing operation that took two lives in Jerusalem.

*   *   *

In 1995, Odeh was living in Jordan, enjoying what she later called "the best period in my life." As she recalled, "I have two jobs, I have a house, I have a car, I have a bank account, and I was happy there."[31] Unfortunately, her father had developed a malignancy and needed to be treated in the United States. Odeh's brother Mustafa, who was living in Stockbridge, Michigan, asked her to move there to take care of their father. As the only unmarried daughter, she agreed.[32]

Odeh applied for an immigrant visa at the U.S. embassy in Amman, providing multiple untruthful answers on the form. Asked to list "all places you have lived for six months or longer," her only answer was Amman, Jordan, omitting her lengthy imprisonment in Israel and the four years she had spent in Lebanon. Most significantly, she denied that she had ever been convicted of "offenses for which the aggregate sentences were 5 years or more," despite her two life sentences for murder and ten years of actual imprisonment.[33]

No one questioned or challenged Odeh's answers. Her visa was issued and she arrived in the United States on April 18, 1995, ready to begin a new life that would eventually lead to citizenship. Her application remained on file, but her false statements would not be discovered for almost twenty years.

1   Palestine

Rasmea Yousuf Odeh has led a difficult life of oppression and dislocation, beginning in infancy when her family was exiled from the village of Lifta on the western outskirts of Jerusalem. Odeh would later say that they had fled following the "massacres and rapes" in the neighboring village of Deir Yassin in April 1948,[1] but in fact the Palestinian women and children of Lifta had been evacuated several months earlier, in advance of the anticipated fighting over the crucial road connecting Jerusalem to Tel Aviv. It is understandable that family lore would conflate the traumatic events of Israel's War of Independence and the ensuing Palestinian Nakba—and a child would have had no reason to ask questions—but the Lifta story is emblematic of the ways in which myth and reality would eventually become inseparable in the narrative of Odeh's life.

As in many Arab villages, life in Lifta was idyllic in the years before 1948. Situated on a slope, it was thought to be the site of the biblical Mei Niftoach, mentioned in the Book of Joshua. Its four hundred houses, built of limestone from a local quarry, wound past a central square featuring a spring-fed well and fecund mulberry, almond, fig, and cherry trees, where people would gather on warm evenings for storytelling, sports and games, and the occasional wedding.[2]

Lifta's population of around 2,500 made it one of the two largest communities in the area west of Jerusalem. Blessed with "rich soil and a high rainfall," in contrast to the regions to the north and east, the village's terraced hills were covered with olive and lemon trees, and its extensive fields were devoted to wheat, barley, vegetables, and grapes. Most Liftawis worked in agriculture, but there were also artisans, merchants, laborers, and teachers.[3]

The British army wrested Jerusalem from the Ottoman Empire in 1917, the same year that the Balfour Declaration committed the British Empire to the establishment of a "national home" for the Jewish people in Palestine. A wave of Jewish immigration followed, known among Zionists as the Third Aliya, as refugees fled the disruptions of World War I and the chaos of the Russian Revolution, both of which contributed to an outbreak of increasingly deadly pogroms.

The League of Nations established the British Mandate for Palestine in 1922, fulfilling the promise of the Balfour Declaration.[4] Jewish immigrants and British administration brought considerable economic activity to Palestine. A lucrative quarry made Lifta a "vital hub for the growing construction industry," as the Arab villages expanded eastward and Jerusalem's increasing Jewish population spread toward the west along newly "improved roads and pavements."[5] Eventually, Lifta became "effectively folded" into metropolitan Jerusalem, and all but "physically intertwined" with several growing Jewish neighborhoods.[6]

Relations between Arabs and Jews were tense but mostly peaceful, until suddenly they were not. In late August 1929, fighting erupted as Jews and Arabs contended for access to Jerusalem's holiest and most contested site—al-Buraq for Muslims and the Western Wall (then known as the Wailing Wall) for Jews. The violence eventually spread throughout Jerusalem and across Palestine as Muslims attacked Jewish homes, schools, and shops, killing at least 133 Jews and injuring hundreds more. The British military responded forcefully, killing 116 Arabs.[7]

A few days before the outbreak at the holy sites, one of Lifta's "wealthy landowners" had killed a Jew suspected of trespassing, which may have contributed to the village's reputation among the British authorities as the home of "trouble makers" and "a place of not very good repute . . . from a Police point of view."[8] More alarmingly, a group of about one hundred men from Lifta, under the leadership of their apparent mukhtar, attacked Jews in the Mahane Yehuda neighborhood, raking them with rifle and pistol fire and causing at least one death, until they were driven off by the British police.

Similar attacks continued, with Liftawis leading an assault on the Jewish suburb of Beit HaKerem. British reports refer to the "disruptive Arabs of Lifta," calling it "as bad a village as there was around Jerusalem."[9] The violence was worse in Hebron and Safed, where most of the killings occurred, but the Liftawis' role in what came to be called the Buraq Revolt could not soon be forgotten.

* * *

In the late 1940s, Lifta had a mosque, an elementary school for boys and girls, a bus station, a small shopping district with two coffeehouses, and a social club, as well as a shrine to the rebel Shaykh Qasim al-Ahmad, who had led an unsuccessful uprising against Egypt in 1834.[10]

The Odeh home was comfortable and the family relatively prosperous. Yousuf Odeh, Rasmea's father, was a trader, or merchant, with "a lot of property" and her extended family had "homes and a lot of land." But as Odeh later explained in a 2013 interview, "when the Zionists occupied Palestine . . . we lost everything."[11]

In November 1947, against the backdrop of the Holocaust and the near destruction of European Jewry, the United Nations voted to partition British Mandatory Palestine into independent Jewish and Arab states.[12] What followed was, in the words of the pro-Palestinian scholar Michael Palumbo, an "irrepressible conflict," in which the Palestinian Arab Higher Command vowed that the establishment of a Jewish state was to be "resisted by force."[13]

The fighting began almost immediately, as Arab forces attempted to deprive the Jewish community in Jerusalem of food, arms, and other supplies from Tel Aviv. To the misfortune of Lifta's residents, the village was located along the main road between Tel Aviv and Jerusalem, which was destined to be heavily contested. Jerusalem's defenders, acutely aware of the 1929 attacks, saw Lifta and the adjacent villages as obvious choke points that had to be secured.[14] As early as November 30, Palestinian families recognized the danger and began leaving the villages west of Jerusalem as "preparatory to [military] operations on the part of the Arabs."[15]

Armed attacks on Jewish-owned shops and buses began on December 1, leading to retaliation by the Haganah, antecedent of the Israel Defense Forces (IDF), as well as by the more extreme paramilitaries IZL and Lehi.[16] On December 2, the mukhtar of Lifta was warned that "the village would be bombed" if it was used as a staging point for attacks on Jews. Further evacuations, by truck and on foot, began two days later. According to Israeli historian

Benny Morris, the inhabitants of Lifta were instructed by the Arab authorities to send away their women and children "in order to make room for incoming militiamen."[17] The Liftawis believed they would be leaving only temporarily, perhaps even "just for a day," and therefore took no possessions with them.[18]

By mid-December, Arab snipers in Lifta were harassing traffic on the Jerusalem–Tel Aviv road, leading first to warnings and then to returned fire from IZL forces. The evacuation of families continued, while "armed irregulars and Arab Legionnaires" held their positions along the road. Not everyone in Lifta was enthusiastic about seeing their village turned into an armed camp and their homes used to attack Jews, but there was little the elders could do to stop the "daily exchanges of fire."

As with almost everything connected to the war, there are conflicting accounts of the escalation in and around Lifta, but one thing seems certain. On December 27, Jewish paramilitaries destroyed a gasoline station on the outskirts of Lifta, which they believed had been the source of sniper fire and whose owner had been providing the Arab militia with reports on the passage of Jewish convoys. Retaliation came quickly in the form of a grenade attack on a Jewish bus, leading in turn to a counterattack on a Lifta coffeehouse in which six Arab men were killed. The fighting spurred further evacuations. By the beginning of January there were almost no Palestinian civilians left in Lifta, and even the young men had relocated to Ramallah by early February.[19]

Fighting along the Jerusalem road continued and intensified, culminating on April 9, 1948, with the attack on Deir Yassin by the paramilitaries IZL and Lehi, in which scores of unarmed Palestinians—reports range well upward from one hundred—were slaughtered. According to a later investigation by the Haganah Intelligence Service, "The conquest of the village was carried out with great cruelty. Whole families—women, old people, children—were killed" and young women were raped.[20] The resulting panic led to even greater flight by Palestinian civilians, who took refuge behind Jordanian lines, eventually numbering in the hundreds of thousands.[21]

Deir Yassin lay only slightly south of Lifta, linked by a dirt path and so close that the two villages shared a school until 1943,[22] but the Lifta civilians were already safely in Ramallah by the time of the massacre. Odeh's family would have been in the initial wave of refugees, whose relatively orderly evacuation by truck, expected to be temporary, was at the urging of Arab authorities rather than in terrified response to the Deir Yassin atrocities or in the "expulsions at gunpoint" that took place a few months later.[23] But the result was the same. As early as February 7, 1948, David Ben-Gurion remarked that the entryway to Jerusalem, including the village of Lifta, had been cleared of Arabs who would never be allowed to return.[24]

Like exiles the world over, former residents of Lifta recalled their lost home as a paradise. The village must have had its share of troubles, but those paled beside the hardships encountered in Ramallah, where the Odeh family and many others found themselves. The distance between Lifta and Ramallah is under fifteen miles and could be traveled in less than a day, even on the jammed and pitted roads encountered by the refugees in 1948. Eventually separated by an armistice line between Israel and Jordan, both locales had been part of the British Mandate for Palestine and before that the Ottoman Sanjak of Jerusalem. Ethnically and linguistically, the populations were virtually identical—Odeh's father had been born in Ramallah—but the Lifta refugees nonetheless encountered a world apart.

Before 1948, in the years of the British Mandate, Ramallah and its twin town of al-Bireh comprised a thriving market and cultural center with a combined population of about eight thousand. The sudden influx of refugees, many of whom arrived destitute, more than tripled the population within a matter of months,[25] creating a humanitarian crisis that the municipal authorities, and later the Jordanians, were ill-equipped to handle. Employment was scarce and housing all but non-existent, requiring the newcomers to crowd into tents and scavenge for food. At first, the Lifta refugees complained that the locals were "mocking them" for their misfortune.[26] With the end of hostilities in April 1949, and the subsequent Jordanian annexation of the West Bank, resumed a semblance of normality.

* * *

Only an infant when her family fled Lifta, Rasmea Odeh came of age in an environment overwhelmed with refugees and struggling to adjust to a new reality. At first, her extended family of eighteen—"grandparents, uncles, aunts, children"—squeezed into a tent. Her father, having been a trader in Lifta, "tried to scrape together a living by selling small goods in the streets," and her uncle also "earned some money selling materials but it wasn't enough."[27] Even the basic necessities of life were lacking. Supplies from the United Nations Relief and Works Agency for Palestine (UNRWA) did not last through the month, and the children sometimes had to search through garbage dumps for food.[28] Some family members "tried to return to Lifta to retrieve a few household goods," but were unable to cross the militarized armistice line. Other Palestinians, Odeh said in a 1980 interview, had been "killed trying to recover their possessions."[29]

Odeh has said that she remembers little of her childhood, "except for the suffering."[30] She saw her mother's weeping and asked why she cried all the time. "I cry because the Jews came from every corner of the earth and took everything we had and now we have nothing to live on" was the answer.[31] In the early 1950s, Odeh's father moved to the United States, where he found work in a Michigan factory and eventually became a naturalized citizen. His remittances brought some financial stability to the family. They were able to rent a small two-room apartment for the large extended family while still sometimes turning to the UNRWA.

Even then, Odeh would ask, "Why, mother, do we not have a house like our neighbors?" Her mother would reply that they owned a house more beautiful than the others, but they had to leave it and could not go back. "We were concerned for your safety; we protected you from danger."[32]

As a young child, Odeh did not understand where her father had gone, even when she was told he was in America. "I missed my father," she said, and "I kept looking for the place where he was hidden." According to Odeh's family, she used to get lost in the streets of Ramallah, asking people "Where is America? I'm looking for America and can't find it." That was the beginning of her political awareness:

> To my child's understanding the return of my father was linked to the return of
> Palestine—one was gone because the other was lost. I never lived my childhood
> but spent my time with adults, asking them how to get back Palestine. And I
> saw everyone else living in the same conditions so I felt that if we were all in the
> same state then we had to solve the problem.[33]

Odeh's solution was to begin attending underground Communist meetings, which she claims to have done at age twelve, in opposition to the Jordanian government and as a way of working "for the return of Palestine." A year later, she joined the Arab Nationalist Movement (ANM), founded in Beirut by George Habash and Wadi Haddad in 1958, and a predecessor to the Popular

Front for the Liberation of Palestine (PFLP). There was a strong current of anti-Semitism in the early ANM, evidenced by its bombing of a Beirut synagogue, and even writers sympathetic to Habash have acknowledged his "anti-Jewish" stance.[34]

According to Odeh's 1980 interview with a sympathetic Lebanese journalist, she believed that the ANM was the "political party that was most concerned with the problem" of Palestine.[35] By the early 1960s the ANM had embarked on "commando operations" and the "creation of a clandestine infrastructure complete with arms caches," intended to advance "Palestinian armed struggle in coordination with Arab revolutionary action," eventually to be directed at reactionary Arab regimes in addition to Israel.[36] It is not clear how much of this Odeh understood as a young teenager, but she knew enough to keep her activities, illegal under Jordanian law, hidden from her family. That was "quite easy," she later explained, "because my mother was alone and had six children to look after."[37]

In 1964, Yousuf Odeh returned from the United States.[38] He had been severely injured in the factory where he was working, and the proceeds from the insurance settlement, together with savings from his brother Khalil, were sufficient to purchase a home in al-Bireh for the extended family.[39] Odeh's mother wore a traditional Palestinian dress and hijab, but contemporary photographs of Rasmea, including one in her high school yearbook, show her in fashionable western clothing with well-styled, uncovered hair. Rasmea did well in school, while maintaining her affiliations with the Communists and ANM, both of which were assertively secular.

In May 1967, Egypt took aggressive action against Israel, evicting U.N. peacekeepers from the Sinai Peninsula and blockading the Straits of Tiran from use by Israeli shipping. The latter was a *casus belli* for the Israelis. On June 5, just as Odeh was completing her high school exams, the Six-Day War began when the Israeli Air Force launched simultaneous attacks on Egyptian and Syrian air bases, destroying most of their planes on the ground. After some hesitation, in the unrealized hope that Jordan would not join the fighting, Israeli ground troops occupied Ramallah the next day and soon took over the entire West Bank.[40]

Odeh's experience of the war was horrific and life-changing. Her father had gone to Jericho, where the climate was said to be better for his health, and the family set out on foot to join him. "We've always been separated in life," said her mother, "at least let's die together." Walking for forty-eight hours "through the hills and through the field [sic]," Odeh was horrified to see the many "corpses burnt by napalm" and the "charred bodies, so appallingly burnt we couldn't tell if they were civilian or military." After twenty days in Jericho, they walked back to Ramallah to find that their home had been damaged by an artillery shell and then "looted by Israeli soldiers" who had taken everything of value.[41]

The Israeli conquest displaced hundreds of thousands of Palestinians, including many who were already refugees from 1948. Those who remained in Ramallah and the West Bank despised the occupation. Like all military occupations, it depended, in the words of Morris, "on brute force, repression and fear, collaboration and treachery, beatings and torture chambers, and daily intimidation, humiliation, and manipulation." Resistance began almost immediately in the form of stone-throwing demonstrations and strikes, which were harshly suppressed by the Israeli forces. The "clear lesson" for the Palestinians was that civil disobedience would be quickly crushed, and "the only real option was armed struggle."[42]

Odeh took that lesson to heart. She joined the stone throwing, "to protest against the desecration of mosques and against the looting," but she had already become "convinced that military action was more important than social or political work" as the means of Palestinian liberation.[43] The routed Jordanian army had "left behind large stocks of weapons and ammunition" that were quickly claimed by would-be insurgents who stashed them in "makeshift caches dug in gardens and courtyards, in nearby caves, and in the fields." Yet more arms were smuggled into the West Bank from Jordan, replacing supplies as quickly as the Israelis could discover and destroy them.[44]

Odeh was determined to "take part in the struggle," which at first involved getting "theoretical—visual—training" in weapons use. She "wanted to actually fire a gun, not just study diagrams of firing mechanisms," but that would have required going abroad to meet up with one of the guerrilla organizations. Her conservative parents, however, were protective of their daughters, and they refused, for the time, to allow her to leave.[45]

Meanwhile, Palestinian exiles began to infiltrate the West Bank and organize resistance. Yasser Arafat himself traveled incognito across the West Bank on a motor scooter, establishing cells in Nablus and Ramallah.[46] Demonstrations continued through the summer and into the fall, as well as "dozens of sabotage and other attacks against Israeli targets."[47] Israeli reprisals were swift and brutal, including arrests, beatings, searches, and house demolitions. By the end of 1967, over 1,100 Palestinians had been detained without trial, and at least two hundred had been killed by the military.[48] Arafat's hoped-for popular uprising collapsed, which only intensified the frustration, resentment, and anger of Palestinian youth. "The streets were full of Israelis," Odeh recalled, "swaggering, looking as though they owned the place." She and her friends stood "glaring at them, hate showing in our eyes," but there was little they could do when the Israeli soldiers "waved us off with their submachineguns."[49]

Odeh finally overcame her parents' objections by applying to medical school at the al-Arabia University in Beirut.[50] According to her 1980 interview, she had to "cultivate" an informer in order to get her travel permit. The West Bank was shot through with informants and collaborators, including municipal officials who had been approved by the Israeli military authorities, so it is quite understandable that Odeh sought the help of someone with contacts in the military government—what Americans call clout and Israelis call "protekzia." On the other hand, Israel was, in the early years, heavily invested in portraying the occupation as benign, so obtaining a study permit may not have been as complicated as Odeh believed.

In any case, Odeh took advantage of her time in Beirut, and not only for education. She made what she thought was surreptitious contact with guerrilla leaders in Amman and Beirut,[51] including Dr. Haddad, a physician who had been born in Safed, in the Galilee, and exiled during the 1948 war. Haddad was one of the founders of the ANM, which Odeh had joined in Ramallah. On December 11, 1967, around the time he was meeting with Odeh, Haddad and Habash, another Beirut-trained physician, joined with several other guerrilla organizations—Heroes of the Return and Youth of Revenge—to form the PFLP.[52] From the beginning, the PFLP was "forthrightly Marxist" and dedicated to "revolutionary violence" against Zionism as the only path to Palestinian liberation.[53] As Morris put it, the PFLP "was to lead the field in international terrorism."[54]

Odeh was living in Lebanon at the time of her 1980 interview by Soraya Antonius, having only recently been released from prison in Israel. It was long before she had any thought of moving to the United States, and she was not reticent about her relationship to Haddad, whom she described as "responsible for military affairs in the PFLP."[55] In that role, Haddad was, as the

New York Times put it, "the strategist behind the Palestinian guerrilla movement's hijacking of airliners."[56] Haddad was known to be responsible for the first such hijacking, of an El Al flight in July 1968, as well as the spectacular commandeering of four planes—all of which were eventually blown up on the ground—in the 1972 operation that came to be known as Black September. He is thought to have a hand in planning numerous other hijackings, including a Lufthansa flight in October 1977, when he was already terminally ill, and, perhaps most memorably, the hijacking of an Air France plane to Uganda in 1976, which resulted in the successful Israeli rescue mission at the Entebbe Airport.

All of that was in the future, however, when Haddad met with Odeh at his Beirut headquarters. At the time, he was more interested in recruiting young militants for "small-scale, well-planned operations" in Israel and the West Bank.[57]

Odeh's meeting with Haddad appears to have been observed by Israeli agents in Beirut, who made note of her associations and activities.[58] Returning to the West Bank after her first year at the university, Odeh did not suspect that she had been under surveillance. Her naïveté—or was it recklessness?—would soon have a profound impact on her life and family.

2 Resistance

When Rasmea Odeh returned to Ramallah in 1968, at the end of her academic year in Beirut, she was already committed to the PFLP, although not yet ready to engage in what she described as "military work." That would come soon enough. In the meantime, she devoted herself to aboveground "social services type of work in which I was trying to find food and clothing and homes" for refugees who had been "forced out of their homes into other towns and other villages but not necessarily outside of Palestine."[1] She helped organize the local Girl Guides and worked on literacy projects with her (again, unrelated) friend Aisha Odeh.[2]

Odeh devoted much of her energy to "the women's problem" within her own society. She could not tolerate the way women were treated, "forbidden to come and go, to act freely, to marry as she pleases; just an armchair for men." According to her "Marxist principles," Odeh believed that traditional "religion gave a false understanding of reality [that impeded] women's liberation."[3] She and her PFLP colleagues refused to accept the traditional status of women and were instead determined to "awaken her awareness and will to struggle, and to give her the assurance that she has the same gifts as men and can be strong and active."[4]

Odeh had managed to go to high school and then university over the objections of an older generation. Her grandfather believed that only her male cousins should go to school, forcing Odeh "to challenge him." As she explained, "I used to walk two to three kilometers to school because I knew he wouldn't give me money for the bus."[5] But even obtaining formal education was not enough for a Palestinian woman because "my father can still marry me off as he chooses." An educated woman could "finish school and return home and do nothing because there aren't many job opportunities for women, and because they are frightened that people may talk about them."[6] In contrast, Odeh herself "always wanted to prove that women are equal to or better than men."[7] Ironically, the Israeli occupation brought a new social role for Palestinian women:

> The Israeli didn't differentiate between the sexes when he shot at demonstrators, or when he searched a house, or when he made an arrest. So danger changed the girls. Then the economic situation—inflation, unemployment—affected everyone. Twelve-year-old children began leaving school to help their fathers earn enough to [support] their families. Men were no longer the only breadwinners.[8]

The result was an "enormous change" in women's situation in the West Bank, and the "reality of the occupation strengthened their resolve." Reacting to the "daily danger," many women "stopped thinking of how to please men, and began to think of building social structures, of fighting the occupier, of the future." At first, "men opposed this state of affairs, but then they were forced to accept it."[9]

Women's activism played an essential part in resisting the Israeli occupation, both aboveground and in military work. As one Palestinian writer put it, women "took the lead in the early years of the post-1967 era while the national will was debilitated." One of the first mass anti-occupation demonstrations was led by women in Jerusalem, only to be forcibly dispersed by Israeli police.[10]

The legendary Abu Iyad, a founder of the Palestine Liberation Organization (PLO) and second-in-command to Yasser Arafat, acknowledged the "daring and self-sacrifice" of female operatives, who "won the admiration of everyone, even those who looked down on them." Young women, and even schoolgirls, were on the front lines of anti-occupation demonstrations. And when the demonstrations turned violent, "they were the first to fight back when the police attacked."[11]

Women of all ages were able to operate an intelligence network, and they were especially valuable as couriers and smugglers. Their "voluminous traditional clothing" could hide weapons—including stones, Molotov cocktails, and firearms—as well as leaflets, funds, and the "illegal Palestinian flag." Israeli soldiers were well aware that women were the "chief weapon carriers," but their searches would draw "angry mob[s] of Palestinian Muslim men, outraged that their women were being physically violated."[12]

In time, the female fighters overcame "the prevailing mentality in a conservative society." Thus, "one of the side effects of the Resistance was to promote the emancipation of women, and as a corollary, men's liberation from fossilized traditions."[13]

There was never a time when the Palestinian population acquiesced in the occupation of the West Bank. Guerrilla operations included frequent attacks on Israeli military personnel and occasionally civilian targets. These early attempts to inspire a popular rebellion, however, were thwarted by the oppressive measures adopted by the Israeli military, which included the roundup of "network after network" of suspected militants, over one thousand of whom were imprisoned by the end of 1967.[14] The Israeli dragnet almost succeeded in capturing Arafat, raiding his Ramallah headquarters only to find he had escaped scant hours earlier, leaving a still boiling teakettle behind.[15] Even acts of civil disobedience were treated harshly, as one senior Israeli military official condescendingly explained, "The Arabs are intimidated by force, and a firm hand will settle them down."[16]

The "firm hand policy" may have been successful in the short term but it ultimately caused only bitter resentment. As the Israeli writer Rafik Halabi noted, the unyielding repression served to ignite tempers throughout the occupied territories. House demolitions, for example, "might have deterred property owners, but it infuriated the young people," contributing to a tense situation that was literally destined to explode.[17]

*   *   *

In late 1967, George Habash and Wadi Haddad founded the PFLP, espousing Marxist–Leninist revolution throughout the Arab world and dedicated to intensifying the armed struggle against Israel. The PFLP immediately began recruiting operatives among "students, young intellectuals, and white-collar professionals," not only to conduct guerrilla operations but also to mobilize the "Palestinian population to participate in protest activities and hold school and business strikes."[18] The PFLP called for "striking the enemy interests wherever they are," including "economic as well as military targets of the enemy camp." Their tactics would eventually include "skyjacking and bombings in and out of Israel." As Habash once put it, "to kill a Jew far from the battleground has more of an effect than killing 100 of them in battle."[19]

Recruiting for the Palestinian resistance got a boost in March 1968, when a massive Israeli military incursion into Jordan met with near defeat. Responding to the bombing of a school bus, the IDF mounted an attack on a complex of guerrilla bases in and around the Jordanian village of Karameh (which means "dignity" in Arabic) expecting to destroy it in short order.[20] Instead, the Israelis encountered furious and effective resistance by the Palestinian forces, supported by artillery and armor from the Jordanian Legion. Although the Israelis succeeded in inflicting the most casualties—there were thirty-three Israeli dead versus a combined 240 for the PLO and Jordanians—the IDF was compelled to withdraw without completing any of its main objectives. The outcome was hailed as a victory among Palestinians and more importantly as "proof of the IDF's vulnerability."[21]

The victory at Karameh—which included the destruction of eight Israeli tanks and the downing of a jet—"reinforced and accelerated" Palestinian resistance, as the image of the "downtrodden displaced person" came to be replaced by the "young, vigorous, intelligent, self-sacrificing guerrilla warrior" known as the *fedayeen*.[22] As historian Benny Morris put it, "the instant legend was to have an immediate result." Thousands of young Palestinians, "abandoning high school and university," flocked to guerrilla groups, especially Arafat's Fatah but also the PFLP.[23] Abu Iyad was likely exaggerating when he claimed that "5000 new recruits applied to join Fatah within the next 48 hours," but perhaps not by much.[24]

For some observers, the Battle of Karameh signaled a transition from Palestinian resistance to revolution.[25] That is a matter of interpretation but it definitely marked the beginning of intensified and widespread assaults on Israeli targets—in the occupied territories, Israel itself, and around the world—by fighters from across the spectrum of Palestinian organizations.[26] Israeli casualties mounted throughout 1968 as guerrilla strikes of one sort or another steadily increased.[27] According to Abu Iyad, who was in a good position to keep track, such operations rose "from a monthly average of 12 in 1967 to 52 in 1968 [and] 199 in 1969."[28]

Odeh was still attending university in Beirut at the time of the Battle of Karameh but she returned to Ramallah shortly afterward, never to resume her studies in Lebanon. She would later claim that the Israelis had arbitrarily refused to allow her to leave the West Bank,[29] but it is equally likely that the exit denial was due to her known association with Haddad and the PFLP. In any case, Odeh had by then become committed to future military action.[30] In the words of the Arab feminist academic Nahla Abdo, she would be "among the first generation of Palestinian fighters to join the armed struggle."[31]

The PFLP made good use of its new recruits. Establishing itself as the most aggressive, daring, and ideological of the Palestinian guerrilla factions, the PFLP adopted a strategy of "selective terrorism," consisting of "carefully planned acts of violence against specific targets and for a specific purpose" that transcended international borders.[32] Its earliest operation—an attack on Israel's international airport at Lydda—was a spectacular failure. A captured guerrilla gave up the names of his comrades and nearly two hundred PFLP operatives were consequently arrested before the end of 1967.[33]

On July 23, 1968, PFLP fighters launched the first of the organization's signature airplane hijackings, commandeering El Al Flight 426, en route from London to Tel Aviv via Rome. One of the three hijackers entered the unlocked cockpit and pistol-whipped the copilot, while the other two held the cabin crew and passengers at gunpoint. Under orders from the commandos, the pilot diverted the flight to Algiers, where the non-Israeli passengers were released. Negotiations between the Algerian and Israeli governments lasted almost six weeks and ended with the exchange of sixteen Palestinian prisoners in return for the plane and hostages.[34]

By late 1968, PFLP operations had become alarmingly violent, in both Europe and Israel, including an attack on an El Al plane at Athens Airport. Jerusalem was especially on edge, following a November car bombing in the Mahane Yehuda market that killed twelve people and left another fifty-two injured. The new year did not bring relief. Another El Al airliner was attacked on the ground at Zurich Airport on February 18, killing the pilot and three passengers.

*   *   *

Friday mornings are always a busy time in Jewish West Jerusalem, as shoppers hurry to make preparations for the coming Sabbath. This is especially the case in winter, when the sun sets early and all commercial activity must end. So it was on February 21, 1969, as customers filled Supersol, the largest supermarket in Jerusalem, making their last-minute purchases for Sabbath meals.

Then, just before 11:00 a.m., with around 150 people crowding the aisles, a powerful blast went off on a shelf across from the meat counter, ripping through the ceiling. Debris flew like shrapnel, as cans, bottles, shards of glass, and decorations for the Purim holiday tore through the store. Frightened shoppers realized immediately what had happened; it was the eighth such civilian-site bombing in Israel since the 1967 war. They rushed in shock for the exits but a panic was averted when the store manager took the loudspeaker, making himself heard over the screams and weeping of the wounded and called on everyone to remain calm.[35]

Emergency responders arrived within minutes, including units from the police, civil defense, ambulance, and fire brigades. They quickly secured the premises and brought the wounded—who included an Auschwitz survivor and a U.N. attaché—to the hospital.[36] As dozens of security personnel began searching through the rubble, they located the source of the blast in the cooking oil section, where the three-kilogram device had been hidden in an apricot jam can.[37] An alert officer prevented a further disaster when he noticed a round candy tin in the wine section that appeared to be out of place. Opening it, he discovered six explosive charges with a British pencil timing device set to go off during the rescue. Army sappers dismantled the bomb, noticing that the tin was a brand sold by Supersol, which would have made it easier for the bombers to carry it past the guard and into the store.[38]

There was nothing the medic crews could do for Edward Joffe and Leon Kanner, who were killed in the explosion. The two young men were agriculture students at Hebrew University and had been purchasing supplies for an upcoming field trip. Immigrants to Israel—Joffe from South Africa and Kanner from Uruguay—both had served in the IDF before enrolling at the university. Kanner had been wounded twice in the Six-Day War and had also participated in the action at Karameh. The friends had recently taken an apartment together at the City Hotel in East Jerusalem, where they were known as studious and shy. Emblematic of Israel's immigrant culture, their common language was Hebrew, rather than Joffe's native English or Kanner's native Spanish.[39]

Emotions were already raw in Israel when the Supersol bomb went off, only three days after the airport attack in Zurich and a few months after the Mahane Yehuda market attack. The situation became even more tense when it was learned that another bomb had been located earlier that morning on the outside of Jerusalem's British Consulate, seemingly in retaliation for the recently announced arms sale from the United Kingdom to Israel. Fortunately, the one-kilogram bomb, hidden in a cigar box, was noticed by the consulate's gardener who then called the police. It was harmlessly detonated in an empty field only thirty minutes before the deadly supermarket blast.[40]

The potential for "private vengeance" against Jerusalem's Arab population was well understood by the police. The earlier Mahane Yehuda bombing had set off riots, as angry mobs of young Israeli Jews had rampaged through Arab neighborhoods, beating up anyone they could get their hands on.[41] The Jerusalem authorities were determined to prevent a similar outbreak of violence, setting up roadblocks at the entrances to Arab neighborhoods and escorting Arab workers safely home from their jobs. Two young Palestinian newspaper vendors sought protection from an Israeli cab driver, who drove them to the Damascus Gate at the edge of the Old City. Speaking at the darkened Supersol, with Moshe Dayan and Abba Eban also in attendance, Mayor Teddy Kollek reassured the public that "95 percent of Jerusalem's Arab residents opposed such acts of violence, whatever their political views."[42]

Other than that, however, the official treatment of Jerusalem's Arabs was far from benevolent. The police were not shy about announcing their "roundups" of Arabs, with the total number of reported detentions ranging from forty to two hundred, depending on the source, in an apparent effort to locate the presumed 5 percent of the population sympathetic to terrorism. In most cases the interrogations were concluded quickly, with the detainees released within hours. In the first few days, for example, about 150 Arabs were subjected to custodial questioning—that being the most frequently reported number—of whom only fourteen were remanded an additional fifteen days for further investigation.[43] The almost arbitrary nature of the roundups could only have heightened anger and resentment among the Palestinians, who rightly felt like they were being treated as scapegoats even if the Israeli police made what they considered good-faith efforts to discharge non-suspects as quickly as possible. The divide between the two populations was inevitable. For the Israelis, the roundup of

Arabs was a necessary survival measure; to the Arabs, it was discriminatory oppression.

*   *   *

Jewish religious tradition calls for funerals to proceed on the day following death, unless it is the Sabbath. The joint interment of Edward Joffe and Leon Kanner was therefore held on Sunday, February 23. Over five thousand mourners, many of them students, gathered at Hebrew University and accompanied the coffins in a slow and silent procession to the cemetery on Har Hamenuhot in West Jerusalem.

At graveside, Deputy Premier Yigal Allon addressed the hushed crowd, which included family members, students, faculty, soldiers, and kibbutzniks, promising that terrorism would not stop the flow of new immigrants, such as Joffe and Kanner, to Israel. "Those responsible for this latest outrage," Allon warned, "should remember that the arm of the Israel Defense Forces is long, and that their deeds will not go unpunished." Hebrew University President Avraham Harman spoke in a voice choked more with emotion than anger, saying that "the whole family of the Hebrew University and the citizens of Jerusalem mourn these two boys who were killed together." The chairman of the Student Union then called upon "all the foreign students in our midst to make the effort to stay with us, and to those Jewish students in the Diaspora to come and join us in our struggle."[44]

Kanner's coffin was carried to his grave on the shoulders of paratroopers, while Joffe's was borne by university students.[45] The two friends were buried side by side, their tombstones carrying identical inscriptions in Hebrew: "Here lies our son and brother, of blessed memory. We will remember you forever." A stone marker spans the two graves, reading,

> "These beloved and dearest in life are also together in death . . ."
> Their spark of life was extinguished by a cruel hand in Jerusalem
>   on the third day of Adar, 5729
> May their Souls be bound together in the eternal chain of Life

The opening quotation, from the Book of Samuel, is David's lament over the death of Saul and Jonathan.[46]

Israelis make a point of quickly returning to normal following terror incidents, so the Jerusalem Supersol was reopened on Sunday even as Joffe and
Kanner were being laid to rest. Police barriers were removed and people
allowed to enter the premises, some to make purchases and others just to view
the damages. The ceiling in the rear of the store was still torn open and scorched
black and there was a hole in the floor at the blast site, but the shelves had been
restocked and there were no other traces of the explosion. Many of the customers brought flowers for the staff, and each of the young women at the checkout
counters was given a bouquet. Among the first shoppers to enter the store was
a young student who had been injured in the bombing. His face still covered in
bandages, he explained, "I had to come back, I had to show myself and others."[47]

The PFLP immediately took credit for the bombing, as it had for the earlier
attack at Zurich Airport. In a typically exaggerated communique from Amman,
the PFLP announced that "27 Jews were killed and 65 injured, 14 of them
gravely, in an explosion at the Jerusalem supermarket," while announcing plans
for a "major offensive" within the next few weeks. "We are now able to strike
when and where we wish against Israel, whether inside occupied territory or
abroad," the PFLP boasted.[48] As if to underscore the seriousness of the threat,
two more bombings shook Israel the following day. One was at the British
consulate in East Jerusalem, which evidently had remarkably poor security,
where an explosive charge had been placed on an exterior window sill. No one
was hurt but the adjacent kitchen and storeroom were wrecked and all of the
building's windows were shattered. The other blast was at the market in Lydda,
a town ten miles southeast of Tel Aviv and adjacent to Israel's international
airport. There were no shoppers in the market, which was closed at the time;
two Palestinian workers were slightly injured.[49]

Foreign Minister Abba Eban repeated Allon's funeral warning, emphasizing Israel's right "to act in self-defense and to react against these gangs as
she sees fit." Vowing to "pursue these organizations until they are destroyed,"
Menachem Begin, also a cabinet minister, added that a "defending nation must
use all the means at its disposal to reach them."[50] The Israel Air Force made
good on the threat, swooping over two Palestinian bases in Syria, "pounding
them with bombs and leaving behind mounds of blazing rubble."[51] Israeli intelligence identified the two camps—called El Hamme and Massaloun—as Fatah
centers for training and recruiting guerrillas, evidently unconcerned that the
PFLP, not Fatah, had been behind the airport and supermarket attacks. The

Syrian government claimed that the bases were actually "civilian population centers," in which women and children had died. Israel countered with an equally unverifiable statement that the strike had killed as many as 150 "saboteurs." It may be that Fatah provided the most candid report, announcing that nine of its fighters had been killed and twenty-nine wounded, which was confirmed by foreign journalists.[52]

Meanwhile, the investigation into the Supersol bombing made steady progress, and it was not long before it led to the Odeh house in al-Bireh.

3 Interrogation

Shortly before midnight on February 28, barely a week after the Supersol bombing, Israeli security officers were banging on the door of the home Yousuf and Khalil Odeh had built for their families in al-Bireh. Like police everywhere, the Israelis chose to conduct their raids late at night to increase the chances of finding all of their targets at home, preferably asleep in bed and therefore less prepared to resist or flee.[1] The tactic worked as planned in this case, as Rasmea and her relatives had already retired when the nine officers—including two women—came bursting into the house.

In a later account, Odeh described Israeli soldiers breaking through the door of the bedroom she shared with her two sisters, Fatima and Leila. At age twenty-one, Rasmea was the middle sister; Fatima, then almost twenty-seven, was paraplegic, and Leila was the youngest at only seventeen. All three young women were torn from their beds, with no opportunity to change from their nightclothes, and allowed only to grab a coat as they were hustled to a waiting jeep. Rasmea's cousin and uncle were arrested later in the night, and the entire group was eventually transferred to the interrogation building at Jerusalem's central police station, known as the Russian Compound to Israelis (after its origin as a nineteenth-century pilgrims' hostel) and feared as "Moskobiya" by Palestinians.[2]

Rasmea's father watched as the soldiers rifled through the house, upsetting furniture and spilling the kitchen containers of oil, rice, and flour onto the floor.[3] It did not take long for the Israelis to discover a cache of weapons and explosives hidden in the stairwell, including grenades, detonating cord, pencil-fuses, three and a half demolition bricks weighing 700 grams, and four 200-gram sticks of gelignite. Elsewhere in the house, the search turned up other suspicious items, including numerous batteries (which could have been used for timers) and three receipts from Supersol, dated February 11 (seeming evidence of mission reconnaissance in preparation for the bombing). Finally, a note found under Rasmea's mattress contained the name of another suspect. The items were all inventoried and photographed and the explosives destroyed.[4]

Rasmea and Yousuf Odeh both later admitted the recovery of explosives from their house in al-Bireh, Yousuf claiming he had been unaware of them and Rasmea insisting they had been planted.[5] It would indeed have been doubtful that a practiced commando would leave so much incriminating evidence in such an obvious and accessible location, but the early Palestinian resistance cells, including the PFLP's, were notorious for recruiting amateurs with little training, few security instructions, and no operational experience, which in turn made them easily compromised and captured.[6] As Abu Iyad put it, "Our losses could be attributed to at least two factors: the efficiency of the Israeli secret service and the carelessness of our fighters" who took too many "useless risks" such as keeping materiel in their homes.[7]

The Israeli security operations were indeed effective. Odeh believed that the midnight raid had been aimed specifically at her—saying that the soldiers had shouted "Where's Rasmiya? Where's Rasmiya?"— as they searched the house.[8] That was entirely possible, and the presence of two police women in the search party suggests that their objective had always been to arrest Rasmea no matter what evidence they found.[9]

Israeli intelligence had "taken over both the files and the stool pigeons of the former Jordanian administration,"[10] which might well have included information on Rasmea's clandestine involvement with the ANM in its pre-PFLP days. Odeh herself believed that "someone had given my name under torture," which was also a possibility. By the time of her arrest, the Israeli investigation had been going on for a week, and around 150 Palestinians had already been roughly interrogated, a number of them having admitted involvement with Fatah or the PFLP. A police spokesman must have exaggerated when he reported that 143 suspects had "without exception" cooperated in the investigation, but there can be little doubt that names were named and may have included Odeh's.[11] Among many other *fedayeen* security lapses, no efforts were made to conceal their identities from each other, and the "formal structure" of the PFLP cells made them even easier to be "rolled up."[12]

The most probable conjecture, however, is that the Israelis had flagged Odeh as a potential PFLP operative dating back to her known association with Wadi Haddad in Beirut. The additional information from surveillance and informants, one of whom was apparently among her PFLP confederates, would have confirmed those suspicions.[13] The week's delay in searching the al-Bireh house was likely because its owners—Yousuf and Khalil Odeh—were both U.S. citizens who could not be included in one of the usual indiscriminate roundups.[14]

One thing is certain about events following the raid: Rasmea's beating by the security team did not begin until she was outside her home.

*   *   *

Odeh has recounted her mistreatment by the Israelis on numerous occasions, at length and in detail. The "slapping and punching" started as soon as she was placed in the police car. She was driven first to the local jail in Ramallah, where she was held handcuffed and blindfolded for two hours, before she was brought back to the car and driven for a long time to a place that seemed very far away. In fact, she had been taken to central Jerusalem, a distance of only about twelve miles, but the circuitous route was evidently intended to disorient her.[15]

When the blindfold and handcuffs were removed, Odeh realized she was in Moskobiya, where she was surrounded by ten or twelve security agents—known in Arabic as *mukhabarat*—in plain clothes, with a uniformed soldier stationed at the door. Israel has multiple security services—including the Shin Bet or Shabak, military intelligence or Aman, and a special police unit called Latam—all of which were likely involved in the interrogation at one time or another. Israeli interrogators intentionally wear plain clothes and use pseudonyms, so Odeh was never able to identify the individuals by their particular organization. Whoever was present that morning, they immediately began beating her, using a wooden stick on her body and an iron bar on her head, before the questioning even began. According to Odeh, she was able to endure the punishment for half an hour before she started screaming and fighting back, which caused the officers to handcuff her again, while cursing her in Arabic.[16]

Even then, the actual interrogation had not begun. Instead, other prisoners in the "torture factory," as Odeh called it, were paraded before her, all of them bruised and staggering, while she was asked if she recognized them. Denying that she had any contacts with "commandos in the resistance," Odeh claimed to be a university student who was home for the Eid al-Adha holiday, which was about to begin.[17] Her denials brought more beatings, as she was slammed against the wooden partitions that framed the otherwise empty room. When she passed out, the agents revived her with buckets of cold water, a process that continued through the morning and into the afternoon.[18]

Only when Rasmea's father was brought into the room did she realize that he had also been arrested. "Save your daughter," he was instructed, as they hit him. "Say what you know." The agents told Rasmea that her two sisters were also in Moskobiya and they too had been beaten, including paralyzed Fatima. The abuse of Rasmea continued in front of her father, amid threats that their house would be blown up. "To save your house from destruction, let your daughter tell what she knows." Finally, Yousuf Odeh broke down, fearful for his home and children. "We can't stand any more," he said. "Please tell what you know." But Rasmea remained stoic. "I said I knew nothing and they took my father away."[19]

That was only the beginning, as the interrogation entered a new phase. Odeh was taken from the barren room into an office, where she was allowed to sit on a chair. Identifying himself as an Iraqi Jew, a new interrogator spoke to her "gently and pleasantly" in Arabic, explaining that he liked Palestinians and had good relations with them. While they were speaking, Odeh could hear "screams and groans" from victims in an adjoining room. "Do you hear?" asked the interrogator. "Confess so that the same won't happen to you." Rasmea insisted that she had nothing to confess, but the interrogator kept pressing her. "I'll write it for you," he said.

Then, in Rasmea's account, she "dictated an imaginary story about how there had been explosives made in the house, but someone had come and taken them, a person swathed in veils so I didn't know whether it was male or female, nor did I know where the explosives were to be taken." The interrogator wrote it all down in Hebrew and read it back to Rasmea. She signed the confession, although she could not understand or read Hebrew at the time.[20]

Even after Odeh's initial confession, the brutality continued day and night for seven to ten days, taking increasingly pitiless forms.[21] "They used to show me people I knew who had been tortured," she said, and then "they tortured me in front of a girl I knew so that she would confess." They showed her men hanging by their wrists, and a man whose gaping head wound had turned gangrenous. One detainee had been stripped completely naked and was subjected to "electric shocks all over his body, in particular in his head, chest and genitals." Only "five minutes later, I learned that he was dead."[22] They made Odeh watch when they set dogs on prisoners, and they brought in her fiancé, Yakoub Odeh, who had been battered so badly that she did not recognize him, even though "he had never done a single military operation in his life."[23]

As her incarceration at Moskobiya wore on, Odeh was subjected to all manner of creative and humiliating abuses. One day, she said, a female soldier in civilian clothes "stamped all over my body, my face, my head, with her high-heeled shoes on."[24] The "good cop" from the office interrogation sometimes intervened. During one savage beating with a wooden stick, another officer tried to disarm her tormentor, which Odeh thought "was only a farce."[25] When she was "boxed on the ears" until she could not hear, a different interrogator followed up with a "nice act," in which he promised rewards for her cooperation. "You're a pretty girl," he said. "You should be out having fun, why ruin your life?" There were also promises of leniency, such as "Join us and we'll release you and you can go to the US and we won't demolish your house." Then they would play tapes of other prisoners "confessing and implicating" Odeh, intended to weaken her resolve.[26]

Worst of all was the sexual torture. "Israelis know how sensitive we are about these matters," she explained in her 1980 interview, "and they used the sexual aspect in order to frighten the girls and to make families refuse to let their daughters participate in the struggle." In its mildest form, the sexual tactics involved only innuendo. "They told my father that my activities were not political, but sexual, and showed him men that they said I had slept with."[27]

Soon enough, the innuendo turned brutal:

> They stripped me and took me to a room where men were suspended from the ceiling. They handcuffed me to the hooks in the ceiling—it was a pulley system which could be raised and lowered—and they chained my feet to the ground, wide apart and raised me so only the tips of my toes touched the ground. They said they had been going to rape me but I was too dirty for them and they would instead get some prisoners who hadn't seen a woman for a long time.[28]

On the most horrific occasion "they stripped me and threw me on the floor" in a room full of men. "They laughed at my nakedness and kicked me, beat me with sticks. . . . Then they got a wooden stick, not a smooth one, and pushed it into me to break the hymen." Odeh's will was only defeated when they brought her father into the room and tried to "force him under blows to take off his clothes and have sexual relations with me."[29] "She isn't your daughter, she's your wife," they told him. Yousuf screamed and "they beat him till he lost consciousness." Only then did Odeh fully break down, in order to keep them "from continuing to torture her father."[30] On agreeing to do whatever the Israelis asked, "They took me to the supermarket and the British Consulate and told me to point out where the bombs had been placed. I didn't know so they showed me and had me photographed standing on the sites."[31] Even after her confession the torture did not stop, said Odeh, as she was subjected to repeated incidents of beating and sexual assault. In total, Odeh spent forty-five days in Moskobiya, twenty-five of them in solitary confinement.[32]

The narrative of Odeh's interrogation under torture is long and gut-wrenching but must be considered in weighing the truth of her account.

*　*　*

There have been many accusations of torture against Israeli interrogators dating back to the period immediately after the Six-Day War, including those raised by an Amnesty International investigation conducted from December 1968 through January 1970. Amnesty concluded that there was *prima facie* evidence of maltreatment of some prisoners, including possible beating, kicking, suspension by handcuffs, electric shocks to the genitals, and use of attack dogs. The Israeli government vigorously denied every allegation, stating that its own investigation found "no substance" to the charges and emphasizing that "Israel is a state in which the Rule of Law prevails."[33]

It is in the nature of torturers to deny their work, which is conducted in the shadows and behind closed doors, if only to make it impossible to confirm. As Amnesty International put it, "the confrontation between the individual and the limitless power of the state, between the torturer and his victim, takes place in the darkest recess of political power."[34] Paradoxically, the very secrecy of "enhanced interrogation" also makes it possible for subjects to embellish or exaggerate their ill-treatment, especially when they are politically motivated.

There seems no doubt that Rasmea Odeh was callously abused during her interrogation. Even Israel's defenders have recognized that security prisoners were subjected to "severe handling," including the "elementary bullying necessary to persuade terrorist suspects that the interrogators are not to be trifled with."[35] Odeh's account goes far beyond mere coercion, however, including unspeakable sadism by her interrogators that was met by heroic, weeks-long resistance to even the most extreme torments.

Since her release from prison in Israel, Odeh has provided three lengthy narratives of her life, including her arrest and interrogation, accounts of which are available in English. She testified for three sessions of a U.N. Special Investigating Committee in 1979;[36] she gave an extensive interview to the Lebanese journalist Soraya Antonius, which was published in 1980;[37] and she spoke for eighteen hours with Chicago psychologist Dr. Mary Fabri in 2014.[38] In addition, Odeh testified at her original trial in Israel, parts of which have been translated into English;[39] she spoke more briefly to Israeli journalist David Krivine in 1977 for publication in the English-language *Jerusalem Post*;[40] and she appears for a few minutes in two Palestinian video documentaries with English subtitles.[41] Given Israel's refusal ever to make interrogators available for interviews,[42] these accounts can only be evaluated by the means used, for example, by reporters for the British newspaper the *Sunday Times* for their 1977 investigation of alleged Israeli torture: the consistency of reports, "corroboration of verifiable details," and other circumstantial evidence.[43]

There are many inconsequential discrepancies across Odeh's three post-prison interviews, as would always be expected among statements given decades apart—with the earliest one more than ten years after the events themselves—and for different purposes. The U.N. testimony was part of an ongoing investigation into mistreatment and torture, the Antonius interview was for publication in a pro-Palestinian journal, and the Fabri interview was part of a psychological evaluation for use in Odeh's defense at trial. None of the three provided an exact chronology, nor could a precise sequence be expected from someone who had been traumatized, blindfolded, and held incommunicado.[44] For the most part, however, those three accounts are internally consistent, detailing the same series of torturous beatings, abuses, and sexual assaults, leaving little question about the totality of the treatment Odeh suffered at the hands of her interrogators.

On the other hand, there are also some serious inconsistencies and implausibilities in Odeh's stories, both internally and compared with externally verifiable facts, especially in her Israeli trial testimony and the *Jerusalem Post* interview, that undermine some of her most extreme claims and therefore indicate exaggeration.[45]

* * *

Apart from Rasmea herself, only one other person has provided an on-the-record eyewitness account of the worst of her abuse by the Israelis. In 1977, British reporters for the *Sunday Times* interviewed Yousuf Odeh about his daughter's interrogation. The elder Odeh explained that he had been arrested in 1969 along with his three daughters. During his detention at the Russian Compound, "the interrogators arranged a series of confrontations between members of the family, seemingly as a pressurizing device." They made Yousuf watch as Rasmea was beaten:

> When they took me back . . . Rasmiah wouldn't stand on her own feet. She was lying on the floor and there were blood stains on her clothes. Her face was blue and she had a black eye. Then she was picked up by two soldiers, and at that moment I started crying and screaming and they blindfolded me and I think she was taken away.[46]

The *Sunday Times* reporters were impressed by the consistency of Yousuf's account, noting that "it squares with the pattern thrown up by other testimony," but they were even more influenced by "Odeh's manner in giving it," which they took as a sign of credibility:

> As his recital continued, Odeh became visibly distressed. He began to breathe rapidly and the muscles in the side of his neck were twitching. . . . He began to cry. At last he said to our interpreter: "I wish I had died rather than see this thing . . . It's a question of honour . . . It is alright, interpret, why not?"[47]

At that point, Yousuf lost his composure. When he was able to continue, he described an incident when he was taken into an interrogation room, "to find Rasmiah naked and handcuffed." One of the interrogators told him to have sex with her. "Don't even think of that," he said. "I would never do such a thing."

> They were beating me and beating her and we were both screaming. Rasmiah was still saying: "I know nothing." And they spread her legs and shoved the stick into her. She was bleeding from her mouth and from her face and from her end. Then I became unconscious.

It was reasonable, in 1977, for the reporters to equate emotiveness with veracity, although that seeming connection has long since been disproven in psychology research. In any case, both Rasmea and Yousuf Odeh have given multiple versions of events that are inconsistent with the sexual abuse incident he related to the *Sunday Times* and which she later repeated before the U.N. Special Committee.

On March 10, 1969, Yousuf Odeh was interviewed by a U.S. consular officer tasked with investigating the treatment of American citizens. At the time, Yousuf had been in custody for ten days, which was well after Rasmea's confession had been reported in the Israeli press. Following the interview, the consular officer sent a diplomatic cable to the Department of State in Washington, which primarily concerned attempts to prevent the demolition of the Odeh home in al-Bireh. The consular cable made no mention of torture, much less sexual abuse with a stick, which Yousuf surely would have reported in the custodial interview:

> Odeh complains of uncomfortable, overcrowded jail conditions but he apparently receiving no rpt [repeat] no worse than standard treatment afforded majority detainees at Jerusalem jail.[48]

The *Sunday Times* reporters interviewed only Yousuf Odeh, but Rasmea later spoke to David Krivine of the *Jerusalem Post*. She repeated the story of hymen-breaking, but she told Krivine that her father had not been there at the time. "Only the Israeli interrogators" were present, she said.

As an Israeli, Krivine might be accused of biased reporting. He was not unsympathetic to coercive interrogation for the purpose of locating hidden explosives caches or a detainee's accomplices at large, although he held that "grilling is one thing, torture another." Nonetheless, his account includes what lawyers and judges call *indicia* of reliability. Again, regarding the stick incident:

> I pressed further. Did the stick not injure her, tear her flesh, cause her to bleed? Her answer makes one wonder: "It is hard to say. I was menstruating at the time."

Until that time, there had been no report in either the Israeli press or the *Sunday Times* that Odeh had been menstruating during the interrogation. Krivine's account could have come only from Rasmea herself, if indeed she had said it. Two years later, in her testimony before the U.N. Special Committee, Odeh confirmed that she was menstruating at Moskobiya.[49] In 2014, in the course of her psychological evaluation, Odeh told Dr. Fabri that during the "seven to ten days" of her interrogation "she was menstruating and she was denied any sanitary products and she was not allowed access to a bathroom or any other way to clean herself."[50] There was no way Krivine could have known of Odeh's menses during interrogation unless she told him about it, which supports the authenticity of the quotations in his *Jerusalem Post* article.[51]

Yousuf and Rasmea Odeh also testified in the course of her Israeli trial, as part of the local equivalent of a motion to suppress her confession, recounting multiple incidents of sexual coercion, beatings, and other physical abuse. Years later, both Yousuf and Rasmea described an incident in which the Israelis attempted to compel them to have sex—with father and daughter stripped naked in the same room—but their testimony at trial told only of threats, related to them separately. On direct examination, Rasmea testified,

> Abu Anni [the interrogator's pseudonym] threatened me with rape and said that my father would be brought in to rape me as well and also that he will bring men who have not seen girls for a long time. They did not rape me and I fell. I didn't know what happened. When I woke up they disappeared.[52]

Taking the stand at the Israeli trial, Yousuf testified that the investigators threatened to demolish his house if he couldn't get Rasmea to talk. He had difficulty maintaining his composure as he described being "ordered to hit his daughter" while she begged to be taken to a room where her father would not have to hear her screams.[53]

Israeli law formally disallows involuntary confessions, and Odeh's public suppression hearing, or "trial within a trial," as it is called in Israel, was held in multiple sessions over several months. Odeh and her counsel evidently believed that there was some chance of excluding her confession on the ground of coercion, or perhaps they simply wanted to take the opportunity to expose Israeli interrogation methods. In either case, there would have been no reason for witnesses to omit the dramatic confrontation of the naked father and daughter, if indeed such a thing had happened. Merely threatening them was bad enough, of course, but the far more graphic and horrifying story emerged only years later in situations where there was no opportunity for cross-examination.[54]

There are other implausibilities in Odeh's post-prison narratives. Her claim of seeing other prisoners attacked by dogs is inconsistent with the geography and architecture of the Russian Compound, which also serves as Jerusalem's central police station. Growling dogs would not escape notice there, given that the courtyard is open to the public and nearly always crowded with people arriving to obtain official documents such as identity cards and driving licenses or to visit the lost and found department. Odeh's claims of receiving electric shocks—and once witnessing an electrocution—are also questionable. The *Sunday Times* reporters heard many similar accounts from other prisoners (although none of fatalities) but noted that electric shocking was the specialty of interrogators at a remote, secret location known as Sarafand (where it would also have been more feasible to use attack dogs without attracting attention). It therefore seems more likely that Odeh had heard of dogs and electricity from other prisoners and later added the details to enhance her own story.

Finally, Odeh told Antonius that her confession had been written out in Hebrew, which she signed even though she could not read or understand it:

> I dictated an imaginary story about how there had been explosives made in the house but someone had come and taken them, a person swathed in veils. . . . I signed the Hebrew text in Arabic; at that time I knew no Hebrew.[55]

In fact, Odeh's eight-page confession was completely handwritten in Arabic and neatly signed in the same language. It was entered in evidence at her Israeli trial and later provided to the U.S. Department of State pursuant to a mutual cooperation treaty. There can be little question that the Arabic confession (which has been translated by the U.S. Justice Department) is the one Odeh mentioned to Antonius. It includes the very scenario about bomb preparation that she recounted in the 1980 interview:

> [The bomb maker] left the house around seven and later after him in like a quarter or half an hour, a person came that I did not know, as he was veiled with a red kufiyah and he took both boxes from me after he asked me to give him the stuff.[56]

Putting aside, just for now, the very real issues of accuracy and coercion, it is demonstrably untrue that Odeh was compelled to sign a Hebrew-language confession that she could not read.[57]

The *Sunday Times* reporters heard numerous torture allegations against Israel and concluded that "some, even many" had likely been fabricated, "but not all of them."[58] The same can be said of Rasmea Odeh's narrative of physical and sexual abuse. Many of her most extreme claims may have been invented, exaggerated, or embellished—but not all of them.

4   Roundups

Beyond Moskobiya's walls, an Israeli special investigation team kept working on the Supersol bombing. Police sappers displayed the captured weapons and explosives to the press, including British-made pencil timing devices, a booby trap detonator, Russian and Czech hand grenades, coiled ignition wire, and various firearms. Some of these items had been taken from the Odehs' house in al-Bireh and much had been retrieved from other "homes and courtyards" in Jerusalem and the West Bank.[1]

Meanwhile, the relentless interrogations and roundups of Arabs continued—mostly out of sight—with great urgency. Jerusalem had experienced four bombs in quick succession, with two more in other locations. Only the Supersol attack had been fatal, but there was no telling where the next explosion might occur or how lethal it might be. For the police, there was no greater priority than discovering the extent of the "sabotage cells" and arresting any members still at large. According to an official announcement, issued on March 1, the "extensive investigation and searches" had been able to fix responsibility for at least the British Embassy bombing on the PFLP, with more disclosures yet to follow.[2]

It took only one more day for additional information to emerge. On Sunday, March 2, at 9:30 a.m., the police escorted "two girls from Ramallah"—meaning Rasmea Odeh and Aisha Odeh—through the Supersol for the purpose of reconstructing the bombing operation. Sunday is the first day of the Israeli work week, and the store was already crowded with customers attending to their post-Sabbath shopping. According to police accounts, the two detainees "pointed out the spot in the cooking oil section where they had placed a charge concealed inside a tin of conserves, and a shelf where a second charge was concealed inside a biscuit tin."[3] The initial police statement did not say which part each of the young women played in the operation, although it later emerged that Rasmea had organized the bomb-making, while Aisha and a third comrade—Rasheida Obeideh, who was never apprehended—had actually planted the explosives.[4]

Despite the confessions of two of the main perpetrators, another forty or fifty suspects—accounts vary—were still being detained for questioning. Among the detainees were three prominent Palestinian professionals, which sent shock waves through both the Jewish and Arab communities, although for different reasons.

The arrestees were Rev. Elia Khader Khalil Khoury, the rector of St. Andrew's Episcopal Church in Ramallah, attorney Bashir el Khairy, also of Ramallah, and Dr. Nabih Assad Muammar, who was the chief surgeon at the "Moslem Charitable Hospital" in the Abu Tor neighborhood of East Jerusalem. The three had long been suspected of engaging in illegal political activities. Rev. Khoury was known to be "militantly anti-Israel" and had refused to hold mass since the 1967 war, as a sign of protest against the occupation.[5] Even so, they had not previously been directly tied to underground military cells.

Arab religious leaders, including the Muslim Grand Mufti and the Anglican Bishop of Jerusalem, attempted to intervene on behalf of the notables, who occupied important positions in Palestinian society. They were rebuffed by Israel's national police minister, who explained the gravity of the charges. Based on information gathered in the investigation, including the interrogations of Rasmea and Aisha, it was believed that attorney el Khairy had been a PFLP recruiter in Ramallah and Rev. Khoury had been a crucial link between the Ramallah cell and the PFLP operational heads in Amman, including a woman named Widad Qumri, who was originally from East Jerusalem.[6] Rev. Khoury, moreover, was alleged to have smuggled money, communications, and explosives from Jordan to the West Bank and to have driven the conspirators from Ramallah to Jerusalem in his "old model Hillman," where Dr. Muammar was thought to have allowed his hospital address to be used as the delivery point for explosives in camouflaged medicine boxes.[7]

If the arrests succeeded in angering Palestinian society, they evidently did little to discourage additional bombings. There was yet another explosion on March 6, this time at the Hebrew University cafeteria. The one-kilogram bomb, which was planted in a window box, sent broken glass and debris across the cafeteria packed with 250 students during lunch hour. The fragments injured thirty-six students, seven of them severely enough to be hospitalized. In what had become almost a routine, the PFLP claimed credit for the bombing in a radio broadcast from Beirut.[8]

In Jerusalem, it did not escape notice that Hebrew University had been the school of Edward Joffe and Leon Kanner, who had been murdered only two weeks earlier, or that it was probably the most integrated institution in Israel (then as now) enrolling Jewish, Muslim, and Christian students, any of whom might have been among the victims. The rector of the university condemned the "despicable act aimed at sowing destruction and death in a place devoted to research and learning." Once again, the police were forced to set up road-blocks "between the Israeli and Arab sections of Jerusalem to head off possible reprisals" by angry mobs.[9]

Still in custody in the Russian Compound, Odeh was interrogated about the Hebrew University bombing and asked if she had any information about the possible perpetrators. In later years, she would claim to have remained silent. In fact, she provided dozens of names to the police.

*   *   *

The so-called ticking bomb scenario is often used as a thought experiment in academic discussions on the permissibility of torture. Many accomplished political and academic figures have accepted its premise, including Prof. Alan Dershowitz, former Judge Richard Posner, and the late Justice Antonin Scalia.[10] In the spring of 1969, however, the ticking bomb was not a hypothetical in Israel. At least seven bombing attacks had been launched by the PFLP in the space of only a few weeks, and only by the grace of fortune had the death count been limited. Another explosion might occur any day, and the public's luck was bound to run out.

The Arab roundups had been sweeping, if not wholly indiscriminate, because the police were determined to turn every possible stone; the questioning had been at least temporarily custodial in order to extract information from an oppressed and unwilling population. The serious interrogation of actual suspects was only secondarily for the purpose of gathering evidence for a later prosecution. Much more urgent was the need to head off additional bombings before they could occur. An Israeli government commission explained the difference:

> The police investigation is aimed at collecting evidence against individuals within the society, suspected of criminal offenses, and its purposes are to have the accused convicted so that he will change his ways, to deter him and others from committing future crimes, and to give him the punishment he deserves. Whereas the goal of the GSS [General Security Service, or Shin Bet] interrogation is to protect the very existence of society and the State against terrorist acts directed at its citizens, to collect information about terrorists and their modes of organization and to thwart and prevent the perpetration of terrorist acts whilst they are still at a state of incubation.[11]

In Israel, ticking bombs were nothing like an intellectual exercise. Given the exigencies, interrogations could quickly turn from simply coercive to viciously brutal.

Accusations of abuse by Israeli interrogators began almost at the outset of the occupation, including Amnesty International's findings of *prima facie* evidence of torture, covering the period 1968–1970.[12] During this same period, the Israeli attorney Felicia Langer repeatedly sent letters to the Ministry of Security complaining that her Palestinian clients had been subjected to torture while in custody and during interrogation. The mistreatment included severe beatings, especially to the genitals and feet, strangulation, use of an "electrical appliance," dousing with cold water while naked, and burning with lighted cigarettes.[13]

Other investigations, stretching over a long period of time, led to the same conclusions about the routine mistreatment, always coercive and sometimes amounting to torture, of prisoners under Israeli interrogation.[14] David Krivine's response to the London *Sunday Times*, defending Israel against accusations of torture, nonetheless conceded that "physical force is applied by the security services where necessary," which he left undefined, under a cloak of "rigid secrecy."[15] Even the U.S. Department of State gingerly recognized "documented reports of the use of extreme physical and psychological pressure during interrogation."[16] For many years, Israel's stock response was simply to issue a blanket denial. Regarding the 1977 *Sunday Times* investigation, for example, Israel's London embassy issued a statement calling the report "horror fiction," insisting that there was "no evidence whatsoever on the actual use of torture."[17]

In fact, many of the same tactics were used at the Russian Compound—that is, Moskobiya—to train Israeli intelligence officers in resisting torture. "We spent three and a half horrible days there without sleep, handcuffed, blindfolded," reported one agent-in-training. "For part of the time, we were handcuffed to a chair with our arms behind us in a position that tensed our entire bodies; part of the time, they chained us to the ceiling, forcing us to stand on tiptoe. During the interrogations, policemen and Shin Bet agents beat us and spit on us. I heard that they even urinated on one guy." It would be naïve to think that the implements of torture—chains, pulleys, hoods, and more—were housed at Moskobiya exclusively for training purposes.[18]

The official torture denials finally became fully untenable in 1987, when an Israeli government commission headed by former supreme court justice Moshe Landau determined that interrogators from the General Security Service (abbreviated in English as GSS; in Hebrew, the Shin Bet or Shabak) had routinely lied in court about the treatment of detainees or otherwise concealed the coercive measures used to extract confessions.

In the case that led to empaneling the commission, the Israeli defendant, himself an IDF officer, asserted—and the prosecution witnesses falsely denied—that he had been slapped, kicked, shaken, thrown to the ground, ordered to strip and doused with cold water, deprived of sleep, made to stand in stress positions, and threatened with the arrest of his mother and wife. Although the Landau Report ultimately authorized the use of "moderate physical pressure" as necessary to "the effective interrogation of terrorist suspects," it tacitly admitted that even more brutal measures had been employed in the past and banned their use in the future.[19]

As explained by the Israeli journalist Ronen Bergman, the Shin Bet "had used illegal tactics since the 1960s":

> Shin Bet interrogators feared, not without cause, that if they did not squeeze information out of the captured prisoners more Israelis would be killed. What began as intimidation and humiliation during interrogation evolved into outright physical and psychological torture: mock executions, sleep deprivation, forcing prisoners to endure painful stress positions and extremes of heat and cold.[20]

The Landau Commission's implicit acknowledgment of strong-arm interrogation techniques would come too late to help Rasmea Odeh. She raised many of the same charges in her own trial, seeking to exclude the evidence of her confession, only to have them baldly denied by prosecution witnesses and predictably rejected by the court.

*　*　*

Two Palestinian undergraduates were arrested on March 15 for the Hebrew University cafeteria bombing. The police announced that the students, both fourth-year humanities majors, were part of the PFLP "network uncovered in the wake of the Supersol bombing," meaning that they had been named by Odeh or one of the other detainees already under interrogation. That students would place a bomb at their own school was alarming to university authorities.

Hebrew University's Arab students were especially troubled by several inflammatory articles in the Israeli press that seemed to spread "hate and suspicion between Arab and Jewish students." They issued a statement condemning the "poisonous and irresponsible articles" and appealing "to their Jewish colleagues and to the Israeli public" not to regard the actions of the two arrestees "as reflecting on the other 170 who study at the university," including twenty-two from the West Bank and Gaza. One Israeli Arab student, stressing the distinction "between nationality and nationalism," explained that Hebrew University was "one of the few, if not only, places in Israel where Arabs always encountered an extremely fair attitude." In a television interview Prime Minister Golda Meir warned against generalizing as to "the involvement [of Israeli Arabs] in terrorist activities" just because a few had "taken part in sabotage." As a precaution, the Hebrew University administration took "measures to prevent harm coming to its Arab students," which fortunately proved unnecessary.[21] Nonetheless, a number of Arab students were detained for questioning, and they were not released for over a week.[22]

With each new set of arrests and interrogations, the security service believed they were Identifying much of the network of PFLP cells responsible for the spate of bombings. At a press conference, it was announced that the network was headed by Nayef Hawatmeh, who had recently broken with the PFLP to form the yet more militant Democratic Front for the Liberation of Palestine, explaining that "the split was not paralleled in the West Bank and East Jerusalem cells."[23] That was just the sort of improbable information most likely to be extracted under torture, when frantic detainees would mention every name they could think of and there could be no realistic verification.

Other than taking credit for the operations, the PFLP had no interest in providing anything other than disinformation about the bombings, as in an interview granted to a reporter for the London *Sunday Telegraph*. On March 15, the same day as the Hebrew University cafeteria arrests, Eric Downton was in Jordan, interviewing Qumri at the PFLP headquarters on the outskirts of Amman. Described by PFLP operatives as "something of a legend," Qumri's story included both truth and fiction, in an evident attempt to help Rev. Khoury and the other detainees in Israeli custody.

Under the watchful eyes of "young guerrillas carrying Russian sub-machine guns," Qumri explained her background to Downton, including her birth in what became Israel and her family's dispossession in 1948. Having grown up in East Jerusalem, which was then part of Jordan, Qumri spent some years studying English literature at Damascus University. She returned to East Jerusalem, where she was teaching at an all-girls school when the Israelis captured the city in the 1967 war. She continued teaching, while becoming increasingly involved with the PFLP, finally becoming "a full-time agent," carrying weapons and messages between Jordan and the West Bank. "We, the Popular Front," she said, "plan to increase our attacks on the Israelis . . . in all parts of the world. We will make more attacks on El Al planes at international airports."

According to Downton's article, "it was Miss Qumri who placed the bomb which killed two Israelis and wounded many others in a crowded supermarket three weeks ago." She claimed to have entered the Supersol "carrying a large shopping bag" that concealed the two bombs. "While pretending to examine purchases she slipped them on to shelves behind goods on display, releasing the timing devices as she did so." Qumri then paid for some items she had taken and walked out of the store, waiting for the first bomb to explode about fifteen minutes later. She concluded with an account of her escape:

> Afterward she stayed underground for some time, but returned to Amman after it became known that the Israelis, through astute interrogation of suspects, had pinpointed her as responsible for the attack.[24]

The Israelis weren't buying it. The security service was well aware of Qumri.[25] She had been identified as the PFLP operative who had "given the order" from Amman for the Jerusalem bombings, although she had not carried out the operation itself. Rather, her role had been coordinating the transfer of money and explosives into the occupied territories, in this case, it was believed, with the help of Rev. Khoury, whom Qumri was now attempting to exonerate. Qumri herself was known to have fled the West Bank for Jordan the previous September after one of her other operatives had been caught smuggling explosives—in a suitcase with a false bottom—across the bridge from Jordan.[26] The two women who did plant the bombs in the supermarket, Aisha Odeh and Rasheida Obeideh, both later recounted their stories in Arabic language documentaries with no mention of Qumri.

There was one aspect of Downton's article, however, that the Israeli security service would have appreciated, if they had noticed it at the time. Qumri conceded that Israel's "astute interrogation of suspects" was able to pinpoint members of the PFLP cell, with no mention of torture.

Astutely or otherwise, the Israeli interrogators had strong incentives to separate the truly culpable suspects from the other prisoners—not out of concern for the rights or well-being of Palestinians but rather as a matter of efficiency and sheer survival. In an environment where the capture of perpetrators is essential to public safety, there are good reasons to release those detainees who have not been reliably implicated in attacks. As Krivine pointed out in his response to the *Sunday Times* series on torture, false confessions and sweeping prosecutions may lead investigators up blind alleys, wasting time, energy, and funds that could be better used apprehending the operatives still at large and plotting further operations.[27] That had little to do with fair-mindedness, and not even necessarily with justice, but rather was a simple calculation of cost and effectiveness. It made the most sense for the security services to concentrate on the identifiable guerrillas while releasing anyone else who could safely be freed.[28]

So it was that Rasmea's relatives—father Yousuf, sister Fatima, cousin Nuha, and uncle Khalil—were all released without charges or bail after several weeks in custody. (Her sister Leila would remain in administrative detention for over a year, ultimately to be released without charges as well.) Although they had all been in the house where the explosives were found—and in Fatima's case, in her bedroom—there was apparently no other evidence of their involvement and the cases were therefore dropped.[29] However ruthlessly they pursued likely suspects, the Israeli authorities had little interest in extending detentions that did not interdict active plots or develop prosecutions.

Freedom, however, was bittersweet for the extended Odeh family. Their house had been blown up while they were in custody, a measure routinely taken by Israel in cases where buildings had been used to plan or execute terror operations. Yousuf and Khalil were American citizens, but even intercession by the U.S. consulate was not enough to keep them from being rendered homeless.

Among the Odehs of Lifta, only Rasmea would be indicted for the supermarket and consulate bombings.

* * *

The first formal remand order against Odeh and ten others, allowing their continued custody and interrogation, was issued by the Jerusalem Magistrate's Court on March 18. Odeh later described the hearing as "a mere formality," held in "a room they called a court [before] one man who said he was the judge." She told him that she did not admit any guilt but he ruled that she was "to be imprisoned."[30] The hearing was indeed a summary proceeding, in a closed courtroom without defense counsel. Although barred from the proceeding, the Israeli press reported, based on information provided by the police, that all of the defendants "alleged ill-treatment in jail, but they did not give details."[31] The absence of details seems unlikely, as Odeh and the other suspects would later show themselves quite determined to describe their abusive interrogations, but the police and court obviously had their own reasons to squelch those accusations for as long as possible.

Meanwhile, the investigation continued to develop. The police followed Obeideh's trail to a house in the West Bank town of Nablus, where she stayed for several days in mid-March, and then to the nearby Balata refugee camp where "a prearranged vehicle met her to take her over the border into Jordan." Once safely in Amman, Obeideh attempted to mislead the Israeli investigators, announcing on PFLP radio that she alone had placed the explosives at Supersol and none of the people "arrested by the Israeli authorities after the incident had anything to do with it."[32] The police also learned of an earlier attempt to bomb the supermarket, in early January, also by two young women from the West Bank. The pair, who belonged to a PFLP cell in Nablus, brought their explosives to the store only to discover that it was closed for the afternoon break. Unfamiliar with Jerusalem, they disarmed their bomb and abandoned it in the adjacent park.[33]

Not every lead panned out. Despite the earlier accusations of complicity in the Supersol bombing, charges were dropped against Dr. Muammar when it was determined that there was "not sufficient evidence" to tie him to the attack. As he was reportedly suffering from a chronic illness, the physician was released from administrative detention and granted a travel permit for exit to Jordan.[34]

In what had appeared to be a stronger case, Rev. Khoury was also released from jail. Newspapers had reported that his arrest had been "on suspicion of incitement and conspiracy with hostile organizations" and that "under the cloak of his cloth [he] had been a go-between carrying funds to Palestine Liberation Front cells." Rev. Khoury claimed that he did not know that the consignments he carried included subversive materials, and the prosecutors were eventually unable to confirm additional charges that "he had driven the car which brought the saboteurs and their bombs to the supermarket." As there was not sufficient evidence to bring him to trial, Rev. Khoury was also "allowed to cross the border into Jordan"—that is, deported—on the unenforceable condition that he "refrain from any anti-Israel activity in other countries."[35]

Rev. Khoury's discharge was highly controversial within Israel, as it was widely believed that it had been due more to pressure from the Anglican Church, and perhaps the British Consulate, than to his actual innocence.[36] Hearing rumors of the planned release, Joffe's bereaved parents sent protest telegrams to Prime Minister Meir and Defense Minister Moshe Dayan. Once Rev. Khoury had been freed, they issued a statement complaining that earlier police announcements "did not square" with later reports of insufficient evidence to bring him to trial. "Either the authorities or the press are not telling the truth," they said, rejecting a police document, shown to them by Dayan himself, detailing the asserted shortcomings in the evidence against Rev. Khoury. The Joffes remained certain that "other factors had been important" in the release of Rev. Khoury and Dr. Muammar, whom they considered "principals of the murder gang."[37]

5   Lydda

Repairs to the charred Supersol ceiling were finally completed in mid-May, eliminating the last reminders of the explosion that had greeted shoppers for the previous ten weeks. In observance of the restoration the store management held an hour-long briefing for employees on security measures.[1]

By coincidence, an indictment for the bombing had been announced just the previous day.[2] The indictment named Rasmea Odeh on five counts, charging her as an accomplice and conspirator in the Supersol bombing, as well as the "main perpetrator" in placing both consulate bombs. Aisha Odeh was named as the "major offender" in the supermarket bombing, along with Rasheida Obeideh, who was described as "an escaped offender." A third defendant, Yakoub Odeh, was charged only with conspiracy.[3] All three were also indicted for unlawful membership in the PFLP, and two others were named in the indictment for lesser offenses unrelated to the bombings.[4]

The proceedings were to be held in the town of Lydda, about ten miles southeast of Tel Aviv and thirty miles from Ramallah. Lydda was a tragic locale for Palestinians, having been the site of the most extensive expulsion during the Nakba of 1948. Odeh's family would have known many Lydda refugees who had resettled in Ramallah, and the trip from the West Bank to attend the trial, which required a military permit, might well have taken them past the ruins of Lifta or other depopulated Arab villages.

A military court system had been established in 1967, shortly after Israel took control of the West Bank and Gaza in the Six-Day War. The court's jurisdiction extends to all Palestinians from the occupied territories, with the primary purpose of adjudicating security offenses. Defendants may be prosecuted for violations of various military orders or, as in Odeh's case, under the Defense (Emergency) Regulations that were enacted by the British in 1945 and adopted by Israel following independence. The provisions of the Defense (Emergency) Regulations are severe, truncating procedural protections, allowing prolonged administrative detention without trial, and providing punishment for activities such as joining organizations, attending meetings, and distributing literature—ordinarily protected in a democratic society. Ironically, Jewish organizations initially protested the Defense (Emergency) Regulations when they were first promulgated during the British Mandate, but their continuation has been seen as necessary and uncontroversial by successive Israeli governments faced with the challenges of Palestinian resistance.[5]

The military courts have never had any legitimacy among Palestinians, for whom they represent simply one more arm of the occupying power. The judges have always been Israeli Jews, as have nearly all of the prosecutors, with Israeli Druze providing the occasional exception. Conviction rates range upward of 95 percent, overwhelmingly as the result of plea bargains.[6] For most arrested Palestinians, therefore, it could fairly be said that the interrogation was the *de facto* trial, as confessions almost invariably led to guilty pleas.[7]

Nonetheless, defendants in military courts retained the right to challenge their confessions in a proceeding similar to a suppression hearing in the United States. As explained by the Landau Commission,

> When the accused's confession during interrogation is the main evidence against him, the accused's plea of not guilty in Court is tantamount to an allegation that his confession was obtained by improper methods, and is therefore invalid and inadmissible as evidence against him. Such an allegation necessitates the conducting of a "trial within a trial" on the admissibility of the confession.[8]

The "trial within a trial"—also called a "little trial," or *mishpat zota* in Hebrew—is held before the same judges who decide guilt or innocence. As the Landau

Commission put it, "the 'trial within a trial' constitutes the essence of the trial itself, and the verdict in it is in effect a decision in the entire trial, against the accused or in his favor."[9]

The prosecutor begins the little trial by presenting the defendant's written confession, including the "name and particulars" of the person who took the confession, the location of the interrogation, and a statement "noting that the accused was informed of his right not to say anything if he so wishes" and that the confession was translated and read aloud to the accused. Voluntariness, however, is a far more flexible concept in Israel than in the United States, as military courts "have found a considerable degree of coercion during interrogation to be consistent with a 'free and voluntary' confession."[10] Regarding security cases, the Landau Commission recognized "physical pressure . . . as an interrogation tool of the utmost importance."[11] Thus,

> The effective interrogation of terrorist suspects is impossible without the use of means of pressure, in order to overcome an obdurate will not to disclose information and to overcome the fear of the person under interrogation that harm will befall him from his own organization, if he does reveal information.
>
> Interrogation of this kind is acceptable under the law . . . and we think that a confession thus obtained is admissible in a criminal trial.[12]

The Landau Commission did place limits on the acceptable degree of coercion, noting that a confession obtained by physical abuse, or in a way that arouses feelings of moral repugnance, will ipso facto be disqualified.[13] But even that restriction came eighteen years after Odeh's "trial within a trial."

*   *   *

When the three-judge military court convened for the Supersol case on June 4, 1969, the prosecution table was already stacked high with ammunition found at the Odeh home in al-Bireh. An inventory of the materiel was introduced, listing two attack grenades, three Russian explosive bricks, a package of detonating cord, four sticks of plastic explosive, three British pencil timers, and multiple batteries from five countries.[14]

Represented by Israeli attorney Eli Cohen and Palestinian lawyer Ali Rafa, Odeh complained that her confession had been "extracted by force" and that she had confessed "only because she wanted some respite from being tortured and to prevent [another] young girl from being tortured as well."[15]

Thus, the first order of business was to determine the admissibility of Odeh's confession. In reality, it was the only order of business. The confession was detailed and extensive; if admitted, there was no chance of an acquittal. It was the prosecution's legal burden to establish that the confession had been freely given.

The main prosecution witness was Sgt. Ezra Kalish, who testified that he had participated in the midnight raid at the Odeh home, collecting the various munitions and devices. Along with a police woman, Kalish had awakened Odeh and searched her bedroom where he found explosives and PFLP literature. He then escorted her from Ramallah to Jerusalem, where they arrived at the Russian Compound around 4:00 a.m. Kalish implausibly asserted that he showed consideration for Odeh by allowing her to "rest" in his office before beginning his questioning two hours later.[16]

Odeh would claim that she had been viciously beaten during that same interval by men wielding wooden sticks and an iron bar. The prosecution vigorously denied inflicting any such abuse but the time gap certainly fit the pattern later identified by the Landau Commission, in which prisoners were brutalized outside the presence of their official interrogators, who could then truthfully testify that confessions had been given to them without physical coercion:

> Concerning the circumstances of obtaining and taking the confession, only the policeman who engaged in this at the end of the interrogation process would be brought to court to testify. He could testify in all good faith and conscience that at the stage in which he was involved, i.e. taking down the confession, everything went smoothly and the accused indeed made his confession voluntarily and of his own free will, as required by the law. The entire interrogation procedure preceding this stage, i.e. the interrogation by GSS [General Security Service, or Shin Bet] interrogators, would not be raised in court at all, and no GSS interrogator was called as a witness in trials within the trial.[17]

Whatever Kalish knew or didn't know about the actions of the GSS agents, he testified that he was "the only one who collected" the statements from Odeh, which was no doubt true as a matter of formal procedure. The torturers—for whom Kalish was the scribe—were not to be named or acknowledged.

In any case, Odeh quickly confessed to Kalish that she had set the Supersol bomb, either to end the abuse or, also likely, to divert the investigation away from her comrades whom she believed to be at large. This led, as Kalish explained, to the site visit to Supersol, where Rasmea and Aisha "reconstructed" the operation for the police.[18] Rasmea's reconstruction had involved feigning knowledge of the explosion's location. She had indeed visited the supermarket a week before the operation—she had apparently purchased the jam that was used to hide the device, as evidenced by the receipts found in her bedroom—but she had not been involved in planting the bomb itself. Kalish evidently figured out that Rasmea's initial statement had been contrived. "She worked with me for 6 days of oral interrogation," he testified.[19] It was only after Rasmea retracted her involvement in the actual bombing, and detailed her role in the preparations, that Kalish instructed her to reduce her confession to writing.

The greatest surprise came on the second day of Kalish's testimony, when he revealed the extent of Rasmea's cooperation with the prosecution. According to Kalish, she had eventually implicated dozens of PFLP operatives, including her codefendants Aisha and Yakoub, and Rasheida, who had escaped to Jordan. She also named the two students who had been arrested for the cafeteria bombing at Hebrew University, having known of their preparations in advance of the operation. In all, Kalish said, Rasmea's disclosures had led to eighty arrests in Ramallah, Nablus, Hebron, Bethlehem, and other locations in the West Bank.[20]

In Kalish's narrative, Rasmea had been motivated by her resentment of two PFLP leaders, who, she believed, had given up her name during their own interrogation. When told the names of the two men who were said to have betrayed her—identified by Kalish as Khalil Abu-Hadiga and Abdul Hadi Odeh—Rasmea responded, "If these are the heroes of the Popular Front, our movement is doomed. Look who are the people who are trying to free Palestine."[21]

The testimony about Rasmea's own betrayals brought turmoil to the courtroom. The other defendants, along with their friends and relatives, turned their backs on her, but the worst reaction appeared to come from Rasmea's own family. According to reports in the Hebrew-language press, a loud argument erupted between Rasmea and her father, who pushed away her extended hand. The shouting intensified when the court recessed. The Odehs eventually made their peace, and Yousuf would soon testify on his daughter's behalf, although the Israeli reporters did not mention the reconciliation in their stories.[22]

Kalish concluded his testimony by denying that Rasmea had ever been stripped and beaten during her interrogation. He claimed to have been with her constantly and said she had been confined in his office with a policewoman standing guard, rather than in a detention cell. Kalish added that he had "no reason to beat her, since she gave the police information which led to the capture of the rest of the gang."[23] Neither Kalish nor the military court, nor any of the Israeli journalists in attendance, appeared to recognize the witness's implicit acknowledgment that beatings could be used to force cooperation from a more recalcitrant prisoner.

The prosecution concluded its case by stressing that Rasmea was accused only of "assisting in planning" the Supersol bombing while "taking an active part in planting bombs only in the British consulate."[24]

* * *

Seeking to exclude her confession at the trial within a trial, Rasmea began her testimony with the flat assertion that "Kalish lied when he said I wrote this under my own free will." She described being beaten on the head and shoulders until she fainted and on "every part of my body" until her legs became paralyzed. She was doused with water to keep her awake, and then the beating would begin again.

Worse than the beatings, she was subjected to "sexual torture." In handcuffs, she was stripped naked by an interrogator named Marcus, who "took off my clothes and tore my blouse," before exposing her to a series of naked men. She was repeatedly threatened with rape by "men who had not seen girls for a long time." An interrogator named Abu Anni, whom she called "a fat tall Jew with a moustache and blue eyes," said he would rape her himself, and then switched tack, saying he "will not rape me but will bring my father in to rape me."[25] She had been violated with a stick that was inserted into her body.[26]

Rasmea acknowledged that two other prisoners had implicated her in preparing explosives, but she did not blame them for her confession. Rather, she testified that her resolve was shaken by the mistreatment of her family. She learned on the very first night that her father was in solitary confinement and her sisters were in a cell with prostitutes. She feared that her father would never be released, until he was brought in to urge her to confess, which led to her initial admission, which later proved false, of planting the Supersol bomb. The interrogators did not believe her Supersol story and so continued torturing her because "they knew it was not correct."[27]

Finally, after seven days, her father begged her to tell the interrogators "what they want to hear and they'll stop the torture and at the same time release him and my sisters." Rasmea complied. "My father's condition was also very bad. I obeyed my father and told them what they wanted to hear."[28] The result was a handwritten confession, in Arabic, eight pages long. Rasmea described the process, many years before the Landau Commission brought the GSS practice to light: "those who tortured me . . . told Kalish what they wanted me to write." Then, he "didn't allow me to write down any word he didn't want me to. He tore up many pages because he didn't want them."

"After I confessed," which was on March 7, "they didn't torture me any longer."[29]

On cross-examination, the prosecutor pressed Rasmea on the circumstances of her two confessions, initially on March 1, when she falsely admitted placing the Supersol bomb, and again on March 7, when she described the full details of the operation. If the police had only wanted her to admit guilt, why would they continue torturing her after the first confession, which had been more than sufficient to convict her?

Boxed in by the facts, Odeh had no choice but to concede that "they didn't believe what I said earlier," thus acknowledging that the interrogators, however brutal, were actually seeking an accurate story.[30] She was naturally, and understandably, less truthful in response to direct accusations. She denied any involvement in military work and said that she had "nothing to do" with the bombing at the British consulate, both of which she would admit in her 1980 interview with Soraya Antonius. She also claimed never to have met Rasheida Obeideh, whom she would later acknowledge as a comrade in a television documentary.

Yousuf Odeh also testified on his daughter's behalf. Displaying the same emotiveness that later impressed the *Sunday Times* reporters—described by the military court as "hysterical" outbursts—he claimed that two policemen "that I would be able to identify in a crowd fifty years from now" had forced him to beat Rasmea to get her to confess. Confirming Rasmea's own testimony, he described one of the interrogators as "tall, broad-shouldered, with a curly red moustache." Fearing that Rasmea was "going to die," he begged to be taken to another room where he could "not hear her screams." On cross-examination, he denied that any explosives had been found in his home, claiming that the numerous batteries including those with soldered thread had been for his grandson's toys. He acknowledged urging Rasmea to confess, in the futile hope it would prevent his house from being destroyed.[31]

*   *   *

The military court predictably rejected Odeh's claims, concluding that she had "lied and invented fantastic stories about the horrible things done to her" in order to justify her betrayal of her friends. As in virtually all such cases, the defendant's complaints of torture didn't matter in the face of the interrogator's "institutionalized lying." As later explained by the head of the Shin Bet interrogation department, "The judges believed us, of course. Because some of the Arabs tended to exaggerate their descriptions of what we did, refuting it all was no problem at all."[32]

The judges fully credited Sgt. Kalish's testimony, noting that he had seen Odeh "at least once a day" during the investigation. "He heard no screaming and described as a lie her stories of fainting, hitting with a stick, and pouring water to revive her." Rather, she had from the very beginning taken upon herself "the responsibility for the terrorist act carried out by another young woman." Thus, the court concluded that Odeh had "reported from her own free will detailed information about all she knows."

Odeh's confession would be received in evidence.[33]

The eight-page confession was written in Arabic on lined paper, with no strike-throughs or other visible signs of shakiness or indecision. Although not strictly chronological, it included the details of Odeh's involvement in the bombings, beginning with her recruitment to military work—*fida'i* in Arabic—while a student in Beirut. Her PFLP contact had quizzed her on the absence of armed operations in the West Bank and suggested that the reason was "the shortage of explosives and weapons," even though "enthusiasm and youth are available." Stopping in Amman en route home to Ramallah, Odeh met with another operative and agreed to act as a courier, first for communications and later for explosives.[34]

In Ramallah, Odeh received her instructions from Widad Qumri, who tasked her with hiding explosives—"some shaped like soap bars and some others like fingers"—and detonators, which she obtained from Rev. Elia Khader Khalil Khoury. She was also introduced to a person "familiar with explosives" who could later help her assemble the devices "because I had no prior experience and I like to make use of what I had."

In great detail, Odeh described her reconnaissance of the Jerusalem Supersol:

> Ten days prior to the explosion I went with a girl called Rashidah from Jerusalem to check out the location and we selected the spot where we were going to install the explosives in, and we bought a lot of stuff from there; like the jam jar which we bought in the afternoon as we entered the store twice; first at noon time and second time in the afternoon. . . . At that point we had picked some items, we paid for them and we left with our receipt. We went back again in the afternoon with the items we bought earlier still with us. It was like an experiment for us; are we going to be asked about the items we already have with us or no? As we entered, no questions were asked and so we decided to carry it again with us. . . . There were apricot jam cans, we bought one with some other items and I asked my friend Rashidah about the spot to put it back and she said either here back to its place or over there in the place where we saw cans of oils, and the latter is a better choice.[35]

Everyone met at Rasmea's home on the day of the operation, which had been chosen because her other family members were all in Jericho. Aisha and Rasheida arrived first, at around 6:30 a.m., followed by an explosives expert whom she called Hani. They prepared three devices, two for the supermarket and one for the consulate, installing the timing pens and soldering the cans shut. Aisha and Rasheida left for Jerusalem at 8:00 a.m., and Rasmea followed an hour later. Only that afternoon, upon returning to Ramallah, did Rasmea learn from a newscast that the Supersol operation had succeeded but the bomb at the consulate "did not explode and the operation failed."

As Rasmea explained it, "this failure pushed me to put more explosives again." She returned to Jerusalem four days later and placed another bomb— "two blocks of explosives and also two fingers of flexible explosives"—in a flower pot on the consulate window sill.

At the bottom of the confession, Rasmea wrote "This is all I know and I do not know anything else, and I voluntarily wrote it with my own hand writing and without any pressure." Then she signed her name.

*　*　*

Rasmea Odeh has consistently claimed—both at her Israel trial and later in the United States—that she had been tortured into making a false confession. The document itself certainly shows signs of having been shaped by her Israeli interrogators. It actually consists of two parts, separately signed, with the second far more detailed than the first. In addition, there is a prologue to the second section, stating "I want to clarify the truth with all what happened with me in this case; my connection with al-Jabah Al-Sha'biah—The Popular Front—and the operations I did and was responsible for."

The unavoidable implication is that the formal interrogator, probably Kalish, had been unsatisfied with the first segment and demanded that she provide further details, specifically tying the operation to the PFLP. The second segment also has two subject captions—"The Supermarket Operation" and "The Way I Obtained the Explosives"—that were much more likely to have been dictated by Kalish than included spontaneously by Odeh. It is likewise obvious that the GSS had extracted more information from Odeh than was included in her written confession. Although she implicated about a dozen others in writing, including her codefendants Aisha and Yakoub, there were nowhere near the eighty names that Kalish attributed to her in his testimony.[36]

On the other hand, the most important aspects of the confession have all been corroborated in the years since the trial. Rasmea, of course, told Antonius that she had indeed placed the bombs at the British consulate, and she told Amal Kawar that she had been active as a guerrilla and belonged to the PFLP. Both Aisha and Rasheida confirmed on video that they had prepared the Supersol bombs along with Rasmea, just as in her confession. Moreover, Aisha's Arabic-language memoir confirmed that the bombs had been prepared at Odeh family's house in al-Bireh with the aid of an "explosives expert," just as Rasmea described it in her confession.[37]

Tellingly, there are details in the confession that could have come only from Rasmea herself and could not have been intentionally supplied by the interrogators. For example, Rasmea's confession recounted her reaction to the Six-Day War, in terms nearly identical to her description to Antonius in 1980:

> I recalled that jinxed day which was 6/6/67 when we fled to the City of Jericho walking on feet, and after 10 days we went back that very same way—walking on feet.

Most significantly, Rasmea told Kalish that she had recruited Aisha, whom she knew from Girl Guides, into the cell:

> I told her that I'm intending to do an explosive operation along with another colleague of mine. . . . After a conversation with her I saw her strong enthusiasm for any Fida'i Action. . . . I told her you can come to my place on Thursday, which was the date with Rashidah and Hani to prepare the explosives in my home.[38]

In a 2004 documentary, Aisha thanked Rasmea for "dragging" her into military work, to which Rasmea replied, smiling, "military work was in you."[39]

The Israeli judges were not interested in the fine details of transcribing admissions, much less in determining how much of Odeh's confession had been directed by Kalish or the other interrogators. Having found the confession admissible, in conjunction with the physical evidence, the court entered a guilty verdict on January 22, 1970, noting that Rasmea had taken "a central role in this affair":

> [T]he defendant discovered activity in many areas while she was a member of the terrorist organization, "Popular Front for the Liberation of Palestine." She maintained in her home a considerable number of explosives, maintained connections with many of the active members of the organization and opened her home to the members of the gang in order to prepare explosives and made her home available on the morning of the assassination in order to prepare the explosives. . . . This defendant executed 2 terror acts at the British Consulate. . . .As it is told in her confessions, this defendant had a central role in this gang and had a hand in all the branches of operations.[40]

An observer from the International Committee of the Red Cross, who had been present during the proceedings, told a reporter that the court had "given the accused every chance of defending themselves" and concluded that there had been "a fair trial."[41]

The military court was unmoved by defense counsel's plea for lenience, based on Odeh's youth and difficult life as a refugee. "Due to the circumstances of the current security situation, the courts need to grant full attention to deter active offenders in order to protect the public."[42] Rasmea Odeh received the maximum sentence: two terms of life imprisonment and an additional ten years for membership in the PFLP. The sentences were retroactive to the date of her arrest, as meaningless as that was for terms of life. As it happened, however, she would ultimately serve almost exactly ten years before she was released in a prisoner exchange with the PFLP.

6 Neve Tirza

Rasmea Odeh and Aisha Odeh were not yet Hebrew speakers when they arrived at the Neve Tirza prison, so they could not have appreciated the grim irony of its name, evoking both a biblical oasis and a lengthy waiting time. Built in 1968, Neve Tirza would be Israel's only women's prison for the next twenty years, incarcerating almost two hundred female criminal and security prisoners from both Israel and the Palestinian territories.[1]

Part of a larger complex that includes the Ayalon men's prison, Neve Tirza could only be entered through a high, solid wall, leading to a boxy main building painted dull white. The prison's basic rooms each held six inmates on spare metal bunks in a space of about 185 square feet—there were also some two-person rooms of about 80 square feet—in long metal sheds, each with its own toilet and cold-water shower. The isolation cells were far smaller, with barely enough room for one person to turn around.[2] There were some amenities that were not usually found in men's prisons. The female inmates were allowed to wear their own clothes, rather than uniforms, and they were permitted to have small appliances, including televisions, in their rooms. Extra food could be purchased in the canteen, but outside food was prohibited, with the incongruous exception that Palestinian prisoners could receive olive oil from their families while Israeli inmates could not.[3]

At first, the Palestinians, who numbered only fifteen to twenty, were housed among the Israeli prisoners whose crimes ranged from petty theft and drug possession to robbery and murder.[4] Because the Palestinians considered themselves political prisoners, guilty only of resistance to occupation, they scorned the Israeli prisoners as merely common criminals. Palestinian accounts of Neve Tirza refer derisively to the Israeli inmates as "whores and prostitutes" or "mental cases," with little or no recognition of the social and family hardships that had ultimately landed them in prison.[5]

Indeed, there was a paradoxical class difference between the populations. Although members of an oppressed minority, most of the Palestinian women came from educated or middle-class backgrounds: Rasmea had been a university student; Aisha was a teacher; others were the children of prominent professionals. Virtually all of the Palestinians belonged to resistance organizations in which they had studied Marxism or other political theory. Their offenses had been driven by nationalist or revolutionary devotion rather than poverty, addiction, or despair. Thus, the Palestinians believed they "demonstrated more civility, intelligence, and self-respect than the Jewish inmates."[6]

The Israeli women, in contrast, almost all came from poor and chaotic backgrounds. Over half of them were drug addicts and nearly 90 percent had been subjected to domestic violence or sexual abuse. "They were the victims in their family," and many had been thrown out of their homes, never knowing secure living conditions or personal safety. Although none of the women were in prison for prostitution—which was not a felony in Israel—many had engaged in sex work at some point in their lives because of coercion or desperation. Others had simply been promiscuous, bearing children out of wedlock, which was enough to condemn them in the eyes of the Palestinians, whose own society was far less permissive.[7] If the Palestinian prisoners were revolutionaries by choice, most of the Israeli women were criminals by circumstance.

Class resentments, however, played at most a small role in the Israelis' hostility toward the Palestinian prisoners. Far more significant was an evident combination of racism, xenophobia, religious bias, nationalism, and, as they would have explained it, patriotism, which generated numerous incidents of violence. After all, many of the Palestinian prisoners had been convicted of murder, or attempted murder, of Israeli civilians. They included not only the Supersol bombers Rasmea and Aisha Odeh but also others like Mariam Shakhshir, who had been convicted for her role in the Hebrew University cafeteria blast.[8] Whatever solidarity or commiseration there was among the Israeli prisoners, it did not extend to convicted terrorists.

The attacks on Neve Tirza's Palestinian prisoners began almost immediately. As Rasmea put it, "the Israeli girls were full of hate against us" and often expressed a desire to "kill all the saboteurs," as the Israeli prisoners called the Palestinians. They "threw lighted cigarettes and poured dirty water and refuse and garbage on our belongings and on our clothing." Then it got worse. "There were attempts to kill one of us" by a prisoner who "stole a knife from the kitchen," and there was also a "plan to assassinate" Rasmea herself with an iron bar. Fortunately, she learned of it in advance and was able avoid the ambush.[9]

The kitchen was the most dangerous locale, where the Israeli prisoners had access to sharp implements, scalding water, and heavy pans, which they often used against the Palestinians assigned to meal duty.[10] Even the garden was not safe. One Palestinian prisoner working in a vegetable plot was grabbed from behind and strangled until her face turned blue, accused by an Israeli inmate of sneaking a cucumber instead of placing it in the required basket. The assault was in full view of the guards, who did nothing, and only the intervention of the other Palestinians foiled the attack.[11]

The Palestinian women were certain that the Neve Tirza authorities were complicit in the assaults by Jewish inmates, motivated by their own animosity toward the Palestinians. The prison warden, according to Rasmea, told the Palestinian prisoners that they were "black-hearted killers of children" and accused them of race hatred and anti-Semitism. Reflecting on this to her friend Aisha, Rasmea "started crying non-stop [and] then she burst out like a volcano":

> They want us not to hate them? They want to deny us our emotions and memory the same way as they denied us our homes, land and our dignity? . . . Or is it that the occupation does not exist, it is just a fabrication and we just imagine it?[12]

Referring to the Israeli women as "stooges for the most part," Rasmea told the U.N. Special Committee that "the principal cause was not the Israeli detainee[s] . . . the whole issue really was the policy followed by those responsible for running the prison." The guards, she said, "organized the activities of the Israeli girls, that is to say, their provocation, which was to increase the tension in the prison and among us." According to Rasmea, the warders wanted to cause fights between the inmate groups in order to direct the Palestinian "struggle against the enemy into other channels, that is instead of struggling against the administration we would fight other prisoners."[13]

The attacks were at their worst when there was news coverage of guerrilla actions, "particularly as a result of a military operation with successes of the Palestinian organization in occupied and non-occupied territories." These provided the administration, according to Rasmea's post-release testimony, "some justification to assassinate us" by provoking the Israeli prisoners, "or to render our lives really infernal, a hell within the walls of the prison."[14]

Rasmea was speaking in code, which should have been recognized by the members of the U.N. Special Committee in 1979. Successful "military operations" were terrorist attacks, such as the 1974 Ma'alot "incident," as Aisha termed it, in which Palestinian guerrillas seized an elementary school in northern Israel and killed twenty-two children whom they had taken hostage.[15] Because the PFLP considered all of Israel to be occupied, actions in "non-occupied territories" thus referred to aircraft hijackings and other raids—such as the 1972 Munich Olympics attack—in Europe and elsewhere.

Prisons everywhere are regrettably, if inherently, violent, with gangs and factions routinely taking every opportunity for reprisals against real or imagined enemies. In a setting already as tense and volatile as Neve Tirza, it is easy to understand, though of course not to defend, the Israeli prisoners' determination to retaliate against the vulnerable Palestinians, especially if the latter had been cheering the "successes" of guerrilla operations against civilians.

Whether or not the authorities incited or encouraged the attacks by Israeli prisoners, they did little or nothing to prevent or redress them. Even when the guards directly observed the violence, "the Israeli girls were not punished in any way." Instead, the Palestinian victims would be told that the Israeli perpetrator was "touched," as Aisha put it, and therefore could not be punished. "The prison authorities told us they had no control over the feelings of the Israeli girls because they were suffering from what happened outside the prison."[16]

Complaints about ill-treatment, inflicted by guards or other prisoners, were seldom investigated, unless the injury to the Palestinian was too grave to ignore. In those cases, there might be a "mock inquiry," as Rasmea called it, in which the "testimony was written down in a report, but in actual fact it was a farce." Complaints to the Red Cross only made things worse, as then "the treatment became more cruel."[17] Although foreign journalists were allowed in the prison, Palestinian inmates would be punished for describing "the reality in which we lived." Odeh once detailed the nature of her interrogation to a Norwegian journalist, after which "my treatment became harder and harder and I was no longer allowed to have [personal] clothing in the prison."[18]

∗ ∗ ∗

Two years after Rasmea and Aisha arrived at Neve Tirza, a separate wing was built for the Palestinian security prisoners—who eventually numbered as many as fifty—which afforded them some relief from violence but not from discrimination.[19] The Israeli prisoners were allowed many privileges that were denied to the Palestinians. Unless they were in isolation, the Israeli inmates "could walk about wherever they wanted in all the different sections of the prison," while the Palestinians "were prevented from leaving the section reserved for us" and were confined to a small courtyard when they were not in their rooms.[20] In addition to greater visiting privileges, the Israelis were allowed to use the telephone but Palestinians were not.[21]

The Palestinians were deeply troubled by religious bias. "I don't remember any of our public holidays being respected," said Aisha. On the first holiday in Neve Tirza, the prisoners "asked to stay together and pray as a group [but] this was refused." Instead, they were forced to remain in their rooms and denied visits with family members who were waiting outside the walls. On another occasion—Eid al-Mawlid, the birth of the Prophet—the Palestinians were ordered to vacate the room where they had gathered so that it could be used by Israelis. The guards refused to listen when the Palestinians attempted to explain that it was a religious holiday. "We are now going to put you in cells," they said, "because you are questioning our decision."[22]

The Israeli prisoners, in contrast, "had every freedom. Every Saturday people would come from outside, candles were lit on the Sabbath, on all the Israeli holidays the rabbi would come and pray with them." On Jewish holidays, the prison would provide special food and bring in singing groups.[23]

The Palestinians considered many of the restrictions arbitrary, calculated more to humiliate them than to enforce order. To them, it seemed obvious that the prison administration regarded any Palestinian sentiments as a threat to authority. Although the Palestinians were forbidden to sing "national songs or songs that spoke of Palestine," the Jewish inmates were allowed to sing "Zionist songs and sometimes they brought in special bands to sing these songs or even theater companies to act plays that expressed Zionist ideas."[24] There were even futile attempts at political conversion:

> We would get Israeli lecturers who spoke Arabic and would speak to us about the kibbutz movement, the Histadrut, Zionism. . . . We got folklore troupes who sang songs about Israel, actors who performed plays extolling Zionist heros [sic] and deeds, and so on. I think they thought this would change our minds.[25]

"Even the word 'Palestine' was prohibited," Rasmea told Soraya Antonius in 1980. "Once a child among the visitors sang a song which mentioned Palestine and the prisoner being visited was not allowed visits for three months." On another occasion, related by Aisha, the Palestinian women continued singing national songs after being ordered to stop. The guards came into the room, "shut the doors and then dragged each girl into the cells. When they shut the doors on us they had gas that they sprayed into our faces. . . . [O]ur faces seemed to be burning and it made us cry."[26]

The Palestinian women were also denied books and newspapers that the administration considered subversive. "We got books on Herzl, and Golda Meir and Eban, and Zionist accounts of Palestine, while any book by an Arab on Palestine, or any Marxist or progressive books were forbidden." At one point, according to Rasmea, even paper and writing implements were confiscated, as well as the exercise sheets from her economics textbook.[27]

Most serious, however, was the inadequate medical care. Palestinians' complaints were often met with a shrug and a doctor's insistence that there was no actual problem. Even serious illnesses and injuries—from bleeding ulcers to shrapnel wounds—were left untreated or misdiagnosed. "I have many comrades in the prison who were sent to the hospitals for medical examination . . . but the reports always said that there was no health problem." Rasmea believed that to be a form of payback, further punishing the Palestinians for their resistance activities. The "hospital physician's first question is not 'What is your complaint, what are you suffering from?' but . . . 'rebel or not.' Depending on the answer, he will decide what treatment is to be given."[28]

Even sympathetic physicians were often unable to provide adequate care. On one occasion Rasmea met with a doctor who was "compassionate and could have treated me" but the head nurse removed her from the room. "The nurse said that I was an assassin, a criminal, and that I did not deserve any medical treatment or care."[29]

Prison medical care is shamefully poor all over the world, so it is impossible to know whether the Palestinians were victims of discrimination or abuse rather than routine carceral neglect. Not for the last time, Odeh took advantage of a sympathetic audience, advancing some complaints that seem nearly impossible to believe. On one occasion, according to Rasmea, who said that by then she "knew Hebrew quite well,"

[T]wo people who were involved in a military operation were brought to the hospital under the supervision of frontier guards. They were put in a room next to mine and I found out by listening to the conversations of the soldiers . . . that it would have been easy for a doctor to save the arm of the first one and the leg of the second one. But the doctors amputated their limbs so that they wouldn't become involved in any more military operations.[30]

Although the story exploits the template of wanton Israeli barbarity—which persists to this day in florid rumors of organ harvesting—it was so far-fetched that even the Special Committee chairman, who had otherwise been supportive throughout Odeh's testimony, balked at accepting it.

* * *

Having been convicted only for acts of resistance, as they saw it, the Palestinian prisoners continued their resistance at Neve Tirza. As explained by the Canadian-Palestinian sociologist Nahla Abdo, this was especially true for women like Rasmea and Aisha whose "strong determination of resistance . . . drew its strength from local, national, and international experiences." Having been born near the time of the Nakba, these women had "memories that directly impacted on their growing up Palestinian." They had also been exposed to "revolutionary literature and to practical military training," which made them "part of the revolutionary era of the time."[31] Thus,

For most women political detainees, the prison was deemed to be a *site of resistance*. . . . For Palestinian women, moving from life under occupation to prison was synonymous with moving from the "large prison" to the small one.[32]

Abdo can be forgiven for minimizing the immeasurable difference between living in, say, Ramallah and confinement at Neve Tirza. It is a common rhetorical excess to compare prisons to other oppressive, but still unconfined, environments, and there can be little doubt that every woman would have immediately chosen freedom as quickly as possible. Abdo is right, however, that the Palestinian prisoners did not simply accept the conditions that they deemed abusive and discriminatory. Rather, they engaged in a series of strikes and protests beginning in 1970, just as Rasmea and Aisha were getting their own bearings at Neve Tirza.[33]

Prisoner protests, including frequent work stoppages and hunger strikes, were initiated in response both to individual injustices and to larger political issues.[34] In one instance, related by both Rasmea and Aisha, a Palestinian prisoner was sitting on her upper bunk after the doors had been locked for the night. A guard told her to get down from the bunk, but the inmate refused, saying she "had the right to sit on her bunk." The guards then dragged her out of the room and "they beat her and sprayed gas on her." The other Palestinian women protested this treatment to Red Cross, resulting in an investigation with mixed results.[35]

The Palestinian women had better success with other protests, some of which were related to work details. The women refused to work in the kitchen on Israeli Independence Day every year, as part of a "demonstration protesting their independence and our colonialism." Sewing assignments were common, usually related to the needs of the prison. On one occasion, however, they were ordered to sew IDF uniforms, which led to an extended strike during which they would only sew Palestinian embroidery. The administration responded by confiscating "books, pencils, and notebooks" but finally relented after fifteen days, and IDF uniforms were never assigned again.[36]

Strikes and work stoppages often resulted in a test of wills. The prisoners would object to some form of mistreatment, the authorities would respond by imposing greater punishments, such as the denial of visits or the removal of radios from their rooms, and the prisoners would in turn intensify their own protest, sometimes in the form of hunger strikes.[37] In the face of continuing protests, the Neve Tirza administration constantly needed to find new penalties. One creative punishment, ironically, was disallowing prisoners from working in the garden.

According to Abdo, "despite the forced nature of labor" at Neve Tirza, women did not mind working in the flower and vegetable gardens because it brought them in touch with places from which Palestinians had been exiled in the Nakba. "Working on the land has in fact connected women to their geographic or territorial identity." Although they could not visit their own birthplaces, "being in prison inside the 1948 boundaries . . . was considered by these women to be a blessing."[38]

Few if any prisoners ever actually described Neve Tirza as anything close to a blessing, but Rasmea did explain the importance of the land in her 2004 video interview:

> Prison is a harsh place. You can't see further than the walls surrounding you . . . .
> I remember an incident when my punishment was to prevent me from working in the prison garden because they knew how much I loved the land and how much I enjoyed it. They used to try to take that pleasure away from me.[39]

Rasmea committed the ultimate act of resistance on June 14, 1975, when she tried to escape by "digging under the outside wall of the compound."[40] Discovered by a routine patrol, she was quickly captured and returned to custody. It is hard to imagine that Rasmea attempted the jailbreak on her own—how much digging could one person do? where would she have gone alone in Israel?—but no one else was apprehended with her.[41] If she had any confederates, this time she did not betray them.

Rasmea was initially charged with "partial escape," which was a criminal offense. The prosecutor decided against pursuing the new case, however, given that she was already serving a double life sentence. Instead, Rasmea was "exiled," as she put it, to a more severe prison in Gaza (which was then still under Israeli occupation).[42] It is understandable that Rasmea considered her stay in Gaza to be an exile. Unlike Neve Tirza, there was no women's section in the prison, and the few female inmates were held in a single cell, thus depriving Rasmea of the community and support network she had developed over the previous five years.

If conditions at Neve Tirza were harsh, in Gaza they verged on unbearable. The women's cell was windowless, cold, and damp, with a "door made of open bars that let the cold in."[43] The walls were painted dark brown and a strong light was left shining day and night, which, along with the "terrible stench," made it almost impossible for the women to sleep.[44] The prisoners were allowed outside for only thirty minutes each day and then only in a tiny courtyard smaller than the cell itself. Certain books had always been subject to confiscation at Neve Tirza, but in Gaza the prisoners were allowed no books at all.[45] The guards were even more arbitrary in Gaza, imposing punishments for imaginary infractions.

After three months, Rasmea was finally allowed to return to Neve Tirza only because her health had deteriorated so badly in Gaza.[46]

∗   ∗   ∗

That was the Palestinian account of life in Neve Tirza, in which the prison was a site of relentless discrimination, deprivation, and torment. Needless to say, the administration would tell a different story, in which the Palestinian prisoners were a constant problem: uncooperative, recalcitrant, and disobedient. All prisoners have complaints about the conditions of incarceration but the Palestinians repeatedly raised the stakes with protests and work stoppages, which only made it more difficult to manage an already combustible environment.

According to Rasmea, the first Palestinian hunger strike began only four or five months after her arrest, while she was still awaiting trial. That would have been in the summer of 1969, only about a year after the prison had first opened. The demands were for "increased visitors and more often than once a month" and for more books, better food, and increased hours of exercise in the courtyard. "We also wanted to be treated as political prisoners instead of criminals."[47] Although the demands were understandable, the prison administration no doubt regarded the hunger strike as an unreasonable rebellion, aimed at undermining discipline. Everyone in prison wants more visitors and books, and definitely better food, but the Palestinian women would have appeared to be insisting on special treatment based on the nature of their own offenses.

Upon arriving at Neve Tirza, for example, the prison director cautioned Aisha that the Palestinians "were considered as prisoners who were only to obey orders given by the warders, and if we disobeyed we would be punished." Aisha replied that "we had rights that we wanted to exercise . . . and that we were political prisoners." The director took the retort as defiance, informing Aisha, "You are only criminals and you are going to be treated like criminals."[48]

In their testimony before the U.N. Special Committee, Rasmea and Aisha referred repeatedly to strikes and protests, as well as complaints to the Red

Cross and various journalists. The dates of the incidents, which included multiple hunger strikes, are imprecise, but they appear to have occurred frequently throughout their ten years at Neve Tirza, sometimes over seemingly typical incidents of incarceration such as restricted visiting hours and insufficient access to linens.

It would not be easy for the two sides to reach an accommodation, as they saw the world from completely different angles. To the Israelis, the Palestinians were, in fact, "killers of children," whose political motives only made them more dangerous. The description was not inaccurate, as the Neve Tirza prisoners included women who, despite initial denials, have later admitted to setting bombs that killed civilians of all ages.[49] The Palestinians, however, saw themselves as patriots, unfairly held captive by an oppressive power. Thus, confrontations were almost inevitable over incidents such as singing "national songs," which Palestinians regarded as spirit-lifting and prison authorities viewed as acts of incipient rebellion.[50]

Both Rasmea and Aisha complained to the U.N. Special Committee, for example, that the Israeli inmates could leave the prison during Jewish holidays but Palestinians were not afforded the same privilege.[51] This may have seemed like unfair discrimination to the members of the Special Committee, none of whom questioned the basis for the disparate treatment. The Neve Tirza authorities, however, obviously had good reasons to keep the Palestinians in continuous custody. The Israeli "common criminals," who were serving fixed sentences, could be relied upon to return to prison, and in any case could be fairly easily apprehended if they violated the terms of their furloughs. The Palestinians, however, always considered themselves resistance fighters who denied the very legitimacy of the Israeli government. They could hardly be expected to voluntarily return to prison, especially those, such as Rasmea and Aisha, who were serving life sentences. A furloughed PFLP member was not merely a flight risk, she was a flight certainty. Rasmea demonstrated as much by attempting to escape, and her PFLP comrades outside the prison engaged in repeated commando operations aimed at coercing her release.

From the administration's point of view, the most dangerous situations were likely to arise from concerted actions by the prisoners. Work stoppages and hunger strikes could be managed, but the risk of an uprising could never be discounted due to the prisoners' connections to the various guerrilla factions that continued to attack Israeli targets. Thus, subversive materials were banned, including the "progressive books" demanded by the strikers, and prisoners were forbidden to hold meetings. Nonetheless, the Palestinian women were determined to "organize our programme," advance "the aims of our revolutionary movement," and otherwise replicate the training they had received in "military camps" before their arrests.[52]

Fears of a possible rebellion were not misplaced, given the inmates' continuing adherence to organizations committed to armed struggle. "Newly arrived security inmates declare or choose an allegiance to one of the Palestinian political factions, which remain their primary affiliations in prison life."[53] Indeed,

> Rather than serving as a deterrent and a punitive framework for breaking the PLO's strongest cadres, Israel's prisons were transformed into higher "academies," as the inmates called them. . . . The uninitiated received instruction (albeit theoretical) in the use of arms and explosives.[54]

As Abdo observed, the women in Neve Tirza had joined the resistance with a "commitment to the national cause and love for the homeland." The majority "belonged to the leftist parties and a few were members of Fatah [or] Islamic Jihad." Most maintained their affiliation throughout their incarceration, though it was not unknown to change allegiance, as Aisha did, switching from the PFLP to the still more radical Democratic Front for the Liberation of Palestine.[55] According to Rasmea, the administration "would try and create dissensions between the girls who belonged to Fateh and the PFLP and other organizations. But we were determined to keep our *sumud*," or steadfastness.[56]

Solidarity with Fatah and the PFLP inspired *sumud* among the Palestinian inmates, but it represented something entirely different to the Israelis, against a backdrop of deadly airport, embassy, and synagogue attacks. And, of course, there were airplane hijackings intended to force the release of Palestinian prisoners, some of which were conducted specifically in the name of Rasmea Odeh.

7 | Freedom

On September 6, 1970, PFLP guerrillas commandeered four passenger airplanes, setting a record for simultaneous hijacking not matched until September 11, 2001. Two of the planes—Swissair Flight 100 and TWA Flight 741—were ordered to fly to Dawson's Field, an abandoned British airstrip in the remote Jordanian desert. As the Swissair flight landed and taxied to a stop, a female hijacker, flying under a forged Costa Rican passport issued to "Miss Fernandez,"[1] made a radio announcement in English:

> The Popular Front for the Liberation of Palestine informs you that its Commando Unit is now in complete control of the DC-8 plane, flying for Swiss Air, Flight number 100, on its way from Zurich to New York. Task Force Rasmieh Odeh who has taken over command of this plane [sic].[2]

Another of the hijacked planes, Pan Am Flight 93, was taken to Cairo. The fourth attempted hijacking, of El Al Flight 219, failed when Israeli air marshals shot and killed one of the commandos while disarming the other and taking her into custody. The flight made an emergency landing in London, where the captured hijacker was identified as the seasoned guerrilla Leila Khaled, who was already famous for her successful hijacking of a TWA flight in 1969. Speaking from a British jail, Khaled announced, "I am the leader of the hijack. My name is Leila Khaled and a member of the PFLP and from the unit of Rasmieh Odeh, a Palestinian woman prisoner."[3]

It was no small accolade to be the namesake of a PFLP task force. There were thousands of Palestinians imprisoned or detained in Israel, including about fifty women in Neve Tirza, but Khaled and "Fernandez" had singled out Rasmea Odeh as their role model. The *fedayeen* in another hijacking had named their unit after Che Guevara, indicating Odeh had been honored for her military work as a guerrilla rather than simply as a random victim of the Shin Bet.

The four hijackings, with a fifth one a few days later, were masterminded by Wadi Haddad, who had personally recruited Odeh to the PFLP only a few years earlier.[4] Haddad led a ten-person intelligence staff that kept scrupulous track of "airline routes, schedules, passengers and airport security measures" while another squad trained in "aerial navigation and aircraft mechanics."[5] The one thing Haddad and his subordinates had not sufficiently planned for, however, was success.

Holding hundreds of hostages in the Jordanian desert turned out to be far more complicated than Haddad and the PFLP had anticipated. The first problem lay in the pure logistics of feeding and caring for so many people, including children and the elderly, for which no arrangements had been made in advance. Ultimately, and far more seriously, the Jordanian government considered the hijacking a challenge to its own authority, which eventually precipitated the civil war known as Black September. In the meantime, disorganization within the PFLP and dissention with other Palestinian resistance organizations made it almost impossible to present a consistent set of demands in exchange for the release of their hostages.[6]

The hijackers eventually settled upon demanding the release of seven PFLP guerrillas, including Khaled, who were held in Britain, Germany, and Switzerland, as well as an unspecified number of Palestinians in Israeli prisons.[7] The PFLP's initial unwillingness to name the Palestinian prisoners, or even attach a number to their demand, made it impossible for Israel to negotiate, even in principle. Eventually, the PFLP negotiator assured a Red Cross representative that they were seeking only "female prisoners" and "particularly important or heroic fedayeen."[8]

Of the thousands of Palestinians in Israeli custody, only Rasmea, and perhaps a few others, fell into both categories.[9] And as the namesake of the hijackers' own task force, Rasmea had briefly become, next to Khaled, the most famous female *fida'i* in the world. (The PFLP later upped the ante by requesting the additional release of two Algerian diplomats detained by Israel since the previous month who had mistakenly booked a flight with a stop in Tel Aviv.)[10]

The standoff eventually ended on September 30 with the release of all hostages. Khaled, whose extradition had been unsuccessfully demanded by Israel, and the other guerrillas were freed from European prisons, as were the Algerian diplomats detained in Israel. Despite extreme pressure from Britain, Germany, Switzerland, and even the United States, Israel refused to budge on its Palestinian prisoners, and Rasmea Odeh remained at Neve Tirza.

*   *   *

The Dawson's Field hijackings were not the last attempt to force the release of Odeh and other PFLP operatives. On May 8, 1972, four guerrillas—three from the newly named Black September organization and one from the PFLP—stormed the cockpit of Sabena Flight 572, then en route from Vienna to Tel Aviv.[11] Once in control of the aircraft, the guerrillas brazenly ordered the pilot to continue the original itinerary and land at Lod Airport (now Ben-Gurion) where they demanded the release of 315 Palestinian prisoners in exchange for the ninety passengers and ten crew members they held hostage.[12]

Negotiations on the Israeli side were handled by Shimon Peres, who was then the transport minister, and Defense Minister Moshe Dayan. While the hijackers were threatening to blow up the plane and everyone on board, the Israelis stalled for thirty hours by pretending to be gathering the hundreds of prisoners, including Odeh. In reality, the Israelis were mustering the elite counterterror unit Sayeret Matkal, which included future prime ministers Ehud Barak and Binyamin Netanyahu in its ranks.[13]

On the morning of May 9, the Israelis brought a group of individuals posing as Palestinian prisoners to the airport and told the hijackers that the Sabena plane had to be serviced by technicians before it could take off. Dressed in white coveralls, sixteen Sayeret Matkal commandos entered the aircraft and swiftly overwhelmed the hijackers, killing the two men and capturing the two women—Theresa Halsa and Rima Tannous. Netanyahu was wounded by friendly fire in the course of the operation, as were three passengers, one of whom died in the hospital.[14]

Halsa, a Palestinian Christian who was born and educated in Israel,[15] later described her motivation:

> I thought I would be shot by Israeli soldiers. Or we were going to blow up the plane if our demands weren't met. I was ready to die because I wanted to make the Europeans and Americans realise that there was a Palestinian people and that they had been treated unjustly by the Israelis. . . . They called us terrorists, but we weren't. The real terrorists were the Israelis who threw the Palestinian people off their land.[16]

Sentenced to multiple life terms in prison, Halsa was incarcerated at Neve Tirza, where she befriended Rasmea and Aisha Odeh.[17] Testifying before the U.N. Special Committee, Rasmea made a plea for Halsa—who was still imprisoned—to receive adequate medical care for an "acute blood disorder," thus returning the favor to a comrade who had sacrificed everything in a failed attempt to free her.[18]

*   *   *

Not every guerrilla operation was aimed at hostage taking; some of them were purely murderous. On May 30, 1972, three members of the Japanese Red Army Faction, trained by the PFLP in North Korea and Lebanon, arrived at Lod Airport on Air France Flight 132.[19] After proceeding through passport control they retrieved weapons hidden in their luggage. The three men immediately began firing automatic rifles and lobbing grenades at arriving passengers, intending "to murder as many people as possible, thereby garnering maximum worldwide exposure."[20] They succeeded in killing twenty-four people, including seventeen Puerto Rican Christian pilgrims, and wounding seventy-two others, before Israeli security killed two of the terrorists and subdued the third. The captured terrorist was twenty-four-year-old Kozo Okamoto, whose name would surface again only three months later.

Shortly before midnight on September 4, 1972, eight Black September commandos held a rendezvous at Munich's central railroad terminal. It was the ninth day of the quadrennial Olympic Games; they would make their move early on the tenth day. The *fedayeen* collected the automatic rifles that had been stowed in station lockers, donned official-looking track suits, and headed for the nearby Olympic Village. Arriving at around 4:00 a.m., the Palestinians appeared to be athletes returning from a night out. They encountered a group of Americans, sneaking back into the compound after curfew, who helped them scale the six-foot fence.[21]

Once inside the perimeter, it took the *fedayeen* only a few minutes to reach the quarters of the Israeli delegation, which were tragically ill-guarded. Storming through the door, the Palestinians killed two Israelis and took nine others hostage. Once the alarm was raised, German police and military units surrounded the building where the guerrillas held their hostages, but the athletes in nearby buildings were not evacuated even after the terrorists threw the body of a dead Israeli wrestling coach onto the plaza. Meanwhile, Olympic events continued to be televised on schedule and were only suspended twelve hours after the initial attack.[22]

In exchange for their hostages, the *fedayeen* demanded the release of 234 prisoners from Israeli custody. The list of names included "Rasmieh Odeh" and "Aishah Odeh," the two female hijackers from Sabena Flight 572, and Kozo Okamoto, the surviving perpetrator of the Lod Airport massacre. In addition, they also demanded freedom for two West German prisoners, Ulrike Meinhof and Andreas Baader, the urban guerrilla leaders of the Red Army Faction.[23] The *fedayeen* threatened to kill one hostage every hour if the prisoners were not quickly released.[24]

Israeli Prime Minister Golda Meir steadfastly refused to negotiate for the release of Rasmea Odeh or anyone else, despite pressure from West Germany and other western governments. Meir's offer to send an Israeli special forces unit was declined, and the West Germans' own plan to storm the residence was abandoned due to lack of adequate preparation. Following a protracted standoff, with multiple deadline extensions, the Palestinians changed their demands. They issued a typewritten "Kommunique" in German condemning the "arrogant attitude of the Israeli military regime" and calling for three aircraft to transport them with their hostages to "a location yet to be determined" (eventually revealed to be Cairo). "Any attempt to interfere with our operation," they threatened, "will end with the liquidation of all Israeli prisoners and the Federal Republic will be blamed."[25]

The Germans initially feigned consent to the Palestinians' demands, providing two helicopters for transportation to a nearby NATO airfield. The German plan was to ambush the guerrillas with sniper fire as they moved from the helicopters to a waiting Lufthansa airplane, but the unit assigned to the task was untrained, undermanned, poorly positioned, and "scandalously under-equipped."[26] The result was a fiasco, in which all of the hostages were killed, as well as five of the eight Palestinians and a Munich police brigadier. The subsequent international condemnation convinced the PLO—but not the PFLP—to cease all military activity outside Israel and the occupied territories.[27]

*   *   *

Haddad had not been involved in the Munich operation, but the bloody failure did not dampen his resolve to free Palestinian prisoners in Israel. It took nearly four years of extensive planning for Haddad to reemerge on the international scene, in an operation that would eventually require "accurate intelligence, meticulous preparations, and coordination with at least two despots, Libya's Muammar Qaddafi and Uganda's Idi Amin."[28] On June 27, 1976, four hijackers—two from the PFLP and two members of the German Revolutionary Cells—seized control of Air France Flight 139 en route from Tel Aviv to Paris, having taken advantage of lax security to board the plane during an intermediate stopover in Athens. The guerrillas ordered the flight diverted to Benghazi, Libya, for refueling and onboarding three more armed operatives.

The ultimate destination was the Entebbe Airport in Uganda, where the hijackers came under the protection of the eccentric dictator Idi Amin. The hijackers soon released 209 passengers, retaining as hostages 83 Israelis and 11 other Jews. They also offered to release the 12 Air France crew members, but the pilots and attendants courageously insisted on remaining with their passengers.

The hostages were brought to a shuttered transit hall where they were surrounded by scores of Ugandan soldiers. Amin himself led the negotiations with Israel, conveying the PFLP's demand for the release of fifty-three prisoners, forty of whom were held by Israel and the others by West Germany, Switzerland, and France.[29] The reduced number—fewer than a quarter as many as demanded at Munich—reflected Haddad's determination to "do what he could to free his people" while attracting maximum international attention.[30] His priorities were his own PFLP recruits, high-profile prisoners, and women. Rasmea Odeh met all three criteria. Others on the list included the Syrian Catholic Archbishop Hilarion Capucci, who had been convicted for using his clerical status to smuggle arms to Fatah cells in Jerusalem, and Kozo Okamoto, still serving his sentence from the Lod Airport massacre. In addition, the hijackers demanded the release of eight Europeans, said to be comrades of Ilich Ramirez Sanchez, better known as "Carlos the Jackal," and the so-called Nairobi Five, who had been apprehended in Kenya in a thwarted bombing plot and later transferred to Israel.[31]

With over a hundred lives at stake, Prime Minister Yitzhak Rabin considered making a deal in violation of Israel's long-standing policy against negotiating with terrorists, but only if he could avoid freeing anyone "with blood on their hands." Shin Bet director Avraham Ahituv insisted that "anyone who has killed a Jew . . . must die in an Israeli prison after being sentenced to life."[32] That would have ruled out Rasmea Odeh, who had been convicted of a double murder, but it turned out to make no difference. There would be no negotiations with the Entebbe terrorists.

On the night of July 3, four Israeli Hercules cargo planes headed to Entebbe Airport, carrying a contingent of Sayeret Matkal commandos under the leadership of Yonatan Netanyahu, brother of the future Israeli prime minister. After landing in the dark, the Israelis quickly overwhelmed the Ugandan sentries, killing several in a firefight. Netanyahu was also killed in the exchange, but the others soon reached the terminal where the hostages were held, killing all eight hijackers. Other members of the assault team seized the airport control tower while another detail destroyed eleven Ugandan fighter jets on the ground, thus ensuring that there could be no pursuit.[33]

The entire operation lasted less than an hour. Of the 106 hostages, 102 were rescued and taken to Israel. Three had been killed by crossfire and one, a British woman who had been hospitalized, was left behind and later murdered. Dozens of Ugandan troops had been killed; several Israeli commandos were wounded, but Lt. Col. Netanyahu was their only fatality.

It would be another two years before the Israeli government would finally agree to negotiate for the release of Palestinian prisoners.

*   *   *

On March 9, 1978, eleven Palestinian *fedayeen* made their way by Zodiac boat from Lebanon to northern Israel. Landing on a beach south of Haifa, they encountered an American tourist, whom they shot and killed. Moving on to the nearby Coastal Road, they sprayed traffic and pedestrians with automatic weapon fire and eventually hijacked two passing busses. By the time Israeli security forces put an end to the terror, thirty-five Israeli civilians had been killed, including thirteen children, along with nine of the eleven Palestinians.[34]

Intended to disrupt the ongoing peace negotiations between Egypt's president Anwar Sadat and Israeli prime minister Menachem Begin, the Coastal Road massacre was the worst terrorist operation ever to occur on Israeli soil (then or since).[35] In response, the IDF launched Operation Litani on March 14, an invasion of southern Lebanon intended to push PLO and other Palestinian guerrilla forces at least ten kilometers away from the border with Israel.

The IDF succeeded in establishing a security zone, at the cost of over a thousand Lebanese and Palestinian lives, eventually extending to the Litani River, patrolled by both Israeli troops and the local, pro-Israel South Lebanon Army. A U.N. peacekeeping force (UNIFIL) arrived on March 23, and a ceasefire was brokered between Israel and the PLO on March 28, although the Israeli occupation continued.

On April 4, a group of six Israeli soldiers and a civilian guide strayed out of the security zone in the vicinity of the Rashidieh refugee camp, on what was later characterized as an unauthorized sightseeing expedition. The Israelis unexpectedly stumbled into a Palestinian guerrilla unit, whose fire crippled their command car and killed four of the soldiers. The civilian and one of the soldiers managed to escape back to Israeli lines, but reserve Pvt. Avraham Amram was captured.

Amram was tortured by his captors, who were from the PFLP—General Command, a splinter group best known for the 1974 massacre of eighteen civilians, half of them children, in the northern Israeli village of Kiryat Shmona.[36] He was taken first to Beirut, where he was shifted from location to location, enduring a fresh beating with every transfer. Amram was eventually moved to Damascus, where he was held in solitary confinement for nearly a year.[37] Israel ended the Litani Operation and withdrew from southern Lebanon in June 1978.

In the meantime, discussions continued between Israel and Egypt, leading to the Camp David accords of September 1978. In the course of subsequent negotiations Sadat repeatedly pressed Begin to offer the Palestinians a "good-will gesture" by releasing prisoners from the West Bank and Gaza. In an American television appearance, Begin "hinted broadly" that Israel would indeed free prisoners if the move did not affect "Israel's security."[38] In fact, Defense Minister Ezer Weizman had been in secret talks with the Egyptians, undisclosed even to the other members of the Israeli cabinet.[39] They eventually reached a deal in which seventy-six Palestinian prisoners, many of them designated by the PFLP, would be exchanged for just one Israeli soldier, Avraham Amram.[40] Many years later, defense attorney Michael Deutsch would tell Odeh's American jury that "normal criminals, people who commit criminal acts, are not released in trades, in prisoner exchanges," about which he was quite right.[41]

∗   ∗   ∗

Sometime after midnight on March 14, 1979, Rasmea Odeh was surprised when military police removed her from her cell at Neve Tirza, blindfolded and in handcuffs. Along with five other female prisoners, including Aisha Odeh, she was shuffled in complete silence to a waiting bus. Given no explanation by the authorities, the women assumed that they were being transferred to another prison, which usually meant worse conditions and additional deprivations. Instead, they were taken to an airfield where, still in blindfolds, they could hear the sound of an idling jet engine. Only then did the women realize that they were going to be freed, although they were still unaware of the details of the exchange. They were not allowed to take any of their belongings, and they were given no opportunity to say goodbye to their comrades who, as Rasmea put it, "had become part of me."[42]

"Up until the very last minute," Rasmea later recounted, "the Israelis behaved meanly." While waiting on the tarmac, still handcuffed and blindfolded, "they told us that if we wanted to go to the bathroom to do it right there, in the open." That was a final act of humiliation, Rasmea assumed. "I suppose they wanted to photograph us and show that Palestinians are animals, without shame."[43] Ill-treatment of Palestinian prisoners can never be discounted in Israel, but Odeh was going to be seated on a Boeing 707, along with sixty-five other prisoners for a five-hour flight to Geneva, Switzerland, where there would be further delays before they could be released. Given the limited toilet space on the aircraft, as well as the complex logistics of escorting shackled prisoners to and from the restrooms, the offer of a final opportunity to use the tarmac could be at least partially explained as necessary for convenience and sanitation, rather than sheer callousness or degradation. If demeaning photographs were taken—which happens in wartime, as we know from Americans' contemporary experiences in Iraq and Afghanistan—none have ever surfaced in public.[44]

Although the Israelis had agreed to release seventy-six Palestinians, there were only sixty-six on the flight to Geneva, six of whom were women. Ten prisoners had chosen to be released to the occupied West Bank, where the Israelis agreed they could live in freedom. One of those was Mariam Shakhshir, who had been convicted for the bombing at the Hebrew University cafeteria in which no one had been gravely injured. Having received a life sentence for the two Supersol murders, Rasmea was not given the option of remaining in Palestine; Theresa Halsa, also serving a life sentence for her role in the Swissair hijacking, was not released at all.[45]

The sixty-six Palestinians were kept blindfolded and handcuffed as they were led one-by-one onto the chartered civilian aircraft. Once seated, their feet were shackled to the floor and they were ordered to remain silent. Infractions— either talking or attempting to see under their blindfolds—were met with beatings, although one prisoner reported that the blows were not severe.[46] There was a Red Cross representative on the plane, perhaps a physician, as recalled by one prisoner. Although the representative was not allowed to intervene on the prisoners' behalf during the flight, he reassured the Palestinians that "things will be O.K." and asked them to spread an encouraging word among themselves.[47]

* * *

The logistics of the Geneva Airport exchange were excruciatingly complex. Amram arrived from Damascus at about 7:30 a.m. in a Russian-made Bulgarian airliner, still in the hands of his captors from the PFLP—General Command. The Israeli flight landed about ten minutes later, and the two planes parked on opposite sides of airport, nearly a half-mile apart and well out of sight of each other. It took Red Cross representatives almost three hours to arrange the actual transfers, due to a "climate of unbelievable suspicion and distrust" on both sides. Security was tight, as Swiss police ringed the two aircraft and kept photographers and reporters far away from the site.[48]

Red Cross officials shuttled back and forth between the planes, finally reaching an agreed protocol. Amram would not be allowed to deplane until half of the Palestinians had been seated on an airport passenger bus. That process was slow and painstaking, as the Israeli authorities and Red Cross representatives double-checked the identity of each prisoner before they were allowed to leave the plane. As a final indignity—"meanness, right up to the last," according to Odeh—the soon-to-be former prisoners were roughly kicked or shoved as they exited the aircraft in Geneva.[49]

Only after the first thirty-three Palestinians were on the bus, confirmed by walkie-talkie, was Amram permitted to take a seat in the waiting Red Cross minivan, which then drove halfway to the Israeli plane. Once it was confirmed that the remaining Palestinians were on the bus, the transfer was concluded, with the vehicles crossing paths as they drove between the two aircraft. Amram went straight aboard the Israeli plane, but the Palestinians were required to wait another forty minutes, some of them crowding the gangway, while their identities were again checked, this time by officials from the PFLP—General Command.[50]

The Israeli flight finally departed at around 11:30 a.m. The Bulgarian plane left about thirty minutes later, on a flight plan for Tripoli, Libya, with Rasmea Odeh on board.

8   America

The freed prisoners landed in Libya where they were hosted at a "festive reception," but they did not remain there.[1] Instead, they traveled onward to Lebanon, where so many other displaced Palestinians had sought refuge. In Beirut, the PFLP singled out "Comrade Rasmea Odeh" among the released detainees who were praised for their "rush to join with the troops of the revolution" and "resolve to persist in the march toward total liberation." The official PFLP magazine published a full-page poem about Odeh:

> She raises her fist in the face of the occupier
> > to issue her ruling that the revolution continues
> And she reads a prophecy of the gun
> > that daylight is at the threshold of the moment.[2]

Although many female ex-detainees had difficulty finding rewarding jobs, Odeh obtained employment in Beirut providing educational and health services to Palestinian refugees, similar to the work she had done in the West Bank before her arrest. She was also employed in a research center.[3]

After four years in Lebanon, Odeh was "able to go back to Jordan," where she lived until immigrating to the United States in 1996.[4] Her years in Amman, Jordan, were "the best period in my life," Odeh later testified. "I have a house, I have a car, I have a bank account," she said, "and I was happy there."[5] In addition to work, Odeh was also able to complete her education in Amman. She enrolled in English classes and studied at several universities, eventually receiving a law degree from Al-Ahliyya University in 1990.[6]

During the years 1979–1995 she was admired in the Arab world as one of the first four female Palestinian activists who had departed from the "women's frameworks" to become active guerrillas. The other three were Aisha Odeh, Rasmea's accomplice in the Supersol bombing; Fatima Bernawi, who had placed a bomb at a movie theater in West Jerusalem and later became the highest-ranking woman in Fatah and a member of its Revolutionary Council; and Leila Khaled, famous for having participated in two airplane hijackings and later a member of the Palestine National Council. All four were celebrated for their "fighting careers," and not as random victims of Israeli persecution.[7]

In her interview with Soraya Antonius, conducted in Beirut shortly after her release from prison, Odeh declared that she would "remain part of the cause." She vowed to "play my part in it," adding that "without struggle nothing can be achieved for a good life." Odeh kept her promise. Through her years in Amman, Odeh remained an activist, never denying or repudiating her involvement in guerrilla work. At the time of her 1990 interview with the American academic Amal Kawar, Odeh was a member of the PFLP Central Committee.[8] No one writing on Palestinian women questioned her past participation in "armed struggle," and she gave Arabic-language television interviews recounting her involvement in "military work."[9]

The acknowledgments ended, however, when Odeh received a call from the United States.

Odeh had stayed in touch with her older brother Mustafa in Stockbridge, Michigan—a U.S. citizen who had received a PhD in political science and owned a restaurant in nearby Jackson—visiting him for four months in 1988–1989. In 1995 Odeh's father was diagnosed with cancer, and the family thought it best for him to receive treatment in the United States. Odeh's mother had passed away eleven years earlier, her sisters were all married with families, and Mustafa, with a business and eight children, was in no position to be a caretaker as well. It was therefore decided that Rasmea, as the only unmarried sister, would relocate to the United States to care for their father there. It was a commitment that she made somewhat reluctantly, but family is family the world over.[10]

Because her father and brother were American citizens, Odeh qualified for permanent residence under the family unification provision of the Immigration and Nationality Act. The visa process required three visits to the U.S. embassy in Amman to provide the necessary documentation, before she was finally ready to file her completed application.[11]

On December 28, 1995, Odeh submitted her four-page "Application for Immigrant Visa and Alien Registration."[12] The misleading or untruthful information began on the first page, where she listed her place of birth as "Lifta, Jordan." National locations are admittedly tricky for Palestinian refugees, who do not want to accept the legitimacy of Israel in any part of historic Palestine. On the other hand, Jordan has never exercised or claimed sovereignty over Lifta, even during the period when it annexed and controlled the West Bank in 1948–1967. By falsely claiming to have been born in Jordan—where there might well have been a village named Lifta as far as a U.S. consular officer could know—Odeh intentionally obscured her connection to Israel. Tellingly, she listed her parents' birthplaces as "Palestine," which she could also have done for herself had she not been intent on concealing her past.

The deception continued on the second page, where she was required to provide "all places you have lived for six months or longer since reaching the age of 16," and corresponding dates. Odeh's response listed only "Amman Jordan," stating that she had lived there continuously since 1948.[13] She made no mention of Neve Tirza, in Israel, where she had been incarcerated for ten years, or even Ramallah, al-Bireh, or Beirut (where she lived at least twice) or Syria (where she may have lived for "less than a year").[14]

The most serious falsehoods were in response to a series of Yes/No questions on pages three and four of the application, which covered the applicant's possible criminal history. The questions asked if she had ever been "convicted of 2 or more offenses for which the aggregate sentences were five years or more," whether she had "ever been arrested," whether she had ever "been in a prison," or whether she had "ever been the beneficiary of a pardon or amnesty." Despite her arrest and two murder convictions carrying life sentences, her ten years at the Neve Tirza prison, and her subsequent release by amnesty (a legal technicality in Israel that enabled the exchange), Odeh untruthfully checked only the "No" boxes, thus suppressing the most significant facts in her background.[15]

Following her submission of the completed application, Odeh appeared at the U.S. embassy for an interview with a consular officer who had reviewed the file. Placed under oath and speaking through an Arabic translator, she confirmed all of the information in her application. If Odeh had answered the criminal history questions truthfully, her file would have been referred for further investigation to the U.S. State Department's visa office in Washington, DC, with no action taken in Jordan. But because Odeh falsely answered "No," her visa application was approved at the American embassy in Amman on January 25, 1995, and signed by Raymond Clore, chief of the consular section.[16]

Rasmea Odeh arrived in Detroit on Royal Jordanian Flight 267, via Montreal, on April 18, 1995. She was ready to begin a new life in the United States, believing that her past as a convicted terrorist and prison inmate would not follow her.

*　*　*

Odeh lived with her brother in Michigan, caring for her father and occasionally working as a cook in Mustafa's restaurant, called Steve's Ranch after his American nickname. She also visited family members in Chicago, which led to an incident in late 2002 that gave her a new direction in life. While sitting in a Chicago park, she noticed that a young Arab girl, perhaps six or seven years old, was sitting and crying while all of the other children were happily playing. Odeh approached the girl and asked her why she was not playing with the others. "I can't," the child answered, because "my mom didn't allow me to play with the boys."[17]

Recalling her organizing and social service work among Palestinian women in Ramallah, Odeh asked the child for her address. The next day, she went "to knock on the door of the family." As she has recounted many times, Odeh asked the woman why her daughter was not allowed to play with the other children. It turned out that the woman "was living in fear of raising her daughter in America and that there were many other Arab immigrant women who shared the same struggle."[18]

"Are you the only one who has this problem not to let your kids communicate with the other kids?" Odeh asked.

"No," answered the frightened woman. "All of us we don't want to communicate with anybody."

Odeh asked if the woman would agree to have coffee with her the next day and to invite some Arab neighbors to join them. At the meeting, as Odeh later described it,

I discussed about the problem, how it's scary to isolate their kids because if they want to do bad things they can do it when they go to the school, but we have to let them grow up in a good environment and trust them, educate them in a good way to be a good citizen in the future and not isolate them.[19]

The experience was transformative for Odeh. After almost eight years in the United States, she had made three trips back to Jordan, where her life had been so good. Her father and brother had passed away, and she had been thinking of returning permanently to Amman.[20] But now she realized that there was a role for her to fill in the Arab and Palestinian community of Chicago. In her childhood in Ramallah, she recalled, she could not find anyone to "help my family and help my mother" who cried all night. And so she "felt it isn't for me not to go to find my interest, but I have to help the people here."[21]

Odeh resolved not only to stay in the United States but also to become a citizen. "So I decide from that moment to ask for . . . naturalization."[22]

*   *   *

The application for naturalized U.S. citizenship is called an N-400. Odeh completed her form and submitted it on June 2, 2004, this time listing her birthplace somewhat more accurately as "Jerusalem, Jordan."[23] It was only on the seventh page that a series of entirely false answers began. There were at least nine of them, each question including the word **EVER** in bold-face capital letters, beginning with the first one:

> Have you **EVER** been a member of or associated with any organization, association, fund, foundation, party, club, society, or similar group in the United States or any other place?

Odeh answered "No," notwithstanding her membership in the ANM and the PFLP, both clearly organizations or parties, which she had acknowledged in her 1980 interview with Antonius. In fact, she had described the ANM as the "political party that was most concerned with the problem" of Palestine, and she had been a member of the PFLP Central Committee until at least 1990.[24]

The next question asked, "Have you **EVER** been a member of or associated (*either directly or indirectly*) with . . . The Communist Party [or] a terrorist organization?" Again, Odeh answered "No," although she had told Antonius of attending Communist Party meetings in Ramallah, beginning at age twelve, and the PFLP had been designated a terrorist organization by the U.S. Department of State since 1995.[25] Despite the PFLP's history of violent guerrilla warfare and its oft-stated goals of destroying Israel and overthrowing "reactionary" Arab regimes,[26] she also answered "No" to the question, "Have you **EVER** advocated (*either directly or indirectly*) the overthrow of any government by force or violence?" (The italics in both questions are in the original.)

Odeh then falsely answered "No" to each of the following five questions,[27] as though her arrest, conviction, and imprisonment in Israel had never existed:

Have you **EVER** committed a crime or offense for which you were not arrested?

Have you **EVER** been arrested, cited, or detained by any law enforcement officer . . . for any reason?

Have you **EVER** been charged with committing any crime or offense?

Have you **EVER** been convicted of any crime or offense?

Have you **EVER** been in jail or prison?[28]

The above questions required the applicant to answer "Yes," according to the instructions, "even if your records were sealed or otherwise cleared or if anyone, including a judge, law enforcement officer, or attorney, told you that you no longer have a record." There was obviously no exception for release through a prisoner exchange or by amnesty nor for an arrest, conviction, or imprisonment that the applicant considered oppressive, unfair, or unjust. If the latter were claimed, however, the applicant could answer "Yes" and set out the details in the space provided for explanation, which Odeh left blank.[29]

Finally, Odeh answered "No" to two additional questions:

Have you **EVER** given false or misleading information to any U.S. government official while applying for any immigration benefit or to prevent deportation, exclusion, or removal?

Have you **EVER** lied to any U.S. government official to gain entry or admission into the United States?[30]

Her 1994 visa application, of course, had contained a series of false and deceptive answers about her personal background and criminal history, making Odeh's last two responses on the N-400 untruthful along with all of the others.

As the final step in the naturalization process, Odeh appeared for an in-person interview in Detroit on November 3, 2004, conducted by adjudication officer Jennifer Williams. Following brief introductions, Williams placed Odeh under oath for a review of the written application. The entire interview was conducted in English, as the law required, with Williams making sure that Odeh understood everything.[31] As Odeh later testified, Williams was very kind and sympathetic toward her, trying to "finish the interview as quickly as possible and to be easy for me as well."[32]

Williams reviewed each section of the application with Odeh, giving her an opportunity to make changes or corrections to any of her responses. Odeh made no significant corrections, and Williams therefore circled each checked box as Odeh confirmed her answers.[33] When they came to questions fifteen to twenty-one, which covered "Good Moral Character" and included the questions about crimes and imprisonment, Williams read each question aloud, explaining, as she had been trained to do, that they covered crimes committed "anywhere in the world."[34]

The interview also included an examination for English language proficiency and a ten-question civics test, covering issues in U.S. history and government. Odeh passed both tests, signed her N-400 under oath, and Williams then approved the application. Odeh was sworn in as a U.S. citizen on December 9, 2004, receiving a Certificate of Naturalization issued the same day.[35]

Odeh's father and brother had died shortly before she was naturalized, so she joined other family members in Chicago, where she followed up on her plan to devote herself to helping the people in the Arab community.

Chicago

Odeh's skills as a leader and grassroots organizer made her an important and much-admired figure in Chicago's Arab and Muslim community. In early 2005, she began working as an AmeriCorps volunteer at the Arab American Action Network (AAAN) on the southwest side, with the hope of addressing, as the filmmaker Nehad Khader put it, "the pervasive difficulties faced by newly arrived immigrant women that ranged from overt racism, isolation, and gender violence to a critical lack of social support and restricted access to social services."[1]

The Arab Community Center, a precursor to the AAAN, had been founded in 1972 as an organization where "Arab Americans of all generations" could find services and connections, as well as a "safe political and social space" for gathering together. By the early 1980s, the Center was also an important location for political organizing. "My folks started bringing me here in 1982, during the first Israeli war on Lebanon," said Hatem Abudayyeh, who is now the executive director of AAAN. "Organizers were giving us up to date news on the resistance. . . . It shaped my political views and raised my consciousness, not only about issues related to Arabs and Palestinians, but also about local and global struggles for liberation."[2]

The AAAN was founded in 1995, succeeding the Arab Community Center, as "new models of organizing" became necessary in the wake of the Gulf War. The organization was determined to provide a "secular and inclusive voice" for "reducing the social and political isolation experienced by Arab Americans and assisting them in becoming active participants and leaders in American society." The organization grew and professionalized through the 1990s, creating projects promoting advocacy, education, youth outreach, social services, and the arts.[3]

The events of September 11, 2001, created greater urgency for the AAAN in response to "discriminatory policies and backlash" against Arabs and Muslims, including an arson attack that destroyed its offices and forced relocation to temporary quarters. The organization was increasingly called upon as the "voice of Arab Americans in Chicago," leading to the establishment of coalitions with "other oppressed and immigrant communities." An increasing emphasis on activism and social justice was accompanied by a revised vision statement calling for the development of an "Arab-American community whose members will have the power to make decisions about actions and policies that affect their lives; access political power as well as social and economic services; and live in a context of equity and social justice."[4]

The AAAN was finally able to move back into its own building—known as the *Markaz*, Arabic for "Center"—in August 2004, shortly before Odeh arrived to volunteer. She found a vibrant and essential organization with both full-time and part-time staff and an annual budget approaching $500,000. AAAN program areas included adult education, youth education (including a hip-hop program for high school students), family services, domestic violence intervention and prevention, and cultural arts.

As Odeh later explained, the organization has programs for "each age in the family," beginning with six-year-old children, continuing through the teen years and into adulthood. "We focus on the family to educate them," she said, "beginning from their families, their communities, and in the society as well." Odeh was proud of her work with AAAN to provide assistance in the area of social services, helping "the needy people" fill out applications for public aid and for medical cards and to obtain other benefits including (ironically) "citizenship exam preparation."[5] Most important for Odeh was her work with the Arab Women's Committee.[6]

* * *

Sometimes called the Domestic Peace Corps, AmeriCorps is a program of the U.S. government that places and supports individuals in non-profit organizations across the country, where they "address critical community needs like increasing academic achievement, mentoring youth, fighting poverty, sustaining national parks, [and] preparing for disasters." Members, as they are called, commit to service for terms ranging from three months to a year or longer, receiving a stipend for living expenses. AmeriCorps members have been placed in national organizations such as Habitat for Humanity, the Red Cross, Boys and Girls Clubs, and Teach for America, as well as local community groups such as the AAAN.[7]

Odeh joined the AAAN as an AmeriCorps volunteer in 2005, working with the nascent Arab Women's Committee, which had been organized in a series of "small, in-depth discussions and trainings . . . on key issues facing the Arab-American community." Focusing on English language and citizenship classes, the Arab Women's Committee also "lobbied around immigration and public benefit policies in the working-class neighborhoods of the southwest side."[8]

That was only the beginning. After two years with AmeriCorps, Odeh became a full-time employee of the AAAN, eventually advancing to a position as the organization's associate director and head of its Family Empowerment Program. Under her leadership, the Arab Women's Committee became a dominant force in Chicago's Arab community. "Rasmea was the one who really expanded it, took it off the ground," said Suzanne Adely, one of the original organizers. "She was the right person for the job as she can quickly connect with the community, and she serves as a real role model." With characteristic energy and commitment, and deploying a "personalized, relationship-based strategy" she had developed before coming to the United States, Odeh went door to door in Arab neighborhoods, even cold-calling Arab names from the telephone book, eventually recruiting over six hundred women from Palestine, Iraq, Yemen, Egypt, Syria, and other countries.[9]

The foremost goal of the Arab Women's Committee has been women's empowerment. "We are doing our best . . . to strengthen the woman because the woman is the base of the family," Odeh once explained. "We focus on this to let the woman [be] independent, strong, to be active in their society as well and not depending on . . . public aid services." Rather than remaining in traditional women's roles, "they have to be active and take decisions and share decisions that affect their lives."[10] The Arab Women's Committee thus emphasized "civil and human rights training so that they understand what their rights are here as immigrants," while focusing as well on "cases of domestic violence within Arab-American communities."[11]

That was a daunting task, as Arab women, especially immigrants, faced numerous challenges in Chicago. As explained by Louise Cainkar, professor of social and cultural sciences at Marquette University, "the discrimination and prejudice that Arab women . . . endure in the United States make for an American experience that is not easy. Women are heckled on the street and children face bullying, starting in elementary school."[12] A common experience, described by Prof. Nadine Naber, has been "the anti-Arab racism and Islamophobia they confronted in their interactions with the US medical industry, their children's schools, their neighbors, and their local playgrounds."[13]

Odeh's approach to the many problems facing Arab women was to develop "a politics of the collective, based upon dialogs that build a sense of confidentiality and safety among the women." By sharing their stories, the women were better able to cope "with the aftermath of war and displacement and problems that arose with their spouses upon migration to the US."[14]

Among the projects of the Arab Women's Committee, initiated or expanded by Odeh, perhaps the most original was the writing workshop, in which immigrant women were encouraged to share their stories "to help them cope with the traumas of war, displacement and re-settlement."[15] One such workshop was attended by sixty women from nearly every Arabic speaking country, many of whom "had to walk by themselves through a polar vortex snowstorm to get there." Odeh inspired the women to "turn to one another with matters that often remain undiscussed" in their community, such as "the increased patriarchal oppression they faced" after immigration and their husbands' "increasing control over their bodies and their movements." One woman described her marital problems, and how they were compounded by her neighbors' hostility and disrespect of her hijab.[16]

Odeh's approach relied heavily on the arts to draw out the women's experiences. She called upon them to write down their immigration stories, sometimes in the form of poems and plays, which she hoped to publish in book form. Odeh herself also wrote short plays, something that she had also done at Neve Tirza, one of which was performed at an International Women's Day celebration. According to an observer, the play focused on the "gender-related struggles" in a multi-generational Arab immigrant family. "The audience was engrossed, laughing and commenting throughout the performance, perhaps because they rarely see their own life struggles thus affirmed in the US." Following the performance, Odeh asked each of her workshop students to read aloud from something they had written. A Yemeni woman went first. "I love my teacher," she read to the group.[17]

The admiration of her students was no doubt prompted by Odeh's willingness to share her "own story of sexual assault," which enabled her "to foster a level of trust about gender injustice," leading to open discussions of otherwise taboo subjects. Again, in the words of Prof. Naber, "She tells her truth. They tell their truth. They confide in her. She confides in them." Thus, Odeh's work with the Arab Women's Committee encompassed "a radical feminist politics where the struggle to end state violence *and* intimate partner violence happens together . . . challenging injustice and hierarchy, and bringing in more and more people in the creation of an ever-larger base."[18]

*　*　*

Odeh's exemplary organizing work among Arab Americans was also recognized in Chicago's wider community. Her writing workshops were funded by a grant from the University of Illinois Institute for Public Policy and Civic Engagement, and she received an award from the Chicago Human Relations Council.[19] Most significantly, the Chicago Cultural Alliance named Odeh an Outstanding Community Leader of the year in 2013. The Chicago Cultural Alliance is an "active consortium of 43 Chicago-area cultural heritage museums, centers and historical societies who span 30 neighborhoods and nine suburbs in the Chicago area and represent over 30 different cultures from around the world." The Alliance's "core members" range from the American Indian Center to the Ukrainian National Museum and include the AAAN. Its mission is "to connect, promote, and support centers of cultural heritage for a more inclusive Chicago," where "cross-cultural dialogue and collaboration are an integral part" of the city's civic fabric.[20] Criteria for the Outstanding Community Leader Award include helping "shape a more genuine and encompassing representation of his/her community" and embracing "the values of inclusion and tolerance in making a more culturally vibrant city."[21]

Odeh was nominated for the Outstanding Community Leader Award by the AAAN, a founding member of the Alliance, and was chosen by a vote of all forty-three core members.[22] The award was presented at the Alliance's annual MOSAIC fundraiser, which featured a video biography of Odeh. Speaking in Arabic, with simultaneous English translation, Odeh described her early life and education, including her family's dispossession. Stating that she was born in "the historical city of Jerusalem"—rather than Lifta—"which is sacred to the three monotheistic religions," she explained that her family had "lost everything" when the "Zionists occupied Palestine." She told of how she had been prevented from continuing her studies in Beirut and therefore remained in Palestine, working with "the internally displaced" who had been "forced out of their homes into other towns and villages but not necessarily outside of Palestine." Odeh's presentation skipped ahead to her work in Chicago, "supporting the empowerment of women" and helping them "learn to be a part of American society." She concluded by expressing her pride in the accomplishments of the members of the Arab Women's Committee, many of whom had become leaders in the community in their own right.[23]

Odeh emphasized her "case management social services type of work" in Palestine, in which she was "trying to find food and clothing and homes for these internally displaced." In fact, Odeh's social service work in the Israeli-occupied West Bank could not have lasted more than about ten months or so, during the period between early June 1967 and late February 1969, and excluding her year of medical school in Beirut. Her video narrative did not mention her transition, in the same short time frame, from social service to "military work" or her membership in the ANM and recruitment to the PFLP. Although she alluded briefly to living in Lebanon and Jordan, Odeh said nothing about her ten years in an Israeli prison.

The Chicago Cultural Alliance award video was not the only time Odeh sanitized her background for an American audience, constructing the appealing myth of having spent years engaged in social services in occupied Palestine when she had actually been incarcerated at Neve Tirza. Until recently, an example could be seen on her "Activist Profile," posted on the AAAN website, which cited her extensive experience and "advocacy in Jordan and Palestine," continuing,

"In Palestine," she says, "we helped women face a difficult political situation. We taught them how to deal [with challenges], how to live. When the schools closed, we taught their kids. Where there was a curfew, we brought them food.

When they were giving birth and the Israeli soldiers refused to let them through checkpoints, we tried to take them [to the hospital ourselves]." [Quotation marks and brackets in original][24]

Those were noble endeavors, but they were not Odeh's. There were only few months between her return from al-Arabia University and her arrest for the Supersol bombing, when she was mostly preparing for her military work, and she could not have participated in all of the activities she claimed. Frequent school closings and constant checkpoints, for example, were not instituted in the occupied West Bank until the outbreak of the First Intifada in late 1987, by which time Odeh had been in prison for over eight years. It is disputed whether Israelis have routinely delayed Palestinian ambulances at checkpoints other than for valid security reasons, but the roster of women who helped circumvent post-Intifada roadblocks did not include Odeh. And if she ever distributed food under a curfew in Ramallah, it was more likely imposed by the Jordanians rather than the Israelis.

In many ways, it is understandable that Odeh would portray herself as the personification of Palestinian women under occupation, even to the extent of taking credit for acts of nonviolent resistance carried out by others. Odeh's AAAN Activist Profile, however, omitted her nearly unique status in the resistance as one of the first four women to be "an active guerrilla."[25] Later, when she did become an "icon of the Palestinian liberation movement," Odeh's myth-building assumed new and more expansive expressions.[26]

Exaggerations and omissions aside, Odeh's years at the AAAN were admirable. Working as a full-time community organizer, she also served as an in-person Obamacare Navigator.[27] Although her duties often required her to visit families in the evening, she was able to obtain a master's degree in criminal justice at Governors State University. Yet more impressively, her leadership of the Arab Women's Committee accomplished something that no one had done before, bringing the "anti-violence feminist movement" into conversation with immigrant Arab women. In the words of Prof. Naber, Odeh had "created an environment that feels safe where [Arab women] can reveal things you don't tell anyone else because you would be too scared."[28]

As one immigrant woman put it, "She works without reward or personal profit. All she cares about is supporting and protecting us and our families."[29]

There is no telling how much more Rasmea Odeh could have achieved in Chicago if the U.S. Department of Justice had not intervened.

*   *   *

In the early morning hours of September 24, 2010, dozens of FBI agents, supported by SWAT teams, conducted simultaneous raids at the homes of seven leftist activists in Minneapolis, Chicago, and Grand Rapids, Michigan, as well as the Twin Cities office of an organization called the Anti-War Committee. Pursuant to search warrants, the agents spent many hours tearing apart rooms and turning the premises upside down before hauling away computers, files, notebooks, cell phones, passports, and "box after box of address books, family calendars, artwork and personal letters," as well as various household items and even children's toys.[30] Before leaving, they served subpoenas on fourteen individuals, commanding them to appear before a grand jury in Chicago the following month. Nine more subpoenas were eventually issued to, as the recipients became known among their supporters, "the Midwest 23."

The FBI operation had actually started more than two years earlier, in the spring of 2008, as an investigation into a possible plan to disrupt the Republican National Convention, to be held that year in St. Paul, Minnesota. An undercover informant had infiltrated the Freedom Road Socialist Organization (FRSO) and had fed the FBI meeting notes and the names of members, some of whom also belonged to labor unions and organizations including the Anti-War Committee, the Colombia Action Network, and the Palestine Solidarity Group—Chicago.[31] There were in fact large-scale demonstrations at the convention leading to some arrests, but there was no violent disruption. Nonetheless, the FBI continued its investigation of the radical groups and individuals that had come under surveillance, many of whom had proudly "traveled to Colombia or Palestine to learn firsthand about US government funding for war and oppression."[32] The FBI's suspicions of links to Revolutionary Armed Forces of Colombia (FARC) and the PFLP were fueled by surreptitious recordings made by its covert operative.[33]

An FBI spokesman at the time stated, "The warrants are seeking evidence in support of an ongoing Joint Terrorism Task Force investigation into activities concerning the material support of terrorism." One of the targets protested the "outrageous fishing expedition," explaining that "we barely have money to publish our magazine. We might write about [revolutionary groups] favorably, but as for giving them material aid, nothing."[34]

The FBI's "Operation Order," accidentally left behind at one of the search sites, identified the investigation as "predicated on the activities of [named subjects] in support of the Revolutionary Armed Forces of Colombia (FARC)." Interrogations were to cover membership and activities of the FRSO, the Anti-War Committee, and the PFLP. Sample questions included, "Have you, anyone from the FRSO, or anyone you know, ever given anything intended for the PFLP?"[35] The applications for the search warrants, filed only the previous day, stated that the investigation was based on violations of the U.S. Criminal Code section prohibiting the provision of "material support or resources to designated foreign terrorist organizations."[36] The efforts of the FBI's Minneapolis Joint Terrorism Task Force's investigation to establish "probable cause" that the targeted individuals had attempted, provided, or conspired to provide "material support to a Foreign Terrorist Organization" are found in the forty-three-page supporting affidavit of Special Agent John Thomas. According to Thomas, the FRSO referred to the FARC and PFLP as part of their own family of "commies fighting for national liberation" and on that basis provided "material support" through "donations to individual members of foreign terrorist organizations, through unions operating as fronts . . . and through 'delegations' composed of FRSO members" visiting foreign countries[37]

The warrants themselves authorized the seizure of any evidence of travel "to and from Palestine" or to any other foreign location in support of foreign terrorist organizations, "including, but not limited to FARC and PFLP." The warrants also sought "materials related to the identity and location of recruiters, facilitators, and recruits" to the FRSO and the Anti-War Committee.[38] The grand jury subpoenas further required production of all pictures, videos, correspondence, and records of payment relating to any trip to, or communications with, "Colombia, Jordan, Syria, the Palestinian Territories, or Israel."[39]

Seven of the Midwest 23 were Palestinian Americans, including Abudayyeh (whose home was also searched), then as now the executive director of the AAAN in Chicago. Clearly a major target of the investigation, Abudayyeh was suspected of ties to the PFLP, including illegal "material support." Ominously for him, the grand jury subpoenas to some of the others insinuated that he had been a conduit to the PFLP, demanding production of "all records of any payment provided directly or indirectly to Hatem Abudayyeh [or] the Popular

Front for the Liberation of Palestine."[40] At one point, Abudayyeh's bank accounts were frozen, and it took him three years just to recover the personal property and papers that had been seized from his home.[41]

None of the Midwest 23 cooperated with the grand jury subpoenas, shielded by the Fifth Amendment's testimonial privilege. The government did not pursue immunity grants, which might have led to contempt citations, but did continue to hold out the possibility of indictments for providing material support to foreign terrorist organizations. In the end, no charges were brought against any of the Midwest 23, although the government would find, in the words of one of Odeh's later supporters, a "consolation prize."[42]

*　*　*

Rasmea Odeh was not one of the Midwest 23. Her home was not searched and she was not subpoenaed for grand jury testimony. To her misfortune, however, a sharp-eyed FBI agent came across her name in the course of the broader investigation into the FRSO, Abudayyeh, and AAAN.[43] Ironically, the FBI's attention may have then been drawn to Odeh due to the appearance of unrelated organizations with similar names in the search. The FRSO had made a series of financial transfers to the PFLP-linked "Palestinian Women's Union," which was also called the "Women's Committee" in conversations secretly recorded by the undercover informant.[44] The latter name was easily confused with Odeh's Arab Women's Committee in Chicago, mentioned frequently in AAAN promotional materials. Whatever the reason, the U.S. Department of Justice began an investigation into Odeh's naturalization, coordinated by the U.S. Attorney's Office for the Northern District of Illinois.[45] After some difficulty, relevant documents concerning Odeh's arrest, trial, and imprisonment were located in Israel, translated into English, and provided to the American prosecutors pursuant to a Mutual Legal Assistance Treaty of 1998 (MLAT).[46] Odeh's fingerprints from the Neve Tirza prison were compared to her naturalization application; internet searches located newspaper articles about her imprisonment as well as the video made by the Chicago Cultural Alliance. Finally, an agent of the Department of Homeland Security intercepted Odeh at Chicago's O'Hare International Airport on July 31, 2013, as she was returning to the United States from a visit to Jordan and Jerusalem. She was taken aside for a "secondary interview," which was surreptitiously videotaped.[47]

Odeh was arrested on October 22, 2013, charged with unlawful procurement of citizenship, a felony punishable by ten years in prison.[48] Shortly afterward, she attended a "People's Thanksgiving Dinner," where she received the "Nelson Mandela Award" from the FRSO. Only recently released on bond, Odeh was in apparent good spirits as she delivered her acceptance speech. "I need your support," she told the seventy people in attendance, "and we all need each other's support to stand strong and continue."[49]

10 Indictment

A Detroit grand jury returned a sealed indictment against Rasmea Odeh on October 17, 2013, charging her with a single count of "Procurement of Citizenship or Naturalization Unlawfully," in violation of 18 U.S. Code § 1425(a).[1] The General Allegations in support of the indictment began with a description of the PFLP, including its 1995 designation by President Clinton as a "foreign terrorist organization." The allegations continued by detailing Odeh's arrest, trial, and imprisonment in Israel, as well as her release in the 1979 prisoner exchange. Finally, the General Allegations set out the specifics of Odeh's immigration and naturalization applications, including most of her many false answers.[2] Although it would not become fully evident until later, the indictment strategically omitted any allegation that Odeh had falsely answered the question: "Have you **EVER** been a member of or in any way associated (*either directly or indirectly*) with . . . a terrorist organization?"[3]

Following her arrest, Odeh was brought before the U.S. District Court for the Northern District of Illinois. She was represented by local lawyer James Fennerty. A longtime stalwart of the leftist National Lawyers Guild, Fennerty began his career with the Wounded Knee Legal Defense Committee for the American Indian Movement in the early 1970s and had frequently represented numerous other radicals and activists.[4] He was proud to have been involved with the Palestinian American community for over forty years, "working on various cases." He had known Odeh since 1984, he and his wife having met her on a trip to Jordan, only a few years after her release from prison in Israel.[5] That was long before Odeh had ever contemplated immigrating to the United States, when she was still acknowledging her past military work and her status as one of the PFLP's first four female guerrillas.[6]

Fennerty secured Odeh's release that day on $15,000 bail, with the additional conditions that she surrender her passport and abide by a travel restriction limiting her to the greater Chicago area (other than for attendance at court dates in Detroit).[7] Because Odeh's naturalization proceeding had been in Detroit, the case was then officially transferred to the Eastern District of Michigan.[8]

Odeh's first court appearance in Detroit was for her arraignment on November 13, 2013. She was accompanied by Chicago attorney Fennerty as she stepped into a courtroom packed with her friends and supporters. Magistrate Judge Laurie Michaelson was unfailingly polite to the defendants in her court—all of whom were people of color and all, except Odeh, were men—treating "everyone who came before her with notable kindness and courtesy." The day's order of business included detention hearings and bail revocation proceedings for defendants in custody, as well as arraignments for some who, like Odeh, were free on bond. Other than Odeh, the defendants were nearly all indigent, as a federal public defender was appointed for all save one.[9]

Detroit attorney William Swor stepped forward with Odeh when her case was called by the clerk, apparently acting as "local counsel" for the purpose of arraignment. The charge was read aloud—unlawful procurement of citizenship—and Odeh was informed of the potential ten-year prison sentence. Odeh "stood mute" when asked for her plea, which the ever-considerate Judge Michaelson recorded as a plea of not guilty, while also re-entering the conditions for bond.[10]

Immediately after the hearing, Odeh and Fennerty addressed the hundred or so people from Chicago, Milwaukee, Grand Rapids, and Detroit who had come to court in a show of solidarity. Fennerty emphasized the importance of public support as the case moved forward, while Odeh spoke only briefly, but emphatically, saying, "Thank you from me. It means a lot for me and my people!"[11] The most expansive speaker was Hatem Abudayyeh, Odeh's colleague and the executive director of the AAAN. In what would be a running theme for the duration of the case, Abudayyeh sought to link Odeh's defense to anti-U.S. government and anti-Israel political causes:

The immigration charge is a pretext to go after her. Just as the U.S. government used political repression against African American, labor and other movements in the past, it is now repressing movements for social justice in our country again today. The U.S. and Israeli governments are angry because we are effective at organizing and changing attitudes of the people in this country about war and occupation in the Middle East. The boycott, divest and sanctions movement against Israeli Apartheid is growing and spreading; making a dent. The U.S. government is not able to criminalize the political activity of the Anti-War 23 and they will not be able to do it to Rasmea Odeh either![12]

Six days later, attorney Swor entered his written appearance, indicating that he had undertaken full representation of Odeh.[13] A 1972 graduate of the Wayne State University School of Law, Swor is one of the preeminent criminal defense attorneys in Michigan. He has successfully represented defendants in numerous widely publicized and highly charged cases, including, as noted on his website, "international money laundering accusations, parents accused of murdering their children, business men accused of drug trafficking, and Americans accused of terrorism and plotting to overthrow the American government," as well as a Canadian businessman "accused of attempting to smuggle cocaine into the United States [and] a father accused by the state of Michigan of murdering his eleven-month old son."[14]

The grandson of Lebanese immigrants and an Arabic speaker,[15] Swor did not shy away from controversy. He worked with "the ACLU challenging the federal government's attempt to deport hundreds of Iraqis who are lawfully in the United States" and he was "lead counsel for 19 Arab men who were rounded up immediately after 9/11 and falsely accused of conspiracy to engage in terrorism against the United States."[16] He has been honored for his outstanding criminal defense work by the Arab American Chamber of Commerce (2010), the American Civil Liberties Union (2006), the National Lawyers Guild (2005), and the Defense Attorneys of Michigan (2004).[17]

Never one to be intimidated by a tough or politically challenging case, Swor nonetheless saw scant hope for Odeh's acquittal. There was no question that she had been convicted and imprisoned in Israel and that her answers had been clearly false on both her visa and citizenship applications. Swor therefore proceeded immediately to plea negotiations with Jonathan Tukel, the assistant U.S. attorney assigned to the case, without even filing pretrial motions.[18]

Negotiations between Swor and Tukel continued into the spring of 2014, leading to a written plea offer from the prosecution under the Federal Rules of Criminal Procedure.[19] Under the terms of the offer, Odeh was to plead guilty to the offense and accept the revocation of her citizenship and subsequent deportation, but with no prison sentence. In addition, the judicial "order of removal" from the United States would be delayed for 180 days so that she could "facilitate her travel arrangements from the country." The latter provision was significant, because a conviction for unlawful procurement of citizenship, either by guilty plea or trial, would ordinarily have been followed immediately by "mandatory immigration detention."[20]

Swor advised Odeh to take the deal, explaining its favorable terms. Although "she would have to surrender her United States citizenship . . . the government would forego taking her into custody and would give her a period of . . . up to 180 days to facilitate her own departure."[21]

In the meantime, however, Odeh continued to confer with Fennerty and other attorneys in Chicago, as well as her friends and advisers, who strongly disagreed with Swor's approach and began planning to present a novel defense.[22] Swor was a lawyers' lawyer, highly skilled at his profession and devoted to Odeh's legal representation. His advice had been sound, but there were also political considerations for the Palestinian movement, which called for more aggressive tactics. The arrest of a beloved community leader whose offense, if any, was decades in the past presented an irresistible opening for an organizing and publicity campaign condemning Israel. Even an advantageous guilty plea, and especially an early one, would let that opportunity to go to waste.

Within one day of Odeh's arrest, the AAAN had circulated a statement, signed by over fifty organizations, protesting the indictment as a "clear signal that federal authorities, along with Israel and its supporters in the U.S., are continuing to search for ways to intimidate and silence those . . . who speak out for Palestinian rights." The statement disingenuously said only that Odeh had been "convicted by the Israeli military court system in 1969 for her alleged association with a leftist Palestinian nationalist group." It made no mention of the deaths in the Supersol bombing and neglected to identify the "nationalist group" as the PFLP.[23]

Given the fast track for the statement, none of the organizations could possibly have known anything about the merits of the case against Odeh. Nonetheless, they all apparently believed that her "activism against the Israeli occupation [and] her community activism in the U.S." had made her "the target of this indictment." The signatories to the statement included both mainstream organizations, such as the Center for Constitutional Rights and the Council on American–Islamic Relations, and leftist groups such as the International Jewish Anti-Zionist Network, the Red Sparks Union of Vancouver, and the International League of People's Struggles—all of them protesting the presumed "persecution of Palestinian American activist Rasmea Odeh."[24]

Organizing on Odeh's behalf continued in the following months, repeatedly asserting that her arrest was one more example of the FBI's "discriminatory enforcement of laws against advocates for Palestinian rights."[25] The United States Palestinian Community Network (USPCN) published its own statement in *Jacobin* magazine, a self-described "leading voice of the American left, offering socialist perspectives on politics, economics, and culture."[26] The USPCN statement "unequivocally" rejected all charges against Odeh, as "nothing but a pretext to criminalize her" and the entire Palestinian community. The indictment itself was denounced as proof that "federal law enforcement in the US is working in coordination with Israel and its occupying army to harass, repress, and sow fear in Palestinian communities and their supporters here."[27]

Eventually, there would be rallies, meetings, and fundraisers for Odeh in locations from Florida to California, virtually always condemning the supposed link between Israel and the FBI. Speaking at an event in Chicago, attorney Michael Deutsch, who had represented members of the Midwest 23, said that the situation "appears to be the Department of Homeland Security behaving in a discriminatory fashion, targeting Arabs, Muslims, and Palestinians for selective prosecution," and adding ominously, "We know that the U.S. government works closely with Israeli officials."[28] The Odeh defense was a successful organizing effort, drawing support not only from leftist and pro-Palestinian organizations but also from more mainstream organizations such as the Peace and Justice Committee of the Episcopal Diocese of Chicago.[29]

*   *   *

All of the political momentum would be lost, of course, if Odeh were to accept Swor's prudently negotiated plea bargain. Speaking on Chicago's WBEZ radio, however, Fennerty stressed that Odeh had pled not guilty and explained that her attorneys were exploring the defenses that could be raised. "She has a right to have a jury trial," he emphasized, "and she can exercise that right if she wishes to go to trial."[30] Nonetheless, reports circulated that Odeh was planning to cut a deal, which seemed confirmed in late April when the court canceled a scheduled pretrial conference and instead set the case for a "plea hearing."[31]

The scheduled plea hearing was held in Detroit before U.S. district judge Paul Borman, on May 21, 2014, with the implicit expectation that Odeh would accept the agreement and plead guilty to the charge. Instead, attorney Swor informed the court that "Miss Odeh has advised me that she does not wish to accept the government's plea offer, that she intends to go to trial." Swor explained that he had received a written plea offer from the prosecution, and an explanatory worksheet from the federal sentencing guidelines, and that his client "has had the opportunity to review them individually and with me, along with Mr. James Fennerty [who is] an attorney in Chicago who has known Miss Odeh for more than two decades, along with at least one other attorney."[32]

Swor and his client had discussed the proposal "at great length," and he had given her his own recommendation, covering "the ramifications of a plea and the ramifications of a trial." Odeh had evidently been somewhat undecided "as recently as last evening . . . and this morning she advised me that she had determined that it was in her best interest to proceed to trial."[33]

It was then necessary for Borman to confirm that Odeh had indeed been informed of the government's written offer, which he took as an opportunity to reassure her that Swor had been required to advise her of the proposed agreement, which did "not in any way mean that he is not with you in your corner."

Odeh had other ideas. She acknowledged that Swor had explained the agreement to her. "Maybe Mr. Swor thought this deal is in my best interest, but I think the other choice is better for me," she said. "That's why I consulted with many attorneys," Odeh continued. "That's why I'm expressing my feeling and asking to change Mr. Swor and get a different attorney."[34]

Judge Borman was not pleased. The trial date was already set for June 10, just three weeks away, and bringing in a new lawyer would disrupt the court's crowded schedule. He tried to explain Swor's role in the plea bargain. "Let me just emphasize again that the fact that he advised you of a plea does not mean [he] doesn't represent you as he should."

"My choice is to go through a trial with a new attorney," Odeh replied. "That's why I'm asking the Court to allow me or give me this chance to defend myself and to choose and retain an attorney." She had not yet settled upon a new lawyer, she said, but she had "almost" chosen "an attorney to represent me in trial."

Many judges would have refused to allow new counsel so close to the trial date, but Borman realized that he was dealing with a high-profile case and was wary of possible missteps. He gave Odeh one week to appear in court with her new lawyer, cautioning her that the time for filing pretrial motions was over. "We're going to set a trial date," he said.[35]

The new lawyer Odeh chose was Deutsch, the doyen of the left-wing bar in Chicago, who appeared with her in court on May 28. A founding partner of the legendary People's Law Office, Deutsch had represented radicals and revolutionaries—including Black Panthers and Weathermen—since the mid-1960s and had received awards from the National Lawyers Guild, the Council on American–Islamic Relations, and the AAAN. Deutsch's lengthy resume included defense of the prisoners in the Attica prison rebellion and a successful clemency petition for Puerto Rican nationalists who had been convicted of shooting five members of the U.S. Congress.[36] Most recently, he had been counsel to several of the Midwest 23—including Abudayyeh, whose activities may have alerted the government to Odeh's problematic naturalization application.[37]

Borman welcomed Deutsch to the case but cautioned him that "the motion cutoff date has expired" and would not be reopened. That put Deutsch in a jam, because, as he told the court, his predecessor had "decided early on that this case was going to get resolved by a plea and then he didn't file any motions." Now that his client had rejected the plea, Deutsch argued that motions would be necessary to "adequately or competently represent Ms. Odeh," adding,

> So I'm asking the court to give me the time to prepare for trial, which means discovery, having her evaluated by an expert, which I've already identified who that would be, and give me a trial date in the fall.[38]

Borman would only go so far, noting the continuity of Odeh's representation, in that Fennerty had been involved in the case from the time of arraignment and had also been present for two of the hearings in Detroit. He told Deutsch that he could have time for discovery and a psychological examination, but no other motions. "And then we have a trial date of October 21."[39]

* * *

Judge Borman's ruling notwithstanding, there was no way the case could go to trial without consideration of pretrial motions on evidentiary and procedural issues. The prosecution began with a volley of motions aimed at shaping the conduct of the trial itself, both by squelching potential defenses and obtaining the admission of crucial government evidence.

Lead counsel for the government was Tukel, chief of the National Security Unit in the U.S. Attorney's Office for the Eastern District of Michigan, where he handled terrorism, terrorist-financing, export control, and similar cases.[40] He was best known for the successful prosecution, and eventual guilty plea, of Umar Farouk Abdulmutallab, the so-called "underwear bomber," for which he received the U.S. Department of Justice's highest award.[41] Tukel took a severe approach to the Odeh case, showing little flexibility and making no accommodations to the defense unless required by law or ordered by the court. He was despised, in turn, by Odeh's supporters, who called him, among other epithets, a racist, a right-wing ideologue, and a "zionist," evidently using the lower case as an expression of contempt.[42]

The prosecution filed three significant motions on July 10. The first motion was preemptive, asking the court to prohibit Odeh from introducing a claim of selective prosecution, even though no such defense had yet been raised by opposing counsel. Nonetheless, the prosecution argued that Odeh and her supporters had "undertaken a wide-ranging media campaign [asserting] that defendant is a victim of selective prosecution by the government."[43] More significantly, a second motion sought the admissibility for trial of "Foreign Evidence," including the Israeli court records of Odeh's arrest, trial, conviction, and imprisonment.[44]

In his most aggressive step, Tukel moved to virtually cripple the anticipated defense case by excluding Odeh's claims of torture in Israel and innocence of the underlying crime. "Evidence of defendant's factual guilt or innocence for crimes of which she was convicted in a foreign country . . . is irrelevant to the question of whether or not she truthfully answered questions on her U.S. naturalization application." Moreover, the motion continued, "claims of torture have no relevance to the offense charged here, which is predicated on the historical fact" of conviction in Israel. Again citing public statements by defense counsel, the prosecution argued that "the validity, by American standards, of a foreign conviction is not relevant to whether it was required to be disclosed in a naturalization application." To rule otherwise, Tukel continued, would permit the defendant "to redefine 'conviction' on her own terms [and] her own standards of due process."[45]

Defense counsel countered with a motion of their own, seeking to bar any evidence of Odeh's "arrest, conviction and imprisonment in 1969–70 by the Israeli military court system as this system does not operate in accordance with fundamental fairness, due process or international law." Likewise, the defense sought to preclude use of the words "terrorist" or "terrorism," because "resistance to an illegal and belligerent occupation by the Israeli government is not terrorism."[46]

The defense motion was accompanied by a fifteen-page brief that was seemingly aimed more at the public than the court. It began with a short history of the 1967 war, in which "about one million Palestinians, previously under the relatively benign control of Egypt and the Kingdom of Jordan, became subject to a belligerent occupation and a new legal system to enforce its control over the conquered civilian population." The brief continued with an account of Odeh's arrest and brutalization, including "25 days of horrific and unspeakable torture" in which she was handcuffed "to hooks in the ceiling" and "raped with a stick numerous times." The representations were exaggerated, going beyond even Odeh's own descriptions of her violent and abusive treatment; for example, she had never claimed, as did the brief, that she had been "repeatedly raped with sticks" by Israeli interrogators "over a 25 day period."[47] But accuracy was not the point, and the brief effectively served the purpose of getting Odeh's allegations into the court record, as the premise for arguing that "A United States court cannot allow the product of such an inhumane and illegal proceeding to be given any recognition."[48]

The prosecution and defense continued jousting through the summer and early fall of 2014, repeatedly filing motions, cross-motions, responses, and replies on these and similar issues, as their interactions became increasingly rancorous—including minute-by-minute arguments over precisely when required notices had been served on pending motions. Before the court could rule on the most crucial matters, however, Deutsch and Fennerty made an unusually aggressive move challenging Borman's qualifications to hear the case as part of a strategy that combined dynamic political organizing with hardline legal representation.

11 Organizing

The takeover by Michael Deutsch and James Fennerty turned the case into a full-bore political trial, an approach that was eagerly embraced by Rasmea Odeh and her allies.[1] Where William Swor had seen only bleak prospects for acquittal, they saw an opportunity for political organizing that extended far beyond the courtroom. Although there could be no denying that Odeh had omitted her conviction and prison sentence during her immigration and naturalization proceedings, the new defense strategy was to turn the tables on the prosecution by focusing on the "horrific torture" Odeh had experienced at the hands of the Israelis and in effect place Israel on trial for its oppression of the Palestinians.

Odeh and her allies rallied her base among leftist and Palestinian organizations, with major support from the USPCN and the FRSO, while the newly formed Rasmea Defense Committee worked on building a coalition among broader community groups. Eventually, the defense committee included over thirty-five other organizations, many of them Arab or Palestinian, but also including JVP, the Korean American Resource and Cultural Center, the Latino Organization of the Southwest, the National Boricua Human Rights Network, and the National Lawyers Guild.[2]

No one was more important to Odeh's defense than Hatem Abudayyeh, the executive director of AAAN, co-founder of the USPCN, and a frequent speaker at meeting, rallies, and fundraisers in many cities. A Chicago native, Abudayyeh is the son of Palestinian immigrants who were themselves leading activists in the Arab American community. His father "experienced fighting" in Israel's 1948 War of Independence, which led to the Nakba, and his grandfather participated in the 1936 "Arab Revolt in Palestine" protesting Jewish immigration under the British Mandate.[3] Abudayyeh's wife, Naima, is from the West Bank. One of her brothers died in an Israeli prison during the First Intifada and another was incarcerated for three years. His family's history, and Naima's experience under occupation, intensified Abudayyeh's commitment to Palestinian rights issues, leading him to see his work at AAAN as "a job that starts when I wake up in the morning and ends when I go to sleep."[4]

Abudayyeh's politics slant sharply to the left. Well before Odeh's arrest, he condemned the U.S. "military fronts opened up in Palestine, Lebanon, Iraq, Colombia, the Philippines, Haiti, and parts of Africa and Latin America" and lauded the insurgents ambushing American troops with IEDs in Iraq, "where the resistance is standing up to U.S. power."[5] He has proudly described his political inheritance as the "Syrian Ba'athists, Iraqi Ba'athists, the Arab National Movement, the Nassirites."[6] Writing regularly in the publication of the FRSO, he has also supported the inclusion of Hamas in a Palestinian unity government, which may partially explain his inclusion by the FBI in the Midwest 23.[7]

Under Abudayyeh's leadership, AAAN had become "a very political organization" devoted to "challenging systems of oppression." Although allowing that "we don't advocate kicking the Jews out of Palestine," Abudayyeh has been adamant that "we want a dissolution of the concept of a Zionist state."[8] The Odeh defense was therefore "critically important" to the "battle against Israel for the hearts and minds of the world," which had to be won "both in the courtroom and in the streets."[9] As Abudayyeh saw it, "This case is a political attack on the Palestine liberation movement, and that means we need a political defense as much as a legal defense."[10] Deutsch agreed, condemning what he believed to be "close collaboration between the US and Israeli Justice Departments."[11] He told a group of demonstrators at the courthouse that their presence "is as important as my work in the court."[12]

The "political defense" of Odeh rested in fairly equal parts on truth, exaggeration, and outright myth. She was beyond question a sympathetic figure, sixty-six years old at the time of her arrest, having lived peacefully in the U.S. for nearly two decades. Her work among Arab American immigrants had been exemplary, and her supporters missed no opportunity to mention her Outstanding Community Leader Award from the Chicago Cultural Alliance.

Odeh's supporters stressed that her Israeli conviction had been handed down by a military court system that lacked guarantees of due process and in which over 98 percent of Palestinians were found guilty, making the U.S. prosecution a "politically-motivated witch-hunt."[13] Or as Deutsch repeatedly put it, the indictment was simply "unfair."[14]

It did not seem that way to Terry Joffe Benaryeh, the niece of bombing victim Edward Joffe. In a column for the Associated Press, Benaryeh described the impact of Joffe's murder on her family. Detailing the video evidence of Odeh's guilt, she expressed the "sheer agony" of seeing her celebrated as a "pillar of her community." Even so, she recognized that Odeh might have been tortured, as she claimed, which would have been "horrific and unacceptable." Benaryeh called on Odeh's supporters to "acknowledge her past and her crimes" and to stop defending her, which of course could never have had any effect.[15] There was no way for a victim's relative to break through the ever-expanding myth.

Odeh's torture at the hands of the Israeli interrogators was made yet more compelling by consistent exaggerations that went beyond even her own claims. Many of Odeh's allies asserted that she had been brutally tortured for twenty-five days—some stated even forty-five days—including repeated rapes.[16] Odeh's actual treatment was bad enough, including sexual abuse, but her own testimony in Israel, given in an attempt to suppress her confession, was that the torture stopped after seven days and the rape incident occurred only once.

Nor was Odeh arrested "along with 500 other Palestinians" following the Supersol bombing.[17] Although there were indeed roundups of Palestinians, the true number was closer to 150, nearly all of whom were released after questioning with only fourteen actually arrested.[18] Nonetheless, the notion that Odeh was scooped up in an indiscriminate sweep of many hundreds implied that she was simply a loser in Israel's persecution lottery, rather than a suspect identified through an evidence-based murder investigation.

Some statements of support for Odeh omitted all mention of the Supersol bombing, asserting instead that her Israeli conviction had been only for seemingly nonviolent offenses. The Peace and Justice Committee of the Episcopal Diocese of Chicago, for example, wrote that "Rasmea's activism against the Israeli occupation in the 1960s resulted in her imprisonment in Israeli prisons for ten years."[19] Likewise, the Critical Ethnic Studies Association held that "Rasmea was arrested by Israeli occupation forces for her community organizing."[20] According to Muhammad Sankari of Chicago's Coalition to Protect Peoples Rights, the "immigration charge is nothing but a pretext. . . . Rasmea is being targeted because of who she is, a Palestinian Arab Muslim woman who continues to organize for Palestinian freedom and liberation."[21]

In another example of exaggeration, attorney Fennerty declared in interviews that "she had her jaw broken" during interrogation and that "she was left nearly blind from years in solitary confinement but slowly regained her sight after her release."[22] Fennerty had known Odeh since meeting her in Jordan in 1984, and presumably had extended opportunities to speak with her, so it is disconcerting, to say the least, that his allegation went far beyond anything Odeh herself had ever described.[23]

The various exaggerations may be irrelevant in one sense, especially in the context of a leftist political campaign. After all, what difference does the number of Palestinian detainees make or whether Odeh was tortured for eight or twenty-five days? On the other hand, the embellished accounts were crucial in fashioning an idealized Rasmea Odeh who was absolutely innocent of any crimes and had no connection to organizations like the PFLP. Instead, she was targeted almost at random in a joint Israel–U.S. scheme "to harass, repress, and sow fear in Palestinian communities and their supporters."[24] In the oft-repeated words of Abudayyeh, the idealized Odeh "has committed no crime and the government has no case."[25]

At least some of Odeh's supporters knew better, and they occasionally let slip their awareness of her renown as a PFLP operative. Within weeks of Odeh's arrest in 2013, the USPCN issued a statement calling her "a living legend in the eyes of thousands across the world," whose "influence spans continents." Later statements from the same organization called Odeh "a Palestinian icon, known worldwide as a leading representative of the legitimate Palestinian struggle for self determination, independence, and the Right of Return," and "a legend to millions of Palestinians who continue to organize for their rights of liberation, equality, and return."[26] Even a year later, a statement from the Rasmea Defense Committee identified her as one of the most famous political prisoners "in the history of the Palestine liberation movement."[27]

Needless to say, Odeh had not become an international icon, historically famous, legendary, and revered by millions, by leading writing workshops on Chicago's southwest side. Rather, she had been long celebrated among Palestinians, evidently including the USPCN, for her "fighting career" as one of the first female guerrillas in the West Bank and as the namesake, on a par with Che Guevara, of a PFLP hijacking crew.[28] The Palestinian Prisoner Solidarity Network praised her as "a member of the Popular Front for the Liberation of Palestine in the '60s [who] helped women face a difficult political situation" in Palestine, evidently unaware that membership in the PFLP alone was sufficient to revoke her U.S. citizenship, given that Odeh had omitted it from her naturalization application.[29]

Odeh herself was more careful not to subvert the narrative of her newly acquired myth. At Deutsch's instruction, she gave no interviews, even to friendly journalists, and made only brief comments when she spoke in public for fear that she might reveal something damaging to "the politically sensitive nature of her case."[30] What she confided to her lawyers and close colleagues remains unknown.

12 Recusal

Michael Deutsch brought his own flair for the dramatic to Rasmea Odeh's case. On July 14, 2014, the defense filed a bold "Motion to Recuse the Honorable Paul D. Borman," asserting judicial bias and seeking the disqualification of the judge "from ruling on any substantive motions or presiding over the trial." Odeh's Detroit-based lawyers had not questioned Borman's impartiality. In pursuing the plea negotiations, William Swor had been willing to let the court decide whether his client would be sentenced to any prison time, and William Goodman, who served as local counsel for Deutsch and Fennerty, told Borman that it was "a pleasure always" to appear in his court.[1] Swor and Goodman had to be circumspect, as they would have other clients before Borman in the future, but the Chicago attorneys faced no such constraints.

On the rare occasions when recusal motions are presented in federal court, they are usually framed in impersonal terms in order to avoid offending the judge. This was not one of those motions. Instead, it began with a reference to Borman's family: "Like his father before him, the Court is a life-long active supporter, fund raiser and promoter of the State of Israel." The gratuitous insertion of Borman's father, which could have no bearing on recusal, was seemingly calculated more to animate Odeh's partisans than to convince the court to keep an open mind.

The recusal motion then detailed Borman's various connections to Israel, including his receipt of the Fred Butzel Award from the Jewish Federation of

Metropolitan Detroit. Borman had been "instrumental in bringing hundreds of Detroiters to Israel," including state legislators, the motion continued, and he and his wife had been recognized as "Builders of Israel" for making lifetime contributions of over $3 million.

The judge's support for Israel required disqualification, argued Deutsch, because the defense sought to exclude evidence of Odeh's conviction and imprisonment on the ground that the "Israeli military legal system . . . is not consistent with fundamental fairness, due process and international law." More provocatively, the motion continued,

> Further, defendant asserts that she was subjected to 25 days of horrific torture including electro-shock and multiple rapes. Ms. Odeh's [sic] asserts that her treatment at the hands of the Israeli security and military was "shocking to the conscience," and cannot be used in any way in a United States court. . . . Ms. Odeh suffers from post-traumatic stress syndrome as a result of her prolonged, brutal and sadistic torture at the hands of Israeli government agents.[2]

The same grounds were reiterated in a supporting brief. "The defendant's claim of bias emanates from the Court's personal and extra-judicial support and deep commitment to the State of Israel," the brief explained. A reasonably objective person, it continued, would question the court's impartiality to fairly decide whether "Ms. Odeh was horrifically tortured and the relevance of these claims to her defense."[3]

Under the applicable federal statute, recusal is necessary if the judge's "impartiality might reasonably be questioned."[4] Deutsch argued that the defense met that standard:

> Given the Court's deep personal and active commitment to the support and defense of the State of Israel, and the issues raised by Ms. Odeh's [motions], her opposition to the use of Israeli military court system documents, and her defense at trial it cannot be disputed that this Court's "impartiality might be reasonably questioned."[5]

The defense stance became even more confrontational several days later, with the filing as a "Supplemental Document" of the tax records of a private charitable foundation called "The Bormans' Inc. Fund." Among the listed grants for

2006 there was a $2,000 contribution to "Friends of the Israel Defense Forces," along with other grants to Congregation Shaarey Zedek, Jewish Home & Aging Services, the Karmanos Cancer Institute, and the Henry Ford Health System, among others, with a total of just under $22,000.[6]

The prosecution objected to the recusal motion, arguing that "The State of Israel is not a party to this case and has no legal stake in its outcome." Moreover, Borman's involvement with Israel had not been shown to be "other than as a tourist and as a fundraiser for a Detroit-area Jewish charity." The government's supporting brief pointed out that "Travel to Israel has a large religious aspect to it for both Jews and Christians," and that the "Builders of Israel" award was given not only for contributions to Israel but also for furthering "the rescue, rehabilitation and education of millions of Jewish people in our community and around the world."[7]

Judge Borman was deeply offended by the recusal motion, which he blasted as "innuendo and rank speculation" about "my faith and my heritage." His charitable activities, leading to the Butzel Award, had been "to further the Jewish community's interest and involvement in programs to alleviate hunger, to promote local African-American Jewish relations and Arab-American Jewish relations," and, contrary to the defense assertion, they were unrelated to the "Israeli military legal system in the Occupied West Bank [sic]." As to the $2,000 donation to the "Friends of the Israel Defense Forces," and the $3 million in Builders of Israel contributions, those had actually been made by the judge's cousin, also named Paul Borman. The court therefore denied the motion without allowing oral argument.[8]

*   *   *

Odeh's supporters reacted angrily to Borman's denial of the recusal motion, calling his decision "strident" and charging him with hypocrisy. According to defense committee spokesman Hatem Abudayyeh, Borman was "falsely covering Zionist ideology" with Judaism. "We opposed Judge Borman not because of his Jewish faith, but because of his decades of support for the state of Israel," he said. "Rasmea overcame vicious torture by Israeli authorities while imprisoned in Palestine in the 70s [and] we need a judge willing to listen to a defense that puts Israel on trial for its crimes against Rasmea, and against all Palestinians."[9]

A *Fight Back News* story described Borman as "anxious" and "visibly confused" at the hearing, arguing that the court "cannot possibly judge a trial fairly when he is politically, financially and emotionally invested" in Israel. "We know that this judge is an ardent supporter of the Israeli occupation," said Jess Sundin, one of the Midwest 23, stressing the "need to pressure him to offer some bit of fairness in a trial that is all about the crimes Israel committed against Rasmea Odeh."[10] The recusal motion was not completely without effect. It had again explicitly recounted Odeh's claims of twenty-five days of torture, including rapes and electro-shock, which fulfilled the defense objective, as Abudayyeh explained, to "put everything on the public record as much as possible."[11]

Speaking to about 150 supporters outside the courtroom, Deutsch characterized Borman's ruling as "saying he was just a Jewish person providing support for Jewish organizations." Deutsch expressed his continuing concerns about the court's impartiality toward Odeh and his fear that adverse rulings on future motions regarding her torture by Israeli interrogators "will be stopping her from mounting a defense."[12]

From a legal perspective, the recusal motion appeared to have backfired badly, angering the judge while accomplishing nothing for the defense. The request itself was not outlandish. The applicable federal statute requires disqualification whenever a judge's impartiality "might reasonably be questioned," with the issue to be determined from the perspective of "a reasonable person with knowledge of all the facts."[13] It was conceivable that a judge with Borman's pro-Israel history might choose, out of an abundance of caution, or perhaps an exceptional concern for public perception, to step aside from the politically charged case of an accused Palestinian guerrilla, and it would not have been unprecedented for the court to err on the side of recusal.

But the defense motion seemed intentionally inflammatory, beginning with an unwarranted comment on the judge's father, inserting the unnecessary details of Odeh's suffering, asserting that the court had a "personal bias" in favor of Israel and against the defendant, and mistaking the judge for his cousin (which was presumably unintentional, though unforgivably sloppy).[14] It was therefore predictable that Borman would react as he did, indignantly dismissing the motion as one that "strikes at the very heart of a Federal Judge's [*sic*] pledge to administer impartial justice, and does so with careless and rank speculation."[15] The resulting vehemence of Borman's opinion could only have appeared to disadvantage Odeh even further. But perhaps that was the tactical purpose of the motion in the first place.

*   *   *

Then lightning struck. Less than two weeks after denying Odeh's disqualification motion, Judge Borman stepped aside from the case. As Borman explained, the naturalization fraud indictment against Odeh had not provided the specifics of her Israeli conviction, and the defense recusal motion had been based only on his "charitable giving [and other] work on behalf of the Jewish Federation of Metropolitan Detroit," which provided an insufficient factual basis for recusal. Upon beginning his research on other pending motions, however, Borman sought out the original Israeli indictment, which included the exact location—Jerusalem's Supersol—of the lethal bombing. That was enough to change his mind, because "at the time of the 1969 bombing, my family had a passive financial investment connection to Supersol."

Borman explained that his family had never had any involvement in Supersol's operations and that there was no present investment of any sort, and he stressed that he had no bias against Odeh and could "faithfully and impartially" preside over the case. Nonetheless, he recognized that the contemporaneous investment in Supersol "could be perceived as establishing a reasonably objective inference of a lack of impartiality in the context of the issues presented in this case."[16] Thus, his recusal was necessary under the terms of the federal statute.

Odeh's supporters greeted Borman's recusal as a great "victory for the defense," boasting that he had been "forced to remove himself from the case."[17] According to one inaccurate report, Borman had responded to "defense documents showing he had an undisclosed Israeli business interest," and another asserted that Borman had "revealed" his family's business interests in Israel that had "all along" been the basis of the recusal motion.[18] Abudayyeh summed it up: "This is great news. It's proof that we were right."[19] And Odeh's defense committee declared that its "claims of pro-Israel bias had been vindicated."[20]

In fact, the claims of Borman's alleged bias had been thoroughly refuted. Although the defense motion had relied only on generalities, based on information from the Jewish Federation website (and, erroneously, a cousin's tax records), Borman had taken the initiative to learn the precise details of Odeh's

Israeli conviction and had then investigated his family's passive investments dating back over forty years. In other words, the judge had scrupulously explored connections that the defense had not raised. He then disqualified himself on the basis of possible perceptions—as the statute required—rather than any actual prejudice against the defendant. The defense got what it wanted, but the true vindication belonged to the court and the judicial system.

Following court procedure, the case was randomly reassigned to Judge Gershwin Drain, who would face a slew of complex motions as soon as the file hit his desk.

* * *

The defense lawyers were heartened when the Odeh case was assigned to Judge Drain. An African American native of Detroit, Drain had been a scholarship football player at Western Michigan University before attending law school at the University of Michigan. He had been a federal public defender for twelve years, trying almost 150 cases to verdict. He then served as a state court judge for twenty-six years, including ten years during which he presided exclusively over felony prosecutions. A lifelong Democrat, Drain was appointed to the federal district court by President Obama in 2011.[21] "I think we're in a much better situation with the new judge than the old judge," said Deutsch.[22]

Judge Drain inherited a formidable stack of filings and cross-filings from both parties, none of which had been resolved by Borman before his recusal. The most pressing issue involved the admissibility of the documents provided to the prosecution by Israel. Both parties sought advance rulings in their favor, pursuant to competing motions *in limine*. (A motion *in limine* requests a ruling on an item or line of evidence, either excluding or allowing it, in advance of trial; literally "at the threshold.")

Although it was unquestionable that Odeh had been convicted of murder in Israel and imprisoned for ten years, courts may proceed only on the basis of legally admissible evidence. Simple testimony about Odeh's conviction would have been excludable as hearsay, and the defendant herself could not be called as a government witness due to the Fifth Amendment. Thus, the entire prosecution case rested on the official records from Israel, which had been produced under the terms of the MLAT. Even so, the documents had to be authenticated—that is, shown to be genuine—in order to meet the standard for admissibility. The prosecution considered this a straightforward matter, clearly amenable to a ruling before trial.[23]

Defense counsel saw things in a completely different light. Their own motion *in limine* was unconcerned with the terms of the MLAT but instead sought to exclude any evidence from Israel as the product of a military court system that "does not operate in accordance with fundamental fairness, due process or international law" that is "based on the use of systematic torture, denial of meaningful access to counsel and lack of impartial judges."[24]

A brief in support of the defense motion provided another opportunity to spell out Odeh's brutalization at length, over nearly four pages, much of it consistent with her earlier statements, but also including some of the by-then-familiar embellishments. Deutsch detailed Odeh's subjection to "25 days of horrific and unspeakable torture, day and night," beatings "throughout her body with fists and clubs," being "subjected to electric shock where electrodes were placed on [*sic*] breasts and genitals," being handcuffed "to hooks in the ceiling," being "raped with a stick numerous times," continuous beatings even after signing her confession "in Hebrew, a language she did not read or understand," and more. As substantiation, the brief referenced the Landau Commission Report of 1987 and also appended a 1979 investigation by Amnesty International and a 1978 cable from a U.S. consular official in East Jerusalem, both reporting systematic torture of detainees in Israel but neither mentioning Odeh herself.[25]

The contrast could not have been more extreme. To the prosecution, the admission of Israeli documents was routine and unexceptional, offered only to prove what should have been an uncontested fact. To the defense, everything about the Israeli occupation was illegitimate, and admission of any records would be "shocking to the conscience."

Judge Drain agreed with the prosecution. The Israeli documents had been "properly authenticated" and "produced in accordance with the Treaty," he ruled, and thus "do not require further authentication and are admissible."[26]

In a companion motion, the prosecution also sought to exclude all evidence of "claims of innocence" and "allegations of torture," arguing that the immigration and naturalization questionnaires asked about "all convictions, valid or invalid," and that "claims of torture have no relevance to the offense charged here, which is predicated on the historical fact" of Odeh's conviction.[27] The defense countered that Odeh "has the right to testify . . . that she was tortured and that affected" her answers to the naturalization questions.[28]

Judge Drain did not mince words. He fully accepted "as credible Defendant's claims of torture," noting "the inhumane circumstances of her detention in the West Bank" and expressing his distress at the "deplorable physical and emotional abuse" that Odeh endured during her detention. Nonetheless, Drain held that "the validity of Defendant's conviction is not an issue for the jury's determination," and he had no intention of "retrying" the Israeli convictions, no matter how unfairly they may have been obtained.[29] The only issue before the court, Drain explained, was whether Odeh had "truthfully answered on her Naturalization Application." Thus, only the "mere fact of a conviction" was relevant and not whether Odeh was "innocent or was convicted based on a coerced confession."[30]

In another blow to the defense, Drain declined to distribute a questionnaire to the prospective jurors, seeking their views on U.S. foreign policy in the Middle East, their "experiences, feelings, impressions, or beliefs about the United States support for Israel," and their knowledge of "the causes of the Israeli-Palestinian conflict." The questionnaire would obviously have been an opportunity to search for sympathetic jurors predisposed to Odeh's case but Drain saw through the stratagem and determined to limit jury *voir dire* to open court.[31]

* * *

While Deutsch was justifiably discouraged by Judge Drain's rulings, Odeh's political supporters were absolutely infuriated. The USPCN accused Drain of handing down "a series of outrageous and unjust decisions [that] no fair minded person can accept." It was inconceivable that Drain could find Odeh's torture allegations "credible" and still exclude testimony about her brutal interrogation and coerced confession. The organization called for unspecified "determined and collective action" in response.[32] Others were yet more blunt about Drain's "vicious" rulings. "We must fill the streets around the courthouse in Detroit [and] pack the courtroom during the trial," said the FRSO. "If there is to be a measure of justice in this case, we are the ones who must provide it."[33]

That sounded like a threat to prosecutor Jonathan Tukel, or so he claimed. From the start of the case Odeh's supporters had shown up at the courthouse for all of her appearances. They held spirited rallies on the steps, holding signs, waving banners, and listening to speakers who proclaimed Odeh's innocence and condemned the injustice of the charges, but there were no reported incidents of disruption or misconduct in the courtroom. Even so, Tukel filed an aggressive motion directed at the demonstrators, seeking to prevent their supposed improper efforts to influence the jury pool.

Tukel's motion asked the court to "empanel an anonymous jury" and also for "partial sequestration" (requesting that the jury be directed to assemble at an off-site location, then to be transported to the courthouse in a van with covered windows). In support, the motion cited an interview with Abudayyeh in which he called for "filling the courtroom every day [and] rallying outside," so that "our posters and our banners and our chants about, you know, justice for Rasmea" could "sway the opinions of the jurors."[34] Tukel noted that Odeh herself had addressed some of the rallies, which he provocatively called a "protesting mob" and a "hoard [sic] of supporters."[35] Odeh's defense committee believed that Tukel's descriptors for the "spirited and dignified protests" carried "a distinctly racist, and anti-Arab undertone."[36]

Drain granted the prosecution motion to have the jurors enter and leave the courthouse in a sealed van. He also entered orders barring spectators from "wearing or carrying any clothing, buttons, or other items in the Courthouse" with messages of support for Odeh and prohibiting individuals from "passing out literature" related to the case.[37]

The defense had argued effectively, however, that Tukel had "concocted baseless allegations" of jury interference and there was no need for an anonymous jury, given that Odeh's supporters had always been "well-behaved" in the courtroom.[38] Judge Drain agreed. He denied the request for an anonymous jury and upbraided the prosecution for misstating the controlling law and failing to include relevant information in its motion.[39]

Finally, Deutsch had moved to preclude the prosecution from referring to Odeh as a "terrorist" or using the word "terrorism," on the ground that "resistance to an illegal and belligerent occupation by the Israeli government is not terrorism" and the term would therefore be "highly prejudicial."[40] Deutsch was hoping that the court would implicitly validate the Supersol bombing as a legitimate act of resistance, but Judge Drain wouldn't bite. Instead, he simply observed the problem of prejudice inherent in the term. "The American public," the court noted, "is particularly emotional when it comes to terrorism and the threat of terrorism," and the terms would therefore "have an undue tendency to improperly influence the jury's verdict." (In a later ruling, Drain also prohibited the term "freedom fighter," although neither party had requested it.)[41]

Those were small victories for the defense, which had otherwise been nearly crippled by Drain's rulings. There was still one remaining opportunity, however, to introduce evidence of Odeh's torture. It would have to be through an imaginative procedural back door that had only occurred to the defense lawyers after they were fully immersed in the case.

13 PTSD

Shortly after Rasmea Odeh was arrested, both Michael Deutsch and James Fennerty gave interviews as members of her "legal team," although neither was then formally representing her in Detroit. It was obvious that they had not yet resolved the central dilemma in the case, which was how to construct a viable legal defense in light of the indisputable facts. In an interview on Chicago Public Radio, Fennerty said they were "exploring many options" for the defense, but he quickly changed the subject when asked if she had made false denials on her citizenship application.[1]

At a lengthy press conference, called by the AAAN and conducted at the People's Law Office, Deutsch was more expressive, though still evasive, when a reporter asked him if Odeh had indeed lied on her immigration papers. "It depends on what a lie is," he replied.[2]

Deutsch proceeded to conjecture potential lines of defense, quite reasonably declining to settle on one so early in the case. His preferred defense at the time appeared to be a theory of "selective prosecution," in which Odeh's arrest had been "politically motivated [due to] prejudice against Muslim people fueled by the Israeli lobby." He pictured a conspiracy, in which the U.S. government, working "closely with the Israeli government," had known at the time of Odeh's naturalization that she had been in prison but delayed acting for its own dishonorable reasons. "They should have denied her citizenship then," he said, "but they didn't do that. They waited."[3]

"Before we ask her if it's a lie, I want to know why the government singled her out," Deutsch continued. If he could get the case dismissed for selective prosecution, "she wouldn't have to answer whether she lied or not." When he was pressed about the defense, Deutsch responded,

> When they ask were you ever arrested, are they asking if you were ever legitimately arrested, or whether you were arrested under a fascist regime, or whether you were arrested in a place where you had no rights? [4]

With only the slightest hint of the psychological defense to come, Deutsch explained to a reporter that Odeh's failure to disclose her imprisonment "is not a lie if you interpret it in the proper way."[5]

*　*　*

By the time Deutsch took over the case on May 28, 2014, he had a better idea of which lines of defense were more likely to be allowed, although he remained "circumspect" about his strategy when speaking to the press.[6] Without making any direct commitments or disclosures that might help the prosecution, he tipped his hand when he appeared for the first time before Judge Borman. Even though prohibited from filing pretrial motions, Deutsch advised the court that "Miss Odeh needs a psychological evaluation" and that he had already identified an expert who could conduct it.[7]

In fact, Deutsch was temporizing. Fennerty had retained Dr. Mary Fabri, a clinical psychologist, months earlier, on March 5, for the purpose of determining whether Odeh had a psychological disorder that could "affect her interpretation of questions about being arrested, convicted, or in prison on an application for naturalization."[8] Fabri had already interviewed Odeh twice, for a total of six hours, by the time Swor was discharged as counsel, but she had not yet settled on her conclusions. They would meet another four times before Deutsch revealed the substance of his proposed psychological defense to the prosecution and the court.

Fabri is one of the preeminent experts in the United States on the treatment of torture victims. She was one of the founding clinicians at the Kovler Center in Chicago, where she had served for twelve years as director (and then senior director) of Torture Treatment Services and International Training.

She also held positions at other organizations concerned with the treatment of torture victims, including the Torture Abolition and Survivor Network and the National Consortium of Torture Treatment Programs. She had consulted on torture care in Kurdistan, Rwanda, Guatemala, Sri Lanka, and Haiti and was widely published in her field.

Fabri spent a total of eighteen hours with Odeh, taking an extensive history and conducting a rigorous evaluation that included administering psychological tests that constituted the "gold standard" for determining the presence of post-traumatic stress disorder (PTSD). In her seventeen-page report, Fabri recounted Odeh's torture narrative at length, including specific details of shocking brutality and sexual assault.[9] Fabri found Odeh to be extremely credible because she "provided high levels of detail when describing traumatic experiences that remained consistent over time."[10]

With her long experience as a treating clinician, it would never have been Fabri's practice to fact-check her patients or verify their claims from external sources, which of course would have undermined the therapeutic relationship. After all, it is "important for the therapist to believe the patient's story of the traumatic experience," which may be seen either as empathy or a form of "deliberate credulousness."[11] It is evident that Fabri brought some of that sensibility to her assessment of Odeh, as she unquestioningly included incidents in her report that were manifestly untrue.

Fabri reported that Odeh's torture was prolonged because she "had no information to share," which is contradicted by Odeh's own admission, in the 1980 Soraya Antonius interview, that she had personally placed a bomb at the British consulate in Jerusalem. Likewise, Fabri accepted Odeh's claim that she was never "told why she was being detained," even though she had been taken for a walk-through at the Supersol on the day after her arrest. Fabri also recounted that Odeh's torture had continued for forty-five days, even after she confessed, despite Odeh's own trial testimony in Israel that the torture had ended following her second confession on day seven.[12] It is understandable, of course, that Fabri did not conduct any independent research on Odeh's background and prior statements, but her trusting acceptance of Odeh's exaggerations and falsehoods does cast doubt on her ability accurately to evaluate her subject's credibility.

Nonetheless, Fabri concluded that Odeh was suffering from chronic PTSD, attributed to "the 45 days of interrogation and torture" that were "highly consistent with Ms. Odeh's self-report of traumatic events (arrest, interrogation, torture, and imprisonment in 1969)."[13] According to Fabri, torture survivors may employ strategies of "avoidance (and sometimes even denial) of thoughts, feelings, and activities associated with the trauma" in order to "keep reminders at a distance." Thus, she opined "to a reasonable degree of psychological certainty" that "someone with PTSD would cognitively process questions about the past to avoid recalling traumatic experiences, such as torture, that are at the root of one's disorder."[14] Significantly, Fabri did not apply that generalization to the distinct facts of the Odeh case, expressing no opinion as to what Odeh did or did not understand when she completed her visa and naturalization applications.

On July 18, 2014, Deutsch filed Fabri's affidavit with the court, which he intended to serve as the basis for a defense of "diminished capacity."[15] As Deutsch explained it, Fabri's testimony would establish that Odeh suffered from PTSD and "that it could have affected her interpretation and understanding of the questions and her answers." There was more to it than that, however. Deutsch had a broader strategic use for Fabri's opinion, which was to introduce the otherwise prohibited evidence of Israeli brutality: "The expert will testify that the defendant suffers PTSD as a result of the horrific torture she received at the hands of her Israeli captors, and will explain to the jury how this condition could have affected her intent" in answering the immigration questionnaires. Quite candidly, Deutsch argued that he wanted "the jury to know that she was tortured, that her alleged confession was the product of this torture, and that she suffers a mental disorder as a result of such torture."[16] It would be a perfect work-around of Drain's other rulings, if the court would allow it.

The prosecution objected to Fabri's proposed testimony, arguing that the alleged unconscious cognitive processing was irrelevant because "criminal responsibility must be judged at the level of the conscious." Moreover, Fabri's testimony about Odeh's torture would be impermissible hearsay under the Federal Rules of Evidence, as "it would be a virtual invitation for the jury to make a decision based on sympathy and on whether or not it believed defendant had been tortured, not on whether or not she had given false information to secure her naturalization."[17] The prosecution's legal argument was technical and complicated, relying on a precedent that preemptively disallowed expert psychological testimony for "general intent" crimes, which do not require an intention to achieve the specific result of the unlawful act. (A more lenient admissibility rule applied to "specific intent" crimes.)

Judge Drain wanted to hear from Fabri herself before deciding whether she could testify at trial, so an evidentiary hearing was held on October 21, 2014.

* * *

Deutsch called Dr. Fabri as the first and only witness at the evidentiary hearing. Following introductory questions about her background and qualifications, Fabri testified to her opinion that Odeh had been "truthfully relating" her "multiple ongoing experiences of torture," which she found "very credible."[18]

Fabri explained her theory that trauma victims "work really hard to develop filters that help keep the reminders out [so that] during periods where someone is not stressed or distressed, those filters work pretty well" and eventually become "automatic." The filtering phenomenon, not mentioned in her initial report, would in turn cause survivors "to narrow their focus to keep the painful memories back."[19]

The direct examination then turned specifically to Fabri's assessment of the defendant, which continued to expand well beyond the information in her initial assessment.

Q. Did Ms. Odeh tell you why she answered "no" to the questions about her arrest, conviction, and imprisonment on her citizenship application?

A. Yes. What she told me was that when she read the question, she thought it meant during her time living in the U.S.

Q. Now, in your opinion would a person with chronic PTSD typically interpret a question in a way in which your brain would cognitively filter recalling past trauma?

A. There's a strong possibility that that would be a protective way that narrowed focus would have them look at the question in a narrow way so that it would be interpreted, during my life in the U.S., not to include, my life back home where these terrible things happened to me.

Q. So, the fact that Ms. Odeh interpreted the questions on her citizenship application to exclude her traumatic past, is that consistent with someone suffering from PTSD?

A. Yes, it could be.[20]

Fabri was willing to provide Odeh's purported explanation about her "no" answers on the naturalization form—although that information was not mentioned anywhere in her seventeen-page report—but she would only go so far. At least for the time being, she balked at providing a definitive opinion about the specific effect of Odeh's PTSD, stating only that there was a "strong possibility" that it "could" have impacted her interpretation of the citizenship questions. That would change later.

On cross-examination, Jonathan Tukel established that Fabri could not say whether Odeh had actually filtered out or misinterpreted the questions on the naturalization application. "I don't know what went on in her mind," Fabri conceded. "I don't know because I wasn't there."[21] That opinion would also change later.

It did not take Judge Drain long to make up his mind. Accepting the prosecution position on general intent crimes, he issued his opinion just six days after the evidentiary hearing, ruling against the admission of "the testimony of a clinical psychologist concerning her conclusions with respect to Defendant's defense related to post-traumatic stress syndrome."[22] It was a resounding victory for the prosecution, but the basis for the court's ruling—a flat prohibition on psychological testimony rather than a specific ruling on Dr. Fabri's theory—would create serious problems later in the case.

Deutsch's initial optimism about Judge Drain had been misplaced. Although he had taken some solace in having informed the court "about the history and about the context of this case," he was demoralized by Drain's harsh rulings on the pretrial motions. "By precluding from the trial any mention of torture, the court has gutted the heart of Rasmea's defense and makes a fair trial impossible," he told a reporter.[23]

Speaking a few days later on Chicago Public Radio, Deutsch was even more despondent, repeating that Drain's rulings had "gutted" Odeh's case, and using terms like "hamstrung," "cut out at the knees," and "cut out the heart of our defense." Worst of all was the lost opportunity to present "evidence of Israeli torture . . . in a U.S. courtroom." Odeh had turned down a very favorable deal, Deutsch explained, because "she was insistent that she wanted to tell her story about what happened to her and who she was; and now on the eve of trial we're seeing that she's not going to be able to tell her story in any kind of full and fair way."[24]

The only hope, as Deutsch saw it, "is that there will be some jurors that will understand and see the injustice of the whole prosecution."[25] He would learn the answer soon enough, as the beginning of the trial was only four days away.

14 Prosecution case

Opening statements in United States v. Odeh were set to begin on the morning of November 5, 2014. A jury of six men and six women, including two African Americans, had been efficiently chosen the previous day. The initial panel of thirty-two was described by an Odeh supporter as "overwhelmingly" white, which seemed surprising in downtown Detroit, given that Wayne County was "mostly Black and Arab."[1] The U.S. District Court, however, had jurisdiction over the entire eastern half of Michigan's lower peninsula, comprising thirty-four counties, many of which are majority white. Judge Drain had closely questioned the prospective jurors about their potential prejudices for or against Palestinians and Muslims, excusing those who admitted that they could not be fair in a case involving a bombing, but he refused the defense request to ask detailed *voir dire* questions specifically about the Middle East conflict. One of the defense attorneys later complained that "this case arose from the Six Day War and the roundups that took place after it, and [Drain] didn't ask a single question about Israel."[2]

In keeping with the court's earlier order, the jurors had been brought to the federal building in vans with their windows covered, entering through the basement garage. Drain provided a "neutral explanation" for the unusual secrecy, telling the jurors, who surely suspected something, only that the security measures were necessary to avoid attention from the press. In fact, the court had shielded the jurors from about one hundred of Odeh's supporters who were gathered at the front entrance to the courthouse, chanting their opposition to the Department of Justice: "DOJ, let's be clear, Rasmea is welcome here."[3]

The courtroom itself was filled with reporters and security officers, with the remaining seats going to Odeh's supporters who had traveled from across the Midwest to attend the trial, although most of the latter had to watch the proceedings on screens in the "overflow courtroom" that Drain had arranged to accommodate them.[4]

There were four lawyers seated with Odeh at the defense table, all of whom knew each other from the National Lawyers Guild. Michael Deutsch and James Fennerty, both veterans of over forty years in Chicago's criminal courts, had been representing Odeh in one way or another ever since her indictment, and they had fully taken over the case when she rejected the plea bargain the previous May. Local counsel William Goodman had his own long history with radical causes in Detroit, as the scion of a storied left-wing family. His late father, Ernest Goodman, had been for nearly seventy years the go-to lawyer for union organizers and Communist Party members (real and imagined) and had represented a Michigan state senator in the first political denaturalization case of the McCarthy era.[5] The fourth lawyer, Dennis Cunningham, was a late addition to the defense team, having only recently arrived from San Francisco. A former partner of Deutsch at the People's Law Office, Cunningham was nationally prominent for successfully raising political defenses in high-profile trials.[6] Although the mean age of the defense lawyers was over seventy, they represented Odeh with the visible energy and passion of youthful believers.

The prosecution side was more reserved, although no less devoted to the case. Lead counsel Jonathan Tukel, a career prosecutor, worked not to show his disdain for the band of defense attorneys. A staunch conservative and member of the Federalist Society—he had befriended and defended right-wing firebrand Ann Coulter when they were classmates in law school—Tukel had been the object of rancorous insults from Odeh's supporters.[7] If he was troubled by the epithets routinely thrown at him—"racist," "fascist," and "zionist," the latter often in lower case as an obscure left-wing signifier—he rarely let it be seen. Tukel was assisted by Mark Jebson, a by-the-book trial lawyer and immigration law specialist, on secondment from the Department of Homeland Security. As an in-court representative of the government, the prosecution chose Special Agent Stephen Webber of the Department of Homeland Security, who would sit at their table throughout the trial. The lead investigator in the case, Webber would also be the first prosecution witness.

Once everyone was in place and introduced, Drain gave the jury some preliminary instructions and then turned to the attorneys for their opening statements.

*   *   *

Jebson's opening statement for the prosecution was simple and straightforward. He began by thanking the jurors for their service, noting that our judicial system could not operate without such "dedicated citizens." With that, he pivoted to Odeh's crime—"obtaining her U.S. citizenship illegally"—explaining that she had "lied about . . . her criminal record during the entire citizenship process."

Like all good trial lawyers, Jebson developed a theme in his opening statement, and it was not subtle: Odeh was a liar. She had lied on her visa application, she had lied on her naturalization application, and she had lied finally during the in-person citizenship examination. In the course of about thirty minutes, Jebson used variations on the words lying, false statement, and perjury nearly forty times.

Jebson told the jury that Odeh had been convicted in Israel for the two bombings in Jerusalem, including one that killed two people, and for membership in the PFLP, using fingerprints from Neve Tirza to prove that the defendant was truly the same person as the one convicted and imprisoned in Israel. He then showed the jury slides of the documents Odeh had signed under oath, noting each place where she had falsely answered questions about her criminal history. Jebson dwelled a bit on the citizenship application, Form N-400, showing the jury each question, with the word **EVER** in bold capital letters, where Odeh had denied having been arrested, charged, convicted, or imprisoned. He then observed that she had made seventeen minor changes on the form during her in-person examination, but none of them corrected her false answers. Jebson promised that the immigration officer who interviewed Odeh—Jennifer Williams—would testify about her invariable practice of explaining the entire process, including emphasizing that the "ever" questions covered "anywhere in the world."

That brought Jebson back to Odeh's crimes in Israel. "We're not here to redo the 1969 bombing case," he said. "She is not on trial here for being a member of the PFLP." The only issue for the jury, Jebson concluded, is whether Odeh procured her citizenship illegally by intentionally providing false answers throughout the process.[8]

* * *

Judge Drain had indeed cut the heart out of the defense case but that did not stop Deutsch from trying to make his point, even if that meant "push[ing] against the strict boundaries Judge Gershwin Drain has placed on the trial," as reported in the *Electronic Intifada*.[9] Realizing that he had only limited time before an inevitable objection, Deutsch began his opening statement to the jury with a quick rebuke to the prosecution and the court:

> The one thing that you didn't know and the judge didn't tell you and, of course, the government didn't tell you is that Ms. Odeh was convicted by a military court that was occupying Palestinian land after the invasion by the Israeli army into Palestine, and judges who sat on that court were soldiers.

Deutsch continued in that vein, all but taunting the prosecution and testing the court's patience, by asserting that both were "part of the system." In contrast, "Rasmieh Odeh embodies essentially the modern history of the Palestinian people." In 1948, she was driven from her home along with seven hundred thousand people, and again in 1967 "the Israeli military came . . . and she had to suffer again the loss of her home." Conceding that Odeh had been arrested, Deutsch explained that it had been part of "a massive sweep, 500 people were arrested and Rasmieh Odeh was one of them." Neither statement was exactly true. Odeh had not lost her home in 1967 and only eighteen people were arrested following the Supersol bombing (of about 150 who were detained only for questioning) but Deutsch proceeded with his narrative, uninterrupted to that point.

Prohibited from mentioning torture, Deutsch resorted to implication. Odeh "had no access to a lawyer for 45 days. She was interrogated extensively, and you can use your imagination as to what interrogation . . ."

That was too much. Jebson's quick objection was firmly sustained by Drain. "We're not going to get into the conviction or the trial of what happened back then. She doesn't get a second trial on that issue," he ruled. The judge then reprimanded Deutsch for his comment about "the system."

I want you to be careful about what you say and how you say it, because you also kind of implied that I wasn't being neutral here and being independent. I just want you to be careful about how you say and talk about the case and, again we're not going to retry that case from back then. . . . I just want to make sure we keep it straight here.

Admonished but not chastened, Deutsch told the jury that he would like to be "talking about what happened to her back then and the legitimacy of the case that gave her a life sentence. But the Court has made a ruling . . . and I can't get into it."

Only after another objection did Deutsch move on, taking the unusual step of committing his client to waive the Fifth Amendment by testifying on her own behalf. Of course, the defense had no other way to explain the false denials on her immigration and naturalization applications. Deutsch therefore told the jury that it was Odeh's English-speaking brother who had filled out the visa application, which she was unable to read. And the incorrect answers on the naturalization exam were the result of a misunderstanding. Odeh thought that the questions referred only to her life in the United States. "She'll testify that she never, never thought that they were asking her about what happened 40 years ago in Israel Palestine [sic]."

In conclusion, Deutsch returned to the conspiracy theory that he had first raised at a press conference in the days shortly after Odeh's arrest. He reminded the jury that Odeh had been naturalized in 2004 and was not accused of lying at that time. Then, "in 2013, nine years later, they charge her with lying. Why? Ask yourself why? Maybe you'll find out, maybe you won't. But that is something you should think about." Another objection ended Deutsch's intimation of sinister forces at work, and he quickly wrapped up with a request for a not guilty verdict.[10]

* * *

Deutsch was stopped by the court before he could fully articulate his conspiracy theory, blaming Israel and the "Israel lobby" for Odeh's arrest,[11] but Angela Davis was under no such constraint when she published an op-ed in the *Detroit News* on the first day of the trial. Identified in the newspaper as "a renowned activist and distinguished professor," Davis opined that Odeh's prosecution had been "politically motivated [and] clearly designed to disrupt the Chicago Palestine human rights community" which had "effectively raised awareness of Israel's apartheid system and its violation of international laws." The case "reeks of political payback," she charged, "in light of success [sic] of the Boycott, Sanctions and Divestment campaign" against Israel. In Davis's view, the only reason for prosecuting Odeh had been "retaliation for the growing successes of the Palestine solidarity movement."[12]

In fact, the Israeli government had been decidedly cool about cooperating in the U.S. prosecution of Odeh and had done nothing to initiate the case. The Department of Justice's initial request for documentation had actually been stalled in Israel with the explanation that the records from forty years earlier, most of which were handwritten, could not readily be retrieved. It took considerable persistence and the local assistance of the Israel Law Center, an Israeli NGO, before the police reports and transcripts could be found in deep storage in a government archive.[13]

I have been informed by one confidential source that the Israelis simply had little interest in Odeh. Having rid themselves of her in 1979, they were content to leave her alone in Chicago.[14] A different confidential source, however, suggested that the Israelis were actually skittish about exposing their interrogation methods at trial in the United States.[15]

In 2007, a Palestinian named Muhammad Salah had been acquitted in Chicago on charges of providing material support to Hamas, a designated terrorist organization, after he contended that his earlier confession in Israel had been the product of extended torture. The Israeli government had cooperated in the Salah prosecution, bringing Shin Bet interrogators to Chicago, where they were allowed to testify using code names in a closed courtroom, only to see the defendant found not guilty of the major charges.[16] Salah, who was believed to be a high-ranking Hamas member, was infinitely more important to the Israelis than Odeh. Having been burned once in the Salah trial, the Israelis were understandably reluctant, according to my informant, to have their interrogation methods again subjected to cross-examination in what they regarded as merely a routine immigration case.

Salah's successful defense attorney had been Michael Deutsch.[17]

*   *   *

The first prosecution witness was Special Agent Webber, of the Department of Homeland Security, who had conducted an investigation of Odeh beginning in 2010, concerning "allegations of possible naturalization fraud" based on her "criminal history."[18] Under direct examination by Tukel, Webber described the stages of his investigation, beginning with a search of various government databases until he located Odeh's immigration file.

Tukel then took Webber methodically through the documents in Odeh's file, including her citizenship and visa applications, showing slides to the jury as the witness explained the significance of each exhibit. Deutsch could only watch in frustration when the naturalization application—Form N-400—was displayed on the screen, with a half-page enlarged, showing Odeh's answers to four fateful questions.

Had she ever been arrested, cited, or detained? Had she ever been charged with committing any crime? Had she ever been convicted of a crime? Had she ever been in jail or in prison?

"What were the defendant's answers to those questions?" Tukel asked.

"She answered 'no' to all of them," Webber replied.[19]

The next step in the investigation was to obtain Odeh's records from Israel and to have them translated from Hebrew to English. Again, Tukel showed the jury slides of the relevant documents, as he walked Webber through the evidence of Odeh's arrest, indictment, conviction, sentence, and imprisonment. Webber also identified the two sets of fingerprints proving that the person imprisoned in Israel was the same person on trial in the courtroom.

Tukel next turned to Odeh's visa application, filled out in Jordan. Webber read one question to the jury from a slide: "List below all the places you have lived for six months or longer since reaching the age of 16."

"And her answer," Tukel requested.

"Amman, Jordan," Webber answered.

"In what country was Odeh in prison?"

"Israel."

"Per the exhibits, is [Jordan] a truthful answer?"

"No, it's not."[20]

The direct examination had until that point been steady, understated, and inexorable, sticking closely to the documents that exposed Odeh's false statements. But Tukel finished with a flourish, using testimony from Webber to lay the foundation for Odeh's interview in the documentary *Women in Struggle*.

Emphasizing that the video had been made in 2004, the same year as Odeh's citizenship application, Tukel played a short clip for the jury, after assuring the court that it was "solely about her time in prison."[21] The jurors then saw a much younger Rasmea Odeh, though clearly the same person as the defendant in the courtroom, with a superscript in English, reading "Rasmieh Odeh: Sentenced for life, spent 10 years in prison." Speaking in Arabic, with English subtitles, she said,

> Prison is a really harsh place; you can't see further than the wall surrounding you at a very short distance. . . . I remember an incident when my "punishment" was to prevent me from working in the prison garden because they knew how much I loved the land and how much I enjoyed it.[22]

There could have been no better proof of Odeh's false answer to the imprisonment question, and Tukel was quite content to leave it at that. "I don't have any further questions for Agent Webber," he told the court.

On cross-examination, Deutsch wasted no time pointing out that Webber was part of the "prosecution team," who had just moved from the prosecution table to the witness stand. He then moved on to his conspiracy theory, asking Webber "what steps had been taken in 2004" to investigate Odeh when she applied for naturalization and "what caused you to initiate an investigation five years later in 2009?"[23]

Stymied by an objection, Deutsch pivoted to another approach, asking Webber whether he had conducted "any kind of independent investigation as to whether there was fairness in the military courts in Israel." That drew another objection, as well as a reproach from the court. Judge Drain reminded Deutsch that he had already excluded the "due process fairness issues" and sternly cautioned him to "abide by the rulings that I've made."

Deutsch is a dolorous figure, visibly weighed down by his decades of challenging the political power structure, representing radicals, revolutionaries, and assorted ordinary criminal defendants, only occasionally getting what he once called "a little bit of justice." He is also a brilliant lawyer, well able to conjure traps and surprises when least expected by his courtroom adversaries. If there is a wizardry comparison to be made, Deutsch would be Tolkien's Gandalf the Grey—ancient, wise, commanding, unpredictable, and ineffably saddened by the power of the forces arrayed against him. In the real world, he made his bones in Chicago's brawling criminal courts, so he was not intimidated by scoldings from the bench.

Deutsch's cross-examination turned next to Webber's July 2013 interception of Odeh at O'Hare Airport as she was returning from a trip to Jordan, an interaction that had been oddly omitted from the investigator's direct testimony. After Deutsch intimated that Webber had interviewed Odeh under a pretense while secretly videotaping her, it became apparent why the defense, rather than the prosecution, was introducing evidence of the airport encounter. Deutsch read out a transcript of Webber's questioning of Odeh:

> Agent: When you came to this country, did you tell anyone about spending your
> time in an Israeli jail?
> Odeh: No, I don't like to speak about this.
> Agent: So when you applied for your green card or your citizenship, you never
> told anyone about it, did anyone ever ask?
> Odeh: No one asked, nobody asked me.
> Agent: But when you filled out the paperwork for immigration, did you ever
> say that?
> Odeh: No, nobody asked me. I don't know.[24]

That was the groundwork for the PTSD defense, or it would have been if the court had not ruled against it. Before she was indicted, and even before she knew of the investigation, Odeh told Webber that she tried to suppress her memory of imprisonment in Israel and she had not understood the immigration and naturalization questions to be asking about foreign arrests.

Deutsch had one last point to make. "She had never been arrested in the United States, correct?"

"As far as I know, yes," answered Webber.

*   *   *

The next government witness was Raymond Clore, a career State Department officer whose assignment in 2014 was with the Office of Space and Advanced Technology. Clore had previously been a consular officer, whose postings included Haiti, Cameroon, Canada, Jerusalem, and, during 1993–1996, Amman, Jordan. In Jordan, Clore's responsibilities included supervising the two "immigrant visa officers" who were responsible for interviewing applicants and forwarding reports. It was Clore's responsibility to review and approve applications—a total of about fifteen thousand in his three years in Amman—as he had done in Odeh's case on January 25, 1995.

Displaying a slide of Odeh's visa application, Tukel directed the witness's attention to a number of corrections that would have been made during the visa officer's interview as well as Odeh's statement that she had not been assisted in completing the forms. Clore testified that a truthful admission of "criminal history" would have halted the process, at which point Odeh's application would have been referred to the State Department in Washington, DC. Odeh would have been asked for "more details" to "see if there was some kind of exemption" available, given the nature of her offenses.[25]

Tukel concluded the brief examination by asking whether Odeh's arrests, convictions, and imprisonment would have affected her eligibility for a visa to enter the United States. The answer, as expected, was "Yes."

Deutsch used the cross-examination to support Odeh's claim—which she would later make explicit in her own testimony—that her brother had actually filled out the application, which her poor English did not allow her to read and understand. He noted that there were misspellings on the application, which indicated, as Clore agreed, someone who was not fluent in English. Clore also agreed that an application could have been brought into the consulate already filled out. And he finally established that Odeh's application had been signed in only one of two required places.

With that successful cross-examination sequence accomplished, Deutsch turned persistently to a prohibited line of questions.

"How did you deal with Palestinians who were swept up and prosecuted by the military court?" he asked.

The predictable objection was sustained.

"Did you come across a lot of Palestinians that had been through the process of being arrested and prosecuted—"

Another objection sustained.

And finally, "Did you make any differentiation between people who were convicted in the Israeli courts and military courts?"

Without objection, Clore replied, "Not that I remember."

* * *

Douglas Pierce's witness appearance, his testimony stretching over two sessions of court, would be the prosecution's longest. Pierce had been an adjudication officer in the Detroit office of the Immigration and Naturalization Service and its successor, the U.S. Citizenship and Immigration Service, since 1995. He became supervisor of the Naturalization Unit in 2006. He had trained many other adjudication officers, including Williams, who conducted Odeh's interview.[26] Under direct examination by Jebson, Pierce provided the jury with a lengthy overview of naturalization, including a history of the relevant government organizations and a step-by-step description of the entire process, from visa to swearing-in.

Pierce testified that there are certain "stop signs" in the process that can render an applicant ineligible, including, of course, commission of a crime involving moral turpitude. Even then, however, an honest applicant could seek a waiver. The crime might be "determined to be [a] purely political offense," or the applicant might show "that they've completely reformed." On the other hand, someone who lied on an application would not be "allowed to come into the United States," with no exceptions.[27]

"How about a conviction for a bombing that killed two people?" Jebson asked. "That would impact naturalization eligibility" was Pierce's understated reply.

In a question intended to preempt Deutsch's conspiracy theory, Jebson asked Pierce why applicants would not be screened for foreign convictions or arrests at the time of naturalization. Pierce explained that the State Department lacked contacts to check with every country in the world, and at most it might be possible to check the databases of "the country that the person is from or they have identified they have been from."[28] In Odeh's case, because of her false answer, that would not have included Israel.

Returning to the case at hand, Jebson displayed Odeh's visa application and asked whether, if the answers had been truthful, she would have been allowed to enter the United States. "Absolutely not," Pierce replied.

Next up was Odeh's naturalization application, which had been reviewed in an interview by Williams. Pierce explained that red notations on the application meant that Odeh made seventeen corrections in the course of the interview and that she had orally confirmed the other answers under oath. Pierce had trained Williams to make sure that applicants understood the questions and to rephrase them if there was any doubt.[29] A stamp indicated that the application had been approved.

"In your opinion," asked Jebson, "why was it approved?"

"It was approved because the applicant provided false information in response to the questions that were asked on the form," Pierce testified.

What if the answers had been truthful?

"We would have referred her case to the immigration and customs enforcement agency [*sic*] for them to pursue deportation or removal proceedings against her."[30]

Pierce's cross-examination was Fennerty's first active involvement in the trial. Fennerty graduated law school only a few years later than Deutsch, but projects optimism where Deutsch is only resolute, and thus seems younger by comparison. He is also shorter than Deutsch and far more cheerful—perhaps Harry Potter to Deutsch's Gandalf—giving the impression that he has seen less and expects more of the world.

The cross-examination started strong, laying the groundwork for Odeh's claim that she had misunderstood the criminal background questions as applying only to the United States. Fennerty established that Odeh had never been arrested or convicted in the United States, and he obtained Pierce's admission that he had testified in a previous case that the naturalization form is a "fairly complex application."[31]

Fennerty was less effective in a line of questioning about an earlier iteration of the naturalization application, which requested disclosure of convictions "in or outside the United States."[32] Pierce, however, simply deflected the implication by pointing out that Fennerty's form had not been used since 1989.

Odeh's defense committee had been raising money for close to a year, but it appeared that none of the funds had been spent on digitization or even photo enlargements. The prosecution had been able to display its exhibits on a large video screen, magnifying relevant sections of Odeh's various applications and highlighting her false answers. The defense attorneys, however, were still working with paper, which required them to seek the court's permission to approach witnesses, while handing them documents that the jury could not immediately see. Fennerty's next point was central to the defense but was blunted by its old-fashioned delivery.

Fennerty's objective was to show Pierce Odeh's own N-400 and point out the question about whether the applicant had "ever" belonged to any organizations "in the United States or in any other place." The idea was to buttress the defense argument that other crucial questions—which also used the word **EVER** but did not say "any other place"—had misled Odeh into thinking it applied only to her life in the United States.

It was a smart move, but it suffered in the execution as Fennerty fumbled with the papers when Pierce asked to see the exhibit before answering questions.

"Sorry, judge," he said, "all my stuff is falling off here."

It did not get much better when Fennerty finally handed the document to Pierce.

"Okay. Can you, can you go to, I believe, it's date stamped 1-4-6-1 is that in the bottom, is that one date stamped?"

That turned out to be wrong. "Take [a] second, judge. Excuse me. . . . Can you turn to, I believe, it's part 10, part 10, number 8, see that on page 7 of the application?"

Questions like this had been handled seamlessly by the prosecution, simply by highlighting the relevant passage on the screen, but now the jurors could only wonder about the content of the document that was causing such confusion. By the time Pierce agreed that there was only one place "on that N-400 where it asks you about any other place," its impact was diminished or lost. The baffling scene was reenacted at even greater length when Fennerty tried to show that other questions on the N-400 did not "mention crimes committed outside the United States."[33]

The cross-examination made a fair point, but it was unlikely that the jurors—unable to see the actual documents under discussion—had been able to follow along as Fennerty shuffled through his papers.

*   *   *

As a naturalization officer in the Detroit office of the U.S. Citizenship and Immigration Service, Jennifer Williams conducted about a thousand citizenship interviews in 2004, including Rasmea Odeh's. Under direct examination by Jebson, she testified that she could not specifically remember her meeting with Odeh but explained she followed "the same procedures every time" she interviewed an applicant.[34]

After putting an applicant under oath, she would proceed to review the entire application, re-asking each question and stopping the interview if it appeared that the applicant did not understand a particular term. As she was trained, Williams testified, she made sure that each applicant understood the scope of the questions about criminal history. Thus, she would ask, "Have you ever committed a crime or offense . . . anywhere in the world," with similar emphasis for the questions about arrests and imprisonment. Jebson drove the point home.

"Would you do that sometimes or every time?"

"Every time."

"Are you're [sic] absolutely positive that you did it every single time."

"I am."

Williams identified Odeh's signature on the application as well as her own signature indicating approval.

"Did you know that she had been convicted of multiple bombings in Israel that resulted in two people being killed?" asked Jebson.

"No I didn't," answered Williams. "I would not have been able to approve it with that information."[35]

Deutsch was skeptical, to say the least, of Williams's claim always to have added "anywhere in the world" during interviews. On cross-examination, he asked the witness if there were any written training materials that included such instructions. "That was verbally taught to us in our training," she answered.

Deutsch pressed the point. "So it wasn't in any document that you had, right?"

After establishing that Williams could not say which of her superiors had trained her to expand on the written questions, Deutsch posed a series of emphatic questions about Williams's non-recollection of Odeh's interview:

"You didn't remember anything about it, right?"

"You can't say you remember asking it to Ms. Odeh in November of 2004, right?"

"As to the specific time when you interviewed her, you don't have any recollection?"

Pursuing the point, Deutsch noted that Williams had made no notations on the N-400 about asking "anywhere in the world," although she had written down some other observations, including Odeh's seventeen corrections, in red ink.

The final government witness was fingerprint expert who compared Odeh's prints on her naturalization application with the prints received from the Neve Tirza prison in Israel. "I determined that the prints were made by one and the same individual bearing the name Rasmieh on the fingerprint card," he testified. There was no cross-examination.

With that, the prosecution rested its case.

15 Defense case

The defense was indeed hamstrung by Judge Drain's earlier rulings, which left only two viable witnesses: Prof. Nadine Naber, who would testify as a character witness, and Odeh herself. Before the defense case could begin, however, Jonathan Tukel requested that Judge Drain explain "the parameters on the rulings [about] claims of torture" and unfair process in Israel.

Michael Deutsch assured the court that "She knows. She knows what your rulings are," adding, "I'm not intending to elicit anything from her."[1] The latter commitment would last only a few minutes once Odeh took the stand, but it would not be an issue in Naber's testimony, which came first.

A professor in the Gender and Women's Studies program and Global Asian Studies program at the University of Illinois, Chicago, Naber was obviously a highly accomplished academic, with multiple advanced degrees, a string of important grants, and four books to her credit. Even so, she was an odd choice for a character witness, as she actually did not know Odeh very well. They had met once about nine years earlier, at a conference, and renewed their acquaintance when Naber moved to Chicago in 2013, less than a year before Odeh's arrest. In Chicago, Naber and Odeh had worked together on a series of workshops for Arab women who told stories and performed plays.

Deutsch began the direct examination by taking Naber through her extensive credentials and her background with Odeh. Naber told the story of the playground encounter that led to Odeh's activism and her unprecedented recruitment of six hundred women to the Arab Women's Committee. The rules of evidence require a rather awkward question of every character witness, using terms of art that Naber evidently did not quite recognize.

"Do you have an opinion as to her reputation in the community for honesty?" Deutsch asked, in the requisite language.

"She has phenomenally created an incredible bond of trust among immigrant women," answered Naber, continuing on to describe Odeh's community organizing work.

Deutsch had to ask the question twice more before he got an answer that fit the rules.

"Rasmieh in my view is one of the . . . most truthful people. She does this work by also telling her own story. . . . She tells her truth. . . . She confides in [the women] and she models truthfulness."[2]

It is questionable whether Odeh had ever actually confided her full truth to Naber and the other Arab women in Chicago, at least before she was indicted and needed public support. Her biography on the AAAN website said nothing about ever having been convicted in Israel nor did an AAAN promotional video in which she featured prominently. She described her family's dispossession in Palestine in her video for the Chicago Cultural Alliance, but she did not mention spending ten years in prison for murder. And of course, she continued to deny plotting the Supersol bombing, which she had never concealed—when living in Lebanon and Jordan—before immigrating to the United States.

It would have been interesting to find out how much Naber actually knew about Odeh's background, including her connection to the PFLP, but Tukel opted not to explore that on cross-examination. Instead, he pointed out only that Naber had not known Odeh in 1969 or 1970. "I was just being born" at the time, said Naber.

* * *

Rasmea Odeh was eager to testify in her own defense, which was the very reason she rejected William Swor's advice to accept a favorable plea bargain. She had waited for over a year since her arrest to tell her full story of Israeli torture and injustice, having refrained from holding a press conference or even granting an interview on the advice of her counsel. Before she could take the stand, however, Judge Drain admonished her as to the limits he had placed on her testimony.

"My rulings have prevented you from going into things like torture and rape and all those kinds of things and I did that because your guilty [*sic*] or innocence in the prior matter, the bombing that you were involved in, is not relevant. So, I'm just cautioning you not to go into those areas."

Odeh protested. "But your honor, it's my case. I have to say about the situation that I have been. It's my life. It's my case."

The court was unmoved. "I ruled already that we can't retry that case . . . And if you get into it, and if you get into it, I'll just have to stop you and if you don't stop, I do have the authority to find you in contempt of court."

Odeh gave a preview of how she intended to testify, informing the court, "I will respect the rules, but sometimes I feel there's some word, I have to say it. I'm not going to say details, but sometimes there's words maybe I can say it, it's automatically going out."[3]

Recognizing that he would have to keep close watch on the defendant's testimony, Drain warned her one more time that "the war that went on is not something that is an issue for us." Then he asked the clerk to administer the oath.

Well over one hundred supporters had come to court for Odeh's testimony, many arriving by bus from Chicago. They first rallied on the steps of the federal building with signs saying "Drop the Charges Now" and chanting "Out of our schools/Out of our mosques/FBI/Go get lost."[4] Defying Tukel's characterization, the group filed peacefully into the courtroom, which was filled to overflowing with supporters when the defendant took the stand.

Deutsch began the direct examination by asking Odeh to describe her work in Chicago with the AAAN, including the awards she had received for organizing the Arab Women's Committee and the story of the little girl at the playground. He continued with her childhood, beginning with her birth in Lifta and detailing the hardships that befell her family in the following years. Some of the spectators were near tears when Odeh described the "dead bodies burned with napalm" outside Ramallah in the 1967 war. Tukel sat still for the lengthy background narrative, which ensured that his eventual objection would be sustained by the court.

Having "set the stage," as he put it, Deutsch turned to Odeh's arrest, signaling to his client that she should do her best to evade Judge Drain's instructions.

"Were you and your family swept up in a mass arrest?" he asked.

"In one week there were mass arrested over 500 from random people was arrested and I have been, me, my father, and other two sisters," she answered. Her "voice cracked" and she began crying when she testified that "my sister was fell down and she died after they beat her. She was 23 years old."[5]

That was not true. Many fewer than five hundred Palestinians were detained for questioning after the Supersol bombing, and Odeh was among only a handful who were actually arrested. Odeh's sister may or may not have been beaten by interrogators, but she lived for years afterward. Nonetheless, Deutsch was concerned only with the big picture. He brought up Odeh's interrogation at Moskobiya and asked "during those 45 days, were you ever given access to a lawyer."

That was finally enough for Tukel, whose objection cut off Odeh's answer. Judge Drain was irritated by Deutsch's blatant attempt to circumvent his ruling, and he became almost angry when the defense attorney tried to justify himself.

Judge Drain: Mr. Deutsch, I told you and I made a previous ruling that we're not going to get into the substance of that case.

Deutsch: I'm not getting into the substance of the case.

Judge Drain: We're not going to retry it.

Deutsch: I'm not retrying it.

Judge Drain: We're not going to get into things that happened there.

Deutsch: I'm not going to get into the substance of the case. I understand your ruling. We can't do that.

Judge Drain: We're not retrying it. And we don't want to hear just one side of the story.[6]

It is seldom a good idea to argue with the judge, but Deutsch wasn't finished. His next two questions were both about Odeh's claim of a false conviction without a fair trial. They both drew objections, which Judge Drain sustained, with an exasperated admonition:

"Okay, Mr. Deutsch, I told you we're not going to get into any due process claims or any rights that you believe or suspect were violated in that process."[7]

Even that did not work. Deutsch turned to Odeh's imprisonment at Neve Tirza, asking whether she had ever "tried to escape from the prison." Odeh was obviously well prepared for it.

"Of course," she said, "any political prisoner try to find—"

Tukel's quick objection interrupted Odeh's response, but she still managed to blurt out her planned answer.

"— their freedom," she said, drawing a wave of applause in the overflow courtroom, while supporters in the main courtroom restrained themselves in silence.[8]

That was three sustained objections in the space of a few minutes. Deutsch had succeeded in introducing perhaps one full sentence of Odeh's political defense, but at the cost, most likely, of considerable annoyance to the jury. Thwarted for the time being, Deutsch moved on to his legal defense, which required Odeh to explain the undeniably false answers on both her visa and naturalization applications.

Turning first to the visa application, filed in Jordan in 1994, Deutsch prompted Odeh to testify that she was unable to read the application due to her poor English and her now-deceased brother Mustafa had actually filled out a draft for her to use in filing the form. Odeh's application had been completed in two different handwritings—evidently Mustafa's and hers—which she explained,

> I told him I can't fill the application. He said I will make it easy for you. He filled part of the form in his handwriting and filled other form the whole question and he told me just copy what is not in this part from the other form. . . . And I didn't read any question because my English was very poor at that time.[9]

Mustafa's involvement was crucial to the defense, so Deutsch asked Odeh to repeat it over and over:

"This application I didn't read it."

"I didn't read anything. I just copy what he put, filled the sample application to me and I just copy it."

"I couldn't read and I trust my brother."[10]

Odeh's claim of English illiteracy in 1994 was superficially plausible, given her imperfect spoken English almost twenty years later. "I graduated from high school teaches just Arabic," she testified. "My English was so poor. I knew just some words and basic sentences."

That was untrue. Odeh's schooling in Ramallah had been during Jordan's rule, and the Jordanian curriculum included mandatory English language study beginning in the fifth grade, for at least six class sessions per week through the end of high school. By the time she graduated, Odeh had received at least two thousand hours of English instruction, teaching her to "read and comprehend English in different contexts with ease and accuracy."[11]

Odeh had been a serious student, so determined to get an education that she defied tradition, walking two or three kilometers to school because her family denied her bus money.[12] She did so well in high school that she was accepted to medical school in Lebanon, where some of her schoolwork was in English. She later took English classes in Jordan, also studying law with some readings in English.[13] Even in prison at Neve Tirza, Odeh spoke with Red Cross officials who conducted their interviews in English.[14] Moreover, the section of the visa application admittedly in her own handwriting is in well-defined cursive letters in the English alphabet, evidencing a level of facility obviously acquired through much practice by someone whose main education was in Arabic.

Odeh's 1996 visa interview was conducted through an interpreter. But whatever her level of spoken fluency, Odeh's ability to understand written English in 1996 certainly extended beyond "some words and basic sentences." Given the extent of her English language education, it is virtually impossible to believe that she had copied her brother's draft without understanding it and even less that she could not read the printed words "convicted," "arrested," and "prison" on the visa application.

The citizenship application was even more problematic for the defense, because there was no question about Odeh's English language ability at the time of naturalization. As part of the interview with Jennifer Williams, Odeh easily passed both the language and civics tests, scoring 100 percent on the latter. Barred from raising Dr. Mary Fabri's PTSD "filtering" theory, Deutsch instead prompted Odeh to testify that she had misunderstood the questions about her criminal background, mistakenly believing that they applied only to her nine years in the United States. That would require a considerable amount of explaining, resulting in an imaginative rationale based on bits and pieces of other questions on the form.

Odeh admitted that she had answered "No" to the questions about her criminal background, but she blamed it on the ambiguity of the questionnaire, claiming she had been misled by a series of other questions that applied only to the United States:

They use "ever" it's bold, but that question said: "Have you ever claimed to be a
    U.S. Citizen in writing or any other way."
I said, "no." Because I understand this about United States.
And: "Have you ever registered to vote in any federal state or local election
    in the United States."
They use "ever" and it's bold, "in the United States." I said, "no."
When I continue the other questions, my understanding was about United
    States. So I continue to say no, no, no.
Never I thought about Israel. . . . If I knew that about Israel, I will say the
    truth.

The evident theory was that having seen the words "ever" and "United States" in
a couple of questions, Odeh therefore believed that the restricted location also
applied in all of the other questions, even when they did not specify "United
States." She explained that as a conscious choice—"my understanding was about
United States"—which was not very persuasive on direct examination and
would come back to haunt her at a much later stage of the case.

Even so, Deutsch still had to deal with Williams's testimony that she always
stressed "anywhere in world" in every interview, which would have included
the one with Odeh. He took the issue head on, asking Odeh to flatly contradict
Williams.

"You heard her testify yesterday that when she asked you about arrests, convictions, imprisonment, she added something orally to the form 'anywhere in
the world' do you remember that?" Deutsch asked.

"I remember exactly what she asked," Odeh replied. "She goes to read the
same questions as is in the form. She didn't add any questions."

"Is it your testimony that she never added to the questions about arrest,
conviction, imprisonment 'anywhere in the world'?"

"With me, no."

"Are you sure about that?"

"I sure. I remember exactly that interview because really she helped me to be
relaxed and she was very kind with me."[15]

The comment about relaxation was not gratuitous. One aspect of Fabri's
theory was that PTSD filters worked best when the individual was calm, but
they would fail—and in Odeh's case bring up memories of Israel—in stress-
ful situations. Although Fabri was not allowed to testify at trial, Deutsch was

thoughtfully making a record for appeal. If only the questioning had been plainly about Israel, he asked Odeh, would she "have answered the question, yes," and given the information to Williams.

Odeh agreed. "It's not a secret that I have been in the jail," she said. "How can I hide this thing. I can't."[16]

That answer was disingenuous. Odeh's past imprisonment may not have been a secret from Hatem Abudayyeh and other friends, and perhaps not from members of the Arab Women's Committee, but she had certainly made every effort to conceal it from the English-speaking public. Before Odeh's arrest, none of her public statements—including two videos produced by the AAAN—made any mention of her bombing conviction, even when telling the story of her exile from Lifta to Ramallah and ultimately from Palestine.

There was one final question in the direct examination.

"At any time either in your visa application or your naturalization application or your interview with Ms. Williams, did you ever knowingly lie?"

"No. Never."

*   *   *

Deutsch had been relatively cautious during the direct examination, attempting to raise his political points while plausibly staying within the letter of Judge Drain's rulings. If he failed, it was because of Tukel's vigilance and the court's refusal to allow much latitude. But caution ended when Deutsch turned Odeh over to the prosecution for cross-examination. He had no control over her answers and she had scant respect for the court's instructions. Tukel knew what to expect from Odeh on cross-examination, as she had virtually announced her intention to interject prohibited answers if given the opportunity.[17]

Tukel did not waste time with pleasantries. His cross-examination immediately challenged Odeh's claims of naïveté and misunderstanding by pointing out that her Jordanian legal education had taught her that "words are very important." Odeh sparred with him, trying to deflect the question by claiming she had never actually practiced law. That was contrary to what she had previously told her friends at AAAN. In an interview shortly after Odeh's arrest, Abudayyeh said, "She has built off her history as a practicing attorney in Jordan, who focused on women's rights."[18]

However she may have used her professional training, Odeh was eventually forced to admit her understanding that "words can have important consequences in the legal documents," including her visa application. When Tukel got to the details of Odeh's embassy interview in Jordan, asserting that a consular officer had reviewed the application with her, the witness had a convenient memory lapse. "Twenty years it's too hard to remember," Odeh said.[19]

Going through the visa application page by page, Tukel made Odeh acknowledge the sections in her own handwriting and pointed out the incongruity of the claim that she had copied only half of the answers from her brother's "sample." Odeh repeatedly insisted that her English had been so "very, very poor" that she had no idea how she was answering when she "had to copy what he sent me."[20]

When it came to the false answer about where she had lived—claiming to have been only in Amman, Jordan, since 1948 and omitting her years at Neve Tirza and in Lebanon—Odeh said that her brother "wrote this because I have Jordanian passport."[21] As Tukel attempted to bring out Odeh's ten years in an Israeli prison, the dam burst.

"It's not right because I [was] tortured and they took—"

Tukel's objection could not keep her from adding "—falsely," as the court reporter was not able to take down every word. Odeh kept trying to finish her outburst, until the court reprimanded her.

"Ms. Odeh, be quiet. Stop now."

Things became even more contentious when Tukel directed Odeh's attention to her naturalization application. Odeh jumped to an obviously well-prepared answer, even before Tukel asked a specific question. She continued with the explanation and would not stop when Tukel tried to re-focus the cross-examination.

They didn't say in Israel. I thought it was about United States and I have been
  nine years in the United States, and I didn't have been in prison.
It wasn't misunderstanding. It was clear they asked about United States because
  there's the other part where . . . the question about United States and they
  use 'ever,' and it was in bold and they said about United States.
They ask the first question and it's bold about United States, then they continue
  to ask the other question, I assumed about United States.
But also they use "ever" about asking about United States.[22]

Odeh's broadside response proved too much, especially her insistence that she hadn't misunderstood the questions but rather had consciously drawn a connection—based on the bolded word "ever"—between those that used "United States" and those that did not. That was the sort of link that Fabri might have explained as a subtle and involuntary psychological phenomenon, but it seemed rote and rehearsed coming from the witness herself. Deutsch and Fennerty had obviously practiced the response with Odeh—as good lawyers do in advance of cross-examination—so they must have believed it was necessary to introduce the argument one way or another. Still, they could not have been happy that their client had jumped the gun by blurting it out before Tukel had even raised the subject.

That was not the last of Odeh's interjections. She continually interrupted the cross-examination with statements tying "ever" to "in the United States," drawing rebuke after rebuke from the court:

> Ms. Odeh, wait for the next question. . . . and let him finish his question before you give your answer.
>
> No. No. No. Just listen to me and just listen for the next question.
>
> Ms. Odeh, wait.
>
> No. No. Wait. Wait. Wait for the next question.[23]

Tukel also realized that he could undermine Odeh's account of relaxation during the citizenship interview. "You said you were very distraught at the time because of the death of your brother when you went in for the interview?" he asked.

"Right," Odeh agreed, without arguing. When Tukel then took her through Williams's questioning, however, Odeh aggressively returned to her talking points about the United States, interjecting in answer to every question:

> But also it's not written in United States or out of United States . . . but all of them my understanding about United States.
>
> I understand it about United States.
>
> Why United States has to ask me if I'm not in United States?
>
> If I'm not in United States they will ask me.
>
> My understood all these questions about United States.[24]

At one point, Odeh declared "I am good citizen here and I do the good and best things in my life here."

That was undoubtedly true, although not exactly as Odeh intended it, and it was the last substantive moment in the contentious cross-examination.

*　*　*

Odeh's testimony drew rave reviews from her supporters, who trusted every word of her account and believed that she acquitted herself as an "iconic and legendary Palestinian figure."[25] Outside the courthouse, Abudayyeh praised her performance on the stand and repeated the charge that "Law enforcement [is] here because the government supports Israel unequivocally, is coming after leaders and institutions in our community, and Rasmieh is one of those people."[26]

Activist journalists reported that Odeh, despite the severe restrictions imposed by the court, had been able to deliver "heartfelt" testimony that brought the "entire courtroom" to tears. According to the *Electronic Intifada*, Odeh answered questions in a "deep and percussive voice." She appeared "calm and unrehearsed" as she proudly withstood a "grueling cross examination," in which she was still able to "touch on the background to her conviction in 1969" and convincingly explain that she did not knowingly give false answers on the visa and naturalization applications.[27]

Not everyone agreed with that assessment. Basil Joffe, brother of the murdered Edward, sat through Odeh's testimony in silence, even as she attempted to interject that she had been falsely convicted. Odeh's supporters saw Joffe's presence as further evidence of a conspiracy, noting his seat "at the bench in the gallery that's been reserved for US attorneys." Joffe's apparently "close contact with the US prosecuting attorneys" was taken as a connection to the Israeli "charge that was brought about by 25 days of torture."[28] In fact, Joffe had emigrated from Israel and was living in Houston, a naturalized American citizen. He attended court with his daughter, Terry Joffe Benaryeh, as representatives of a family that had suffered immense grief. "My parents' lives were also devastated, definitely, and they never recovered until they died," he once wrote.[29] The two survivors sat alone in a row, surrounded by Odeh's supporters, enduring their "hateful looks and the rehashing of a traumatic event" that changed their family forever.[30] To her credit, a reporter for the *Electronic Intifada* sought an interview with Joffe. But having seen Odeh's supporters "condoning the murders that she perpetrated," Joffe realized there was nothing he could say to her.[31]

A reporter for the mainstream press neatly summed up the multiple interpretations of Odeh's testimony. "She's a pro-Palestine activist beloved by many in her adopted home of Chicago; a terrorist in the eyes of Israel; and a liar according to the US Government."[32]

16 Judgment

Jonathan Tukel and Michael Deutsch were both well prepared for final argument, which is "the advocate's only opportunity to tell the story of the case in its entirety, without interruption, free from constraining formalities."[1] The challenge for attorneys is to stress the strong points of their case, recognize and cope with the weak points, and undermine or refute the opposing case, all while relating a persuasive narrative. As the prosecutor, Tukel would speak first, followed by Deutsch for the defense, after which the prosecution would have an opportunity for rebuttal.

Tukel began, as most lawyers do, by thanking the jurors for their service, emphasizing the "sacrifice and the duty" they had undertaken. Then he got right to the heart of the case:

> It's not about the 1969 trial that the defendant had in Israel. It's not about Israel or the Palestinians. It's not about anything that went on in that part of the world. It's about one thing and one thing only. Did she, here in Detroit, when she applied for naturalization, and when she went to speak to Jennifer Williams, did she make false statements regarding her naturalization application?[2]

With the aid of a large video screen, Tukel took the jury through all of Rasmea Odeh's false answers, pointing out the word "**EVER**," capitalized and boldfaced. He stressed Odeh's repeated answers "no," on both forms and in the interview with Williams. "These questions all ask the same thing relating to criminal history," he said. "If any of them are false, they're all false," and there could be no doubt about "her conviction for three bombings which resulted in the deaths of two people and injuries to many more."[3] He reminded the jury that Odeh would not have been eligible for citizenship if she had been truthful on the visa and naturalization applications.

Turning to Odeh's testimony, Tukel reminded the jurors that "people lie to get things that they want" and that the defendant "has a motive to try and explain everything away." Her story, however, depended on "an amazing string of coincidences," beginning with the claim that it was her brother who lied on the visa application, filling it out falsely without telling her, and that Odeh, despite her legal education, took it to the U.S. embassy with no idea of what had been written down. He scoffed at the idea that "she was just copying down something that someone tells her to do [and] that just happens to be the same thing that she misunderstands nine years later on a different form when she applies for citizenship."[4]

How could it be possible, Tukel asked, for Odeh to misunderstand the word "ever," when she spoke English, had degrees in law and criminal justice, and scored 100 percent on her civics test? Especially when the jury "heard from Jennifer Williams," who always said, "have you ever been arrested anywhere in the world?"[5]

Attorneys frequently use analogies to reinforce their arguments, and Tukel was well-versed in that technique. He asked the jury to imagine a couple about to marry in Michigan. The young woman asks her fiancé, "Have you ever been married?" And her prospective husband says, "no."

> So they go ahead and they get married and then many years later a friend of his is visiting and he mentions, hey, do you remember when we were in London at your wedding and we saw the changing of the guard at Buckingham Palace?

The wife is stunned, of course. "I asked you if you had ever been married?"

"I thought you meant in the United States," the imaginary husband answers in his own defense, adding,

> We were talking about where we would send the kids to school, and that was all in the United States. So, I interpreted your question of, have you ever been

married, to mean only in the United States. . . . That all happened overseas. That's not part of the United States.

"Everyone would know that's a lie," Tukel explained, driving the point home, "and that someone got caught telling that lie."[6]

Tukel finished up by emphasizing Odeh's false statements on two instances nine years apart. "As we know," he said, "she was sentenced to two life terms." There was no way to attribute the answers on the visa application as "referring to in the United States because she hadn't been here yet." And as to the naturalization form and interview, Williams had testified that "she adds the words 'anywhere in the world' for those [criminal background] questions every single time she does it, because that's what the training is."[7]

At the beginning of his argument, Tukel had made an implicit promise to the jury by telling them that the case was not about Israel or the Palestinians. He kept his promise, mentioning the Supersol bombing only four times, never for more than a single sentence and only in the context of Odeh's false answers. Tukel concluded by arguing that Odeh had lied again, from the witness stand, because that was "the only way to try to fix the situation she's in now."[8] He thanked the jurors and asked them to return a guilty verdict.

* * *

Deutsch apologized to the jury for standing at the lectern. He preferred to speak to people from right in front of the jury box, he explained, "so they can look at me and I can look at them," but he needed to stay planted near the microphone, which allowed the people in the overflow room to hear the proceedings. That brief moment of introduction unintentionally exemplified the defense case, from the moment William Swor's negotiated plea was rejected. Odeh's legal interests had deliberately been subordinated to political organizing, seemingly with her agreement. Deutsch therefore chose to sacrifice the up-close effectiveness of his advocacy—when his client needed every slight edge she could get—so that the overflow activists could hear his argument. Rallying the faithful, in other words, was momentarily more important than taking the best possible advantage of his well-honed trial skills. Deutsch's location could not have made much, if any, difference in the case, but the tradeoff—favoring communication with the crowd over intimacy with the jury—was surely telling.

Deutsch began his argument in classic defense-counsel mode, by stressing the importance of the presumption of innocence and proof beyond a reasonable doubt, but he quickly turned to Middle East politics, cleverly using Judge Drain's own words to keep himself within bounds of the pretrial ruling. "The judge is going to give you an instruction," he told the jury, that will provide "insight into the government's case." The judge will tell you "that it's not your job to determine whether or not she was in fact guilty or innocent of any crime in Israel [and] we're not going to retry that case in 1969." That was fair enough, and it even seemed to reinforce the prosecution argument, until Deutsch surprised the courtroom with a twist of his own:

But ask yourself why. How many times [the prosecution] told you that she was convicted of a string of bombings in which two people were killed. They must have said that 50 times in this courtroom and Mr. Tukel said it at least 10 times in his closing argument.

And remember . . . this charge comes from a military court in Israel. It comes from a court that sits in judgment of Palestinians by soldiers.[9]

It was an inspired maneuver, exploiting the jury instruction to get at the Israeli military court while accusing Tukel by innuendo—"Ask yourselves why"—of an ominous obsession with Odeh's Israeli conviction. In fact, Tukel had mentioned the bombing just four times, not ten, for a total of less than one hundred words, amounting to no more than a minute or two in his entire argument, and always in the context of Odeh's false statements. But exaggeration had always been a favored tactic of Odeh's defenders.

Deutsch continue pressing his point, testing the limits of Judge Drain's rulings. He told the jury that the Israeli documents—the records of Odeh's conviction and sentence—need not be taken "as what happened in fact." Again relying on the jury instructions, he said, "I would tell you that she's innocent of that, but the judge is telling you it's not an issue for you."[10]

The only issue, Deutsch continued, was whether the government "has proved beyond a reasonable doubt that she knowingly lied" on her visa and naturalization applications and in the interview with Williams. That meant, he explained, that there had to be proof beyond a reasonable doubt that the incorrect answers "were not the result of mistakes, miscommunication, misunderstanding, or ambiguity. That there was no innocent reason."[11]

The "innocent reason," Deutsch argued, was simply her misunderstanding of the naturalization form. "She's been living here legally [for nine years] without any problems with the law. . . . Well, what would you think?" he asked. "In her mind . . . they were asking about the U.S." If only they had asked specifically about Israel, of course she would have provided the information. He continued, reading aloud from the naturalization application, but without a slide or enlargement, stressing that none of the questions "say anything about foreign convictions."[12]

That still left the problem of Williams's testimony that she had added "anywhere in the world" during the naturalization interview, as she had been trained to do. Deutsch pointed out that another prosecution witness, Douglas Pierce, testified that he had trained Williams, and yet he said nothing about such oral instructions. "First of all," Deutsch added, "bureaucrats make mistakes." And despite the many corrections that Williams made on Odeh's application, circled in red ink, "There's no writing in red saying . . . 'anywhere in the world.'" In other words, "There's no proof beyond a reasonable doubt that Ms. Williams asked her those questions."[13]

Deutsch made good use of another prosecution witness, Homeland Security Special Agent Stephen Webber, whose videotaped interview with Odeh went unmentioned in direct examination, only to be probed on cross. "He was trying to entrap her at the airport," Deutsch argued, yet "she didn't lie to him. She didn't try to obfuscate it. She told him, yes, I did it. Why should I lie?" And when Webber asked why she hadn't included that on her immigration forms, she said "they never asked me." Deutsch spent only about a minute on Odeh's visa application, however, saying "her brother filled it out, her brother was educated in English," which may have been "improper conduct" but not a crime.

As he explained to a Chicago radio audience on the eve of trial, Deutsch needed to plant the seeds of doubt among at least "some jurors that will understand and see the injustice of the whole prosecution."[14] Restricted by Judge Drain's evidentiary rulings, he told the jury that he still wanted "to sit down with you in your living room and tell you the full story of the life of Rasmieh Odeh [but] sometimes the court situation [does not] allow that." Nonetheless, he was still going to try.

"You've got to know what she's done in this country for 20 years," he said, pointing to the women in the courtroom "who come all the way from Chicago to show their support, because they appreciate who she is and what she's done for them." Deutsch was arguing beyond the record, as lawyers say, attempting to sway the jury with a show of community support, contrary to his assurances when the prosecution had first moved for a protective order.[15] Tukel let it pass, however, even when Deutsch added "that's very important when you're trying to decide whether she's a criminal."

Next came the conspiracy theory. "Why would the government use all this time and energy to somehow make a criminal out of a woman [when] all she's done is suffer and overcome, overcome that suffering and come and make a life of service to her community?"[16] He asked the jurors to "prevent making Rasmieh Odeh a criminal for something that happened 45 years ago" by finding her not guilty.

Then came Deutsch's final pitch:

> Let me just close by telling you that one of the great privileges of my law and legal career has been representing Rasmieh Odeh. She is an extraordinary woman of great compassion and dignity. And it would pain me, and I think any people who hope for justice, to make her into a criminal after all the work that she's done in her community and [for] her people.[17]

That was an admission of sorts, showing little confidence in the evidence and asking instead for jury nullification. The activists in the courtroom knew what Deutsch was getting at, and they could only hope that the jury did, too.

Tukel took advantage of his rebuttal argument to ridicule the defense case, knowing the Deutsch would not be allowed to say anything in reply. Odeh wants to you believe, he said, that she thought "the U.S. government isn't interested in finding out whether someone who wants to come here has been associated with a terrorist organization before they came here."[18]

Judge Drain instructed the jury, explaining that "the defendant is not on trial for events which occurred in Israel in 1969 or for whether she was a member of the Popular Front for the Liberation of Palestine." Instead, he told them that they should only consider evidence of her arrest and conviction in relation to the current charge that she unlawfully procured her U.S. citizenship, cautioning that conviction required a finding that Odeh made "at least one false statement" and that "she knew it was false, and made it voluntarily and intentionally and not because of mistake or some other innocent reason."[19] With that, the jury retired to deliberate.

* * *

It took the jury less than two hours to find Odeh guilty, returning their verdict just after 11:00 a.m. on November 10, 2014. The spectators in the courtroom sat still as the court polled the jury, confirming that each member had voted to convict. Judge Drain thanked the jurors, adding, "I don't usually comment on verdicts, but in this case . . . I think that your verdict is a fair and reasonable one based on the evidence and the testimony that came in."[20] The jurors declined the court's offer to debrief with the attorneys for both sides, choosing to meet only with the prosecutors.[21]

The jury left the courtroom and, after a few moments of stunned silence, Odeh turned around in her seat at counsel table and shouted to those behind her, "Someday we will find fairness, in some place in the world."[22] There was a more animated scene in the overflow room, where Odeh's supporters gasped in disbelief when the verdict was announced, one woman sobbing inconsolably and another angrily condemning the court as "haram," Arabic for "forbidden."[23]

Deutsch made what he thought was a routine motion to continue Odeh's bond until the date of sentencing, which was likely to be several months away. Tukel, however, shocked the courtroom when he moved instead to revoke Odeh's bond, meaning that she would be taken immediately into custody.

Tempers flared in a testy exchange between counsel. Already feeling burned by the conviction, Deutsch felt that he had been unfairly blindsided by the unusually aggressive motion. Having obviously been caught off guard, he had to ask Tukel for copies of the relevant cases. "That's fine, I'll be happy to," Tukel tartly replied. Judge Drain told the attorneys that he would hear their arguments following the noon recess.

Odeh's supporters rallied on the courthouse steps during the lunch break, chanting her name and "Yes we can" in Arabic, along with rhyming condemnations of the prosecution and the FBI.[24] Speakers assailed the verdict as a travesty of justice and denounced Drain for denying Odeh "a full and fair trial."[25] Speaking through a bullhorn, Deutsch complained about the court, the prosecution, and even the jurors. "That's the kind of jury we had," he said. "They were kept ignorant of 75 percent of our defense and then they didn't even want to hear from us at the end." Hatem Abudayyeh raised the familiar conspiracy theory, charging that the U.S. Attorneys' Offices "are doing the bidding of Israel in the prosecution of Palestinian Americans."[26]

Visibly shaken, Odeh herself addressed the crowd, in Arabic and English, using angry words she would soon come to regret. "We can't find justice in this court," she shouted through a bullhorn. "Maybe in another place, there is justice in this world. We will find it. We will find the justice. Don't worry, we will find it. . . . We have to change this world [and] continue to support Palestine."[27] Breaking her attorney-imposed media silence, now that the trial was over, Odeh told reporters that "the verdict is not justice. The government did not allow us to defend ourselves. . . . It was a racist verdict."[28]

Back in court, Tukel argued that Odeh had become a flight risk, given that her U.S. citizenship would be automatically revoked at sentencing, subjecting her to deportation and possibly to prison. Obviously well prepared for the motion, Tukel cited a 2009 case in which the "likelihood of deportation," which was now facing Odeh, was held to be a factor in finding that the defendant was a flight risk. He also pointed to Odeh's noontime expression of disrespect for the court and her earlier statements, some of them on YouTube, about the unfairness of Drain's rulings. Moreover, "she ignored direct orders of this court" during trial "and went ahead and testified to inadmissible facts."[29] To Tukel, all of this demonstrated that Odeh would also feel free to violate the terms of her bond.

Deutsch could barely contain his anger when the court turned to him for response. "I'm shocked at what the government has argued here," he said. Odeh had lived in the United States for nearly twenty years without even a traffic ticket. What's more, she had been free on only $3,000 bail ever since her arrest, traveling from Chicago to Detroit for every court date and obeying all the conditions of her bond. As to fleeing, Deutsch argued that Odeh's whole purpose in going to trial "is that she wants to stay here." She had an opportunity to plead guilty and leave the country voluntarily, but "she refused that because she doesn't want to leave here." The government's motion was "vindictive," he argued, seeking to punish Odeh "for exercising her right to trial."[30]

Apparently realizing that he had raised his voice, Deutsch candidly explained to the court, "I'm kind of angry about this, because I told her there's no way you're going to be locked up if there's a conviction here," admitting, "Maybe that was wrong of me."

Judge Drain was aghast. "Why did you tell her that?"

"Because I read the law and I saw the facts," Deutsch replied, disrespectfully. "In my opinion as a lawyer there's no reasonable reason why she should be locked up awaiting sentence."[31] Deutsch kept arguing, raising every possible alternative to bond revocation, sometimes repeating himself. He offered to produce witnesses on Odeh's behalf.

"You said that three times," replied Judge Drain, becoming exasperated. "I don't want to hear from them right now."[32]

The court was ready to rule, and it did not go well for Odeh. Drain distrusted Odeh's "truthfulness and candor" when testifying, and he cited her escape attempt from Neve Tirza, which showed him "that if she felt that the conviction was inappropriate or unfair, then she was free to kind of ignore the order of the court." Not an hour earlier, Odeh had told her supporters and the national press that she had not gotten justice from Drain's "racist" court. Alerted by Tukel's argument to Odeh's disrespectful statements, Drain concluded, "I'm not sure that she would really come back for sentencing if her bond was continued."[33] He ordered the marshal to take her into custody.

As she was being escorted to the lockup in handcuffs, Odeh turned to her friends and lawyers in the courtroom. "Don't worry. I'm strong," she shouted.[34]

*　*　*

There is no federal jail for the Eastern District of Michigan, so Odeh was held in the St. Clair County Jail, located sixty miles north of Detroit in Port Huron, under contract with the federal authorities. Conditions in the jail were difficult for the sixty-six-year-old Odeh, both physically and psychologically, nor was she a good prisoner. Perhaps recalling the resistance at Neve Tirza, Odeh became belligerent toward her guards for which she was placed on "lock down" as punishment. In a Skype interview with Dr. Mary Fabri, the psychologist, Odeh blamed the confrontation on a "screaming" guard, whom she accused of a "big lie." Odeh complained to Fabri that the jail was cold and the metal toilet seat was "cold and uncomfortable." She said, "I felt as bad or worse than in the Israeli jail."[35] Odeh's supporters, including Deutsch, consequently claimed that the U.S. Attorney's Office and the Department of Homeland Security had "instigat[ed] the harsh treatment Odeh is receiving."[36] Records from the St. Clair County Jail debunk the conspiracy theory, reporting that Odeh had repeatedly refused orders to return to her cell while insisting that a guard could "not tell her what to do."[37]

Odeh's supporters and legal team launched an intensive campaign for her release on bond, holding rallies and seeking reconsideration from the court.

Defense counsel's motion and supporting brief at times read as though they were aimed more at a political audience than the court, repeating the very facts that Drain had excluded at trial—including Odeh's experience with "ghastly torture" under "illegal military occupation" and her arrest under a non-existent "sweep" of Ramallah—which implicitly complained about his rulings.

Despite several pages of obligatory Middle East political rhetoric, the defense argument did present more convincing reasons to restore Odeh to bail. Regarding ties to the community, a key determinant that Drain had initially found lacking, the motion pointed out that Odeh had two nephews in Chicago and that community members were willing to pledge their homes as security. James Fennerty, who had known Odeh since meeting her in Jordan thirty years earlier, offered to house her and act as her custodian. The motion was accompanied by many letters to Judge Drain recounting the hardships that Odeh was suffering and emphasizing her deep connection to the Arab American community of Chicago.[38]

The bond motion was nearly as hard-fought as the trial itself, with the barest pretense of professional courtesy between counsel. The prosecution response to the bail motion was a broadside attack on Odeh herself, attaching seventy pages of Israeli documents, with English translations, detailing the nature of Odeh's involvement in the Supersol bombing. Drain had excluded such evidence at trial, on behalf of either side. Tukel was taking advantage, however, of an evidentiary backdoor that allowed the admission of hearsay evidence at a bail hearing while arguing that it established Odeh's "serial dishonesty carried out over decades." He reminded Judge Drain of Odeh's outbursts at trial in flagrant disregard of the court's rulings and emphasized Deutsch's own angry remarks following the conviction.[39]

The defense reacted with nearly unrestrained fury, charging the prosecution with "a deplorable slander" and "a relentless, remorseless, and startlingly unprincipled attack of Ms. Odeh's . . . life of suffering and service." The defense fusillade was not wholly unjustified, given the punitive nature of the prosecution motion. But then it lapsed back into conspiracy theorizing, this time accusing the prosecution of "currying favor with the U.S. pro-Israel lobby." Ever political in nature, the defense argued that the Supersol bombing could not have been "terrorism"—rationalizing the murders and almost admitting them—because "people whose land is occupied will resist." The argument was equally dismissive of American law, asserting bluntly that the "the result of [Odeh's] supposed falsehoods in obtaining her citizenship [had] been overwhelmingly positive in the real world."[40]

Judge Drain was unimpressed by Odeh's political stance. Brushing right past her purported distinction between terrorism and resistance, he found that her conviction in Israel "demonstrated a lack of good moral character." He agreed that the prosecution had made a compelling argument concerning her "proclivity for dishonesty, as well as her apparent disdain for this court's orders." But his rejection of Odeh's conspiracy theory did not keep Drain from recognizing that she truly had set down deep roots in Chicago's Arab community, which convinced him that she was "not as significant a flight risk as originally believed."[41] He therefore ordered her released upon posting a $50,000 cash bond, rejecting the offers of several supporters to put up their homes as security.

That was Odeh's first, albeit small, victory in the case. Having been jailed for five weeks, much of it on lockdown, she at least would be free until sentencing.

* * *

When the attorneys approached the bench for Rasmea Odeh's sentencing on March 12, 2015, it was as though they were speaking of two entirely different cases. The advisory federal guidelines called for a sentence of fifteen to twenty-one months, although Judge Drain was free to impose a longer or shorter term. Both parties had already filed sentencing memorandums, with the prosecution asking for a sentence of five to seven years and the defense urging no prison time at all. The defense memorandum also attached seventy-two letters, entreating the court for leniency, from community figures in Chicago and other cities, attesting to Odeh's good character and charitable works. Nearly all of the letters referred to Odeh as a torture victim, some repeating defense counsel's most exaggerated claims. Others were simple pleas for mercy, including an extremely moving tribute from Odeh's nephews in Chicago.[42] Judge Drain also acknowledged receiving "a ton of other letters . . . from all across the country."

Amid the flood of letters sympathetic to Odeh—most of them from writers with no direct knowledge or connection to the case—two letters were very different. Basil Joffe, whose brother Edward was murdered in the Supersol bombing, urged the court to impose a "significant sentence," in light of Odeh's "violent past as a terrorist and her un-repentant [sic] and flagrant violations of US immigration law." Disclaiming any interest in seeing Odeh punished further for her crime in Israel, Joffe explained that the nature of the offense, which had been proven "beyond dispute," was nonetheless "material" to her unlawful procurement of citizenship.[43] The three sisters of Leon Kanner, Miriam, Irit, and Rachel, wrote that Odeh, "in her ongoing fraud opposite the U.S. Immigration Authorities . . . deliberately tried to erase her past crimes and to carry on a life bearing no witness to her devastating actions." They urged the court to see the case in the "severest context" and to "impose the maximal sentence possible."[44]

Although Joffe and the Kanner sisters had more personal links to the case than nearly all of the defense-submitted leniency letters, Deutsch objected to their relevance: "He's not a victim of the crime for which she was convicted," he said of Basil Joffe, adding, without evident awareness of the irony, "They're trying to make a political statement about her."[45]

Deutsch spoke first at the sentencing hearing. Stressing Odeh's good works, advanced age, and frail health, he argued that no good purpose would be served by imprisoning her in advance of her inevitable deportation. He also raised the rejected plea deal, in which she could have been allowed simply to leave the country after 180 days, with no incarceration at all. Imposing a draconian sentence now, he said, would amount to punishing her for exercising her right to trial. Being forced to leave her community and adopted home would be punishment enough.

Soon enough, however, Deutsch stopped simply invoking sympathy and turned again to politics and conspiracies. "Throughout history, people have resisted foreign occupation," he told the court, adding that they "have to resist in any way they can to fight for their land and fight for their people." He claimed, "the American people have been denied the truth about the history of what happened to the Palestinians, the ethnic cleansing, the occupation, the murder and destruction."

Deutsch was not finished. He said repeatedly that Odeh had been "horrifically tortured." He compared her to Nat Turner, Denmark Vesey, Toussaint L'Ouverture, and Nelson Mandela, as one more resistance fighter against injustice and foreign occupation. He conceded that Odeh herself "may have been involved in some sort of resistance activity" but contended that "it doesn't matter in this particular case" and urged the court not "to go back 45 years where [her] country was invaded."

That was surely just what Odeh and her friends wanted to hear, but it was far from certain to persuade court. There was a touch of condescension when

Deutsch urged Judge Drain not to "let this terrorism pandering influence you," but he finished strongly, pleading "with all my heart, and all the heart of the people that have signed letters and demonstrated and come to court" to spare Odeh additional prison time.[46]

Tukel said that he planned to avoid addressing "foreign relations or history," stressing instead that "every single day that she had been in the United States has been illegal. Every single day has been based on fraud." But it did not take long for Tukel to turn to Odeh's convictions in Israel, explaining that her "background is what makes the immigration crime . . . just that much more serious."

"There is absolutely conclusive proof that she was involved in the bombing of the Supersol supermarket," Tukel said. He showed the court clips from the Palestinian documentaries, in which Aisha Odeh and Rasheida Obeideh reminisced with Rasmea about the operation. "She's never expressed contrition for any of the acts," which Deutsch had just attempted to justify. "She has also referred to herself in this court as having been a victim of racial injustice and I think that really shows the character of the defendant."[47]

Rasmea Odeh had an opportunity to redeem herself in the eyes of Judge Drain when he invited her to take the stand for "whatever you want to say about the sentencing." Although she would have been best served by an expression of sincere remorse—at least regarding her contentious testimony at trial— she could not bring herself to apologize.

"I didn't mean to unrespect you," she told the court, but "I really wanted the jury to see the whole picture from my side." She continued to rationalize her violations of Drain's orders, explaining that she had to provide "the whole explanation because of the torture that happened to me over in Israel." Without the "real picture [of] all the torture," she said, the court could not give her "the real justice."

"As a woman in occupied territory," Odeh continued, "everybody was work against the occupation . . . and I was one of my people." Using the PFLP's euphemism for an attack on civilians, she insisted that "I didn't do that operation." Nor was she "responsible [for] what that girl said about me" in the documentary, even though she smilingly accepted the praise for initiating "military work" when she and Aisha sat together in front of the camera. "They want to make me icon, big things," Odeh said, without explaining why anyone would have wanted to falsely glorify her during her 2004 visit to Jordan.[48]

Judge Drain had the last word. He was not impressed by the defendant's non-apology, recalling how she had kept violating his orders despite repeated admonitions. "I don't usually raise my voice in court," he said, "and I had to do that to stop her, and she just decided what she was going to say and went ahead and said it."[49] "My feeling is," Judge Drain added, "you don't have a lot of respect for the law."[50]

Quoting all of Odeh's false answers, he said flatly that she had "perjured herself" when she testified and she "just would not follow my instructions." Speaking directly to her, Judge Drain said,

> I think you lied when you talked about how you viewed the application. You said you thought that [it] only applied or the questions only applied to conduct in the United States, and I don't believe that, and the jury didn't believe it and they convicted you because they didn't believe it.[51]

The judge did not believe Odeh's denial of involvement in the Supersol bombing, and he firmly rejected Deutsch's claim that it had been an act of legitimate resistance, referring to Odeh multiple times as a terrorist. "Ms Odeh's history," Judge Drain said, "does include some terrorist activities," including membership in the PFLP, although he also believed that "she's reformed and she's engaged in positive and constructive activities" since moving to Chicago.[52]

Deutsch's resistance pitch—comparing Odeh to Nelson Mandela and Nat Turner—apparently backfired. Judge Drain found it "disturbing" that the case had been "politicized," with Odeh referring to herself as a "political prisoner." Although recognizing that had been a "rallying point" for her supporters, Drain believed strongly that it was not a political case but it was rather "about honesty and being truthful and saying the right thing under oath."[53]

Although Odeh's supporters believed that their presence—in the courtroom and in the streets—had been essential to her defense, the widespread publicity actually ended up hurting her at sentencing. Drain explained his theory of "general deterrence," which required him to consider "how other people" would react to her sentence:

> If I just said, Ms. Odeh, you can go home, you're going to be deported, that shows that there's no consequences, that there's no risk for lying under oath. A slap on the hand really would not serve any kind of deterrence.[54]

General deterrence was therefore especially important in Odeh's case, given its politicization, because it had become so "high profile [and] a lot of people are looking at the case and a lot of people will act based on what happens here."[55] The rallies and demonstrations convinced Judge Drain that there had to be a significant sentence. Although he barely entertained the prosecution's hyperbolic recommendation, Drain also rejected the defense argument that Odeh's five weeks in jail had been sufficient punishment. "It's not enough for this case," he told her. "You lied under oath in an important situation seeking citizenship in this country."[56]

Rasmea Odeh was sentenced to eighteen months in prison. The prosecution dropped its objection to bail, and the defendant was allowed to remain free pending the outcome of her appeal.

17 Appeal

Rasmea Odeh's conviction and sentence only invigorated her defenders, who were determined to continue their organizing as the case was appealed. The radicals saw the outcome of the trial as "a farce orchestrated by a biased judge," amounting to a "racist attack on Arab Americans."[1] Making the same claims, a "National Week of Action to Defend Rasmea" included fundraisers in many cities, and Students for Justice in Palestine organized events on university campuses.[2] As "emergency meetings" were held around the country, protesters chained themselves to the doors of Oakland's federal courthouse, claiming that Odeh had been the victim of a politically motivated prosecution.[3] A Middle Eastern restaurant in Oakland displayed a full-wall mural of Odeh's portrait, celebrating her as a hero of resistance while also earning a favorable review in the Sunday travel section of the *New York Times*.[4]

Even Odeh's mainstream supporters condemned the prosecution and trial as a "fishing expedition targeting Palestinian American community leaders."[5] When the Arab American Civil Rights League presented its "Justice Award" to Barbara McQuade, the progressive U.S. attorney for the Eastern District of Michigan, who had been nominally in charge of Odeh's prosecution, the Rasmea Defense Committee called for the honor to be rescinded and threatened retaliation if the demand was not met.[6] Marc Lamont Hill, the prominent African American academic and activist, called Odeh's case a cause célèbre, describing her as a "Palestinian freedom fighter being railroaded for her commitment to justice."[7] A "Black-Palestinian" solidarity video, featuring Lauryn Hill and Danny Glover, celebrated Odeh as a symbol of the "Palestinian people [who] have refused to surrender after almost seven decades of continuous struggle against Israeli settler colonialism."[8]

Michael Deutsch and the other defense lawyers were buoyed by the ongoing support, providing evidence that their client had not been forgotten, as well as a small but continuing stream of funds to help cover the cost of pursuing Odeh's appeal. In contrast to the proceedings in the trial court, however, there were no regular court appearances as rallying or publicity occasions. The appellate process consisted mostly of the office work involved in researching and preparing their opening brief, which was filed in the Sixth Circuit Court of Appeals, following an expedited schedule, on June 9, 2015.

* * *

The defense brief advanced three broad claims, following the time-honored approach of making its strongest argument first and at greatest length. Thus, the first thirty pages of the brief were devoted to Drain's evidentiary rulings on PTSD, excluding Dr. Mary Fabri's testimony and prohibiting Odeh from testifying about the consequences of her brutal interrogation. The brief's second section, of about fifteen pages, argued that the records of Odeh's Israeli indictment and conviction had been procured by torture and therefore should not have been admitted in a U.S. court. The final five pages of the defense brief argued that Odeh's sentence was "unduly harsh."

Perhaps because the brief was directed to the confines of appellate chambers, it was for the most part free of the political rhetoric that had suffused Odeh's pleadings in the more public forum of the trial court. Apart from one obligatory mention of the legitimacy of "national resistance to the belligerent illegal occupation," and scattered references to Odeh's torture and abuse in Israel, the brief concentrated on legal issues, seeking to establish that Judge Drain had committed reversible errors in the course of Odeh's trial.

The most important and promising defense argument centered on the exclusion of Dr. Fabri's testimony, which the brief characterized as a "solid, science-based, direct explanation" of how Odeh's PTSD had "blocked her from understanding the time frame in the questions that were answered falsely."[9] It was a straightforward claim, made far more complex by the need to wade through Drain's distinction between general and specific intent crimes. After ten pages of technicalities, the brief returned to its basic point,

> Dr. Fabri's testimony would have provided expert psychological corroboration of Ms. Odeh's factual defense, that her disorder caused her to filter out the association with her traumatic past, by narrowing—automatically, involuntarily, on a non-conscious level—her interpretation of the questions about criminal history, and particularly the time frame referred to by the word "EVER."[10]

Fabri's description of automatic, involuntary, non-conscious filtering was essential to the defense case because it negated the requirement of intentional untruthfulness. That description was unrebutted in the trial court record, due to Drain's categorical ruling—without addressing the validity of Fabri's underlying opinion—against any expert psychology testimony regarding a general intent crime. In fact, Fabri's characterization of "non-consciousness" was even contradicted in the defense brief's introductory Statement of the Case, which said that Odeh "believed at the time" that the naturalization application asked only about crimes committed in the United States and that prior questions with the word "**Ever**" had "reinforced her understanding."[11] The inconsistency went unnoticed at the time.

Odeh's other "state of mind" arguments were pursued at much less length. The defense brief devoted barely more than a page to Judge Drain's limitation on her testimony, prohibiting her from mentioning torture in Israel, and only one sentence to the false statements on her 1994 visa application.[12]

The other two sections of the brief were so succinct as to leave the impression their inclusion was merely *pro forma*. The Israeli court records should not have been admitted, the defense argued, because they were the equivalent of "documents created by a Nazi court operating in occupied France that convicted partisans resisting occupation."[13] And the prison sentence of eighteen months was excessive in light of the "unspeakable torture and sexual abuse" Odeh had already endured.[14]

The defense was bolstered by an *amicus curiae* brief filed on behalf of four organizations devoted to "the rights of victims of torture, including their right to redress and rehabilitation."[15] It was a study in equivocation, strongly supporting Odeh's right to offer psychological expert testimony without ever endorsing Fabri's unique theory of automatic filtering. At various points, in fact, the torture experts' brief described the impact of PTSD as causing the victim to "relive" the experience, rather than filter out the memory, providing examples of conscious or intentional avoidance strategies. At best, the brief allowed that "Dr. Fabri's testimony, if believed, can be found to support a legally acceptable theory" of defense.[16]

*　*　*

The prosecution's appellate brief went down the same rabbit hole, devoting page after page to the general/specific intent distinction, without ever addressing the gist of Fabri's opinion. Consequently, the brief left the impression that there was a potentially valid psychological defense but it had been categorically excluded by a blanket ruling on the classification of the charged offense. Even if technically correct, the prosecution brief failed to expose the deep flaws in the "filtering" theory, which therefore remained superficially attractive to the appellate judges. Why not allow the defense expert to testify about the effects of torture on memory, which seemed only to make sense?

Oral argument was held on October 14, 2015. The three Sixth Circuit judges were extremely skeptical of Drain's ruling. Two of the judges said they didn't understand the general versus specific intent distinction, with one of them calling it "beside the point," while the third judge remained silent. The court was far more concerned with the content of Fabri's proposed testimony. One judge suggested that an expert should be able to testify that Odeh's "mind, interacting with that question, on that date, didn't register with the facts that would lead [her] to say 'no.'" It was "counterintuitive" to believe that Odeh could be guilty "if in her mind, she wasn't lying to the government."[17]

The court's interest in Fabri's theory gave Deutsch an opportunity to characterize it as "powerful" and relevant. The expert, he argued, would have explained how Odeh's PTSD created a filter or "blockage," which would have been "pierced" if the naturalization questionnaire had only asked "were you ever in prison in Israel." Of course, Odeh had already concealed her connection to Israel by lying on her initial visa application, but that point was never raised during the oral argument.[18]

Arguing for the government, Jonathan Tukel had no ready response when a judge likened Odeh's alleged situation to a person with amnesia. Why wouldn't an expert be allowed to testify to the consequences of memory loss, even in a general intent crime? Unfortunately for the prosecution, there was nothing in the record to distinguish Fabri's filtering theory, for which there was no basis in the psychology literature, from the well-documented phenomenon of amnesia.

The appellate court issued its unanimous opinion reversing Odeh's conviction on February 25, 2016. The court ruled that expert psychological testimony was not "categorically inadmissible to negate a defendant's knowledge of the falsity of a statement." Thus, Fabri's proffered testimony was "relevant to whether Odeh knew that her statements were false."[19]

Because Drain had never ruled on the content of Fabri's opinion, the case was remanded to the trial court to determine whether there were other grounds to exclude it. Ominously for the prosecution, however, the appellate court opinion noted that a defendant generally has "the right to the admission of competent, reliable, exculpatory evidence," which seemed to reflect some confidence in Fabri's testimony.[20] The prosecution had actually been too successful in the trial court, thus leaving the record bare of the many reasons to reject Fabri's unfounded filtering theory.

Odeh's supporters were elated by the Sixth Circuit ruling, which Deutsch called "a great victory."[21] Speaking for the AAAN, Hatem Obedayyeh said, "We're very, very happy. All of her supporters are very happy."[22] A representative of the defense committee was more cautious. "This isn't a full victory yet," said Nesreen Hasan. "The conviction wasn't overturned altogether, but at least Judge Drain will be forced to rethink his decision on the torture evidence."[23] Nonetheless, Deutsch was confident that there would be a new trial, with Fabri as the star witness. "I don't see another reasonable reason to exclude the expert testimony," he said.[24]

It was not going to be that easy.

*   *   *

The appellate court ruling—that psychological expert testimony could not be categorically excluded—still left in doubt the admissibility of Fabri's filtering theory. Under the Federal Rules of Evidence and the controlling decision of the U.S. Supreme Court, scientific or medical testimony is only admissible if it is "the product of reliable principles and methods" based on "sufficient facts and data."[25] The standards for admissibility, established by the landmark *Daubert* decision and elaborated by other cases, thus include whether the expert's methods have been validated or subjected to peer review. A witness's "subjective belief" in her theory is not sufficient for admissibility, as there may be "too great an analytical gap between the data and the opinion proffered."[26] Accordingly, Judge Drain scheduled the case for a "Daubert hearing" to determine whether Dr. Fabri's opinion met the specific test for admissibility. If so, there would have to be a new trial in which she could testify; if not, Odeh's conviction and sentence would stand.

The prosecutors had already made one mistake concerning the Fabri testimony, having successfully moved to exclude it—on the general intent theory—without developing a full record. They were determined not to allow that to happen again. Their first step, therefore, was to request their own psychological examination of Odeh, on the ground that it was necessary to effectively challenge or rebut Fabri's proposed testimony. The proposed "government psychological examination would determine whether Odeh's PTSD manifested itself . . . in the way the defense expert claims."[27]

The defense reacted angrily, arguing that "no mental examination at all should be ordered [underlining in the original]" and certainly not in advance of a ruling on Fabri's testimony. "Such a fundamentally adversarial interrogation—obviously designed to debunk her earnest PTSD defense—would gravely threaten a serious aggravation of her symptoms," the defense argued.[28]

Judge Drain granted the prosecution's motion. Fairness required a government psychological examination of Odeh, given that Fabri's opinions had been "based solely on Defendant's statements." Moreover, the claim that Odeh's symptoms would be aggravated by a further examination was "belied by the numerous occasions Defendant has been able to discuss her history in Jerusalem in the media and elsewhere."[29]

But that was not the end of it. Defense counsel fiercely responded with a motion to restrict the location and length of the upcoming psychological examination due to "the distinctive threat of serious further mental and emotional harm." Throwing caution and judicial deference to the wind, the defense motion protested "the cynically dismissive, false assertion by the Government—accepted whole cloth by the Court—that the Defendant has freely discussed her torture in the past." Supported by an affidavit from Fabri, detailing the "suffering the defendant experienced" during eighteen hours of interviews, the defense sought to have the government's examination conducted at a neutral site, with Odeh accompanied by a "trusted companion."[30] The prosecution took that as an invitation to list the many times Odeh had voluntarily described her torture in Israel, including her explicit testimony before the U.N. Special Committee in 1979 and her video interview for *Women in Struggle* in 2004.[31]

Once again, Drain rejected the claim that examination by a government psychologist would be harmful to Odeh, and he also denied her request to be accompanied by a companion. The court did order the evaluation to be conducted at a neutral site, specifying the DePaul Law School if the parties could not agree on a more convenient location.[32]

The government's evaluation of Odeh was conducted by Dr. Ron Nieberding, a clinical psychologist in private practice, over five sessions in early October 2016. Dr. Nieberding, who had previously worked for thirteen years at the federal jail in Chicago, confirmed Dr. Fabri's diagnosis of PTSD but concluded "there is little reason to believe the defendant was experiencing an acute phase of PTSD, marked by severe symptoms at or near the time of the reported offense." As to Fabri's explanation for Odeh's false answers, Nieberding said, "The notion that a reflexive coping strategy characterized as 'cognitive filtering' was the proximate cause of Ms. Odeh's negative responses to questions about her legal past is highly questionable [and] seems implausible."[33]

What followed was a battle of reports. Defense counsel submitted a lengthy affidavit (and later a supplement) from Dr. Hawthorne Smith, the clinical director of the Bellevue/NYU Program for Survivors of Torture, who vouched for the thoroughness of Dr. Fabri's examination and cautiously opined that "the possibility exists that memory repression may play a role in [Odeh's] behavior and the credibility of her sworn statements." Smith saw "no legitimate clinical reason that Dr. Fabri's evaluation not be considered in . . . adjudicating this case."[34] The defense also submitted a shorter affidavit from Dr. James Jaranson, a retired psychiatrist then consulting with Survivors International, who opined that Odeh "could have cognitively processed questions about the past to avoid recalling traumatic experiences."[35]

The prosecution countered with a report from a psychiatrist and two psychologists at the Walter Reed National Military Medical Center, including the chief of the Center for Forensic Behavioral Sciences. The Walter Reed team observed that the concept of "filtering" is not found in the Diagnostic and Statistical Manual of Mental Disorders (DSM-5) or anywhere else in psychology research and that the literature "on PTSD does not support the idea that denial or repression might operate only in response to written stimuli."

Moreover, Fabri's methodology was "insufficient to conclude that the wrong answers on the questionnaires or during the interview were due to automatic filtering secondary to PTSD."[36]

*   *   *

Judge Drain broke the logjam on December 6, 2016, ruling that Dr. Fabri's testimony was admissible and therefore ordering a new trial. It should not have escaped notice that even Fabri's endorsers had carefully avoided validating her theory, instead couching their reports in the language of possibility. Dr. Smith, for example, averred that memories affected by PTSD "may be misfiled, inaccessible, or overly intrusive," the latter phenomenon being the exact opposite of Fabri's filtering theory.[37] But Drain had already been burned once by the appellate court and he was not inclined to take the same chance twice. Quoting the Sixth Circuit opinion that "Dr. Fabri's proffered testimony is relevant to whether Odeh knew that her statements were false," the court declined even to hold a hearing on the prosecution motion to exclude Fabri's opinion testimony.[38] Any further challenge to Fabri's evaluation would have to come on cross-examination at the new trial, which was scheduled for the following spring.

That was the victory the defense team had been waiting for. Odeh would get a new trial where she could present her strongest defense; better yet, Israel's brutal treatment of Palestinian detainees would now play a central role in the case. Not only would Fabri's expert opinion about PTSD be admitted in evidence, but so would Odeh's own testimony about her arrest, torture, and coerced confession, "potentially putting the Shin Bet (Israel Security Agency) itself on trial."[39]

"This is incredible news," exulted Nesreen Hasan of Odeh's defense committee. "The government has gone to great lengths to cover up the details of Israel's torture and crimes against . . . this Palestinian icon. Now the truth will finally be told in open court."

18 Guilty

The admissibility of torture evidence, potentially from both Dr. Mary Fabri and Rasmea Odeh, was a serious blow to the government's case, but the prosecutors soon responded with their own powerful riposte. On December 13, the government obtained a superseding indictment that expanded the scope of the case against Odeh. The original indictment charged only that Odeh had procured her citizenship unlawfully by falsely answering the questions about her past arrest and imprisonment. The new indictment went further by adding allegations that she had falsely answered "No" to two additional questions: Whether she had **EVER** been a member of or associated with any organization "in the United States or in any other place," and whether she had **EVER** been a member of or in any way been associated "with a terrorist organization."[1]

As the prosecutors explained in a memorandum to the court, the new indictment was drafted to allow the government to prove Odeh's often-acknowledged association with the PFLP as well as her involvement in the Supersol and British consulate bombing. Moreover, the prosecutors intended to take the depositions of Aisha Odeh and Rasheida Obeideh, announcing that the Department of Justice had already contacted the Palestinian Authority for assistance in compelling the two co-conspirators to testify.[2] It was far from obvious that the Palestinian women would cooperate, even if they could be located, but a loophole in the rules of evidence might then have made their old video interviews admissible, which would be even more devastating to Odeh.[3]

It was a stunning preemptive strike. If the defense was going to make the case about torture, the prosecution, with the tactical advantage of going first, would turn it into a case unambiguously about terrorism. Odeh's defense committee denounced the superseding indictment as part of a "broader attack" aimed at "the criminalization of the Palestine liberation movement."[4] Michael Deutsch told the *Electronic Intifada* that the new charges were a sign of government desperation, in the hope of circumventing Odeh's PTSD defense.[5]

Deutsch was indeed outraged, almost to the point of sputtering on paper. He and his colleagues attacked the superseding indictment as vindictive and retaliatory, accusing the prosecution of "terrorism-mongering."[6] In a near admission of Odeh's complicity, the defense pleadings repeatedly described the PFLP in glowing terms, such as "a patriotic liberation organization exercising their rights under international law to oppose the foreign occupation of their homeland."[7] With no apparent sense of irony, the defense accused the prosecution of attempting to "convert the new trial into a political one" while concurrently asserting the legitimacy of PFLP resistance, presumably including the hijackings at Dawson's Field and Entebbe, and condemning "the tens of billions of dollars the U.S. government provides to the Israeli occupiers."[8] As the defense failed to add, there is no right under international law to hijack airplanes or bomb synagogues and supermarkets.

If defense spirits had been high following the court's ruling on Fabri's testimony, the superseding indictment brought them quickly back to earth. And that was not the only problem the defense had to confront as they contemplated the retrial.

*　*　*

The government had twice bungled its approach to Fabri's proposed testimony, but the defense could not rely on the prosecutors to make a third unforced error, nor was there any guarantee that Fabri would hold up well under cross-examination. The first prosecution mistake was relying on the categorical exclusion of all psychological testimony, which led to reversal in the appellate court. The second mistake came in the prosecution's choice of experts in the battle of reports following remand. The defense produced affidavits from two experts in support of Fabri's testimony, both of whom had significant clinical experience with torture victims. The prosecution experts, in contrast, were all current or former government employees, with either the Department of Justice or the military, none of whom had any first-hand involvement with torture or PTSD.

It was therefore unsurprising when Judge Drain denied the government motion to exclude Fabri's testimony, relying heavily on the reports of defense experts, while discounting the prosecution experts, whom defense counsel had predictably derided as the team of "army doctors." Obscured by the lopsided confrontation was the sleight of hand used by Drs. Smith and Jaranson to provide some support for Fabri without actually endorsing her method or findings. They accomplished this by emphasizing the well-recognized impact of PTSD on memory, while skipping over Fabri's novel, but previously unknown, theory of automatic misinterpretation.

Perhaps independent experts rather than apparent partisans might have better explained the radical discontinuity—between memory loss and so-called filtering—to Judge Drain, or at least have gotten more of his attention. In the course of my research, years after the trial, I located three nationally prominent experts on PTSD and memory, none of whom had any prior knowledge of the Odeh case. I provided each of them with Fabri's report and supplementary affidavits, without any commentary or other indication of my own views. They uniformly rejected Fabri's opinion out of hand.

Dr. Richard McNally, a psychology professor at Harvard and author of the book *Remembering Trauma*, said there is "no link between misinterpretation and PTSD" and there is no way that "PTSD could lead to misunderstanding" a question. If anything, "PTSD tends to call up the past or remind [a victim] of trauma." Of Fabri's theory, he said, "I don't see it in any way."[9] The cognitive psychologist Dr. Elizabeth Loftus, professor at the University of California, Irvine, author of *The Myth of Repressed Memory*, and widely recognized as the preeminent American expert on the study of memory, was in agreement. She called Fabri's filtering theory "an unknown phenomenon," adding that there is "no literature that suggests PTSD affects the interpretation of memory."[10] Dr. Luan Phan, a neuropsychiatrist specializing in PTSD, and chair of the department of psychiatry and behavioral health at Ohio State University, told me "there is no such thing as automatic filtering of selective events" and "there is no scientific evidence of it."[11]

It is unknown whether Deutsch and the other defense lawyers fully realized the scientific invalidity of Fabri's theory, but they quite evidently had a hand in shaping it—in fact, improving it, from the defense standpoint—as the case proceeded. In her original report, dated July 18, 2014, Fabri opined only in generalities, stating that "someone with PTSD would cognitively process questions about the past to avoid recalling traumatic experiences, such as torture, that are at the root of one's disorder." She offered no opinion at all about Odeh's answers on the naturalization application or at the interview with Jennifer Williams, nor did she say that the avoidance of "traumatic experiences such as torture" would have extended to a far more lengthy experience such as ten years of imprisonment.

Moreover, Fabri's original report included numerous observations that were potentially damaging to the defense, including a reference to Odeh's "recurrent, involuntary, and intrusive memories" of her detention. Odeh told Fabri that "everything makes me remember" the torture, and she specifically denied an "inability to remember," saying "I remember every detail."[12]

Although Fabri's original report was only moderately useful to the defense, if that, it eventually got better. At the evidentiary hearing on October 21, 2014, Fabri testified on direct examination that she found Odeh "very credible" and "she told me . . . she thought [the naturalization questions] meant during her time living in the U.S." Those statements were not in her written report. Deutsch then asked whether "a person with chronic PTSD" would interpret a question to "cognitively filter recalling past trauma?"

Fabri balked at the specificity of Deutsch's question. "There's a strong possibility . . . that it would be interpreted during my life in the U.S.," was as far as she would go.

Deutsch tried again, asking if "Ms. Odeh interpreted the questions on her citizenship application to exclude her traumatic past" due to PTSD.

"Yes, it could be," Fabri answered. The response was still hedged, but at least Fabri's opinion, under Deutsch's direction, had now been linked to the specifics of the naturalization application.

Under cross-examination by Jonathan Tukel, however, Fabri was compelled to admit the limit of her knowledge. "I don't know what went on in her mind," she testified. "I don't know because I wasn't there."[13]

Fabri was not allowed to testify at Odeh's 2014 trial, so the gaps in her opinion were not further explored. Following the reversal in the appellate court, however, Fabri submitted a new affidavit, dated November 14, 2016, that went far beyond both her initial report and earlier testimony.

"This evaluator's professional opinion," she said, "based on more than 25 years working with torture survivor's [sic], is Ms. Odeh did not intentionally lie on the citizenship exam, but instead interpreted the questions based on her understanding of what was being asked and given that she suffers from the long-term psychological and neurobiological consequences of PTSD."[14] Fabri did not explain how her opinion developed from "a strong possibility" in which she could not say "what went on in her mind" to a definitive statement about Odeh's actual intentions at a specific date and time almost ten years before the two had met.

I showed the progression of Fabri's opinion to two nationally prominent forensic psychiatrists, neither of whom had any previous awareness of the Odeh case. Dr. Philip Resnick, director of forensic psychiatry at Case Western University and past president of the American Academy of Psychiatry and the Law, said that a psychologist or psychiatrist would have "no expertise in credibility" and could not "opine on whether someone lied in the past." He criticized people who get into forensics through single issues, noting the "risk of an agenda that influences testimony."[15]

Likewise, Dr. Thomas Gutheil, professor of psychiatry and the law at Harvard, and author of *The Psychiatrist as Expert Witness* and other seminal books on psychological testimony, told me that "no expert can be a truth detector." He said that Fabri should not have given an opinion on the "truthfulness of Odeh's torture claims" nor should her opinion have changed over time "without new data."[16] In the words of one prominent textbook on forensic psychology, it appeared that Fabri had, deliberately or otherwise, created "a diagnosis to fit the behavior."[17]

It would be naïve to believe that the defense attorneys played no part in the dramatic improvements to Fabri's opinion, which ultimately contradicted her previous sworn testimony. At a minimum, defense counsel surely realized how vulnerable Fabri would be under skillful cross-examination by the unrelenting Tukel, which they must have taken into account as they weighed the chances of obtaining an acquittal.

*   *   *

Judge Drain's ruling opened the door to Odeh's own testimony about torture and PTSD, but the superseding indictment also exposed her to cross-examination on the Jerusalem bombings and her association with the PFLP. Even worse for the defense, Odeh's testimony at the 2014 trial stood in sharp conflict with Fabri's description of cognitive filtering.

According to Fabri, Odeh would have automatically filtered the questions about past crimes to exclude everything in Israel, in a process beyond her actual awareness. Fabri was quite emphatic under questioning by Deutsch at the evidentiary hearing:

> Deutsch: So someone suffering from PTSD, do they know at some level they are, are they conscious of filtering their memory?
>
> Fabri: No, because it's automatic. . . . It's not this intentional, I'm not going to do that.[18]

Fabri was even more definite following the appellate court's remand, stating in her affidavit that filtering "is not a conscious intentional act." Thus, Odeh's answers on the naturalization form were "an 'automatic' interpretation without conscious consideration involving choice."[19]

Odeh's own prior testimony, however, had been almost precisely the opposite, stating that she had consciously understood the background questions to apply only to her years in the United States. She explained that the first set of questions with the word "ever" were limited to "in the United States." Then, "When I continue to the other questions, my understanding was about United States. So I continue to say, no, no, no."[20]

On cross-examination, Odeh repeatedly insisted that she had made a conscious decision to answer only about the United States: "They ask the first question and it's bold about United States, then they continue to ask the other question, I assumed about United States."[21]

The jury did not believe Odeh's testimony, and neither did Judge Drain, who called it perjury. But even taking her words at face value, Odeh had committed herself under oath to a story about intentional choice, not automatic filtering, that would be nearly impossible to reconcile in a second trial.

None of that seemed to weigh heavily on Odeh's political supporters, who continued to celebrate the twin victories before the Sixth Circuit and Judge Drain, while casting her as a nationally prominent feminist leader.[22] Following the massive Washington, DC, Women's March protesting the inauguration of President Donald Trump, eight women called for a general strike to be held on

March 8, 2017, International Women's Day. Odeh was one of the signatories. The event—called A Day Without Women—was announced in the *Guardian*, as a protest against both Trump's "aggressively misogynistic, homophobic, transphobic, and racist policies" and the "ongoing neoliberal attack on social provision and labor rights."[23] Odeh's inclusion in the Women's March leadership drew much disapproval,[24] which had no effect on the organizers of the events that were held in cities around the country.[25]

Odeh was loudly welcomed at the Chicago Women's Day rally, receiving two standing ovations when she condemned "Israeli and U.S. policies" and called for resisting attacks on "immigrants, Black people, Arabs and Muslims." She announced that she had been convicted "based on torture evidence, but I won my appeal and am going to a re-trial."[26]

In fact, Odeh's attorneys had been secretly conferring with the prosecutors in Detroit in an attempt to avoid a retrial by pleading guilty. Although the incoming Trump administration had obtained the resignation of U.S. Attorney Barbara McQuade, and every other Obama appointee in top positions at the Department of Justice, the career prosecutors assigned to the Odeh case, including Tukel, remained on the job, which included the undisclosed plea negotiations.

On March 23, 2017, barely two weeks after Odeh's International Women's Day speech, Hatem Abudayyeh announced that she was going to plead guilty to the charge of unlawful procurement of citizenship pursuant to the superseding indictment.[27] Under an agreement with the prosecution, Odeh would face no further incarceration but she would lose her U.S. citizenship and face deportation. The defense committee did its best to spin the decision as "a victory," declaring that the prosecution had "its back against the wall" following the reversed conviction and that the agreement to forego prison showed the weakness of the government's case. Indeed, the prosecutors made the deal because they wanted "to dodge a public and legal defense that puts U.S.-backed Israel on trial for its crimes against Rasmea and its continuing crimes against the Palestinian people." The committee weakly proclaimed that Odeh's defense, despite her forthcoming guilty plea, had already "pushed forward" the liberation of Palestine by putting Israel's "policy of torture and sexual assault on the permanent record in a U.S. court of law."[28]

Contradicting the proclamation of victory was the further explanation that the ascension of the Trump administration, with the Justice Department then under the command of "racist Attorney General Jeff Sessions," made it "impossible for Rasmea to expect a fair trial in US courts."[29] In fact, the change at the top of the Justice Department meant almost nothing. Odeh faced retrial in front of the same Obama-appointed judge with the same mostly Democratic jury pool, and two of the three appellate judges who reversed her conviction had been Republicans. But a rationalization is always needed when an icon abandons principle, and that was the best excuse the defense committee could come up with.

The lawyers knew better. Odeh's chances at retrial were dicey at best. Fabri's much-touted filtering theory rested on a foundation of psychological sand, and it was in evident conflict with Odeh's own prior explanation of her answers on the naturalization form. Odeh's testimony about torture promised to be emotionally compelling, but it would be preceded by prosecution evidence about her terrorist associations, which Drain had already accepted as true. In addition to everything else, Fabri could say nothing about Odeh's false answers on the 1994 visa application at the U.S. embassy in Jordan, when she could not possibly have understood the questions about past convictions to apply to anything other than her indictment and imprisonment in Israel. Unless a future jury was willing to buy the story about Odeh's brother—already debunked and rejected by Drain— those answers alone were sufficient to convict and sentence her once again.

Perhaps because he was located in Detroit, and somewhat isolated from the Chicago-based activists who dominated Odeh's defense, local counsel William Goodman offered a far more realistic and humane explanation for his client's decision to plead guilty. "Her trial was grueling and immensely difficult," he said. "She had to relive things she would rather not have to relive." Another trial would be "grinding" for the by-then sixty-nine-year-old defendant, according to Goodman. "Rather than going through all that and putting herself and her supporters through all that again, she decided this would be the most peaceful course to take," he said, adding that the agreement with the prosecution would still have to be approved by Drain at an April 25 hearing.[30]

"We knew that this was a very difficult case from the get-go," said Abudayyeh, Odeh's spokesman and friend.[31] He did not acknowledge that the deal was almost identical to the one Odeh had defiantly rejected over three years earlier.[32]

*　*　*

Myths die hard. Odeh had been scheduled to address the national membership meeting of JVP, to be held in Chicago during March 31–April 2. The announcement of Odeh's guilty plea only a week before the conference did nothing to dampen her reception by JVP, an explicitly anti-Zionist organization that endorses the economic and cultural boycott of Israel. According to a JVP press release, Odeh had been forced to accept the plea bargain because she had no "real chance for a fair trial" with Sessions as attorney general. "When a leader like Rasmea Odeh . . . chooses to leave a fight, she knows the game is rigged."[33] Perhaps in an attempt to emphasize ecumenicism, the poster for the JVP event showed Odeh in a hijab,[34] although she is a confirmed secularist who considers religion an "impediment to liberation" and does not make a practice of covering her hair.[35]

Writing in a prominent Jewish newspaper, the executive director of JVP defended Odeh's invitation, repeating the story that she had been tortured into a false confession of the Jerusalem bombings. "We are honored to hear from her before she is uprooted."[36] In yet another statement, Rabbi Alissa Wise, deputy director of JVP, issued a blanket refutation of the charges against Odeh. "For me it is simple: I believe her."[37]

Odeh's appearance at the JVP conference was a rousing success. She drew extended standing ovations from the thousand activists in attendance, who shouted "Rasmea, we love you" as she called for the liberation of "historical Palestine . . . from Zionists." Often breaking into tears, Odeh referred to her prosecution as a "torturous ordeal," comparing it to the Nakba experienced by the Palestinian people in 1948. Making it clear that there was no room for the state of Israel in her vision for the future, she promised to continue her struggle "for the establishment of a democratic state on the entirety of the historic land of Palestine."[38] She called for the completion of revolution in Egypt and the Arab world and boasted of participating in the "shut down of O'Hare Airport the day after Pres. Trump's Muslim ban was announced."[39]

There was "not a dry eye in the house" when Odeh finished speaking.[40] No one yet had seen the admissions in her signed plea agreement.

* * *

If there had been any doubt about whether the prosecution or Odeh most feared going to trial, it was dispelled by the written plea agreement executed by both parties. To obtain the advantages of the deal—a recommendation against prison time and a delay of deportation—Odeh had to admit her unequivocal guilt. The thirteen-page document, signed by both Odeh and Deutsch, listed the false statements about her criminal record on both the visa and naturalization applications, with Odeh's acknowledgment that she "knew the statements were false" at the time they were made. In what appears to have been the only concession to Odeh, she was not required to admit membership in the PFLP or association with a "terrorist organization."[41]

In signing the plea agreement, Odeh made a sweeping admission of both wrongdoing and raising a false defense:

> She made the false statements intentionally and not as a result of any mistake, Post traumatic Stress Disorder or any other psychological issue or condition or for any innocent reason, and notwithstanding any other statement or testimony Defendant Odeh may have made at any other time regarding those answers. At the time she made the false statements, Defendant knew that it was unlawful for her to provide false information to the United States Department of State and to United States Citizenship and Immigration Services in connection with her application for Immigrant Visa [sic] and her application for naturalization.[42]

The kicker was that Odeh and Deutsch had been given only thirty days to accept the plea offer on a take-it-or-leave-it basis, demonstrating beyond question that the prosecution held the upper hand.

The Federal Rules of Criminal Procedure required Judge Drain to hold a hearing on the plea bargain, which was set for the afternoon of April 25, 2017.[43] The court began the proceeding by taking Odeh step by step through the written agreement, to make sure that she had read and understood it. Odeh identified her signature and affirmed that she had discussed the agreement with her attorneys. She acknowledged that she was waiving the right to a new trial, which could have included her own testimony, and Fabri's, on the effect of her PTSD. She agreed that her plea had not been influenced by either promises or threats.[44]

Then Drain asked Odeh if she was pleading guilty freely and voluntarily. She answered only that she had "signed the papers." The court asked again, with the same response. Odeh's recalcitrance continued, as the court rephrased the question over and over again, and the defendant replied with variations on her evasive theme: "I think all of this paper said what you want" and "I signed it freely." Odeh was accompanied in the courtroom by five defense attorneys. They must have advised their client that she would need to admit guilt as a condition of her plea, and they were surely growing nervous at Odeh's repeated equivocations. Only on the seventh iteration was Odeh able to make the necessary admission. "I think to sign this it makes me guilty," she told the court.[45]

That finally satisfied Drain, who noted that that the written agreement included "all of the essential elements" of the crime. "So, as you say, it does make you guilty."[46] He accepted her plea and set the case for formal sentencing on August 17.

The entry of Odeh's guilty plea had lasted just under thirty minutes. It took less time than that for her to begin repudiating everything she had just acknowledged.[47] Speaking in both Arabic and English to about fifty chanting supporters on the courthouse steps, she declared "There is no justice, no justice. I didn't have any choice." Ignoring the fact that she had just relinquished her long-avowed intention to put Israel on trial, she added, "My case is Palestine's case."[48]

"Rasmea is not guilty just because Tukel says she is," shouted A'budayyeh, who led the small crowd in a call and response.

"Is Rasmea guilty?"

"No, no! Ras-Me-Ya! Free Palestine, from the river to the sea!"[49]

Representing JVP, Rabbi Brant Rosen spoke directly to Odeh, assuring her that she was not guilty. "We are proud to stand in solidarity with you," he said, "and we will continue to do so."[50]

Deutsch soon provided another layer of justification. "At the end of the day, if we won this case, the government could still deport her," he explained to the *Electronic Intifada*. "The finding of not guilty in the criminal case would not have protected her from a [civil] deportation proceeding by the government." Deutsch was right about that. Unfair as it seems, a criminal acquittal, based on a reasonable doubt, does not preclude a civil suit based on the same facts, where the standard of proof is only a preponderance of the evidence. But that had been true ever since Deutsch began representing Odeh three years earlier. The law, including the risk of successive criminal and civil denaturalization proceedings, had not changed but Deutsch's assessment of the case surely had.

Deutsch was in denial. "A decision was made," he said, "to let her leave with her head held high and with her principles and integrity intact."[51]

Deutsch was scarcely alone in participating in the myth-making. Abudayyeh insisted that "for three and a half years we put Israel on trial in the United States," ticking off a series of accusations against Israel that had never been permitted in evidence in any court.[52] Odeh herself continued to denounce the "phony immigration charge," saying that "because of the racist nature of the justice system in this country, I was forced to accept a plea deal."[53]

Not everyone was deluded about the outcome of the case. "When individuals lie on immigration documents, the system is severely undermined and the security of our nation is put at risk," said the special agent in charge of Homeland Security investigations for Detroit.[54] Steven Emerson, of the Investigative Project on Terrorism, recognized that Odeh's plea agreement had unambiguously abandoned "the torture and post-traumatic stress claims."[55] Tukel maintained that Odeh was still an "icon in the terrorist world."[56]

Basil Joffe summed things up, expressing his "sense of relief that this chapter brings the thing to an end," although there was "no sense of remorse or even a very freely acknowledged guilt. . . . But we're glad that it's over."[57]

Afterword

Although Judge Drain had accepted all of the terms in the plea agreement between the prosecution and defense, a formal sentencing hearing was still required by law. The parties assembled for one last time on August 17, 2017.

Rasmea Odeh had been trying for over three years to tell her story of Israeli brutality and dispossession. She had fired one lawyer, sparred with a federal judge, prevailed on appeal, and ultimately capitulated when Michael Deutsch advised her to plead guilty. It was a bitter tradeoff for Odeh, abandoning her long-sought opportunity to testify about torture as the price of avoiding a lengthy prison term. "It's not a joyful process," Deutsch later explained, "but it's one you sometimes have to choose, weighing all the circumstances."[1]

At sentencing, however, Odeh had nothing left to lose. The outcome was predetermined. She would serve no prison time, but her citizenship would be revoked and she would soon be deported, either to Jordan or some other country of her choice. If she was ever going to speak her mind in court, it would be at the sentencing hearing.

Odeh was well prepared when Drain invited her to the courtroom lectern. Reading from a prepared statement, she launched immediately into an assault on Israel "on behalf of all Palestinian people." Saying virtually nothing about her own guilty plea, Odeh condemned the illegal occupation of the West Bank, including "massacres killing children [and] demolishing schools, homes, hospitals, clinics, and places of worship."

Judge Drain repeatedly attempted to redirect her to the issues at hand, asking her to stop talking about "this historical conflict," but Odeh would not cooperate. "Because I'm not terrorist. My people is not terrorist," she said.

It soon became clear that Odeh meant to justify the Supersol bombing, describing it as "resistance" rather than terrorism. "People have a right to fight for their independence and to [expel] the colonizers and occupiers. . . . Why are the Palestinian [sic] prohibited from struggling for our independence?" Nor did she deny membership in the PFLP, complaining that "the U.S. government calls us the terrorist by placing all of our legitimate resistance . . . organizations on the terrorist list."

Still the Marxist after so many years,[2] Odeh repeated an old PFLP party line, railing against "the manufactured state of Israel [that] has been doing the bidding of the powerful British and U.S. empire." American "military policy, political, and diplomatic support allows [sic] Israel to continue its colonization and military occupation of Palestine."

Finally, after about eight minutes, Judge Drain had enough. "You're really testing my patience," he warned Odeh. "If you keep talking and I have to find you in contempt of court, I'll do that and you may end up being locked up."

Realizing that she had only moments left to speak, Odeh at last turned to her own case. "It was unjust [to] have this case at all because I'm not terrorist. They tortured me. They raped me. They destroy all my houses twice." Then she spoke defiantly to the court. "I think this is my right. I will raise my voice [because] we have the right to struggle for our country." She was done.[3]

Judge Drain asked Odeh to remain at the lectern. "I think you are actually pretty wise in taking the deal," he said, because "it would be easy to justify a lengthier sentence" following a retrial. Drain left no doubt about his assessment of Odeh's defense, "I find it extremely difficult to believe that the PTSD actually caused you to make false statements [and] I just don't think that the PTSD defense that you were putting forth would have in any way succeeded."[4]

With that, the court imposed the agreed upon sentence, with the addition of a $1,000 fine.

* * *

Deutsch had also been allowed to speak at Odeh's sentencing, and he used the opportunity to question the basis for the entire prosecution.

"I suggest that somebody who was concerned about justice would have said, oh, we don't really need to charge this person with an immigration fraud case," he told the court. "It really isn't in the interest of fairness and justice to make this woman have to answer to a court and respond and then face what she now faces, is removal from the country." He argued that the prosecutors should have considered that Odeh had served her community for twenty years and "was beloved by the members of that community . . . and was given awards for that." Acknowledging Odeh's ten years in prison, Deutsch asked, "What did she do? She didn't tell the full history of her interaction with the Israeli government in answering her naturalization questions." No matter the evidence, he concluded, "this is the kind of case that should have been passed by the prosecutor, and said, no, we're going to not charge this woman. We're going to let her continue to do the great work she's doing in Chicago."[5]

It was in many ways the most persuasive argument Deutsch made in the case, although it came too late to matter. For over three years of litigation, the defense lawyers and the defense committee had been pushing a political agenda, condemning Israel and castigating the prosecution, often in conspiratorial terms. The many aspects of the case favorable to the defense, including Odeh's decades of humble service, might have made her more sympathetic—if not to the prosecutor, then to the judge and jury—but they were for the most part swept aside by rhetoric.

At rally after rally, the case was posed in terms of anti-Palestinian persecution, advancing a theory of U.S./Israeli collusion to frame Odeh for a nonexistent crime. And while the rallies had no impact on the outcome of the case, the same attitude was carried over into court.

At trial, Odeh repeatedly violated Drain's order to refrain from talking about her torture at the hands of the Israelis. She attempted to interject her story time and again, fencing with the prosecutor and drawing sharp reprimands from the court. Her conduct undermined her credibility with the jury and caused Drain to sentence her more harshly than he might have otherwise. The memory of Drain's scolding quite evidently played a role in Odeh's eventual guilty plea, as even Deutsch admitted that she was motivated by a desire to avoid greater prison time.

In consequence, Odeh spent three years hoping to tell her story in court, only to be repeatedly frustrated and denied. In the end, she had neither the cathartic satisfaction of placing Israel on trial nor the benefit of presenting herself more sympathetically. Instead, she endured over three years of stress and five weeks of incarceration, only to accept a bargain that had been offered from the outset.

Odeh was not coerced into following this path, which she seems to have taken quite willingly, but neither does she seem to have been counseled away from it. For all their dedication, Deutsch and Fennerty were both clearly committed to using the case as a political platform, thus depriving Odeh of the more objective, and ultimately more valuable, advice she might have gotten if she had stayed with a less ideological attorney.

Deutsch made a good point when he asked why the prosecution had not simply "passed the case." Of course, his hostility toward Israel drove him to discount the severity of the Jerusalem supermarket bombing—and perhaps to approve of it—but Odeh's admirable, decades-long life in the United States surely should have counted in her favor in the eyes of the Department of Justice. And although Deutsch did not mention it, there had been a less drastic measure available to the prosecution.

Rather than pursue a criminal case, with the potential for lengthy imprisonment, the government could instead have brought a civil denaturalization case, which could result only in loss of citizenship and deportation—serious consequences, to be sure, but preferable from the defendant's perspective to prison time preceding deportation.[6] In fact, civil denaturalization proceedings have been used more often than the criminal alternative, including the cases of the Nazis John Demjanjuk, Fedor Fedorenko, and Jakiw Palij, among others.[7] Most recently, the Department of Justice brought a civil denaturalization case against a Palestinian who, like Odeh, obtained U.S. citizenship by concealing a terror-related conviction in Israel.[8]

There are strategic considerations in every prosecutorial decision, leading some cases to be pursued more harshly than others. It is undeniable, however, that the government took unusually aggressive positions in the Odeh case, from requesting an anonymous jury—as protection from hypothetical mobs and hordes—to seeking bond revocation following the initial guilty verdict. Even at the 2017 plea hearing, where the conclusion was foregone, the prosecution introduced information about Odeh's terrorist associations that went well beyond the written plea agreement.[9]

* * *

Judge Gershwin Drain insightfully rejected the myth surrounding Rasmea Odeh, recognizing that it had been built on a foundation of untruths, half-truths, and exaggerations about her past, even as it was reinforced by the benefits of her more recent community organizing. "Rasmieh Odeh lied big time," he observed, while it was also unquestionable that she had also done "a lot of good work. No doubt about that."[10]

But what did Odeh's friends and supporters actually believe? Did they fully accept her denials of the Supersol bombing and claim of enduring twenty-five days (or more) of constant torture before confessing, both of which were contradicted by Odeh's own earlier statements? Were they truly misled by Dr. Mary Fabri's helpfully contrived theory of PTSD filtering, otherwise unknown in the literature on memory and psychology? It seems overwhelmingly likely that most of Odeh's supporters—including Rabbi Alissa Weiss and the thousand cheering members of JVP—accepted her at her word, perhaps having willingly suspended disbelief out of antagonism toward Israel. Rabbi Brant Rosen has written, apparently along these lines, that solidarity with the Palestinians "is not about the specifics" of their struggle for liberation.[11]

Odeh's closest comrades were a different matter. Hatem Abudayyeh and other members of the AAAN claimed that Odeh had never concealed her torture-based conviction and imprisonment by Israel, which must be a mark of honor in Chicago's Palestinian activist community. But had she also confided in them the truth about her involvement in the Supersol bombing? The Palestinian and left-wing activists of Odeh's defense committee certainly would have celebrated that "operation" as resistance, not murder, and definitely not terrorism, if Odeh had ever let slip that she had indeed been a PFLP operative. The early acknowledgment that she was "a Palestinian icon, known worldwide as a leading representative of the legitimate Palestinian struggle for self-determination" was, to put it mildly, a powerful indication that Odeh's participation in armed struggle was not unknown to at least some of her confreres in the United States. At a 2014 press conference, Abudayyeh was asked if Odeh "was disputing that she was involved in the bombing." After an awkward silence, he replied haltingly and evasively, "To be clear, I'm not the person to speak about that."[12]

As a clinician and counselor to torture victims, Dr. Fabri was committed to believing survivors. Skepticism and suspicion would make effective treatment impossible, so it is understandable that Fabri validated even Odeh's most implausible accounts. Given her years of frontline experience, however, Fabri surely recognized the sheer impossibility that Odeh, with no military or other training, had resisted confessing for twenty-five (or forty-five) days of continuous torture. Lisa Hajjar, the acknowledged expert on Israeli military courts, has noted that Palestinian prisoners "with no previous interrogation experience" were "unable to withstand the process," leading to an unprecedented willingness to confess immediately and in great detail, especially "in the first years of occupation."[13] American pilots captured by North Viet Nam, Naval Academy graduate John McCain among them, reported enduring only four days of torture before complying with their captors' demands.[14] Even the slightest curiosity would easily have alerted Fabri to Odeh's exaggeration.

Fabri must also have realized that she had allowed her services to be exploited by defense counsel, as she obligingly provided successive elaborations, expressing ever greater levels of specificity and certitude, as the case progressed. Her ultimate opinion, that Odeh had not intentionally lied at a particular time and date many years before her evaluation, went far beyond accepted professional standards for either forensic or treating psychotherapists.

Deutsch and James Fennerty had decades of experience representing radicals and revolutionaries, as well as more ordinary defendants accused of dreadful crimes. They well understood the principles of confidentiality and zealous representation, which they employed to good effect throughout their careers. Odeh's actual guilt or innocence—of either murder or lying about it—would make no difference to lawyers who were obligated to raise the best possible defenses on her behalf, short of lying or offering false testimony, which is prohibited by the Rules of Professional Conduct. In this case, of course, the defense attorneys were ideologically aligned with their client. Their pleadings described the PFLP as a "patriotic liberation organization." In an interview about the trial, Deutsch denied that "anyone who is defending their land and fighting against a foreign occupation could ever be considered a terrorist. They are usually, in the history of the world, freedom fighters."[15]

Fennerty had known Odeh since 1984, having met her on a trip to Jordan only a few years after her release from Neve Tirza, when he was already deeply involved in the Palestinian community. At the time, Odeh was still celebrated among Palestinians as one of the first female guerrillas of the resistance movement. She had not yet contemplated relocating to the United States, and she therefore had no reason to conceal her involvement in the PFLP, which Fennerty would have known full well.

As lead defense counsel, Deutsch was not required to fact-check his client, and he was certainly entitled to believe her account of unspeakable torture at the hands of Israeli interrogators. He may or may not have known the actual details of Odeh's past military work, although it seems unlikely that Fennerty would have withheld information from his co-counsel in the course of their joint representation. Deutsch surely did know, however, that he had pressed Dr. Fabri to improve her opinion to fit the needs of the case. He was also responsible for Odeh's testimony on direct examination, which Judge Drain called perjury, about the origin of her false statements: first that she had simply copied her brother's draft of her visa application and then that she had misunderstood the word "**EVER**" on the naturalization form.

The defense of Rasmea Odeh required her lawyers to walk a fine ethical line between zealousness and fabrication. The purely psychological defense, based on Odeh's unquestioned PTSD, could have been carefully presented without lying, as the attorneys were entitled to give the benefit of the doubt to both their client and her therapist. The superseding indictment, charging Odeh with concealing her PFLP association, presented a more serious problem. If Fennerty, and through him Deutsch, had been aware of Odeh's PFLP membership, which seems likely, the prevailing rules of legal ethics would not have allowed them to offer her false denial on direct examination. Although their advice to Odeh is unknowable, that dilemma may have influenced their decision to recommend the plea bargain.

*   *   *

Not everyone was ready simply to believe Rasmea Odeh. Mainstream journalists attempted to maintain neutrality, reporting not only the accusations of immigration fraud against Odeh and her Israeli murder convictions but also, without additional commentary, her own allegations of torture and coercion. Others, especially (but not only) conservatives, were completely unconvinced by Odeh's professions of innocence.

Cornell University law professor William Jacobson posted a series of articles on the website Legal Insurrection, debunking nearly all of Odeh's claims. It was Jacobson who first pointed out that Odeh's initial confession came only one day after her arrest, rather than after the asserted twenty-five days of relentless torture. Jacobson took a special interest in the surviving members of the Joffe and Kanner families. He traveled to Israel to meet with them and posted interviews on Legal Insurrection. Jacobson also posted nearly all of the pleadings from the Odeh case, including translations of many documents from her trial in Israel. While Jacobson's reporting can rightly be categorized as partisan, his research in this case was impressive and reliable.[16]

Steven Emerson, of the Investigative Project on Terrorism, also took an early interest in the Odeh case that might be best described as adversarial. He produced a seven-part documentary, titled "Spinning a Terrorist into a Victim," that exposed the exaggerations and distortions undergirding Odeh's defense. Beginning with a video of the Edward Joffe and Leon Kanner funerals in Jerusalem, Emerson's documentary took particular aim at Odeh's backers, exposing their deep hostility toward Israel, indifference to her victims, and the "propaganda machine" that was built up around her. The series included moving interviews with Harold and Basil Joffe, calling Odeh a murderer and a liar, and a former immigration enforcement officer who identified her as an "unrepentant terrorist."

The Investigative Project on Terrorism attempted to interview Odeh at a Chicago rally in 2014, but, as shown in the documentary, she walked angrily away, shouting "Do you mean Israel killed the children" in the Gaza war. A caption on the video reads, "In Odeh's mind, inadvertent casualties caused by Israel are reprehensible. Yet she had no problem killing innocent Israeli civilians in a supermarket."[17]

*   *   *

Rasmea Odeh's guilty plea (and later sentencing) brought a sense of closure to the Joffe and Kanner families, more than four decades after the Supersol bombing. Basil Joffe reflected on "the large gang of supporters who championed her" and expressed satisfaction that "now they're going to have to eat their words."[18] He could not have been more wrong.

Within a week of pleading guilty, Odeh was condemning outright the bargain her own lawyers had negotiated. She drew cheers at a May Day rally when she claimed that she had been subject to a "phony immigration charge" and forced into a racist plea deal.[19] Two weeks later, on the anniversary of the Nakba, Odeh addressed the Students for Justice in Palestine chapter at Northwestern University, saying that her deportation was due to the "racist nature" of the U.S. justice system. Prof. Nadine Naber, who had been Odeh's character witness at the 2014 trial, also spoke, calling Odeh "an embodiment of Arab and Muslim struggles against colonialism."[20] Perhaps most improbably for the defender of PFLP aircraft hijackings, Odeh showed up at Chicago's O'Hare Airport to protest the mistreatment of a passenger by United Airlines.[21]

Oscar López Rivera was the leader of the Puerto Rican paramilitary organization Fuerzas Armadas de Liberación Nacional (Armed Forces of National Liberation, or FALN), which took responsibility for a series of bomb attacks on the mainland, some of them deadly. In 1981, López Rivera was convicted of seditious conspiracy, interstate transportation of firearms, and conspiracy to transport explosives, for which he was sentenced to fifty-five years in prison. President Obama commuted López Rivera's sentence in 2017, after thirty-six years in prison, allowing him to return home to Chicago.

Odeh was there to join the celebration for López Rivera's homecoming, which was also her seventieth birthday. Presenting him with a Palestinian keffiyeh, Odeh praised López Rivera as "an example to all of us." Saying, "I have faced my own criminalization," Odeh promised López Rivera that Palestinians would "fight for what you fight for, self-determination and an end to colonialism and full and complete independence." López Rivera expressed his own support for Odeh as well as "solidarity with Venezuela" in a televised phone conversation with Nicolás Maduro.[22]

Odeh's public appearances continued through the spring and into the summer. On August 12, just before formal sentencing, her supporters held a "Farewell" event, featuring a speech by Angela Davis. The hundreds of activists in attendance cheered as Davis denounced Israel as "the worst possible example of a carceral society."[23] Odeh herself got the usual standing ovation, accompanied by the chant to liberate Palestine "from the river to the sea," when she called on the crowd to keep "organizing until all of Palestine is free."[24] She continued the theme immediately after her sentencing, speaking in Arabic to a crowd of about 150 on the courthouse steps. "I am angry the judge did not let me tell my story. This is not a case about lying on a form. . . . The U.S. is a partner in the crimes of Israel."[25]

Tuesday, September 19, 2017, was Rasmea Odeh's last day in the United States. She spent the morning with a reporter for the *Chicago Sun-Times*, who interviewed her as she packed for the twelve-hour flight to Jordan. "Up until this very moment, I didn't believe they will throw me out," she said. "For the past month, I haven't been able to sleep at night, just crying all the time."[26]

Odeh arrived at the entrance to O'Hare Airport's international terminal, along with about one hundred supporters who held a two-hour rally as police and federal marshals stood watching. Hatem Abudayyeh assured the crowd that "We will liberate Palestine because of the Rasmea Odehs of the world." A representative of JVP praised Odeh's grace and resilience "under this stupid, idiotic attack." Odeh herself said she had "no words for the pain," adding, "This is unjust, inhuman."[27] She maintained her composure until it was time to enter the terminal for departure, as police barred her friends at the door. A single federal marshal accompanied Odeh inside. He would escort her on the flight to Jordan, according to a statement from U.S. Immigration and Customs Enforcement (ICE).[28]

"Upon arrival at the Queen Alia International Airport in Amman, Jordan, she was turned over to Jordanian officials without incident," ICE announced. As she emerged from customs, Odeh was greeted with flowers by over a dozen friends and family members, many of whom she had visited on her regular trips to Jordan over the years.[29] Newspapers in Jordan and Palestine reported on Odeh's return, noting that there had been "a solidarity campaign among the Arab community of America," in which Odeh declared that "the struggle against the occupation will not end."

Uninfluenced by defense committee spin, a Jordanian newspaper wrote that "She joined the Popular Front for the Liberation of Palestine in her youth," adding that "she was active in the popular resistance and then the military resistance." A Palestinian news site got the location slightly wrong but was not reluctant to report that Odeh "had conducted an operation in Mahane Yehuda market, in the heart of Jerusalem, in the year 1969, that resulted in killing of [two] Israelis and injuring nine other Israelis."[30]

There was no reason to deny the obvious truth when writing in Arabic.

Notes

Introduction

1 Charlotte Silver, "Surrounded by Supporters, Rasmea Odeh Pleads Guilty," *Electronic Intifada*, April 25, 2017, https://electronicintifada.net/blogs/charlotte-silver/sur rounded-supporters-rasmea-odeh-pleads-guilty.

2 United States Palestinian Community Network, Odeh Rally, United States Palestinian Community Network, video, 40:26, April 25, 2017, https://www.face book.com/watch/live/?v=1534229493278554.

3 Palestinian Network, Odeh Rally, April 25, 2017.

4 "Jewish Voice for Peace Is Proud to Host Palestinian Organizer Rasmea Odeh," March 7, 2017, https://jewishvoiceforpeace.org/jewish-voice-peace-proud-host-palestinian-organizer-rasmea-odeh/.

5 Charlotte Silver, "Dozens Travel to Detroit to Support Rasmea Odeh as Trial Begins," *Electronic Intifada*, November 5, 2014, https://electronicintifada.net/ blogs/charlotte-silver/dozens-travel-detroit-support-rasmea-odeh-trial-begins.

6 Immigration and Naturalization Act of 1906, Pub. Law No. 59–338, § 15. See Aram A. Gavoor and Daniel Miktus, "Snap: How the Moral Elasticity of the Denaturalization Statute Goes Too Far," *William and Mary Bill of Rights Journal* 23, no. 3 (March 2015): 637, 649, https://scholarship.law.wm.edu/wmborj/vol23/iss3/3.

7 Patrick Weil, *The Sovereign Citizen: Denaturalization and the Origins of the American Republic* (Philadelphia: University of Pennsylvania Press, 2013), 55–65; 18 U.S.C. § 1425 (2019).

8 Weil, *Sovereign Citizen*, 179–80.

9 Under the McCarran Act of 1950, "affiliation within five years of naturalization with an organization that, at the time of naturalization, would have precluded citizenship was made prima facie evidence of an *earlier* lack of attachment to the

principles of the Constitution and so of fraud." Weil, *Sovereign Citizen*, 136, 171; italics in the original.

10 Irina Manta and Cassandra Burke Robertson, "(Un)Civil Denaturalizations," *NYU Law Review* 94, no. 3 (June 2019): 402, https://www.nyulawreview.org/issues/volume-94-number-3/uncivil-denaturalization/.

11 Weil, *Sovereign Citizen*, 178. Weil's figure is accurate as of 2007, under the auspices of the Justice Department's Office of Special Investigations (OSI). Another source informs me that an additional twenty-two denaturalizations were obtained following OSI's 2010 merger into the Human Rights and Special Prosecutions Section. The Nazi cases were nearly all civil. In 2013, however, Divna Maslenjak, a Bosnian Serb, was indicted for violating 18 U.S.C. § 1425 by providing false information on her application and interview for naturalization, when she concealed her husband's involvement in the massacre of eight thousand Bosnian Muslim civilians at Srebrenica. Her subsequent conviction was reversed by the U.S. Supreme Court in 2017 and was remanded to the Sixth Circuit where it remains pending as of this writing. Maslenjak v. United States, 582 U.S. ___ (2017). Another of the relatively rare criminal prosecutions was brought against Gilberto Jordan, who had concealed his participation in the massacre of civilians during Guatemala's civil war. See Weil, *Sovereign Citizen*, 179.

12 Weil, *Sovereign Citizen*, 180.

13 Manta and Robertson, "(Un)Civil Denaturalizations."

14 Seth Freed Wessler, "Is Denaturalization the Next Front in the Trump Administration's War on Immigration?," *New York Times Magazine*, December 19, 2018.

15 Wessler, "Denaturalization the Next Front?" More ominously, the Trump administration also took steps to void the presumed citizenship of American-born individuals accused or convicted of terrorism. Josh Gerstein, "Trump Officials Pushing to Strip Convicted Terrorists of Citizenship," *Politico*, June 8, 2019; Rukmini Callimachi and Alan Yuhas, "Alabama Woman Who Joined ISIS Can't Return Home, U.S. Says," *New York Times*, February 20, 2019.

16 Manta and Robertson, "(Un)Civil Denaturalizations."

17 "Enforcing Apartheid: An Interview with Michael Deutsch," *Jacobin*, November 7, 2014, https://www.jacobinmag.com/2014/11/enforcing-apartheid/.

18 "Testimony of Rasmieh Odeh, June 20, 1979," in United Nations Secretary General, Special Committee to Investigate Israeli Practices Affecting the Human Rights of the Population of the Occupied Territories, *Report of the Special Committee to Investigate Israeli Practices Affecting the Human Rights of the Population of the Occupied Territories* (New York: United Nations General Assembly, 1979).

19 Soraya Antonius, "Prisoners for Palestine: A List of Women Political Prisoners," *Journal of Palestine Studies* 9, no. 3 (Spring 1980): 45.

20 Antonius, "Prisoners for Palestine," 48. In her interview with Antonius, Odeh also implicitly acknowledged her participation in other aspects of the operation, saying that she had confessed "to things I didn't know of, but I didn't confess what I did know." Antonius, "Prisoners for Palestine," 47.

21 Amal Kawar, *Daughters of Palestine: Leading Women of the Palestinian National Movement* (Albany: State University of New York Press, 1996), 24–25, 136.

22 *Women in Struggle*, directed by Canaan Khoury (Ramallah: Majd Production, 2004), video, 56:33, https://www.youtube.com/watch?v=v0Va7-cNxf8. The video was evidently made during Odeh's visit to Jordan in April–May 2004, which she listed on her naturalization application the following November. Application for Naturalization of Rasmieh Yousef Odeh, November 3, 2004, attached to United States v. Odeh, Notice of Filing Government's Trial Exhibits, docket #186. Aisha Odeh was extremely credible on the subject of military work, having been named a member of the Palestine National Council in 1981. Nahla Abdo, "Palestinian Women Political Prisoners and the Israeli State," in *Threat: Palestinian Political Prisoners in Israel*, eds. Abeer Baker and Anat Matar (London: Pluto Press, 2011), 186–87.

23 Sean Nevins, "Rasmea Odeh: Raped and Tortured by Israel, Now Being Prosecuted by the U.S.," *Mint Press*, October 28, 2014, https://www.mintpressnews.com/rasmea-odeh-raped-and-tortured-by-israel-now-being-prosecuted-by-the-u-s/198257/. Khoury is a Palestinian independent film maker whose Majd Production Company was founded in Ramallah in 2000. *Women in Struggle* was exhibited at film festivals in the United States, the Middle East, and Europe and won the American Medical Women's Association Excellence in Media Award. See *Women in Struggle*.

24 The documentary also won an award at the Kazan Film Festival for Muslim Countries. Jillian Kay Melchior, "Rasmieh Gets Justice," *National Review*, November 11, 2014.

25 PATV, "In a Fighter's Home," PATV, Aisha Odeh interview, August 27, 2013, video, 3:39, https://www.youtube.com/watch?v=ySFOBuPXaOI&feature=youtu.be. In a 2012 interview with the Canadian academic Nahla Abdo, Aisha described Rasmea as among "the first generation of Palestinian fighters to join the armed struggle." Nahla Abdo, *Captive Revolution: Palestinian Women's Anti-Colonial Struggle within the Israeli Prison System* (London: Pluto Press, 2014), 69.

26 Aisha Odeh, *Ahlam Bel-Hurriah* [Dreams of freedom], 4th ed. (Amman, Jordan: El-Birony Press, 2016), 70.

27 *Tell Your Tale, Little Bird*, directed by Arab Loutfi (Cairo: Cinema Maa, 1993), video, 1:30:32, https://www.youtube.com/watch?v=wdkoxBjKM1Q.

28 Confidential Department of State Telegram, March 10, 1969, United States v. Odeh, Government's Opposition, Attachment F, document 137. The official report of the search also noted that Yousuf Odeh had been present at the time of the search. The Israeli investigators could not have known the contents of the State Department telegram when writing the search report, nor vice versa, which confirms the accuracy of the admission by the elder Odeh. Search Report for February 28, 1969 (filed June 4, 1969), attached to United States v. Odeh, Government's Response, Exhibit A, 543, document 88–1.

29 "The American Authorities Expel the Struggler Rasmea Odeh from the USA," *Arab 48*, September 20, 2017. "Rasmieh Odeh: An Icon of the Struggle outside Palestine," Palestine Information Center, September 21, 2017. Received translation from Arabic, October 4, 2017. Both stories incorrectly identified Odeh's target as the Mahane Yehuda market, which had been attacked the previous November, rather than the Supersol. They accurately stated the date of the operation and the number of casualties. "Arab 48" refers to Palestine, under the British Mandate, as it existed prior to the establishment of Israel.

30 "Jewish Voice for Peace Is Proud to Host."
31 United States v. Odeh, No. 13-cf-20772, Trial Transcript, November 6, 2014, 110.
32 United States v. Odeh, No. 13-cf-20772, Trial Transcript, November 6, 2014, 110.
33 United States v. Odeh, No. 13-cf-20772, Government Trial Exhibit 2A.

Chapter 1

1 United States v. Odeh, No. 13-cf-20772, Trial Transcript, November 6, 2014, 111.
2 Walid Khalidi, *All That Remains: The Palestinian Villages Occupied and Depopulated by Israel in 1948* (Washington, DC: The Institute for Palestine Studies, 1992), 300–302; Rebecca Stein, "Israeli Routes through Nakba Landscapes: An Ethnographic Meditation," *Jerusalem Quarterly*, 43 (Autumn 2010): 6; Fatima Masri, "Among the Ruins of Lifta, Memory of the Nakba Persists," liftasociety.org, May 14, 2013 (site discontinued).
3 Abdul Jawad Saleh and Walid Mustafa, *Palestine: The Collective Destruction of Palestinian Villages and Zionist Colonization, 1882–1982* (London: Jerusalem Center for Development Studies, 1987), 23.
4 Rashid Khalidi, *The Hundred Years' War on Palestine: A History of Settler Colonialism and Resistance, 1917–2017* (New York: Metropolitan Books, 2020), 34.
5 Rana Barakat, "The Jerusalem Fellah: Popular Politics in Mandate-Era Palestine," *Journal of Palestine Studies* 46, no. 1 (Autumn 2016): 11; Ilan Pappe, *The Ethnic Cleansing of Palestine* (Oxford: Oneworld Books, 2006), 67.
6 Barakat, "Jerusalem Fellah," 9–11.
7 Barakat, "Jerusalem Fellah," 8.
8 Barakat, "Jerusalem Fellah," 13, 15, 18; capitalization in the original.
9 Barakat, "Jerusalem Fellah," 14; Ian Black, *Enemies and Neighbors: Arabs and Jews in Palestine and Israel, 1917–2017* (New York: Atlantic Monthly Press, 2018), 105; Pappe, *Ethnic Cleansing* of Palestine, 67.
10 "Lifta before 1948," Zochrot Project, accessed June 6, 2019, https://www.zochrot.org/en/village/49239.
11 Chicago Cultural Alliance, "Rasmea Yousef Odeh: Outstanding Community Leader," interview with Odeh, in Arabic with English voiceover, Chicago Cultural Alliance, video, 5:36, May 13, 2013, https://www.youtube.com/watch?v=7Xxrl8aj8aQ.
12 Khalidi, *War on Palestine*, 60; Benny Morris, *1948: A History of the First Arab-Israeli War* (New Haven, CT: Yale University Press, 2008), 39.
13 Palumbo was of course quoting William Seward's 1858 speech in the U.S. Senate predicting the coming Civil War. Michael Palumbo, *The Palestinian Catastrophe: The 1948 Expulsion of a People from Their Homeland* (Boston, MA: Faber and Faber, 1987), 37–38.
14 Khalidi, *All That Remains*, 301.
15 Benny Morris, *The Birth of the Palestinian Refugee Problem Revisited* (London: Cambridge University Press, 2004), 119.

16 IZL, which stands for Irgun HaTzvai HaLeumi, is more commonly known in the United States as the Irgun, commanded by Menachem Begin in the years 1943–1948. Lehi, a Hebrew acronym for "Fighters for Freedom," is often pejoratively called the Stern Gang, after its founder Avraham Stern. Both "dissident" groups were more aggressively militant and more right wing than the establishment Haganah. Black, *Enemies and Neighbors*, 109.

17 Morris, *1948*, 96.

18 Testimony of Rasmea Odeh, United States v. Odeh, No. 13-cf-20772, Trial Transcript, November 6, 2014, 102.

19 Morris, *Palestinian Refugee Problem*, 119–21.

20 Morris, *1948*, 125–27; Victor Kattan, *From Coexistence to Conquest: International Law and the Origins of the Arab-Israeli Conflict, 1891–1949* (New York: Pluto Press, 2009), 192. According to Ian Black, Palestinian researchers eventually "revised the number of fatalities to 107, closer to what was described in contemporary Jewish testimony." Black, *Enemies and Neighbors*, 118. In 1987, Palestinian researchers at Bir Zeit University concluded that Arab prisoners, including women and children, had been executed by the IZL and Lehi forces, supported by the mainstream Haganah, and that the survivors had been robbed, but they made no mention of rape. They counted 107 victims, 11 of whom were combatants, identifying them by name. Sharif Kan'ane and Nihad Zeitawi, *Deir Yassin* (Bir Zeit: Bir Zeit University Press, 1987) cited in Benny Morris, "The Historiography of Deir Yassin," *Journal of Israeli History* 24, no. 1 (March 2005): 96. The Palestinian American historian Rashid Khalidi says that "one hundred residents, sixty-seven of them women, children, and old people, were slaughtered when the village was stormed by Irgun and Haganah assailants." Khalidi, *War on Palestine*, 74. In a 2004 interview, Morris said that his research identified evidence of "about a dozen" rapes committed by Israeli soldiers in the 1948 war. "Because neither the victims nor the rapists liked to report these events," he assumed there had been many more. He also found reports of twenty-four massacres and "a great deal of arbitrary killing." Ari Shavit, "Survival of the Fittest? An Interview with Benny Morris," *Haaretz*, January 8, 2004. See also Yoav Gelber, "Three Case Studies of the War in Palestine in 1948," *Tel Aviv Review of Books*, Winter 2019, https://www.tarb.co.il/three-case-studies-of-the-war-in-palestine-in-1948/.

21 Rashid Khalidi, "The Palestinians and 1948: The Underlying Causes of Failure," in *The War for Palestine: Rewriting the History of 1948*, eds. Eugene Rogan and Avi Shlaim (Cambridge: Cambridge University Press, 2001), 13.

22 Khalidi, *All That Remains*, 290.

23 Sari Nusseibeh, *Once Upon a Country* (New York: Farrar, Straus and Giroux, 2007), 47; Black, *Enemies and Neighbors*, 116. Odeh later said that her family fled when she was one month old, after hearing "stories of the massacre of Deir Yassin and the stories of rape." Antonius, "Prisoners for Palestine," 43. Odeh was born on May 22, 1947, according to her visa and naturalization applications, and her family's evacuation a month later would have been long before the Deir Yassin killings, and six months before the fighting even began. United States v. Odeh, Government Exhibit 2A. Of course, a child would have had no way of distinguishing among the waves of

refugees, and Odeh had every reason to associate herself with one of the many great tragedies of the Palestinians. Even West Bank families who were not displaced in 1948 were deeply affected by the reports from Deir Yassin. As recounted by Aisha Odeh, Rasmea's unrelated codefendant from a small village near Ramallah, "as a little child, I would sit with the people in my village listening to the horrendous stories they told about the Deir Yassin massacre." Nahla Abdo, *Captive Revolution: Palestinian Women's Anti-Colonial Struggle within the Israeli Prison System* (London: Pluto Press, 2014), 136. Rasmea's experience was no doubt the same. To this day, "Deir Yassin remains a byword for Zionist brutality that has resonated down the decades and remains a rallying cry for the Palestinian cause." Black, *Enemies and Neighbors*, 118.

24 Morris, *1948*, 196–97; Khalidi, *All That Remains*, 303.

25 The population of Ramallah in 1945 was 5,080 and of al-Bireh was 2,920. The population of Ramallah in 1952 was 17,145; the population of the entire Ramallah subdistrict was 110,076. Separate information for al-Bireh is not available. Sami Hadawi, *Village Statistics 1945, A Classification of Land and Area Ownership in Palestine* (Beirut: Palestine Liberation Organization Research Center, 1970), 64–65; Jordan, Dā'irat al-Iḥṣā'āt al-'Āmmah, *The Hashemite Kingdom of Jordan, 1952 Census of Housing: Statistics for Districts, Subdistricts, Nahiyas, and Principal Towns* (Jerusalem: Hashemite Kingdom of Jordan, 1952).

26 Morris, *Palestinian Refugee Problem*, 120.

27 Antonius, "Prisoners for Palestine," 43. At her 2014 trial, Odeh testified that there were nineteen people in her extended family. United States v. Odeh, No. 13-cf-20772, Trial Transcript, November 6, 2014, 101.

28 Abdo, *Captive Revolution*, 69.

29 Antonius, "Prisoners for Palestine," 43. Odeh was not exaggerating. Morris, *1948*, 294, 301.

30 "Odeh: Outstanding Community Leader."

31 Antonius, "Prisoners for Palestine," 43.

32 Abdo, *Captive Revolution*, 68.

33 Antonius, "Prisoners for Palestine," 43.

34 As'ad AbuKhalil, "Internal Contradictions in the PFLP: Decision Making and Policy Orientation," *Middle East Journal* 11, no. 3 (Summer 1987): 364; As'ad AbuKhalil, "George Habash's Contribution to the Palestinian Struggle," *Electronic Intifada*, January 30, 2008, https://electronicintifada.net/content/george-habashs-contri bution-palestinian-struggle/7332.

35 Antonius, "Prisoners for Palestine," 43.

36 Jamal Nassar, *The Palestine Liberation Organization: From Armed Struggle to the Declaration of Independence* (New York: Praeger, 1991), 86; John W. Amos, *Palestinian Resistance: Organization of a Nationalist Movement* (New York: Pergamon Press: 1980), 77.

37 Antonius, "Prisoners for Palestine," 43.

38 United States v. Odeh, No. 13-cf-20772, Trial Transcript, November 6, 2014, 103. In the Antonius interview, Odeh said that he returned in 1965. Antonius, "Prisoners for Palestine," 44.

39   The house may have been large with eighteen rooms. "Ramallah Girl Being Deported," *Jerusalem Post*, March 23, 1969. It was apparently divided into separate apartments for the two families. Affidavit of Dr. Mary Fabri, July 18, 2014, United States v. Odeh, docket #45, filed July 18, 2014.

40   Michael Oren, *Six Days of War: June 1967 and the Making of the Modern Middle East* (New York: Oxford University Press, 2002), 227.

41   Antonius, "Prisoners for Palestine," 44; United States v. Odeh, No. 13-cf-20772, Trial Transcript, November 6, 2014, 104. The story of walking to and from Jericho is questionable. One of Odeh's sisters was a paraplegic confined to a wheelchair. Special Committee, "Testimony of Rasmieh Odeh," June 20, 1979; United States v. Odeh, No. 13-cf-20772, Trial Transcript, November 6, 2014, 105. It is hard to imagine that they left her behind in Ramallah, or that someone twice pushed her chair the twenty-four-mile distance between the two cities, over roads that were then in constant use by military convoys. Nor does it seem plausible that all eighteen or nineteen members of the extended family—including Odeh's grandparents—made the journey on foot, leaving their house unattended. The account may have been necessary so that Odeh could claim to have seen stacks of napalmed bodies, as there had been almost no fighting in or around Ramallah or al-Bireh. The two towns had been occupied by Israel without significant resistance and with no occasion for extensive shelling by the IDF, as occurred in other locations in the West Bank.

42   Benny Morris, *Righteous Victims: A History of the Zionist-Arab Conflict, 1881–2001* (New York: Vintage Books, 1999), 327, 340–41.

43   Antonius, "Prisoners for Palestine," 44.

44   Rafik Halabi, *The West Bank Story* (New York: Harcourt Brace Jovanovich, 1981), 55–56.

45   Antonius, "Prisoners for Palestine," 44.

46   Mark A. Tessler, *A History of the Israeli-Palestinian Conflict* (Bloomington: Indiana University Press, 1994), 424; Abu Iyad (Salah Khalaf) and Eric Rouleau, *My Home, My Land: A Narrative of the Palestinian Struggle* (New York: Times Books, 1981), 55.

47   Wendy Pearlman, "The Palestinian National Movement," in *The 1967 Arab-Israeli War: Origins and Consequences*, eds. William Roger Louis and Avi Shlaim (Cambridge: Cambridge University Press, 2012), 139.

48   Helena Cobban, *The Palestinian Liberation Organization: People, Power and Politics* (Cambridge: Cambridge University Press, 1984), 38; Morris, *Righteous Victims*, 366.

49   Antonius, "Prisoners for Palestine," 44.

50   "Odeh: Outstanding Community Leader"; Nehad Khader, "Rasmea Odeh: The Case of an Indomitable Woman," *Journal of Palestine Studies* 46, no. 4 (Summer 2017): 62, 63.

51   Antonius, "Prisoners for Palestine," 45.

52   Yezid Sayigh, "Turning Defeat into Opportunity: The Palestinian Guerrillas after the June 1967 War," *The Middle East Journal* 46, no. 2 (Spring 1992): 257.

53   Riad el-Rayes and Dunia Nahas, *Guerrillas for Palestine* (New York: St. Martin's Press, 1976), 37.

54 Morris, *Righteous Victims*, 366.

55 Antonius, "Prisoners for Palestine," 45.

56 Raymond Anderson, "Wadi Haddad, Palestinian Hijacking Strategist, Dies," *New York Times*, April 2, 1978; Khalidi, *War on Palestine*, 113–14.

57 Amos, *Palestinian Resistance*, 78.

58 Mutual Legal Assistance Treaty Document No. 78517, transmitted August 28, 2014. Israeli agents often penetrated "deep inside Haddad's organization." Ronen Bergman, *Rise and Kill First: The Secret History of Israel's Targeted Assassinations* (New York: Random House, 2018), 140, 175.

Chapter 2

1 Chicago Cultural Alliance, "Odeh: Outstanding Community Leader." In her 2013 video interview, Odeh also said that she decided at that point to shift from medicine to law "so that I could learn how to uphold the rights of myself and my family and my people," although she did not actually go to law school until she was living in Jordan many years later.

2 *Women in Struggle.*

3 Loren Lybarger, *Palestinian Chicago: Identity in Exile* (Oakland: University of California Press, 2020), 187.

4 Antonius, "Prisoners for Palestine," 45.

5 Arab American Action Network, "Activist Profiles: Rasmea Odeh," Arab American Action Network, accessed August 4, 2017, (link since removed), http://www.aaan.org/?p=1030.

6 Antonius, "Prisoners for Palestine," 45.

7 Arab American Action Network, "Activist Profiles: Rasmea Odeh."

8 Antonius, "Prisoners for Palestine," 45.

9 Antonius, "Prisoners for Palestine," 45.

10 Mazin Qumsiyeh, *Popular Resistance in Palestine: A History of Hope and Empowerment* (London: Pluto Press, 2011), 117.

11 Iyad and Rouleau, *My Home, My Land*, 60. As a founder of Black September, Abu Iyad handpicked the two guerrillas who led the attack on Israeli athletes at the 1972 Munich Olympics. Iyad and Rouleau, *My Home, My Land*, 106–12. He was later assassinated in an intra-Palestinian struggle.

12 Eileen MacDonald, *Shoot the Women First* (New York: Random House, 1991), 65. MacDonald was writing of the 1989 Palestinian Intifdada, but the same situation also existed in the first years of the occupation. Eric Downton, "Guerrillas Hail Teacher as First Heroine," *Sunday Telegraph*, March 16, 1969.

13 Iyad and Rouleau, *My Home, My Land*, 60.

14 Cobban, *Palestinian Liberation Organization*, 38.

15 Ehud Ya'ari, *Strike Terror: The Story of Fatah*, trans. Esther Yaari (New York: Sabra Books, 1970), 150; Cobban, *Palestinian Liberation Organization*, 38; Mark A. Tessler, *A History of the Israeli-Palestinian Conflict* (Bloomington: Indiana University Press,

1994), 425. In a footnote, Tessler observes that some historians question the accuracy of the Arafat story.

16 Rafik Halabi, *The West Bank Story* (New York: Harcourt Brace Jovanovich, 1981), 63.

17 Halabi, *West Bank Story*, 63.

18 Shaul Mishal, *The PLO under Arafat: Between Gun and Olive Branch* (New Haven, CT: Yale University Press, 1986), 11.

19 Oriana Fallaci, "A Leader of the Fedayeen: 'We Want a War Like the Vietnam War,'" *Life*, June 12, 1970. Some writers have subsequently sanitized this statement, which was made in an interview with Fallaci, intentionally substituting "Zionist" for "Jew." Jamal Nassar, *The Palestine Liberation Organization: From Armed Struggle to the Declaration of Independence* (New York: Praeger, 1991), 88, 89.

20 Rashid Khalidi, *The Hundred Years' War on Palestine: A History of Settler Colonialism and Resistance, 1917–2017* (New York: Metropolitan Books, 2020), 118.

21 Benny Morris, *Righteous Victims: A History of the Zionist-Arab Conflict, 1881–2001* (New York: Vintage Books, 1999), 368–70.

22 Pearlman, "The Palestinian National Movement," 142; partially quoting Rosemary Sayigh, *Palestinians: From Peasants to Revolutionaries* (London: Zed Books, 1979), 144.

23 Morris, *Righteous Victims*, 369; Yehoshafat Harkabi, *Fedayeen Action and Arab Strategy* (London: Institute for Strategic Studies, 1968), 26; Sayigh, *Peasants to Revolutionaries*, 158; Tessler, *Israeli-Palestinian Conflict*, 426. In a 2004 documentary, Aisha Odeh, who was tried and convicted with Rasmea Odeh, said that Karameh "brought great awareness" to potential PFLP fighters in the occupied territories. *Women in Struggle*.

24 Cobban, *Palestinian Liberation Organization*, 42.

25 Sayigh, *Peasants to Revolutionaries*, 147.

26 Kemal Kirisci, *The PLO and World Politics: A Study of the Mobilization of Support for the Palestinian Cause* (New York: St. Martin's Press, 1986), 38; Yezid Sayigh, *Armed Struggle and the Search for State: The Palestinian Movement 1949–1993*, Institute for Palestine Studies (Oxford: Clarendon Press, 1997), 195.

27 Pearlman, "Palestinian National Movement," 142; Qumsiyeh, *Popular Resistance*, 119.

28 Iyad and Rouleau, *My Home, My Land*, 60.

29 "Odeh: Outstanding Community Leader."

30 Antonius, "Prisoners for Palestine," 44.

31 Abdo's description came from a 2012 interview with Aisha Odeh, who was convicted of the Supersol bombing along with Rasmea Odeh and who has proudly acknowledged her own participation in the operation. Nahla Abdo, *Captive Revolution: Palestinian Women's Anti-Colonial Struggle within the Israeli Prison System* (London: Pluto Press, 2014), 9–10, 69. See also Amal Kawar, *Daughters of Palestine: Leading Women of the Palestinian National Movement* (Albany: State University of New York Press, 1996), 24, in which Rasmea Odeh admitted having been among the women "active first as guerrillas."

32 Nassar, *Palestine Liberation Organization*, 89; Samih Farsoun and Christina Zacharia, *Palestine and the Palestinians* (Boulder, CO: Westview Press, 1997), 192.

33 Yezid Sayigh, "Turning Defeat into Opportunity: The Palestinian Guerrillas after the June 1967 War," *The Middle East Journal* 46, no. 2 (Spring 1992): 257.

34 "When Plane Hijackings Were Palestinian Terrorists' Weapon of Choice," *Haaretz*, March 29, 2016.

35 James Feron, "Bomb Explosion in Jerusalem's Largest Supermarket Kills 2, Injures 9," *New York Times*, February 2, 1969; "2 Die, 8 Wounded in J'Lem Terror Outrage at Supersol," *Jerusalem Post*, February 23, 1969.

36 "2 Die, 8 Wounded in J'Lem Terror Outrage."

37 Feron, "Bomb Explosion in Jerusalem's Largest Supermarket"; Police Officer Albert Levi, "Visit to a Bomb Location Report," February 21, 1969, in United States v. Odeh, Government's Response, Exhibit A, 509, document 88–1.

38 "Supersol Blast," *Jerusalem Post*, February 23, 1969; United States v. Odeh, Government's Response, Exhibit A, 511, document 88–1.

39 "Funeral Today of Two Victims," *Jerusalem Post*, February 24, 1969.

40 "2 Die, 8 Wounded in J'Lem Terror Outrage"; "Supersol Blast"; "Jerusalem Supersol Re-opens for Business; 2 Young Bombing Victims Are Buried," *Jewish Telegraphic Agency*, February 24, 1969; Police Officer Albert Levi, "Report re Visit to Location of Explosion," February 21, 1969, in United States v. Odeh, Government's Response, Exhibit A, 511, document 88–1.

41 "Jerusalem Supersol Re-opens for Business"; James Feron, "Many Israelis Angry," *New York Times*, February 23, 1969.

42 "Supersol Blast."

43 "14 East Jerusalem, West Bank Arabs Held by Israel in Supermarket Bombing," *Jewish Telegraphic Service*, February 25, 1969; "14 Remanded for Fortnight as Blast Suspects," *Jerusalem Post*, February 24, 1969; James Feron, "Israelis Warn Arabs," *New York Times*, February 24, 1969. The *New York Times* headline referred to warnings directed at the PFLP and supportive Arab governments, not local residents. Two weeks later, it was reported that eleven of two hundred suspects had been remanded to custody, and the rest released. "Bombing Suspects Remanded," *Jerusalem Post*, March 19, 1969. There may or may not have been overlap between these two groups, but it in any case appears that at least nine out of ten interrogees were released without charges within the legally required fifteen days. Whether this represented a policy of sweepingly overbroad arrests or rather careful questioning and expeditious release of the innocent depends wholly on one's point of view.

44 "Supersol Victims Buried; Allon Promises Vengeance," *Jerusalem Post*, February 24, 1969.

45 "Supersol Victims Buried."

46 The ellipses appear on the marker itself, where there is likewise no other punctuation. William Jacobson, "Rasmea's Victims Then and Now," *Legal Insurrection*, June 10, 2015, https://legalinsurrection.com/2015/06/rasmea-odehs-victims-then-and-now/.

47 "Supersol Reopens; Business as Usual," *Jerusalem Post*, February 24, 1969; "Jerusalem Supersol Re-opens for Business."

48 "Supersol Bomb Victims Recover," *Jerusalem Post*, February 26, 1969; Eric Downton, "Arabs Plan Push," *Sunday Telegraph*, February 23, 1969.

49 "Market Blast Hurts 2 Arabs; Officials Escape Injury in British Consulate Explosion," *Jewish Telegraphic Service*, February 26, 1969; "Supermarket Outrage," *Jerusalem Post*, February 28, 1969. Lydda and the adjoining town of Ramle had been the site of the largest expulsion of Palestinians in the Nakba, with fifty thousand to seventy thousand compelled to leave their homes in July 1948 following the conquest of the region by the Israeli army. Many died on the forced march to Jordanian-held territory, which the Israeli journalist Ari Shavit called "the dark secret of Zionism." Ari Shavit, *My Promised Land* (New York: Spiegel and Grau, 2013), 108.

50 Feron, "Israelis Warn Arabs."

51 "Reply to Fatah," *Jerusalem Post*, February 28, 1969.

52 "Israel's Week," *Jerusalem Post*, February 28, 1969.

Chapter 3

1 Nahla Abdo adds that the late-night arrests were "intended to serve as yet another method of terrorizing the individual and her family." Abdo, *Captive Revolution*, 141.

2 Special Committee, "Testimony of Rasmieh Odeh," June 20, 1979.

3 Affidavit of Dr. Mary Fabri, July 18, 2014, United States v. Odeh, docket #45, filed July 18, 2014.

4 Police Officer Albert Levi, "Report of Destruction of Explosives and Demolition," March 1, 1969, in United States v. Odeh, Government's Response, Exhibit A, 523, docket #88–1; "Search Report for February 28, 1969" (filed June 4, 1969), attached to United States v. Odeh, Government's Response, Exhibit A, 543, docket #88–1; "Beginning of Trial of the Two Women," *Davar*, June 5, 1969.

5 Confidential Department of State Telegram, March 10, 1969, United States v. Odeh, Government's Opposition, Attachment F, docket #137; Special Committee, "Testimony of Rasmieh Odeh," June 20, 1979.

6 Yehoshafat Harkabi, *Fedayeen Action and Arab Strategy* (London: Institute for Strategic Studies, 1968), 26; Yezid Sayigh, "Turning Defeat into Opportunity: The Palestinian Guerrillas after the June 1967 War," *The Middle East Journal* 46, no. 2 (Spring 1992): 251.

7 Iyad and Rouleau, *My Home, My Land*, 56.

8 Antonius, "Prisoners for Palestine," 46.

9 "Israel Tortures Arab Prisoners," *Sunday Times*, June 19, 1977.

10 Iyad and Rouleau, *My Home, My Land*, 56.

11 "Trial Due Soon of 143 Jerusalem Terror Suspects," *Jerusalem Post*, May 4, 1969. The projected trial of over 140 suspects was another exaggeration.

12 Sayigh, "Turning Defeat into Opportunity," 251.

13 The PFLP was riddled with informants and Israeli agents. In later operations, the Mossad was able to "exploit its deep intelligence penetration of Haddad's organization" in dramatic ways. Ronen Bergman, *Rise and Kill First: The Secret History of Israel's Targeted Assassinations* (New York: Random House, 2018), 212.

14 In a 2014 interview, Odeh stated that she and her family were planning to leave the following day for Jericho, which may have been known to Israeli intelligence. If so,

the raid would have been timed to prevent her departure from al-Bireh. Affidavit of Dr. Mary Fabri, July 18, 2014, United States v. Odeh, docket #45, filed July 18, 2014.

15 Antonius, "Prisoners for Palestine," 46.

16 Antonius, "Prisoners for Palestine," 46.

17 Special Committee, "Testimony of Rasmieh Odeh," June 20, 1979, 22.

18 Special Committee, "Testimony of Rasmieh Odeh," June 20, 1979, 23.

19 Antonius, "Prisoners for Palestine," 46; Special Committee, "Testimony of Rasmieh Odeh," June 20, 1979, 23.

20 Antonius, "Prisoners for Palestine," 46–47.

21 Affidavit of Dr. Mary Fabri, July 18, 2014, United States v. Odeh, docket #45, filed July 18, 2014. At the request of defense counsel, Dr. Fabri interviewed Odeh for a total of eighteen hours in three sessions, evaluating her for post-traumatic stress disorder in preparation for testimony on her behalf. In the course of the interviews, Odeh provided her with an account of her 1969 interrogation.

22 Special Committee, "Testimony of Rasmieh Odeh," June 20, 1979, 23.

23 Antonius, "Prisoners for Palestine," 47.

24 Special Committee, "Testimony of Rasmieh Odeh," June 20, 1979, 26. Odeh explained that she knew the woman was a soldier because she saw her later in uniform.

25 Special Committee, "Testimony of Rasmieh Odeh," June 20, 1979, 26.

26 Antonius, "Prisoners for Palestine," 48; British abbreviation in the original.

27 Antonius, "Prisoners for Palestine," 47.

28 Antonius, "Prisoners for Palestine," 48.

29 Special Committee, "Testimony of Rasmieh Odeh," June 20, 1979, 25.

30 Affidavit of Dr. Mary Fabri, July 18, 2014, United States v. Odeh, docket #45, filed July 18, 2014.

31 Antonius, "Prisoners for Palestine," 48.

32 Affidavit of Dr. Mary Fabri, July 18, 2014, United States v. Odeh, docket #45, filed July 18, 2014.

33 Amnesty International, Report on Torture (London: Duckworth in association with Amnesty International Publishing, 1973), 212; capitalization in the original.

34 Amnesty International, Report on Torture, 220.

35 David Krivine, "Flawed Insight on Torture," Jerusalem Post, August 5, 1977; David Krivine, "More Insight on Torture," Jerusalem Post, October 28, 1977.

36 Special Committee, "Testimony of Rasmieh Odeh," June 20–21, 1979.

37 Antonius, "Prisoners for Palestine."

38 Affidavit of Dr. Mary Fabri, July 18, 2014, United States v. Odeh, docket #45, filed July 18, 2014.

39 United States v. Odeh, Government's Opposition, Attachment E, docket #137.

40 Krivine, "Flawed Insight on Torture." The Sunday Times refers to the elder Odeh as Josef and Joseve, but it is clear from the context that the interview was with the father of Rasmea Odeh.

41 Women in Struggle; Tell Your Tale, Little Bird.

42 Krivine, "Flawed Insight on Torture."

43 "Israel Tortures Arab Prisoners." Odeh also testified at her trial in the United States, although she was not allowed to speak about her interrogation and treatment in

Israel. Finally her handwritten confession, the accuracy of which she denies, was translated from Arabic into English and filed in the U.S. prosecution. United States v. Odeh, Trial Transcript, November 6, 2014; United States v. Odeh, Government's Opposition, Attachment I, docket #137.

44   Both the Special Committee testimony and the Antonius interview attempted to place the events of Odeh's interrogation in chronological order, and they are roughly consistent. Fabri's interview, which was conducted for psychological diagnostic and treatment purposes, also presents events chronologically, but it is an after-the-fact summary of three six-hour sessions, rather than an account in Odeh's own words, and therefore likely to be less concerned regarding the sequence of occurrences.

45   In a 1993 Arabic-language video interview, Odeh said, "We used to hear the Jews' propaganda when they talked about the Nazis' torture of the Jews. But in reality what I saw and passed through moment by moment was much more horrible than any kind of torture they ever talked about." *Tell Your Tale.*

46   "Israel Tortures Arab Prisoners," ellipses in the original.

47   "Israel Tortures Arab Prisoners."

48   Confidential Department of State Telegram, March 10, 1969, United States v. Odeh, Government's Opposition, Attachment F, docket #137. Odeh confirmed her father's interview with the U.S. consular officer, although she referred to the "Ambassador" and placed the interview at fifteen days following the arrests rather than the actual ten. Special Committee, "Testimony of Rasmieh Odeh," June 20, 1979.

49   Special Committee, "Testimony of Rasmieh Odeh," June 21, 1979.

50   Affidavit of Dr. Mary Fabri, July 18, 2014, United States v. Odeh, docket #45, filed July 18, 2014.

51   In her testimony before the U.N. Special Committee, Odeh acknowledged speaking with Krivine while she was imprisoned in Israel. According to her testimony, "I mentioned the tortures inflicted on my father in the period when he was interrogated, but the journalist said that he wanted to see my father and interview him. I don't know whether he did or not." The Committee chair asked Odeh if she had read Krivine's *Jerusalem Post* articles, but she avoided answering the question. Odeh did tell the committee that her father had been in the interrogation room during some episodes during and after her torture, but not during the stick incident, saying "on the same day that they tried to tear my hymen they introduced my father into the same room. . . ." The chair then asked if she had ever spoken with her father about the incident, evidently to exclude the possibility of collusion, to which she replied, "No, I never discussed that. Even the court where I spoke about the torture was an ad hoc court where there were no persons other than those concerned with that trial [underlining in the original]." Special Committee, "Testimony of Rasmieh Odeh," June 20–21, 1979. The latter assertion was untrue. Odeh's trial was public, with her father and other family members and friends present in the courtroom, and it was widely reported in the Israeli press, in both Hebrew and English. "Beginning of Trial"; "Supersol Accused Turn Backs on Informer," *Jerusalem Post,* June 6, 1969. In her 2014 evaluation sessions with Dr. Fabri, Odeh described at least eleven incidents of actual or

threatened sexual torture, some of which, contrary to her Special Committee testimony, she had evidently discussed with her father. Regarding the use of a stick to break her hymen, Odeh said "she was aware of others being in the room and later learned that her father had witnessed the sexual assault." Affidavit of Dr. Mary Fabri, July 18, 2014, United States v. Odeh, docket #45, filed July 18, 2014, 6.

52 Military Prosecutor v. Odeh et al., Testimony of Rasmea Odeh, attached to United States v. Odeh, Government's Opposition, docket #137–8. In other transliterations, the interrogator has been identified as abu-Ghanni, Abuhanni, and Abu Hani.

53 United States v. Odeh, Government's Opposition, Attachment H, docket #137.

54 In a 1993 Arabic-language video interview, Odeh tells of being tormented by a female interrogator in thin high heels, who "began to step on my stomach . . . telling me she was preparing me for a man to come and sleep with me." In the video, which includes only a few minutes of what was obviously a longer interview, Odeh says nothing about violation with a stick or threats of compelled sex with her father, although the video interview was thirteen years after Odeh made those charges in her Special Committee testimony and interview with Antonius. It seems unlikely that the video director would have omitted the most horrific accounts of Odeh's torture if she had repeated them on camera. Odeh did say, "There are things one feels shy to repeat, even to oneself. What I am saying are general lines. I am not going into details. The details are much more horrible." *Tell Your Tale.* Other writers have repeated the more dramatic account. "Rasmiye Odeh's father was forcibly involved in his daughter's sexual violation in a complex attempt to shame both of them." Elizabeth Warnock Fernea, *Women and the Family in the Middle East* (Austin: University of Texas Press, 1985), 194.

55 Antonius, "Prisoners for Palestine," 47.

56 United States v. Odeh, Government's Opposition, Attachment I, docket #137.

57 United States v. Odeh, Government's Opposition, Attachment I, docket #137.

58 "Israel Tortures Arab Prisoners."

Chapter 4

1 "Supersol Blast Suspects Held in Round-Up of 40," *Jerusalem Post*, March 2, 1969.

2 "Supersol Blast Suspects Held."

3 "Supersol Crime Reconstructed," *Jerusalem Post*, March 3, 1969.

4 "Forty Members of Terrorist Cells Rounded Up in Supermarket Bombing Case," *Jewish Telegraphic Agency*, March 4, 1969; *Tell Your Tale, Little Bird.* Bomb making materials were also recovered from Aisha Odeh's home, including Russian-, Italian-, and Czech-made grenades. Report of Police Officer Albert Levi, March 3, 1969, United States v. Odeh, Government's Response to Motion for Reconsideration of Bond Revocation, Attachment I, docket #137–10.

5 "Israeli Police Arrest Minister, 2 Professionals, in Market Bombing," *Jewish Telegraphic Agency*, March 5, 1969; "Suspects of the Bombing," *Davar*, March 6,

1969; "Suspects Held in Both U.K. Consulate Bombs," *Jerusalem Post*, March 14, 1969.

6   Spellings of her name vary, including Widad and Wadad, and Qumri and Kaimary.

7   "Suspects of the Bombing"; "Major Terror Gang Seized," *Jerusalem Post*, March 6, 1969; "Terror Chain," *Jerusalem Post*, March 7, 1969.

8   "Israelis Outraged by Bombing of Hebrew U. Cafeteria; 7 Students Injured Seriously," *Jewish Telegraphic Service*, March 7, 1969.

9   "Israelis Outraged by Bombing."

10   Alan Dershowitz, *Why Terrorism Works: Understanding the Threat, Responding to the Challenge* (New Haven, CT: Yale University Press, 2002), 131; Richard Posner, "The Best Offense," *New Republic Online*, September 5, 2002, https://newrepub lic.com/article/66437/the-best-offense; Matt Ford, "Antonin Scalia's Case for Torture," *Atlantic*, December 13, 2014.

11   Moshe Landau et al., *Commission of Inquiry into the Methods of Investigation of the General Security Service Regarding Hostile Terrorist Activity Report, Part One* (Jerusalem: State of Israel Government Press, 1987), 17.

12   Amnesty International, *Report on Torture*, 220.

13   Letters from Felicia Langer to Israel Ministry of Justice, dated November 20, 1968, September 11, 1969, January 27, 1970, and February 3, 1970, reproduced in United Nations General Assembly Special Committee to Investigate Israeli Practices Affecting the Human Rights of the Population of the Occupied Territories, *Report of the Special Committee to Investigate Israeli Practices Affecting the Human Rights of the Population of the Occupied Territories* (New York: United Nations General Assembly, 1970); Felicia Langer, *With My Own Eyes: Israel and the Occupied Territories 1967–1973* (London: Ithaca Press, 1975), 31–34.

14   See, e.g., Amnesty International, *Israel and the Occupied Territories: The Military Justice System in the Occupied Territories: Detention, Interrogation and Trial Procedures* (New York: Amnesty International, 1991); International Commission of Jurists and Law in the Service of Man, *Torture and Intimidation in the West Bank: The Case of Al-Fara'a Prison* (Geneva: International Commission of Jurists and Law in the Service of Man, 1985); Efrat Bergman-Sapir and Rachel Stroumsa, *Public Committee against Torture in Israel: Independent Report to the UN Committee against Torture towards the Review of the Fifth Periodic Report on Israel* (Jerusalem: Public Committee Against Torture in Israel, 2016); Lisa Hajjar, *Torture: A Sociology of Violence and Human Rights* (New York: Routledge, 2013); National Lawyers Guild, Middle East Delegation, *Treatment of Palestinians in Israeli-occupied West Bank and Gaza: Report of the National Lawyers Guild, 1977 Middle East Delegation* (New York: The Guild, 1978); Lisa Hajjar, *Courting Conflict: The Israeli Military Court System in the West Bank and Gaza* (Berkeley: University of California Press, 2005); James Ron et al., *Torture and Ill-Treatment: Israel's Interrogation of Palestinians from the Occupied Territories* (New York: Human Rights Watch, 1994).

15   David Krivine, "Flawed Insight on Torture," *Jerusalem Post*, August 5, 1977.

16   Even more carefully, the State Department report stated that "instances of brutality by individual interrogators cannot be ruled out." United States Department of State, *Country Reports on Human Rights Practices: Report Submitted to the Committee*

on International Relations, U.S. House of Representatives, and Committee on Foreign Relations, U.S. Senate (Washington: U.S. Government Printing Office, 1978), 365–66.

17 "Torture—Israel Replies," *Sunday Times,* July 3, 1977.

18 Ronen Bergman, *Rise and Kill First: The Secret History of Israel's Targeted Assassinations* (New York: Random House, 2018), 102–3.

19 Landau et al., Commission Report, 21–23, 30, 79. In recognition of Israeli political reality, the Landau Commission Report also noted what it termed "false complaints by suspects concerning severe torture" as a common part "of the systematic campaign conducted by terrorist organizations" against the GSS. Landau Commission Report, 87. For the full details of the underlying case, see Nafsu v. Chief Military Advocate, Supreme Court of Israel (1987), accessed July 24, 2019, http://versa.cardozo.yu.edu/opinions/nafsu-v-chief-military-advocate. As the contemporary journalist Ronen Bergman put it, Israeli interrogation methods "included prolonged detention without judicial sanction, and torture; perjury in the courts and concealment of the truth from counsel and judges. Bergman, *Rise and Kill First,* 31.

20 Bergman, *Rise and Kill First,* 281.

21 "Arab Students Condemn Terrorist Involvement," *Jerusalem Post,* March 17, 1969; "Bombing Suspects Remanded," *Jerusalem Post,* March 19, 1969; "Mrs. Meir Says Arab Population Loyal," *Jerusalem Post,* March 19, 1969.

22 "Jerusalem Terror Suspects for Trial," *Jerusalem Post,* March 21, 1969.

23 "Girl, 19, and 30 Others Held for H.U. Cafeteria Blast," *Jerusalem Post,* March 16, 1969.

24 Eric Downton, "Guerrillas Hail Teacher as First Heroine," *Sunday Telegraph,* March 16, 1969.

25 "Suspects of the Bombing."

26 "Major Terror Gang Seized"; "Supermarket Blast by Woman Who Wasn't There," *Jerusalem Post,* March 17, 1969.

27 David Krivine, "More Insight on Torture," *Jerusalem Post,* October 23, 1977.

28 "University Bombing Suspects," *Jerusalem Post,* March 16, 1969.

29 "Ramallah Girl Being Deported," *Jerusalem Post,* March 23, 1969.

30 Special Committee, "Testimony of Rasmieh Odeh," June 20, 1979, 6. Antonius, "Prisoners for Palestine," 49.

31 "Bombing Suspects Remanded."

32 "Woman Claims She Led Supersol Explosion," *Jerusalem Post,* June 4, 1969; "Printer Guilty of Hiding Supersol Bomb Girl," *Jerusalem Post,* June 10, 1969. The man who sheltered Obeideh in Nablus, who was the secretary of the local printers' union, was arrested and pled guilty.

33 "First Sabotage Attempt on Supersol Failed," *Jerusalem Post,* May 14, 1969; "Teenagers Jailed for Attempt on Supersol," *Jerusalem Post,* July 11, 1969. The two would-be bombers were arrested, convicted, and received sentences of seven and ten years.

34 "2 Prominent Terror Suspects Allowed to Go to Jordan," *Jerusalem Post,* April 17, 1969.

35 "2 Prominent Terror Suspects Allowed to Go."
36 "Suspects of the Bombing."
37 "Release of Terror Suspect Protested," *Jerusalem Post*, March 30, 1969; "Questions on Release of Rev. Khoury," *Jerusalem Post*, April 18, 1969.

Chapter 5

1 "First Sabotage Attempt on Supersol Failed," *Jerusalem Post*, May 14, 1969.
2 "Supersol and Cafeteria Indictments Laid," *Jerusalem Post*, May 12, 1969.
3 Yakoub Odeh was described in the press as Rasmea's cousin, and she later referred to him as her fiancé. In her 2013 interview on Palestine Television, Aisha said only that Yakoub, like Rasmea, was from Lifta. Aisha Odeh interview, August 27, 2013.
4 Indictment in Military Prosecutor v. Rasmieh Yusuf Odeh et al., February 26, 1969, attached to Notice of Filing Government's Trial Exhibits, United States v. Odeh, docket #186, filed May 29, 2015.
5 Lisa Hajjar, *Courting Conflict: The Israeli Military Court System in the West Bank and Gaza* (Berkeley: University of California Press, 2005).
6 Lisa Hajjar, a staunch critic of Israel's military courts, estimates that 95 percent of defendants are convicted, while of the convictions, approximately 97 percent are the result of plea bargains. Although Hajjar does not do the math, her figures suggest that of the defendants who do not plead guilty, well over half are not convicted. Hajjar, *Courting Conflict*, 3. Statistics from Human Rights Watch are similar, reporting, for one five-year period, that only 3 percent of defendants had been acquitted. Seventy percent of the convictions, however, had come via plea bargains, which suggests an ultimate acquittal rate of about 11 percent among cases actually taken to trial. James Ron et al., *Torture and Ill-Treatment*, 245. In U.S. federal courts, by comparison, only about 2 percent of felony prosecutions result in trials—90 percent are plea bargained and 8 percent are dismissed—with a conviction rate of over 95 percent at trial. See John Gramlich, "Only 2% of Federal Criminal Defendants Go to Trial, and Most Who Do Are Found Guilty," Pew Research Center, June 11, 2019, https://www.pewresearch.org/fact-tank/2019/06/11/only-2-of-federal-criminal-defendants-go-to-trial-and-most-who-do-are-found-guilty/.
7 Hajjar, *Courting Conflict*, 189.
8 Landau et al., *Commission Report*, 20.
9 Landau et al., *Commission Report*, 20. According to the Israeli lawyer Leah Tsemel, who frequently defended Palestinians in security cases, convictions in military tribunals were "always based on a statement purporting to confess to the offences as charged, no heed being given to the principle that confessions should be supported by corroborative evidence to constitute acceptable grounds for conviction." United Nations General Assembly Special Committee to Investigate Israeli Practices Affecting the Human Rights of the Population of the Occupied Territories, *Report of the Special Committee to Investigate Israeli Practices Affecting the Human Rights of the*

Population of the Occupied Territories (New York: United Nations General Assembly, 1977), 31; British spelling in the original.

10   Human Rights Watch, *Torture and Ill-Treatment*, 243.

11   Landau et al., Commission Report, 30.

12   Landau et al., Commission Report, 79.

13   Landau et al., Commission Report, 65.

14   "Trial Begins of Supersol Accused," *Jerusalem Post*, June 5, 1969; "Beginning of Trial of the Two Women," *Davar*, June 5, 1969.

15   "Trial Begins of Supersol Accused"; "Beginning of Trial."

16   United States v. Odeh, Government's Opposition, Attachments A-D, document 137.

17   Landau et al., Commission Report, 21.

18   "Supersol Crime Reconstructed," *Jerusalem Post*, March 3, 1969.

19   United States v. Odeh, Government's Opposition, Attachments A-D, docket #137.

20   United States v. Odeh, Government's Opposition, Attachments A-D, docket #137; "Supersol Accused Turn Backs on Informer," *Jerusalem Post*, June 6, 1969. Although the number of arrests seems large, the PFLP cells were extremely vulnerable to informers because "no efforts were made to conceal their identities from each other," thus making them easy to "roll up" once even a single operative cracked. Sayigh, "Turning Defeat into Opportunity," 251. Recounting her own arrest, Aisha said she had been asked "Do you know Rasmiyya?" which corroborates Kalish's testimony that Rasmea had indeed given up the names of her comrades. Nahla Abdo, *Captive Revolution: Palestinian Women's Anti-Colonial Struggle within the Israeli Prison System* (London: Pluto Press, 2014), 143.

21   "New Revelations in the Supersol Trial," *Maariv*, June 6, 1969.

22   "New Revelations in the Supersol Trial"; "Testimony of the Father of the Main Defendant," *Hatzofeh*, June 6, 1969.

23   "Supersol Accused Turn Backs on Informer."

24   "The Defendants from the Supersol Bombing Accuse the Police of 'Sexual Torture,'" *Maariv*, November 11, 1969.

25   "Defendants from the Supersol Bombing Accuse the Police"; United States v. Odeh, Government's Opposition, Attachment E, docket #137.

26   "Defendants from the Supersol Bombing Accuse the Police."

27   United States v. Odeh, Government's Opposition, Attachments E and G, docket #137.

28   United States v. Odeh, Government's Opposition, Attachments E and G, docket #137.

29   United States v. Odeh, Government's Opposition, Attachments E and G, docket #137.

30   Nahla Abdo, herself once a political detainee, believes that "the Israeli methods of torture have been and continue to be aimed at 'punishing the suspect, as well as acquiring information about Palestinian political and military organization, obtaining a confession as primary evidence against the accused, and warning and frightening others from further political activity.'" Abdo, *Captive Revolution*, 149 (quoting Raija-Leena Punamaki, "Experiences of Torture, Means of Coping, and Level of Symptoms among Palestinian Political Prisoners," *Journal of Palestine Studies* 17, no. 4 (Summer 1988): 81–96). While none of those effects can be disregarded, Odeh's treatment clearly establishes that obtaining "information about

Palestinian . . . military organization" was the overriding purpose of the interrogation. The interrogators did not accept Odeh's initial confession, itself sufficient as "primary evidence," and the mistreatment stopped once she provided a full account of the operation, which would not have been the case if "punishment" had been their objective.

31 "Supersol Accused Turn Backs on Informer"; United States v. Odeh, Government's Opposition, Attachment H, document 137.

32 Ronen Bergman, *Rise and Kill First: The Secret History of Israel's Targeted Assassinations* (New York: Random House, 2018), 283–84.

33 United States v. Odeh, Government's Opposition, Attachment H, docket #137.

34 United States v. Odeh, Government's Opposition, Attachment I, docket #137.

35 United States v. Odeh, Government's Opposition, Attachment I, docket #137.

36 United States v. Odeh, Government's Opposition, Attachment I, docket #137. Likewise, there was no mention of the arrestees in the Hebrew University bombing. The confession did name Rev. Khoury, but it did not say that he had driven anyone from Ramallah to Jerusalem, and Dr. Muammar was not mentioned at all.

37 Aisha Odeh, *Ahlam Bel-Hurriah* [Dreams of freedom], 4th ed. (Amman, Jordan: El-Birony Press, 2016), 70.

38 United States v. Odeh, Government's Opposition, Attachment I, docket #137; capitalization in the original.

39 *Women in Struggle.*

40 United States v. Odeh, Government's Response to Order, Exhibit A, docket #88–1.

41 "Supersol Saboteurs Sentenced to Life," *Jerusalem Post*, January 23, 1970.

42 United States v. Odeh, Government's Response to Order, Exhibit A, docket #88–1. The conviction and verdict were affirmed on May 5, 1970. United States v. Odeh, Motion in Limine of the United States, Exhibit 7, docket #36.

Chapter 6

1 In 1988, a women's wing was opened in the HaSharon prison.

2 Human Rights Watch/Middle East, *Prison Conditions in Israel and the Occupied Territories, April 1991: A Middle East Watch Report* (New York: Human Rights Watch, 1991), 26, 28. Punishment cells—called *tsinok* in Hebrew—were reported to be too small to allow a prisoner to lie down, but they do not seem to have been used at Neve Tirza. United Nations General Assembly, *Report of the Special Committee*, 1977, 32.

3 Human Rights Watch, *Prison Conditions in Israel*, 34.

4 Special Committee, "Testimony of Aisha Odeh," June 22, 1979, 3.

5 Nahla Abdo, *Captive Revolution: Palestinian Women's Anti-Colonial Struggle within the Israeli Prison System* (London: Pluto Press, 2014), 172; Special Committee, "Testimony of Rasmieh Odeh," June 20, 1979, 5, 6, 10, 12; "Testimony of Afifa Bannoura, June 21, 1979," in United Nations Secretary General, Special Committee to Investigate Israeli Practices Affecting the Human Rights of the Population of the Occupied Territories, *Report of the Special Committee to Investigate Israeli Practices Affecting the Human Rights of the Population of the Occupied Territories* (New York: United Nations General Assembly, 1979); Special Committee, "Testimony of Aisha

Odeh," June 22, 1979, 3, 5; United Nations General Assembly Special Committee to Investigate Israeli Practices Affecting the Human Rights of the Population of the Occupied Territories, *Report of the Special Committee to Investigate Israeli Practices Affecting the Human Rights of the Population of the Occupied Territories* (New York: United Nations General Assembly, 1976), 32.

6   Abdo, *Captive Revolution*, 187.

7   Ram Cnaan, "Notes on Prostitution in Israel," *Sociological Inquiry* 52, no. 2 (March 1982): 115–21; Delia Amar and Menachem Amir, "The Politics of Prostitution and Trafficking of Women in Israel," in *The Politics of Prostitution: Women's Movements, Democratic States and the Globalisation of Sex Commerce*, ed. Joyce Outshoorn (New York: Cambridge University Press, 2004), 144–64; "Women beyond the Walls," *Haaretz*, September 30, 2006; "There's Only One Women's Prison in Israel," *Business Insider*, April 12, 2018; "Behind the Bars in Israel's Only Female Prison," *Jewish News*, March 21, 2019; Nahla Abdo, "Palestinian Women Political Prisoners and the Israeli State," in *Threat: Palestinian Political Prisoners in Israel*, eds. Abeer Baker and Anat Matar (London: Pluto Press, 2011), 64; Special Committee, "Testimony of Aisha Odeh," June 22, 1979, 8.

8   "Girl, 19, and 30 Others Held for H.U. Cafeteria Blast," *Jerusalem Post*, March 16, 1969; Special Committee, "Testimony of Aisha Odeh," June 22, 1979, 7; Special Committee, "Testimony of Rasmieh Odeh," June 20, 1979, 11.

9   Special Committee, "Testimony of Rasmieh Odeh," June 20, 1979, 6, 7, 13; "Testimony of Rasmieh Odeh," June 21, 1979, 4.

10   Special Committee, "Testimony of Aisha Odeh," June 21, 1979, 3; Special Committee, "Testimony of Rasmieh Odeh," June 20, 1979, 13.

11   Special Committee, "Testimony of Rasmieh Odeh," June 21, 1979, 3, 5; Special Committee, "Testimony of Aisha Odeh," June 21, 1979, 4–5.

12   Abdo, *Captive Revolution*, 68–70.

13   Special Committee, "Testimony of Rasmieh Odeh," June 21, 1979, 3, 4, 6.

14   Special Committee, "Testimony of Rasmieh Odeh," June 20, 1979, 10.

15   Special Committee, "Testimony of Aisha Odeh," June 21, 1979, 5. The Palestinian commandos who murdered the school children at Ma'alot had first demanded the release of "twenty of their comrades in Israeli prisons." Ronen Bergman, *Rise and Kill First: The Secret History of Israel's Targeted Assassinations* (New York: Random House, 2018), 190. It cannot be determined whether the names on the guerrillas' list included Rasmea or Aisha Odeh; but if so, that would certainly explain the heightened hostility of the Neve Tirza authorities and the Israeli inmates.

16   Special Committee, "Testimony of Aisha Odeh," June 22, 1979, 6.

17   Special Committee, "Testimony of Rasmieh Odeh," June 21, 1979, 4.

18   Special Committee, "Testimony of Rasmieh Odeh," June 20, 1979, 9.

19   Special Committee, "Testimony of Aisha Odeh," June 22, 1979, 5; Special Committee, "Testimony of Rasmieh Odeh," June 21, 1979, 5.

20   Special Committee, "Testimony of Rasmieh Odeh," June 21, 1979, 5; Human Rights Watch, *Prison Conditions in Israel*, 28.

21   Human Rights Watch, *Prison Conditions in Israel*, 40, 41, 52, 53.

22   Special Committee, "Testimony of Aisha Odeh," June 22, 1979, 6.

23 Special Committee, "Testimony of Aisha Odeh," June 22, 1979, 6, 7.
24 Special Committee, "Testimony of Rasmieh Odeh," June 20, 1979, 13, 14.
25 Antonius, "Prisoners for Palestine," 51.
26 Special Committee, "Testimony of Aisha Odeh," June 22, 1979, 8; Special Committee, "Testimony of Rasmieh Odeh," June 20, 1979, 13.
27 Special Committee, "Testimony of Rasmieh Odeh," June 20, 1979, 13.
28 Special Committee, "Testimony of Rasmieh Odeh," June 20, 1979, 11.
29 Special Committee, "Testimony of Rasmieh Odeh," June 20, 1979, 8.
30 Special Committee, "Testimony of Rasmieh Odeh," June 20, 1979, 12.
31 Abdo, *Captive Revolution*, 168.
32 Abdo, *Captive Revolution*, 167.
33 Human Rights Watch, *Prison Conditions in Israel*, 57.
34 Abdo, *Captive Revolution*, 180.
35 Special Committee, "Testimony of Rasmieh Odeh," June 21, 1979, 3; Special Committee, "Testimony of Aisha Odeh," June 22, 1979, 7.
36 Antonius, "Prisoners for Palestine," 50; Abdo, *Captive Revolution*, 170; Special Committee, "Testimony of Rasmieh Odeh," June 20, 1979, 14.
37 Special Committee, "Testimony of Rasmieh Odeh," June 20, 1979, 14.
38 Abdo, *Captive Revolution*, 180.
39 *Women in Struggle.*
40 Antonius, "Prisoners for Palestine," 51.
41 United States v. Odeh, Notice of Filing Government's Trial Exhibits, docket #186, exhibit 11.
42 Special Committee, "Testimony of Rasmieh Odeh," June 20, 1979, 14.
43 Special Committee, "Testimony of Afifa Bannoura," June 21, 1979, 15.
44 Special Committee, "Testimony of Aisha Odeh," June 22, 1979, 11–12.
45 Special Committee, "Testimony of Aisha Odeh," June 22, 1979, 11–12.
46 Special Committee, "Testimony of Rasmieh Odeh," June 20, 1979, 14.
47 Antonius, "Prisoners for Palestine," 50. A small number of Israeli women at Neve Tirza also demanded to be treated as political prisoners. Barbara Harlow, *Barred: Women, Writing, and Political Detention* (Middletown, CT: Wesleyan University Press, 1992), 114.
48 Special Committee, "Testimony of Aisha Odeh," June 22, 1979, 3.
49 Special Committee, "Testimony of Afifa Bannoura," June 21, 1979, 15.
50 Special Committee, "Testimony of Rasmieh Odeh," June 20, 1979, 13, 14.
51 Special Committee, "Testimony of Aisha Odeh," June 22, 1979, 7; Special Committee, "Testimony of Rasmieh Odeh," June 21, 1979, 5.
52 Special Committee, "Testimony of Rasmieh Odeh," June 20, 1979, 9; June 21, 1979, morning session, 5; Special Committee, "Testimony of Aisha Odeh," June 22, 1979, 8, 9; Abdo, *Captive Revolution*, 89.
53 Human Rights Watch, *Prison Conditions in Israel*, 46.
54 "Israel's Prison Academies," *Atlantic*, October 1989, 26–27, quoted in Human Rights Watch, *Prison Conditions in Israel*, 46.
55 Abdo, *Captive Revolution*, 132.
56 Antonius, "Prisoners for Palestine," 52; spelling in the original.

Chapter 7

1 David Raab, *Terror in Black September: The First Eyewitness Account of the Infamous 1970 Hijackings* (New York: Palgrave Macmillan, 2007), 16.

2 *Tell Your Tale, Little Bird.*

3 United States v. Odeh, Sentencing Memorandum of the United States, docket #161, 17.

4 Sarah Irving, *Leila Khaled: Icon of Palestinian Liberation* (London: Pluto Press, 2012), 53.

5 John M. Lee, "Hijacking Mastermind Is No. 2 in the Popular Front," *New York Times*, September 14, 1970.

6 Raab, *Terror in Black September*, 124, 128–29.

7 Raab, *Terror in Black September*, 85, 205.

8 Raab, *Terror in Black September*, 87.

9 Golda Meir responded that Israel would not release any terrorists, whom she regarded as "murders who had blown up cafeterias and killed civilians." She might have added supermarkets, as the Supersol bombing, with two civilian fatalities, had happened within a few days of the non-lethal explosion at the Hebrew University cafeteria. Raab, *Terror in Black September*, 164.

10 Raab, *Terror in Black September*, 37.

11 Ronen Bergman, *Rise and Kill First: The Secret History of Israel's Targeted Assassinations* (New York: Random House, 2018), 140.

12 Aaron Klein, *Striking Back: The 1972 Munich Olympics Massacre and Israel's Deadly Response* (New York: Random House, 2005), 15.

13 Judah Ari Gross, "When the Prime Ministers Took Down the Hijackers," *Times of Israel*, August 13, 2015.

14 "Two Passengers on Hijacked Plane Seriously Wounded; Terrorists Separate Jews and Non-Jews on Plane," *Jewish Telegraphic Agency*, May 11, 1972.

15 Malu Halasa, "My Cousin, the Hijacker," *Lenny Letter*, January 5, 2018, https://www.lennyletter.com/story/my-cousin-the-hijacker. As the author of this article explains, the family name is variously spelled Halsa, Halasa, or Hales.

16 Stuart Jeffries, "Four Hijackers and Three Israeli PMs: The Incredible Story of Sabena Flight 571," *Guardian*, November 11, 2015; British spelling in the original.

17 Barbara Harlow, *Barred: Women, Writing, and Political Detention* (Middletown, CT: Wesleyan University Press, 1992), 102.

18 Special Committee, "Testimony of Rasmieh Odeh," June 20, 1979, 12.

19 Bergman, *Rise and Kill First*, 141.

20 Klein, *Striking Back*, 17.

21 Klein, *Striking Back*, 40.

22 "Incredibly, they're going on with it. It's almost like having a dance at Dachau." Jim Murray, "Blood on Olympus," *Los Angeles Times*, September 7, 1972; Bergman, *Rise and Kill First*, 149.

23 Klein, *Striking Back*, 49; United States v. Odeh, Sentencing Memorandum of the United States, docket #161.

24   Klein, *Striking Back*, 49; Kay Schiller and Christopher Young, *The 1972 Munich Olympics and the Making of Modern Germany* (Berkeley: University of California Press, 2010), 196–97.

25   United States v. Odeh, Sentencing Memorandum of the United States, docket #161.

26   Schiller and Young, *Munich Olympics*, 200–201.

27   Schiller and Young, *Munich Olympics*, 201.

28   Bergman, *Rise and Kill First*, 202.

29   The hijackers correctly suspected that the so-called Nairobi Five had been transferred to Israel. Bergman, *Rise and Kill First*, 203.

30   Bergman, *Rise and Kill First*, 200.

31   "Hijacking of Air France Airbus by Followers of Popular Front for the Liberation of Palestine – Israeli Action to Liberate Hostages held at Entebbe Airport – Inconclusive Debate at UN Security Council – Ugandan Recriminations against Britain and Kenya – Severance of Diplomatic Relations with Uganda by Britain," *Keesing's Record of World Events* (formerly Keesing's Contemporary Archives), Vol. 22, August 1976.

32   Bergman, *Rise and Kill First*, 204.

33   "1976: Israelis Rescue Entebbe Hostages," BBC: On This Day, accessed October 18, 2019, http://news.bbc.co.uk/onthisday/hi/dates/stories/july/4/newsid_27860 00/2786967.stm; Bergman, *Rise and Kill First*, 207.

34   Bergman, *Rise and Kill First*, 227.

35   See William Robert Johnson, "Chronology of Terrorist Attacks in Israel," current through March 2018, accessed January 14, 2020, http://www.johnstonsarchive. net/terrorism/terrisrael.html.

36   "Massacre of 18 in Kiryat Shemona Continues to Provoke Indignation," *Jewish Telegraphic Agency*, April 18, 1974.

37   "Israel in First Prisoner Exchange with Arab Terrorist Organization," *Jewish Telegraphic Agency*, March 15, 1979; Mark Segal, "Terrorist-held Israeli Freed for 76 Prisoners," *Jerusalem Post*, March 15, 1979.

38   Wolf Blitzer, "Begin, Sadat Split Differences," *Jerusalem Post*, March 27, 1979; Shmuel Katz, "The Bare Realities," *Jerusalem Post*, March 30, 1979.

39   Hirsh Goodman, "Bartering with Terrorists," *Jerusalem Post*, March 23, 1979.

40   The disproportionate trade was extremely controversial within Israel, not only because it appeared to reverse the long-standing policy against hostage negotiations, as had been invoked at Munich, but also because it threatened to set a precedent for even more lopsided exchanges in the future—which indeed it did. Katz, "Bare Realities"; "Trading with Terror," *Jerusalem Post*, March 19, 1979; Goodman, "Bartering with Terrorists"; Ronen Bergman, "Gilad Shalit and the Rising Price of Israeli Life," *New York Times*, November 9, 2011 (detailing the exchange with Hamas of 1 Israeli soldier for 1,027 Palestinian and other prisoners, including 280 who were serving life sentences for murder).

41   United States v. Odeh, transcript of proceedings, November 5, 2014, 42–43.

42   Antonius, "Prisoners for Palestine," 52.

43   Antonius, "Prisoners for Palestine," 52.

44 Male prisoners also reported the command, or invitation, to relieve themselves on the tarmac before boarding the flight, recounting it in less delicate terms. "Go on, shit," a guard told Kamal Hammari. "Go on, do it here." Hammari testified to the U.N. Special Committee that he refused, for fear that "they were taking pictures of us," and that he was beaten as a consequence. "Testimony of Kamal Hammari, June 20, 1979," in United Nations Secretary General, Special Committee to Investigate Israeli Practices Affecting the Human Rights of the Population of the Occupied Territories, *Report of the Special Committee to Investigate Israeli Practices Affecting the Human Rights of the Population of the Occupied Territories* (New York: United Nations General Assembly, 1979).

45 Special Committee, "Testimony of Rasmieh Odeh," June 20, 1979, 11, 12. Halsa was freed on November 23, 1983, when Israel released over 4,700 Palestinian and Lebanese prisoners in exchange for 8 IDF soldiers who had been captured during the 1982 Lebanon War. Jeffries, "Four Hijackers and Three Israeli PMs." Halsa settled in Amman, where she died of cancer on March 28, 2020, at the age of sixty-seven. Miko Peled, "Remembering Theresa Halasa: Revered Veteran of the Palestinian Resistance," *MintPress News*, March 31, 2020, https://www.mintpressnews.com/remembering-theresa-halasa-veteran-palestinian-resistance/266222/. The Israeli record of Odeh's release recounts that "She was requested by the terrorists in prior bargaining encounters." Ministry of Defense, State of Israel, confidential document Gimmel (undated), declassified and retrieved July 8, 2014, transmitted to U.S. Department of Justice by Apostile, August 28, 2014.

46 Special Committee, "Testimony of Kamal Hammari," June 20, 1979, 21; Antonius, "Prisoners for Palestine," 52.

47 Special Committee, "Testimony of Kamal Hammari," June 20, 1979, 21. There were other deadly Palestinian guerrilla operations during this time period in which prisoner releases were demanded—including one in the village of Ma'alot and another in the heart of Tel Aviv—but it cannot be determined whether any of the demands included Rasmea Odeh. Bergman, *Rise and Kill First*, 190, 193.

48 Segal, "Terrorist-held Israeli Freed for 76 Prisoners."

49 "[T]hey gave me a jacket, took off the blindfold, and pushed me down the stairs. That was the last push I took from the Zionists," said Hammari. Special Committee, "Testimony of Kamal Hammari," June 20, 1979, 22. Odeh was less sardonic. "When it landed, as I waited to go out, I received such a blow from behind that I thought my back was broken." Antonius, "Prisoners for Palestine," 52.

50 "Israel Exchanges 66 Palestinians for Soldier Captured in Lebanon," *New York Times*, March 15, 1979; Segal, "Terrorist-held Israeli Freed for 76 Prisoners."

Chapter 8

1 "A New Column Joins the Troops of the Revolution," *Al-Hadaf*, March 17, 1979.

2 "A New Column"; "The Liberated Comrades Meet the Children of Martyrs and School Children," *Al-Hadaf*, April 7, 1979; Hasan Farhat, "For Rasmea Odeh: The

Dawn-Lit Face," *Al-Hadaf*, April 7, 1979. Regarding *Al-Hadaf* as the magazine of the PFLP, see Khalidi, *War on Palestine*, 110.

3   Nahla Abdo, *Captive Revolution: Palestinian Women's Anti-Colonial Struggle within the Israeli Prison System* (London: Pluto Press, 2014), 204; Testimony of Rasmea Odeh, United States v. Odeh, November 6, 2014, 109. Report of Ron Nieberding, 4, United States v. Odeh, docket #213.

4   Odeh also spent some time in Syria during the years 1979–1983, although the exact duration is unknown. She told psychologist Ron Nieberding that she spent "less than a year" in Syria, and she mentioned it only in passing during her trial testimony. Report of Ron Nieberding, 4, United States v. Odeh, docket #213; Testimony of Rasmea Odeh, United States v. Odeh, November 6, 2014, 109.

5   Testimony of Rasmea Odeh, United States v. Odeh, November 6, 2014, 109.

6   Testimony of Rasmea Odeh, United States v. Odeh, November 7, 2014, 21–25. Law is an undergraduate degree in Jordan. Report of Ron Nieberding, 4, United States v. Odeh, docket #213; Mark Mondalek, "The Campaign against Rasmea Odeh," *Jacobin*, October 13, 2015, https://www.jacobinmag.com/2015/10/rasmea-odeh-palestine-israel-midwest-23-bds-fbi/. According to her official profile at the AAAN, she also "worked as a teacher and then a lawyer." Arab American Action Network, "Activist Profiles: Rasmea Odeh."

7   Amal Kawar, *Daughters of Palestine: Leading Women of the Palestinian National Movement* (Albany: State University of New York Press, 1996), 11, 24–25, 134, 135.

8   Kawar, *Daughters of Palestine*, 136.

9   Abdo, *Captive Revolution*, 69; Kawar, *Daughters of Palestine*, 24–25, 136; *Tell Your Tale, Little Bird*; *Women in Struggle*.

11 Odeh was initially informed that she had provided insufficient documentation that she was not "likely to become a public charge," requiring her to return with records from her bank account. Testimony of Rasmea Odeh, United States v. Odeh, November 6, 2014, 120.

12 United States v. Odeh, Notice of Filing Government's Trial Exhibits, docket #186, exhibit 2A.

13 "Amman" and "Jordan" were entered in adjacent boxes on the form, hence the absence of punctuation in the quotation. United States v. Odeh, Notice of Filing Government's Trial Exhibits, docket #186, exhibit 2A.

14 As noted earlier, Odeh told psychologist Ron Nieberding that she spent "less than a year." Report of Ron Nieberding, 4, United States v. Odeh, docket #213; Testimony of Rasmea Odeh, United States v. Odeh, November 6, 2014, 109.

15 United States v. Odeh, Notice of Filing Government's Trial Exhibits, docket #186, exhibit 2A.

16 United States v. Odeh, Notice of Filing Government's Trial Exhibits, docket #186, exhibit 2B. Technically, the consular approval becomes part of an immigrant packet that allows the person to apply for a visa at a port of entry. In nearly all cases, however, as in Odeh's, issuing the actual visa is a formality once all of the documents are in order.

17 Testimony of Rasmea Odeh, United States v. Odeh, November 6, 2014, 110. This story has been told in various iterations. Sometimes the child is ten, sometimes

she is five; sometimes the event happened only once, sometimes it was a regular organizing tactic; sometimes the encounter was related to AAAN organizing, sometimes it occurred years earlier. The only source is Odeh herself.

18 Nadine Naber, "Organizing after the Odeh Verdict," *Jacobin*, January 14, 2015.

19 Testimony of Rasmea Odeh, United States v. Odeh, November 6, 2014, 115.

20 Rasmea Odeh, Application for Naturalization, June 2, 2004, United States v. Odeh, No. 13-cf-20772, Government Trial Exhibit 1A. She would make a fourth such trip in early 2004.

21 Testimony of Rasmea Odeh, United States v. Odeh, November 6, 2014, 116; double negative in the original.

22 Testimony of Rasmea Odeh, United States v. Odeh, November 6, 2014, 116.

23 Odeh was born in 1947, when Lifta was under the British Mandate. East Jerusalem was governed by Jordan during the period 1948–1967, but that never included Lifta, which is on the city's western outskirts. After its depopulation during the 1948 war, the ruins of Lifta became part of Israel and were later incorporated in the Jerusalem municipality.

24 Antonius, "Prisoners for Palestine," 43; Kawar, *Daughters of Palestine*, 136. According to her official biography at the AAAN, her experience before 2004, presumably during her life in Palestine or Jordan, included "work and service in various associations including women's and workers' unions." Arab American Action Network, "Activist Profiles: Rasmea Odeh." Even some of Odeh's supporters, who deny her participation in the Supersol bombing, have conceded that "there is evidence that she was involved in the PFLP." Marguerite Dabaie, "Rasmea Odeh: Woman without a Country," *The Nib*, September 28, 2017.

25 U.S. Department of State, Bureau of Counterterrorism, "Foreign Terrorist Organizations," accessed January 20, 2020, https://2009-2017.state.gov/j/ct/rls/other/des/123085.htm.

26 Riad el-Rayes and Dunia Nahas, *Guerrillas for Palestine* (New York: St. Martin's Press, 1976), 37.

27 She also answered "No" to whether she had "**EVER** received a suspended sentence, been placed on probation, or been paroled?" It is conceivably questionable, however, whether her release in the 1979 prisoner exchange—technically an amnesty—should be considered parole.

28 Rasmea Odeh, Application for Naturalization, June 2, 2004, United States v. Odeh, No. 13-cf-20772, Government Trial Exhibit 1A.

29 Regarding the first question, Odeh admitted to Antonius that she had joined political organizations that were outlawed in pre-1967 Jordan, for which she was never arrested. Antonius, "Prisoners for Palestine," 43.

30 Rasmea Odeh, Application for Naturalization, June 2, 2004, United States v. Odeh, No. 13-cf-20772, Government Trial Exhibit 1A.

31 Testimony of Jennifer Williams, United States v. Odeh, November 6, 2014, 45.

32 Testimony of Rasmea Odeh, United States v. Odeh, November 7, 2014, 17.

33 Odeh made seventeen minor corrections to her application, but none to the crucial questions about her criminal background.

34 Testimony of Jennifer Williams, United States v. Odeh, November 6, 2014, 46.

35 Certificate of Naturalization, December 9, 2004, United States v. Odeh, No. 13-cf-20772, Government Trial Exhibit 10. At the conclusion of the naturalization interview, each applicant is given an opportunity to change his or her name. Odeh elected to changer her name to Rasmieh Joseph Steve, in honor of her brother who had recently passed away. Testimony of Rasmea Odeh, United States v. Odeh, November 7, 2014, 16–17. The certificate was therefore issued under her new name, but she reverted to Odeh and has continued to use her original surname in the following years, including at trial.

Chapter 9

1 Nehad Khader, "Rasmea Odeh: The Case of an Indomitable Woman," *Journal of Palestine Studies* 46, no. 4 (Summer 2017): 64.

2 Nesreen Hasan, "Arab American Action Network's Long Standing History of Serving Palestinians," Palestine in America, August 2016, 29.

3 *Arab Americans Arising: Case Studies of Community-based Organizations in Three American Cities*, National Network for Arab American Communities, accessed January 21, 2020, https://aaan.org/about/history/.

4 *Arab Americans Arising.*

5 Testimony of Rasmea Odeh, United States v. Odeh, November 6, 2014, 97; Arab American Action Network, "ArabAmericanMarkaz," Arab American Action Network, video, 10:15, May 7, 2012, https://www.youtube.com/watch?v=70bn4VitM_8.

6 *Arab Americans Arising*; Hasan, "Arab American Action Network's Long Standing History."

7 Corporation for National and Community Service, "What Is AmeriCorps," accessed February 5, 2020, https://www.nationalservice.gov/programs/americorps/what-americorps; Corporation for National and Community Service, "Sponsor a Vista Member," accessed February 5, 2020, https://nationalservice.gov/SponsorVista.

8 Naber, "Organizing."

9 Naber, "Organizing"; Hasan, "Arab American Action Network's Long Standing History"; Khader, "Indomitable Woman," 64.

10 Testimony of Rasmea Odeh, United States v. Odeh, Trial Transcript, November 6, 2014, 98.

11 Chicago Cultural Alliance, "Odeh: Outstanding Community Leader"; Anna Lekas Miller, "Prominent Palestinian-American Community Activist Arrested," *Daily Beast*, November 1, 2013 (updated July 11, 2017), https://www.thedailybeast.com/prominent-palestinian-american-community-activist-arrested.

12 Louise Cainkar, "Why I Advocate for Leniency for Rasmea Odeh," StopFBI.net, March 11, 2015, http://www.stopfbi.net/2015/3/11/why-i-advocate-leniency-rasmea-odeh.

13 Naber, "Organizing"; "US" so abbreviated in the original.

234   The Trials of Rasmea Odeh

14   Naber, "Organizing"; "US" so abbreviated in the original.

15   Ramah Kudaimi, "Rasmea Odeh Should Be Honored, Not Imprisoned," *Arab
     American News*, March 11, 2015, https://www.arabamericannews.com/2015/03/11/
     Rasmea-Odeh-should-be-honored-not-imprisoned/.

16   Naber, "Organizing"; Testimony of Nadine Naber, United States v. Odeh,
     November 6, 2014, 85.

17   Naber, "Organizing"; "US" so abbreviated in the original.

18   Naber, "Organizing"; italics in the original; Testimony of Nadine Naber, United
     States v. Odeh, November 6, 2014, 86, 90.

19   Testimony of Rasmea Odeh, United States v. Odeh, November 6, 2014, 98; Louise
     Cainkar, "Why I Advocate for Leniency for Rasmea Odeh," Rasmea Defense
     Committee, March 11, 2015, http://justice4rasmea.org/news/2015/03/11/
     why-I-advocate-for-leniency-for-Rasmea-Odeh/.

20   Chicago Cultural Alliance, "About," accessed February 7, 2020, https://www.chi
     cagoculturalalliance.org/about/. There are no Jewish organizations among the
     forty-three core members listed on the Chicago Cultural Alliance website, but I
     have been separately informed that the Illinois Holocaust Museum is an active
     participant and "they were thrilled to have us."

21   Chicago Cultural Alliance, "Outstanding Community Leader Award Nomination
     Form," received February 25, 2020. On file with author.

22   Teresita Aviles Bailey, Chicago Cultural Alliance, email message, February 25,
     2020. Odeh shared the 2013 award with Kerstin Lane, the executive director
     of the Swedish National Museum and honorary Consul General of Sweden.
     Chicago Cultural Alliance, "Kerstin Lane: Outstanding Community Leader,"
     Chicago Cultural Alliance, video, 4:35, May 13, 2013, https://www.youtube.com/
     watch?v=mpOwg-IQCy8.

23   Chicago Cultural Alliance, "Odeh: Outstanding Community Leader."

24   Arab American Action Network, "Activist Profiles: Rasmea Odeh"; quotation
     marks and brackets in the original.

25   Amal Kawar, *Daughters of Palestine: Leading Women of the Palestinian
     National Movement* (Albany: State University of New York Press, 1996), 11, 24–25,
     134, 135.

26   Institute for Global Education, "Justice for Rasmea—September 22 Update,"
     https://www.igegr.org/2016/09/16/justice-rasmea-odeh-september-22-update/.

27   Jillian Kay Melchior, "Convicted Terrorist Worked as Obamacare Navigator
     in Illinois," *National Review*, February 26, 2014, https://www.nationalreview.
     com/2014/02/convicted-terrorist-worked-obamacare-navigator-illinois-jillian-ka
     y-melchior/.

28   Testimony of Nadine Naber, United States v. Odeh, November 6, 2014, 80, 90.

29   Kudaimi, "Odeh Should Be Honored."

30   Charles Davis, "The FBI's Failed Two-Year Campaign against a Group of Non-Violent
     Activists in the Midwest," *Vice*, March 31, 2014; Peter Wallsten, "Activists Cry Foul
     over FBI Probe," *Washington Post*, June 13, 2011; Committee to Stop FBI Repression,
     "One Year Since the September 24 FBI Raids and Grand Jury Subpoenas," *Fight
     Back News*, September 23, 2011, http://www.fightbacknews.org/2011/9/23/one-

year-september-24-fbi-raids-and-grand-jury-subpoenas; Freedom Road Socialist Organization, "Resistance Is the Key: The 2010 FBI Raids on Anti-War and International Solidarity Activists," *Fight Back News*, September 24, 2019, http://www. fightbacknews.org/2019/9/24/resistance-key-2010-fbi-raids-anti-war-and-internati onal-solidarity-activists.

31 Fight Back News, "Fighting Repression 4 Years after FBI Raids on Anti-War, International Solidarity Activists," *Fight Back News*, September 23, 2014, http:// www.fightbacknews.org/2014/9/23/fighting-repression-4-years-after-fbi-raids-anti-war-international-solidarity-activists.

32 Committee to Stop FBI Repression, "One Year since the September 24 FBI Raids."

33 Davis, "The FBI's Failed Two-Year Campaign."

34 Andy Grimm and Cynthia Dizikes, "FBI Raids Anti-War Activists' Homes," *Chicago Tribune*, September 24, 2010.

35 "Operation Order/FBI SWAT-Minneapolis, 415U-MP-70824, accessed February 11, 2020, http://www.stopfbi.net/sites/default/files/CSFR%20May%2018%20doc uments%20ALL.pdf.

36 18 U.S. Code § 2339B.

37 Affidavit of John P. Thomas, September 23, 2010, accessed February 11, 2020, https://vice-asset-uploader-cdn.vice.com/files/1396281030Search_Warrant_Files_ Part_I_r.pdf.

38 Search and Seizure Warrant, United States District Court, District of Minnesota, no. 10-MJ-389-SRN, accessed February 11, 2020, https://vice-asset-uploader-cdn. vice.com/files/1396281030Search_Warrant_Files_Part_I_r.pdf.

39 Subpoena to Testify before Grand Jury, United States District Court, Northern District of Illinois, no. 09—GJ-717, accessed February 11, 2020, http://www. stopfbi.net/sites/default/files/CSFR%20May%2018%20documents%20ALL.pdf.

40 Subpoena to Testify before Grand Jury, United States District Court, Northern District of Illinois, no. 09—GJ-717, accessed February 11, 2020, http://www. stopfbi.net/sites/default/files/CSFR%20May%2018%20documents%20ALL.pdf.

41 Committee to Stop FBI Repression, "U.S. Attorney Escalates Attacks on Civil Liberties of Anti-War, Palestinian Human Rights Activists," *Fight Back News*, May 8, 2011, http://www.fightbacknews.org/2011/5/8/us-attorney-escalates-at tacks-civil-liberties-anti-war-palestinian-human-rights-activists; "FBI Confirms That They Copied Tens of Thousands of Documents Seized from the Homes of Local Anti-War Activists; Originals Returned, Indictments Still Looming," 4strugglemag, November 2, 2011, https://4strugglemag.org/2011/11/02/fbi-con firms-that-they-copied-tens-of-thousands-of-documents-seized-from-the-homes-of-local-anti-war-activists-originals-returned-indictments-still-looming/; "FBI Returns Personal Papers to Hatem Abudayyeh," *Fight Back News*, September 17, 2014, http://www.fightbacknews.org/2014/9/17/fbi-returns-personal-papers-hatem-abudayyeh.

42 "Barry Jonas, of Chicago U.S. Attorney's Office, Refuses to Return Materials from FBI Raid," StopFBI.net, August 8, 2012; Fight Back News, "On the Anniversary of the FBI Raids on Anti-War and International Solidarity Activists, Contribute to

the Defense of Rasmea Odeh," *Fight Back News*, September 24, 2015, http://www.fightbacknews.org/2015/9/24/anniversary-fbi-raids-anti-war-and-international-solitary-activists-contribute-defense-ras.

43 Communication from Confidential Source A, August 7, 2018. According to one of Odeh's attorneys, "What happened was that during that raid of the home of these activists, the FBI came across Rasmea's name at the AAAN and then reached out to the Israelis who immediately provided them with their information on her trial and conviction." Ray Hanania, "Rasmea Odeh Sentenced to 18 Months Prison," *Arab Daily News*, November 11, 2014.

44 Affidavit of John P. Thomas, September 23, 2010, accessed February 11, 2020, https://vice-asset-uploader-cdn.vice.com/files/1396281030Search_Warrant_Files_Part_I_r.pdf.

45 Motion to Dismiss Indictment, United States v. Odeh, docket #48–2, July 23, 2014.

46 Communication from Confidential Source B, February 14, 2020.

47 Discovery Notice, United States v. Odeh, docket #12, filed November 19, 2013. Photographs of Odeh show her visiting the Old City in East Jerusalem, the annexation of which to Israel is not recognized by Palestinians, Jordan, or Arab states.

48 18 U.S. Code § 1425(b).

49 Fight Back News, "Palestinian Activist Rasmea Odeh Given Nelson Mandela Award," *Fight Back News*, December 10, 2013, http://www.fightbacknews.org/2013/12/10/palestinian-activist-rasmea-odeh-given-nelson-mandela-award.

Chapter 10

1 Government's Motion and Supporting Brief to Seal Indictment and Arrest Warrant, United States v. Odeh, docket #1, October 17, 2013.

2 Indictment, United States v. Odeh, docket #3, October 17, 2013.

3 Motion in Limine of the United States to Exclude (1) Evidence Relating to Claims of Innocence of Underlying Foreign Convictions and (2) Allegations of Torture, United States v. Odeh, docket #34, 11, filed July 10, 2014.

4 National Lawyers Guild, "NLG Chicago: Jim Fennerty," undated video, 16:43, ca 2016, accessed February 12, 2020, https://vimeo.com/146698892; Sarah Gelsomino, "News from the Board," National Lawyers Guild of Chicago, March 2012, https://nlgchicago.org/wp-content/uploads/NLGChicagoNewsletter_MARCH2012.pdf; National Lawyers Guild Chicago, "NLG Lawyer Representing CAARPR Activist in Contempt Case," National Lawyers Guild Chicago, March 29, 2019, https://nlgchicago.org/blog/nlg-lawyer-representing-caarpr-activist-incontempt-case/; https://nlgchicago.org/?s=Lawyer+Representing+CAARPR+Activist/.

5 "Local Palestinian-American Faces Prison or Deportation," *Worldview*, WBEZ Radio, Chicago: WBEZ, November 20, 2013.

6 Amal Kawar, *Daughters of Palestine: Leading Women of the Palestinian National Movement* (Albany: State University of New York Press, 1996), 24–25, 136.

7 Order Setting Conditions of Release, United States v. Odeh, docket #7, October 22, 2013.

8   "Local Palestinian-American Faces Prison or Deportation."

9   Ali Abunimah, "Rasmea Odeh's Day in Court," *Electronic Intifada*, November 14, 2013, https://electronicintifada.net/blogs/ali-abunimah/rasmea-odehs-day-court; United States v. Odeh, Minute Entries, November 13, 2013, docket #7 and #9.

10   Abunimah, "Rasmea Odeh's Day in Court."

11   Abunimah, "Rasmea Odeh's Day in Court."

12   Tom Burke, "Big Detroit Rally for Rasmea Odeh's Day in Court," *Fight Back News*, November 13, 2013, http://www.fightbacknews.org/2013/11/13/big-detroit-ral ly-rasmea-odeh-s-day-court.

13   United States v. Odeh, Attorney Appearance for William W. Swor, November 19, 2013. Swor had evidently been appointed the previous day pursuant to the Criminal Justice Act, meaning that the court would pay attorney's fees as well as investigative and expert expenses pursuant to 18 U.S.C. § 3006A. United States v. Odeh, Minute Order, November 18, 2013.

14   "Firm Profile," William W. Swor and Associates, accessed February 12, 2020, http://www.sworlaw.com/profile.html.

15   "William (Bill) W. Swor," ACCESS (Arab Community Center for Economic and Social Services), accessed February 13, 2020, https://www.accesscommunity. org/about-us/william-bill-w-swor; "William W. Swor," AVVO, accessed February 13, 2020, https://www.avvo.com/attorneys/48226-mi-william-swor-762382.html.

16   "William (Bill) W. Swor."

17   "Firm Profile."

18   United States v. Odeh, transcript of proceedings, May 21, 2014, 11.

19   Rule 11(c), Federal Rules of Criminal Procedure.

20   United States v. Odeh, transcript of proceedings, May 21, 2014, 13. In theory, the judge could have imposed a prison sentence of up to six months, but there was an implicit understanding that Odeh would not serve time under the agreement.

21   United States v. Odeh, transcript of proceedings, May 21, 2014, 14.

22   At a press conference, Deutsch, of Chicago's People's Law Office, identified himself as a member of Odeh's legal team. Lauren Zumbach, "Lawyer: Palestinian Community Activist Unfairly Targeted," *Chicago Tribune*, November 12, 2013. Fennerty spoke as "one of Rasmea's lawyers" at a "Town Hall" meeting held at the Aqsa School in Bridgeview, Illinois, a Chicago suburb. "Rasmea's Case and How We Can Help," The Coalition to Protect Peoples Rights, February 7, 2014 (misdated February 7, 2013).

23   US Palestinian Community Network, "USPCN Joins 50 Organizations to Stand against the Persecution of Palestinian American Activist Rasmea Odeh," US Palestinian Community Network, October 24, 2013, https://uspcn.org/2013/10/24/ uspcn-joins-50-organizations-to-stand-against-the-persecution-of-palestinian-am erican-activist-rasmea-odeh/.

24   "USPCN Joins."

25   Maureen Clare Murphy, "Palestinian Arrested in Chicago because of Her Community Activism, Groups Say," *Electronic Intifada*, October 26, 2013, https://electronicinti fada.net/blogs/maureen-clare-murphy/palestinian-arrested-chicago-because-her-co mmunity-activism-groups-say.

26 "Raison d'être," *Jacobin*, accessed February 16, 2020, https://jacobinmag.com/about.

27 United States Palestinian Community Network, "A Statement on the Arrest of Rasmea Yousef Odeh," *Jacobin*, November 11, 2013, https://www.jacobin mag.com/2013/11/a-statement-on-palestinian-activist-rasmea-yousef-odeh.

28 Fight Back News, "Attorney: Why Is Rasmea Odeh Targeted Now?" *Fight Back News*, November 12, 2013, http://www.fightbacknews.org/2013/11/12/attorney-why-rasmea-odeh-targeted-now.

29 "Peace and Justice Committee of Episcopal Diocese of Chicago Stands in Solidarity with Rasmea Odeh," USPCN, March 28, 2014. Similar statements were issued by the executive director of the United African Organization, the Minnesota Welfare Rights Committee, and Fr. Robert Bossie, SCJ of Chicago.

30 "Local Palestinian-American Faces Prison or Deportation."

31 Orders, United States v. Odeh, docket #20, #21, and #22; Josh Gerstein, "Arab Activist Balks at Guilty Plea in Detroit," *Politico*, May 21, 2014; "Contrary to Erroneous Press Reports, Rasmea Odeh Is Not Pleading Guilty," Committee to Stop FBI Repression, May 21, 2014; Hatem Abudayyeh, "Rasmea Odeh NOT Pleading Guilty," US Palestinian Community Network, May 21, 2014, https://uspcn.org/2014/05/21/rasmea-odeh-not-pleading-guilty/.

32 United States v. Odeh, transcript of proceedings, May 21, 2014, 6.

33 United States v. Odeh, transcript of proceedings, May 21, 2014, 6.

34 United States v. Odeh, transcript of proceedings, May 21, 2014, 7–8.

35 United States v. Odeh, transcript of proceedings, May 21, 2014, 11.

36 People's Law Office, "Michael E. Deutsch," accessed February 18, 2020, https://peopleslawoffice.com/about-civil-rights-lawyers/attorney-staff-bios/michael-e-deutsch/.

37 "Victory: Bank Returns Abudayyeh Family Money, Government Involvement Alleged," *U.S. Palestinian Community News*, May 10, 2011; "I am one of the attorneys representing the political activists," Michael Deutsch of People's Law Office to Congresswoman Jan Schakowsky, letter, April 21, 2011 (misdated 2010), April 26, 2011, stopfbi.net.

38 United States v. Odeh, transcript of proceedings, May 28, 2014, 9.

39 United States v. Odeh, transcript of proceedings, May 28, 2014, 10.

40 "Tukel, Jonathan," University of Michigan Law School, accessed February 20, 2020, https://www.law.umich.edu/FacultyBio/Pages/FacultyBio.aspx?FacID=jtukel.

41 United States Department of Justice, "Umar Farouk Abdulmutallab Sentenced to Life in Prison for Attempted Bombing of Flight 253 on Christmas Day 2009," February 16, 2012, https://www.justice.gov/opa/pr/umar-farouk-abdulmutallab-sentenced-life-prison-attempted-bombing-flight-253-christmas-day.

42 Fight Back News, "More Victories for the Defense in Rasmea's Case," *Fight Back News*, June 15, 2016, http://www.fightbacknews.org/2016/6/15/more-victories-defense-rasmea-s-case.

43 Motion in Limine of United States to Exclude at Trial Any Claim, Questioning or Argument in Support of Alleged Selective Prosecution, United States v. Odeh, docket #33.

44 Motion in Limine of United States to Rule Admissible for Trial Foreign Evidence Produced Pursuant to Mutual Legal Assistance Treaty, United States v. Odeh, docket #36.

45 Motion in Limine of the United States to Exclude (1) Evidence Relating to Claims of Innocence of Underlying Foreign Convictions and (2) Allegations of Torture, United States v. Odeh, docket #34. There was also a fourth, less significant, prosecution motion to exclude evidence of the "consequences of conviction."

46 Rasmea Odeh's Motions in Limine, United States v. Odeh, docket #41. In an interview, Deutsch said "people who are fighting against illegal occupation can never be terrorists, they're not terrorists, they're freedom fighters," Interview with Michael Deutsch, video (undated) ca 2016, (link since removed), https://m.youtube.com/watch?v=qCVymVtXLXs.

47 In her lengthy series of interviews with a psychologist retained by defense counsel, Odeh described her torture in detail, mentioning only a single incident of sexual violation with a stick. Affidavit of Dr. Mary Fabri, July 18, 2014, United States v. Odeh, docket #45, filed July 18, 2014.

48 Brief in Support of Rasmea Odeh's Motion in Limine, United States v. Odeh, docket #41, 2, 4, 6, 13.

Chapter 11

1 Arab America, "New Date of October 21st Set for Trial of Rasmea Odeh," Arab America, May 28, 2014, https://www.arabamerica.com/rasmea-yousef-odeh-to-appear-in-detroit-court-on-wednesday-may-28th/. Although Odeh had dismissed Swor on May 21, formal appearances of the new lawyers were not filed until June 9 (Deutsch) and June 27 (Fennerty). An additional appearance was filed on July 3 by William Goodman of Detroit, who until then had been appearing only as local counsel.

2 Rasmea Defense Committee, "List of Organizations," Rasmea Defense Committee, accessed February 19, 2020, http://justice4rasmea.org/defense-committee/.

3 "Board-Staff," Arab American Action Network, accessed February 25, 2020, https://aaan.org/about/board-staff/; Hatem Abudayyeh, "A Palestinian's Tribute to Muhammad Ali," *Chicago Monitor*, July 8, 2016; Loren Lybarger, *Palestinian Chicago: Identity in Exile* (Oakland: University of California Press, 2020), 61, 63.

4 *Independent Lens: The New Americans*, "Palestinian Bride," episode 1, directed by Jerry Blumenthal, Gordon Quinn, Fenell Doremus (Chicago: Kartemquin Films, 2004) video, aired March 29, 2004, on PBS, (link since removed), https://www.pbs.org/independentlens/newamericans/newamericans/palestinian_episode1.html.

5 Fight Back News, "Israel and U.S. Wage War on Lebanon and Palestine," *Fight Back News*, July 22, 2006, http://www.fightbacknews.org/2006/03/hateminterview.htm.

6 Lybarger, *Palestinian Chicago*, 80.

7 Fight Back News, "Israel and U.S. Wage War"; Hatem Abudayyeh, "Victory for the Palestinian People," *Fight Back News*, March 9, 2009, http://www.fightbacknews.org/2009/03/gaza-war-victory-for-palestinian-people.htm.

8   Kristin Szremski, "AAAN's Abudayyeh Struggles to Rebuild after Fire Guts Office," *Washington Report on Middle East Affairs*, January–February, 2002.

9   Dahr Jamail, "Tortured and Raped by Israel, Persecuted by the United States," *Truthout*, September 2, 2014.

10 "Judge Borman Steps Down from the Case of Rasmea Odeh," StopFBI.net, August 12, 2014. Abudayyeh also said, "Winning this case is not limited to a legal strategy." "Replace Pro-Israeli Judge, Say Odeh Lawyers," StopFBI.net, July 16, 2014.

11 Jamail, "Tortured and Raped by Israel"; abbreviation and capitalization in the original.

12 Charlotte Silver, "Judge with Strong Israel Ties Refuses to Step Down in Case against Palestinian-American," *Electronic Intifada*, August 6, 2014, https://electronicin tifada.net/blogs/charlotte-silver/judge-strong-israel-ties-refuses-step-down-case-against-palestinian-american.

13 US Palestinian Community Network, "Critical Ethnic Studies Association Supports Rasmea Odeh," US Palestinian Community Network, May 13, 2014, https:// uspcn.org/2014/05/13/critical-ethnic-studies-association-supports-rasmea-odeh/; Committee to Stop FBI Repression, "Critical Ethnic Studies Association Supports Rasmea Odeh," American Friends Service Committee, May 13, 2014, https://www. afsc.org/event/winning-justice-palestine-middle-east-peace-process-and-bds-mov ement.

14 Lauren Zumbach, "Lawyer: Palestinian Community Activist Unfairly Targeted," *Chicago Tribune*, November 12, 2013.

15 Terry Joffe Benaryeh, "Rasmieh Yousef Odeh Must Not Be Allowed to Continue the Violence," Associated Press, July 29, 2014.

16 Ali Abunimah, "Why Is Obama Administration Prosecuting Sexual Torture Victim Rasmea Odeh?" *Electronic Intifada*, June 10, 2014, https://electronicintifada.net/ blogs/ali-abunimah/why-obama-administration-prosecuting-sexual-torture-vic tim-rasmea-odeh; Charlotte Silver, "US Judge's Pro-Israel Activism challenged in Palestinian Organizer's Deportation Trial," *Electronic Intifada*, July 19, 2014, https:// electronicintifada.net/blogs/charlotte-silver/us-judges-pro-israel-activism-challe nged-palestinian-organizers-deportation; Charlotte Silver, "Court Motion Details Palestinian American Rasmea Odeh's Torture by Israeli Jailers," *Electronic Intifada*, July 31, 2014, https://electronicintifada.net/blogs/charlotte-silver/court-motion-details-palestinian-american-rasmea-odehs-torture-israeli; Josh Gerstein, "Defense Wants Pro-Israel Federal Judge Off Case," *Politico*, July 15, 2014; "Women's Magazine: Labor Day Focus on Immigrant Women (interview with Nadine Naber)," KPFA, September 1, 2014; Azadeh Shahshahani, "Demanding Justice from Chicago to Palestine," *Guild Notes*, Winter 2014, 3; Lybarger, *Palestinian Chicago*, 185.

17 Jamail, "Tortured and Raped by Israel."

18 "14 East Jerusalem, West Bank Arabs Held by Israel in Supermarket Bombing," *Jewish Telegraphic Service*, February 25, 1969; "14 Remanded for Fortnight as Blast Suspects," *Jerusalem Post*, February 24, 1969. Because the roundups were intended to reassure the Israeli public, the police had every reason to exaggerate, rather than minimize, the number of Palestinians detained for questioning.

19 US Palestinian Community Network, "Peace and Justice Committee of Episcopal Diocese of Chicago Stands in Solidarity with Rasmea Odeh," US Palestinian Community Network, March 28, 2014, https://uspcn.org/2014/03/28/peace-and -justice-committee-of-episcopal-diocese-of-chicago-stands-in-solidarity-with-ras mea-odeh/.

20 Committee to Stop FBI Repression, "Critical Ethnic Studies Association."

21 Arab America, "New Date of October 21st Set for Trial of Rasmea Odeh."

22 "Local Palestinian-American Faces Prison"; Jacob Meisner, "Feds: Woman Hid Terror Conviction to Get Citizenship," *Chicago Tribune*, October 22, 2013.

23 Odeh has never claimed to have had her jaw broken. In her U.N. testimony she did describe a short period of traumatic blindness while she was at Neve Tirza, but she said that it fully resolved after about ten days.

24 United States Palestinian Community Network, "Statement on the Arrest."

25 Hatem Abudayyeh, "Judge Paul Borman Recuses Himself from Rasmea's Case," US Palestinian Community Network, August 12, 2014, https://uspcn.org/2014/08/ 12/breaking-judge-paul-borman-recuses-himself-from-rasmeas-case/.

26 United States Palestinian Community Network, "Statement on the Arrest"; US Palestinian Community Network, "Call for Nakba Commemorations to Highlight Rasmea Odeh's Case," US Palestinian Community Network, May 2, 2014, https:// uspcn.org/2014/05/02/call-for-nakba-commemorations-to-highlight-rasmea-ode hs-case/; Eid Saeed, "Make Zakat-Eligible Donation," US Palestinian Community Network, August 12, 2014, https://uspcn.org/2014/07/28/reminder-rasmeas-stat us-hearing-in-detroit-july-31-make-zakat-eligible-donation/; non-punctuation and capitalization in original.

27 "In Travesty of Justice, Rasmea Odeh Found Guilty Despite History of Israeli Torture," *Mondoweiss*, November 10, 2014.

28 Amal Kawar, *Daughters of Palestine: Leading Women of the Palestinian National Movement* (Albany: State University of New York Press, 1996), 11, 24–25, 134, 135; Nahla Abdo, *Captive Revolution: Palestinian Women's Anti-Colonial Struggle within the Israeli Prison System* (London: Pluto Press, 2014), 9–10, 69; *Tell Your Tale, Little Bird*.

29 Robin Strauss, "Rasmea Odeh Conviction Part of US War on Dissent," *Freedom Socialist*, December 2014, https://socialism.com/fs-article/rasmea-odeh-convic tion-part-of-us-war-on-dissent/.

30 Jamail, "Tortured and Raped by Israel."

Chapter 12

1 United States v. Odeh, transcript of proceedings, May 28, 2014, 5.

2 Motion to Recuse the Honorable Paul D. Borman, United States v. Odeh, docket #44.

3 Brief in Support of Ms. Odeh's Recusal Motion, United States v. Odeh, docket #44.

4 See 28 U.S. Code § 455(a). Disqualification of justice, judge, or magistrate judge.

5   Motion to Recuse the Honorable Paul D. Borman, United States v. Odeh, docket #44; misquotation of statute in the original.

6   Motion to File Supplemental Document in Support of Defendant's Motion for Recusal, United States v. Odeh, docket #57.

7   Response and Brief of the United States in Opposition to Defendant's Motion to Disqualify the Honorable Paul D. Borman, United States v. Odeh, docket #53.

8   Opinion and Order Denying Defendant's Motion to Recuse, United States v. Odeh, docket #58.

9   "Judge Borman Steps Down from the Case of Rasmea Odeh," StopFBI.net, August 12, 2014.

10 Tom Burke, "Rasmea Odeh Court Hearing, Judge Borman Refuses to Step Down," *Fight Back News*, August 1, 2014, http://www.fightbacknews.org/2014/8/1/rasmea-odeh-court-hearing-judge-borman-refuses-step-down.

11 Silver, "Judge with Strong Israel Ties."

12 Bill Chambers, "USA vs. Rasmea Odeh: Pro-Israel Judge Refuses to Step Down," *Chicago Monitor*, August 4, 2014.

13 Buell v. Mitchell, 274 F. 3d 337 (6th Cir. 2001).

14 The motion alleged that "as a respected jurist, it is logical that this Court must have made inquiries of Israeli officials about the persistent complaints of torture and illegality of the Occupation and the military court system." Motion to Recuse the Honorable Paul D. Borman, United States v. Odeh, docket #44. The supporting brief sarcastically referred to Judge Borman as someone "who no doubts believes that Israeli is a great democracy and protector of human rights." Brief in Support of Ms. Odeh's Recusal Motion, United States v. Odeh, docket #44; misspellings in the original.

15 Opinion and Order Denying Defendant's Motion to Recuse, United States v. Odeh, docket #58, 10.

16 Opinion and Order of Recusal Sua Sponte, United States v. Odeh, docket #82, August 12, 2014.

17 Fight Back News, "Judge Borman Forced to Step Down in Case of Rasmea Odeh," *Fight Back News*, August 12, http://www.fightbacknews.org/2014/8/12/judge-borman-forced-step-down-case-rasmea-odeh; "Judge Borman Steps Down."

18 Bill Chambers, "USA vs. Rasmea Odeh—New Judge, Next Hearing," *Chicago Monitor*, August 22, 2014; Christine Geovanis, "Judge Borman Steps Down from Rasmea Odeh Case," *Palestine Legal*, August 14, 2014.

19 Charlotte Silver, "Judge in Case against Palestinian-American Pulls out Due to Israel Business Ties," *Electronic Intifada*, August 12, 2014, https://electronicintifada.net/blogs/charlotte-silver/judge-case-against-palestinian-american-pulls-out-due-israel-business-ties.

20 Abudayyeh, "Borman Recuses Himself."

21 "Gershwin A. Drain," Eastern District of Michigan, United States District Court, accessed March 2, 2020, https://www.mied.uscourts.gov/index.cfm?pageFunction=chambers&judgeid=36.

22 "Palestinian American Activist Asks Judge to Drop Charges Based on 'Illegal' US Investigation," *Electronic Intifada*, September 3, 2014.

23 Government's Motion in Limine to Rule Admissible at Trial Foreign Evidence Produced Pursuant to Mutual Legal Assistance Treaty, United States v. Odeh, docket #67.

24 Motion in Limine to Exclude All Evidence Created and Produced by the Israel [sic] Military Occupation Legal System, United States v. Odeh, docket #59.

25 Brief in Support of Rasmea Odeh's Motions in Limine to Exclude All Evidence Created and Produced by the Israel [sic] Military Occupation Legal System, United States v. Odeh, docket #59-1.

26 Order Denying Defendant's Motion to Exclude Evidence Produced by the Israel Military Occupation Legal System [#59], Denying Defendant's Motion to Exclude the Specific Charges and Conviction Emanating from Defendant's Arrest and Prosecution [#60], Granting Defendant's Motion to Exclude Any Reference to Terrorist or Terrorist Activity [#61], Granting the Government's Motion to Exclude Evidence Relating to Claims of Innocence and Allegations of Torture [#66], Granting the Government's Motion to Rule Admissible Evidence Produced Pursuant to Mutual Legal Assistance Treaty [#67] and Granting the Government's Motion to Exclude Any Argument in Support of Alleged Selective Prosecution [#73], United States v. Odeh, docket #117.

27 Motion in Limine of the United States to Exclude (1) Evidence Relating to Claims of Innocence of Underlying Foreign Convictions and (2) Allegations of Torture, United States v. Odeh, docket #66.

28 United States v. Odeh, Motion/Evidentiary Hearing, October 21, 2014, transcript 39.

29 United States v. Odeh, Motion/Evidentiary Hearing, October 21, 2014, transcript 41. Order Denying Defendant's Motion to Exclude Evidence Produced by the Israel Military Occupation Legal System [#59], Denying Defendant's Motion to Exclude the Specific Charges and Conviction Emanating from Defendant's Arrest and Prosecution [#60], Granting Defendant's Motion to Exclude Any Reference to Terrorist or Terrorist Activity [#61], Granting the Government's Motion to Exclude Evidence Relating to Claims of Innocence and Allegations of Torture [#66], Granting the Government's Motion to Rule Admissible Evidence Produced Pursuant to Mutual Legal Assistance Treaty [#67] and Granting the Government's Motion to Exclude Any Argument in Support of Alleged Selective Prosecution [#73], United States v. Odeh, docket #117.

30 Order Denying Defendant's Motion to Exclude Evidence Produced by the Israel Military Occupation Legal System [#59], Denying Defendant's Motion to Exclude the Specific Charges and Conviction Emanating from Defendant's Arrest and Prosecution [#60], Granting Defendant's Motion to Exclude Any Reference to Terrorist or Terrorist Activity [#61], Granting the Government's Motion to Exclude Evidence Relating to Claims of Innocence and Allegations of Torture [#66], Granting the Government's Motion to Rule Admissible Evidence Produced Pursuant to Mutual Legal Assistance Treaty [#67] and Granting the Government's Motion to Exclude Any Argument in Support of Alleged Selective Prosecution [#73], United States v. Odeh, docket #117.

31 Motion and Brief in Support of Request for a Jury Questionnaire, United States v. Odeh, docket #94; Brief of the United States in Opposition to Defendant's Request

for a Written Jury Questionnaire, docket #96; Order Denying Defendant's Motion for Jury Questionnaire, docket #118.

32 US Palestinian Community Network, "November 4, San Jose: Justice for Rasmea Odeh," US Palestinian Community Network, November 3, 2014, https://uspcn. org/2014/11/03/november-4-san-jose-justice-for-rasmea-odeh/.

33 Fight Back News, "Vicious, Unjust Rulings in Case of Rasmea Odeh – Come to Detroit Nov. 4, Stand up for Justice!" *Fight Back News*, October 28, 2014, http:// www.fightbacknews.org/2014/10/28/vicious-unjust-rulings-case-rasmea-odeh-come-detroit-nov-4-stand-justice.

34 Ñ *Don't Stop*, Episode 14, Interview with Hatem Abudayyeh, Ñ *Don't Stop*, video, 10:05, September 10, 2014, https://www.youtube.com/watch?v=nU-e3w1TMQI.

35 Motion of the United States to Empanel an Anonymous Jury and to Take Other Measures Necessary to Ensure an Untainted Jury, United States v. Odeh, docket #97.

36 US Palestinian Community Network, "Detroit U.S. Attorney Threatens Supporters of Rasmea Odeh," US Palestinian Community Network, October 6, 2016, https:// uspcn.org/2014/10/06/detroit-u-s-attorney-threatens-supporters-of-rasmea-odeh/.

37 Order Directing the United States Marshal Service to Partially Sequester the Jury and to Perform Other Duties as Necessary, United States v. Odeh, docket #109; Order Governing Public Conduct, Courtroom Procedures and Decorum, docket #110; Supplemental Order Regarding Public Conduct, docket #121.

38 Opposition to Government's Request for an Anonymous Jury and Other Related Special Prejudicial Security Requests, United States v. Odeh, docket #101.

39 Order Granting in Part and Denying in Part the Government's Motion to Empanel an Anonymous Jury and to Take Other Measures Necessary to Ensure an Untainted Jury, United States v. Odeh, docket #107.

40 Rasmea Odeh's Motions in Limine, United States v. Odeh, docket #41. Deutsch continuously used the term "belligerent" as though it implied something distinctly angry or hostile about the Israeli occupation, when in fact it meant only that the occupation had come about during a war, in which, under international law, the parties are known as "belligerents." In oral argument before Judge Drain, Deutsch asserted that Odeh "was not involved in any terrorist activity. She was not involved in a bombing. She was not a member of the PFLP." Making such denials was appropriate for a criminal defense lawyer, although Deutsch likely knew at least that the latter claim was false. In any event, he also argued that "resisting occupation . . . is legal under international law." United States v. Odeh, Motion/Evidentiary Hearing, October 21, 2014, transcript 41, 42.

41 Order Denying Defendant's Motion for Jury Questionnaire, United States v. Odeh, docket #118.

Chapter 13

1 "Local Palestinian-American Faces Prison or Deportation," *Worldview*, WBEZ Radio, Chicago: WBEZ, November 20, 2013.

2   Arab American Action Network, "Press Conference on Palestinian Activist Rasmea Odeh," CAN TV, video, 32:57, November 18, 2013, https://www.youtube.com/watch?v=vVciKRYfKWY&feature=youtu.be.

3   Arab American Action Network, "Press Conference"; Investigative Project on Terrorism, "Spinning a Terrorist into a Victim – Part 5 – A Spin Strategy Larger Than Rasmieh Odeh Herself," *IPT News*, video, 11:41, October 31, 2014, https://www.investigativeproject.org/4639/spinning-a-terrorist-into-a-victim-part-5-a-spin/.

4   "Press Conference."

5   Lauren Zumbach, "Lawyer: Palestinian Community Activist Unfairly Targeted," *Chicago Tribune*, November 12, 2013. For video of Deutsch's statement, see Investigative Project on Terrorism, "Spinning a Terrorist into a Victim – Part 4 – Rasmieh Odeh's Changing Story," *IPT News*, video, 6:51, October 30, 2014, https://www.investigativeproject.org/4637/spinning-a-terrorist-into-a-victim-part-4-ras mieh/.

6   Ali Abunimah, "Palestinian Activist Rasmea Odeh Rejects US Plea Deal, Prepares for October Trial," *Electronic Intifada*, May 28, 2014, https://electronicintifada.net/blogs/ali-abunimah/palestinian-activist-rasmea-odeh-rejects-us-plea-deal-prepar es-october-trial.

7   United States v. Odeh, transcript of proceedings, May 28, 2014, 8, 9.

8   Affidavit of Dr. Mary Fabri, July 18, 2014, United States v. Odeh, docket #45, filed July 18, 2014.

9   Affidavit of Dr. Mary Fabri, July 18, 2014, United States v. Odeh, docket #45, filed July 18, 2014, 2–7.

10 Affidavit of Dr. Mary Fabri, July 18, 2014, United States v. Odeh, docket #45, filed July 18, 2014, 8.

11 Thomas Gutheil, *The Psychiatrist in Court: A Survival Guide* (Washington, DC: American Psychiatric Press, 1998), 28.

12 Affidavit of Dr. Mary Fabri, July 18, 2014, United States v. Odeh, docket #45, filed July 18, 2014, 3.

13 Affidavit of Dr. Mary Fabri, July 18, 2014, United States v. Odeh, docket #45, filed July 18, 2014, 10, 15.

14 Affidavit of Dr. Mary Fabri, July 18, 2014, United States v. Odeh, docket #45, filed July 18, 2014, 16.

15 Opening Brief in Support of Testimony of Expert Witness, United States v. Odeh, docket #43.

16 Reply to the Government's Opposition to Expert Testimony, United States v. Odeh, docket #52.

17 Response and Brief of the United States in Opposition to Defendant's Proposed Use of Expert Testimony Regarding Diminished Capacity, United States v. Odeh, docket #51.

18 United States v. Odeh, Evidentiary Hearing, October 21, 2014, transcript, 11.

19 United States v. Odeh, Evidentiary Hearing, October 21, 2014, transcript, 14.

20 United States v. Odeh, Evidentiary Hearing, October 21, 2014, transcript, 15–16.

21 United States v. Odeh, Evidentiary Hearing, October 21, 2014, transcript, 43, 53.

22 Order Granting Government's Motion for Reconsideration [#105] and Denying Defendant's Motion for Offer of Proof [#111], United States v. Odeh, docket #119.

23 Ali Abunimah, "Judge Refuses to Dismiss 'Baseless' Charges against Palestinian-American," *Electronic Intifada*, October 3, 2014, https://electronicintifada.net/bl ogs/ali-abunimah/judge-refuses-dismiss-baseless-charges-against-palestinian-am erican; Charlotte Silver, "Judge Deals Major Blow to Rasmea Odeh's Defense," *Electronic Intifada*, October 28, 2014, https://electronicintifada.net/blogs/char lotte-silver/judge-deals-major-blow-rasmea-odehs-defense.

24 "Rasmea Yousef Odeh Goes to Trial," *Worldview*, WBEZ Radio, Chicago: WBEZ, October 31, 2014.

25 "Odeh Goes to Trial."

Chapter 14

1   "Report: First Day of Rasmea Odeh Trial," USPCN, November 4, 2014.

2   Charlotte Silver, "Dozens Travel to Detroit."

3   Ed White, "Jury Picked in Detroit Trial of Chicago Activist," Associated Press, November 4, 2014.

4   "First Day of Rasmea Odeh Trial."

5   Margaret Collingwood Nowak, *Two Who Were There: A Biography of Stanley Nowak* (Detroit, MI: Wayne State University Press, 1989). The founder of one of the oldest integrated law firms in the United States, Ernest Goodman served as president of the National Lawyers Guild and worked with Michael Deutsch on the Attica defense, among many other accomplishments. "Ernest Goodman, 90, Civil Rights Lawyer," *New York Times*, April 2, 1997.

6   Silver, "Dozens Travel to Detroit"; Amber Shelton, "EPIC Honors Civil Rights Attorney Dennis Cunningham," The Northcoast Environmental Center, October 2, 2019, https://www.yournec.org/epic-octnov2019.

7   Jennifer Davis, "Speaking Up," Michigan Alumni Association, Fall 2011, accessed March 11, 2020, http://digitaledition.qwinc.com/publication/?i=78757&arti cle_ id=810272&view=articleBrowser&ver=html5 .

8   United States v. Odeh, transcript of proceedings, November 5, 2014, 16–37.

9   Charlotte Silver, "US Government Focuses on 45-Year-Old Israeli Military Ruling in Trial of Rasmea Odeh," *Electronic Intifada*, November 6, 2014.

10 United States v. Odeh, transcript of proceedings, November 5, 2014, 37–48.

11 "Press Conference on Palestinian Activist Rasmea Odeh."

12 Angela Davis, "Free Rasmea Odeh, Political Prisoner," *Detroit News*, November 4, 2014.

13 Shurat HaDin/Israel Law Center, accessed March 13, 2020, https://www.israel lawcenter.org/about-us/.

14 Communication from Confidential Source B, February 26, 2020.

15 Communication from Confidential Source C, March 2, 2020.

16 Salah was convicted of obstruction of justice in a related civil case and sentenced to twenty-one months in prison. At sentencing, the trial judge said that the jurors had believed the Israeli agents and disbelieved Salah. The defense attorney, however, said he had spoken to jurors who believed Salah. Michael Higgins, "21-Month Sentence for Salah," *Chicago Tribune*, July 12, 2007.

17 Michael Deutsch, "Remembering Muhammad Salah," *Electronic Intifada*, April 26, 2016.

18 United States v. Odeh, transcript of proceedings, November 5, 2014, 52, 55.

19 United States v. Odeh, transcript of proceedings, November 5, 2014, 56–57.

20 United States v. Odeh, transcript of proceedings, November 5, 2014, 66, 67.

21 United States v. Odeh, transcript of proceedings, November 5, 2014, 77.

22 *Women in Struggle.*

23 United States v. Odeh, transcript of proceedings, November 5, 2014, 79, 81.

24 United States v. Odeh, transcript of proceedings, November 5, 2014, 91.

25 United States v. Odeh, transcript of proceedings, November 5, 2014, 116–18.

26 United States v. Odeh, transcript of proceedings, November 5, 2014, 140.

27 United States v. Odeh, transcript of proceedings, November 5, 2014, 137–38.

28 United States v. Odeh, transcript of proceedings, November 5, 2014, 151.

29 United States v. Odeh, transcript of proceedings, November 5, 2014, 154.

30 United States v. Odeh, transcript of proceedings, November 6, 2014, 20–21.

31 United States v. Odeh, transcript of proceedings, November 6, 2014, 25.

32 United States v. Odeh, transcript of proceedings, November 6, 2014, 27.

33 United States v. Odeh, transcript of proceedings, November 6, 2014, 31.

34 United States v. Odeh, transcript of proceedings, November 6, 2014, 44.

35 United States v. Odeh, transcript of proceedings, November 6, 2014, 48.

Chapter 15

1 United States v. Odeh, transcript of proceedings, November 6, 2014, 75.

2 United States v. Odeh, transcript of proceedings, November 6, 2014, 90.

3 United States v. Odeh, transcript of proceedings, November 6, 2014, 93.

4 Gus Burns, "Rasmieh Odeh, Alleged Ex-Terrorist, Takes Stand in Federal Deportation Trial," MLive.com, November 6, 2014, updated April 3, 2019, accessed March 27, 2020, https://www.mlive.com/news/detroit/2014/11/rasmieh_odeh_alleged_ex-terror.html.

5 United States v. Odeh, transcript of proceedings, November 6, 2014, 105; "Report of Trial Day 3: Rasmea Takes the Stand," USPCN, November 6, 2014. Charlotte Silver, "Rasmea Odeh Takes the Stand in Her Own Defense," *Electronic Intifada*, November 7, 2014.

6 United States v. Odeh, transcript of proceedings, November 6, 2014, 106.

7 United States v. Odeh, transcript of proceedings, November 6, 2014, 107.

8 Deborah Dupre, "Rasmea Odeh on Federal Trial in Detroit: Supporters Pack Court," *Voice of Detroit*, November 7, 2014.

9 United States v. Odeh, transcript of proceedings, November 6, 2014, 111.

10 United States v. Odeh, transcript of proceedings, November 6, 2014, 112–13.
11 Nasima Yamehi, "English Teaching and Training Issues in Palestine," *TESOL Quarterly* 40, no. 4 (December 2006): 861; Arab Information Center (U.S.), "Education in Jordan," in *Education in the Arab States* (New York: Arab Information Center, 1966), 82; William Harrison, Clifford Prator, and G. Richard Tucker, *English-Language Policy Survey of Jordan: A Case Study in Language Planning* (Arlington, VA: Center for Applied Linguistics, 1975), 1, 2, 5, 7.
12 "Activist Profiles: Rasmea Odeh."
13 Report of Ron Nieberding, 4, United States v. Odeh, docket #213.
14 Special Committee, "Testimony of Aisha Odeh," June 22, 1979, 7, 11; "Testimony of Rasmieh Odeh," June 21, 1979, 4; "Testimony of Rasmieh Odeh," June 21, 1979, 3.
15 United States v. Odeh, transcript of proceedings, November 6, 2014, 17–18.
16 United States v. Odeh, transcript of proceedings, November 6, 2014, 120.
17 United States v. Odeh, transcript of proceedings, November 6, 2014, 75, 93.
18 Kevin Gosztola, "Political Case Brought against Palestinian Organizer in Chicago for Immigration Fraud," Shadowproof, October 23, 2013, https://shadowproof.com/2013/10/23/activists-targeted-by-justice-department-suspect-arrest-of-palestinian-organizer-for-immigration-fraud-connected/.
19 United States v. Odeh, transcript of proceedings, November 7, 2014, 25–26, 32–33.
20 United States v. Odeh, transcript of proceedings, November 7, 2014, 37–38.
21 United States v. Odeh, transcript of proceedings, November 7, 2014, 46, 49.
22 United States v. Odeh, transcript of proceedings, November 7, 2014, 53–54.
23 United States v. Odeh, transcript of proceedings, November 7, 2014, 62–63.
24 United States v. Odeh, transcript of proceedings, November 7, 2014, 68–71.
25 US Palestinian Community Network, "Report of Trial Day 3"; Silver, "Rasmea Odeh Takes the Stand"; Charlotte Silver, "After Tense Last Day, Jury Begins Deliberations on Rasmea Odeh," *Electronic Intifada*, November 8, 2014, https://electronicintifada.net/blogs/charlotte-silver/after-tense-last-day-jury-begins-deliberations-rasmea-odeh; Nora Barrows-Friedman, "A Political Prosecution: Inside the Trial of Rasmea Odeh," *Electronic Intifada*, November 9, 2014, https://electronicintifada.net/blogs/nora-barrows-friedman/political-prosecution-inside-trial-rasmea-odeh.
26 Burns, "Rasmieh Odeh, Alleged Ex-Terrorist, Takes Stand."
27 US Palestinian Community Network, "Report of Trial Day 3"; Silver, "Rasmea Odeh Takes the Stand"; "Jury Begins Deliberations"; Barrows-Friedman, "Political Prosecution."
28 Silver, "Rasmea Odeh Takes the Stand"; "Jury Begins Deliberations."
29 Jillian Kay Melchior, "Death in the Supermarket," *National Review*, May 21, 2014.
30 Terry Benaryeh, "Bombing Victim's Niece: Rasmea Odeh Is No Hero," *Legal Insurrection*, November 13, 2014.
31 Benaryeh, "Bombing Victim's Niece"; Silver, "Rasmea Odeh Takes the Stand."
32 Burns, "Rasmieh Odeh, Alleged Ex-Terrorist, Takes Stand."

Chapter 16

1   Steven Lubet and J.C. Lore, *Modern Trial Advocacy*, 5th ed. (Boulder, CO: National Institute for Trial Advocacy, 2015), 435.

2   United States v. Odeh, transcript of proceedings, November 7, 2014, 82–83.

3   United States v. Odeh, transcript of proceedings, November 7, 2014, 84, 87.

4   United States v. Odeh, transcript of proceedings, November 7, 2014, 95–96.

5   United States v. Odeh, transcript of proceedings, November 7, 2014, 99.

6   United States v. Odeh, transcript of proceedings, November 7, 2014, 100–101.

7   United States v. Odeh, transcript of proceedings, November 7, 2014, 105, 107

8   United States v. Odeh, transcript of proceedings, November 7, 2014, 107.

9   United States v. Odeh, transcript of proceedings, November 7, 2014, 110–11.

10   United States v. Odeh, transcript of proceedings, November 7, 2014, 111–12.

11   United States v. Odeh, transcript of proceedings, November 7, 2014, 112.

12   United States v. Odeh, transcript of proceedings, November 7, 2014, 113–15.

13   United States v. Odeh, transcript of proceedings, November 7, 2014, 118–19.

14   "Odeh Goes to Trial."

15   Opposition to Government's Request for an Anonymous Jury and Other Related Special Prejudicial Security Requests, United States v. Odeh, docket #101.

16   United States v. Odeh, transcript of proceedings, November 7, 2014, 122–23.

17   United States v. Odeh, transcript of proceedings, November 7, 2014, 124.

18   United States v. Odeh, transcript of proceedings, November 7, 2014, 128.

19   United States v. Odeh, transcript of proceedings, November 7, 2014, 140, 143.

20   United States v. Odeh, transcript of proceedings, November 10, 2014, 7.

21   Diane Bukowski, "Palestinian Heroine, Torture Victim Rasmea Odeh Convicted, Jailed in Detroit, Appeal Planned," *Voice of Detroit*, November 10, 2014.

22   Charlotte Silver, "Defense Promises to Appeal Guilty Verdict against Rasmea Odeh," *Electronic Intifada*, November 10, 2014, https://electronicintifada.net/blogs/charlotte-silver/defense-promises-appeal-guilty-verdict-against-rasmea-odeh.

23   "Chicago Activist Guilty in Terrorism-Related US Immigration Case," *Chicago Sun-Times*, November 10, 2014.

24   William Jacobson, "Rasmea Odeh Conviction: Jury Verdict," *Legal Insurrection*, November 11, 2014; Jillian Kay Melchior, "Rasmieh Gets Justice," *National Review*, November 11, 2014.

25   "Palestinian Woman Found Guilty of US Citizenship Fraud," *USA Today*, November 10, 2014.

26   Silver, "Defense Promises to Appeal."

27   Niraj Warikoo, "Palestinian Woman Guilty of Lying on Citizenship Papers," *Detroit Free Press*, November 10, 2014; Associated Press, "US Activist Found Guilty of Not Disclosing Conviction in Fatal Jerusalem Bombing," *Guardian*, November 10, 2014, photograph; Jess Sundin, "Rasmea: We Will Be Strong," video, 3:08, November 10, 2014, https://www.youtube.com/watch?v=ieFeazVZ78Q.

28   Silver, "Defense Promises to Appeal"; "Chicago Activist Guilty."

29   United States v. Odeh, report of proceedings, November 10, 2014, 12–13.

30 United States v. Odeh, report of proceedings, November 10, 2014, 15–17.

31 United States v. Odeh, report of proceedings, November 10, 2014, 17.

32 United States v. Odeh, report of proceedings, November 10, 2014, 17, 19. Defense counsel later admitted that "the Court was exasperated" upon learning that Deutsch had advised Odeh that she would not be taken into custody upon conviction. United States v. Odeh, Motion and Brief for Reconsideration of Order Revoking Defendant's Bond Pending Sentencing, docket #133, 14.

33 United States v. Odeh, report of proceedings, November 10, 2014, 21–24.

34 Bukowski, "Rasmea Odeh Convicted."

35 United States v. Odeh, Addendum to the Affidavit of Dr. Mary Fabri, docket #160–78.

36 Ali Abunimah, "Rasmea Odeh in Prolonged Solitary Confinement in Michigan Jail," *Electronic Intifada*, December 5, 2014, https://electronicintifada.net/blogs/ali-abunimah/rasmea-odeh-prolonged-solitary-confinement-michigan-jail.

37 William Jacobson, "Rasmea Odeh Wasn't Targeted for Isolation in St. Clair County Jail," *Legal Insurrection*, December 10, 2014, https://legalinsurrection.com/2014/12/no-rasmea-odeh-wasnt-targeted-for-isolation-in-st-clair-county-jail/.

38 United States v. Odeh, Motion and Brief for Reconsideration of Order Revoking Defendant's Bond Pending Sentencing, docket #133, with exhibits 1–4; and Affidavit of Defense Counsel, docket #134. The letters were heartfelt, but some of them appeared compromised. One such letter, for example, came from the 8th Day Center for Justice, a coalition of thirty-eight Catholic organizations dedicated to "a more just and peaceful world," which had awarded Odeh its Sister Mary Elsbernd Award when she was already under indictment and awaiting trial for naturalization fraud. A petition from "members of the Arab Women's Committee" included a significant number of male and non-Arab names among its 250 signatories. Most convincing was the letter from Dr. Mary Fabri, who opined that Odeh's PTSD was intensified by the immediate custody order and explained that pre-sentencing release "would afford Ms Odeh time to prepare psychologically" for incarceration.

39 United States v. Odeh, Response and Brief of United States in Opposition to Motion for Reconsideration of Order Revoking Defendant's Bond Pending Sentencing, docket #137, with attachments A–J.

40 United States v. Odeh, Defendant's Reply to Government's Response to Motion to Reinstate Bail Pending Sentencing, docket #144, 2–6.

41 United States v. Odeh, Order Granting Defendant's Motion for Reconsideration of Order Revoking Bond Pending Sentencing and Setting Conditions of Release, docket #148.

42 Many of the letters followed a template that had been circulated by Odeh's defense committee. US Palestinian Community Network, "Rasmea's Sentencing March 12 – Need Letters for Leniency," US Palestinian Community Network, January 14, 2015, https://uspcn.org/2015/01/14/rasmeas-sentencing-march-12-need-letters-for-leniency/. Other letters added details to the proposed format, not always accurately. Rev. Donald Wagner, for example, falsely asserted that Odeh had signed a "confession in Hebrew," when the actual confession, as entered in the court file,

was plainly handwritten in Arabic. Other letters repeated the claim that Odeh had been tortured for twenty-five or forty-five days, when she herself had testified that the brutality stopped after her confession on the seventh day of interrogation. United States v. Odeh, docket #160–11, #160–13, #160–49, and #160–63. The letter submitted by Odeh's nephews is docket #160–71.

43 William Jacobson, "Victim's Brother: Rasmea Odeh Deserves 'Significant Sentence,'" *Legal Insurrection*, February 15, 2015.

44 William Jacobson, "Sisters of Leon Kanner Seek 'Maximal Sentence' for Rasmea Odeh," *Legal Insurrection*, March 2, 2015.

45 Charlotte Silver, "US Demands Long Prison Term for Rasmea Odeh, Based on Israeli Accusations," *Electronic Intifada*, February 26, 2015, https://electronicintifada. net/blogs/charlotte-silver/us-demands-long-prison-term-rasmea-odeh-based-isra eli-accusations.

46 United States v. Odeh, transcript of proceedings, March 12, 2015, 11–22.

47 United States v. Odeh, transcript of proceedings, March 12, 2015, 22–35.

48 United States v. Odeh, transcript of proceedings, March 12, 2015, 39–45.

49 United States v. Odeh, transcript of proceedings, March 12, 2015, 8.

50 United States v. Odeh, transcript of proceedings, March 12, 2015, 50.

51 United States v. Odeh, transcript of proceedings, March 12, 2015, 53.

52 United States v. Odeh, transcript of proceedings, March 12, 2015, 49.

53 United States v. Odeh, transcript of proceedings, March 12, 2015, 50.

54 United States v. Odeh, transcript of proceedings, March 12, 2015, 53.

55 United States v. Odeh, transcript of proceedings, March 12, 2015, 55.

56 United States v. Odeh, transcript of proceedings, March 12, 2015, 56.

Chapter 17

1 "Odeh's Conviction a Racist Attack on Arab Americans," *Arab American News*, November 12, 2014.

2 William Jacobson, "Rasmea Odeh: DePaul Fundraiser: Conviction," *Legal Insurrection*, February 1, 2015; Catherine Kim, "Organizer Rasmea Odeh speaks at Northwestern for SJP's Israeli Apartheid Week," *Daily Northwestern*, May 16, 2017.

3 US Palestinian Community Network, "November 14, New York City: Emergency Action for Rasmea Odeh," US Palestinian Community Network, November 12, 2014, https://uspcn.org/2014/11/12/november-14-new-york-city-emergency-action-for-rasmea-odeh/; "Activists Lockdown US Federal Court in Support of Tortured Chicago Community Leader," StopFBI.net, November 12, 2014.

4 Rebecca Flint Marx, "An Arab Bakery in Oakland Full of California Love," *New York Times*, November 11, 2017.

5 Dima Khalidi, "Odeh's Guilty Verdict Doesn't Mean Her Battle for Justice Is Over," *The Hill*, November 14, 2014.

6 William Jacobson, "Rasmea Odeh Prosecutor: Justice Award," *Legal Insurrection*, May 1, 2015; Fight Back News, "Tell Arab-American Civil Rights League that Rasmea's Prosecutor Deserves No Award!" *Fight Back News*, April 29, 2015, http://www.fight

backnews.org/2015/4/29/tell-arab-american-civil-rights-leag u e - rasmea-s-prosecu tor-deserves-no-award. The award was not rescinded; it was jointly bestowed by the ACRL and the NAACP on May 1, 2015. Ali Harb, "ACRL, NAACP Honor U.S. Attorney McQuade and Judge Roberts," *Arab American News*, May 8, 2015.

7 Marc Lamont Hill, "Why Every Black Activist Should Stand with Rasmea Odeh," *Huffington Post*, October 13, 2015.

8 Annie Robbins, "New Black-Palestinian Solidarity Video Features Lauryn Hill, Rasmea Odeh, Danny Glover," *Mondoweiss*, October 14, 2015.

9 United States v. Odeh, Defendant-Appellant's Brief on Appeal, 14.

10 United States v. Odeh, Defendant-Appellant's Brief on Appeal, 27–28.

11 United States v. Odeh, Defendant-Appellant's Brief on Appeal, 7.

12 United States v. Odeh, Defendant-Appellant's Brief on Appeal, 8, 30.

13 United States v. Odeh, Defendant-Appellant's Brief on Appeal, 36.

14 United States v. Odeh, Defendant-Appellant's Brief on Appeal, 44.

15 United States v. Odeh, Brief Amicus Curiae [of] Torture Experts International, 1.

16 United States v. Odeh, Brief Amicus Curiae [of] Torture Experts International, 12, 25.

17 United States v. Odeh, audio recording of Sixth Circuit oral argument, October 14, 2015, https://www.opn.ca6.uscourts.gov/internet/court_audio/aud2.php?link=a udio/10-14-2015%20-%20Wednesday/15-1331%20USA%20v%20Rasmieh%20O d eh.mp3&name=15-1331%20USA%20v%20Rasmieh%20Odeh.

18 United States v. Odeh, audio recording of Sixth Circuit oral argument, October 14, 2015, https://www.opn.ca6.uscourts.gov/internet/court_audio/aud2.php?link= audio/10-14-2015%20-%20Wednesday/15-1331%20USA%20v%20Rasmieh%20O deh.mp3&name=15-1331%20USA%20v%20Rasmieh%20Odeh.

19 United States v. Odeh, no. 15–1331, 6th Circuit, February 25, 2016.

20 United States v. Odeh, no. 15–1331, 6th Circuit, February 25, 2016.

21 Charlotte Silver, "Rasmea Odeh May Get New Trial, US Appeal Court Rules," *Electronic Intifada*, February 25, 2016, https://electronicintifada.net/blogs/char lotte-silver/rasmea-odeh-may-get-new-trial-us-appeal-court-rules.

22 Niraj Warikoo, "The Case of Rasmieh Odeh, 68, a Former Resident of Michigan, Became a Flashpoint in the Debate over Israel," *Detroit Free Press*, February 25, 2016.

23 "Decision in Rasmea Odeh Appeal a Partial Victory," StopFBI.net, February 25, 2016.

24 Silver, "Rasmea Odeh May Get New Trial."

25 Rule 702, Federal Rules of Evidence.

26 Daubert v. Merrell Dow Pharmaceuticals, Inc., 509 U.S. 579 (1993); General Electric v. Joiner, 522 U.S. 136 (1997).

27 United States v. Odeh, Government's Motion for and Brief in Support of Mental Examination of Defendant by Government's Expert Pursuant to Rule 12.2(c)(1)(B), docket #201.

28 United States v. Odeh, Defendant's Opposition to the Government's Demand for a Mental Examination, docket #203.

29 United States v. Odeh, Order Granting Government's Motion for Mental Examination of Defendant by Government's Expert Pursuant to Rule 12.2(c)(1)(B), docket #207; capitalization in the original.

30 United States v. Odeh, Motion for Disclosure of Government Expert and for Modification of Court Order Needed to Protect the Defendant from Additional Harm, docket #208; capitalization in the original.

31 United States v. Odeh, Government's Opposition to Defendant's Motion for Disclosure of Government Expert and for Modification of Court Order, docket #209.

32 United States v. Odeh, Order Granting in Part and Denying in Part Defendant's Motion for Disclosure of Government Expert and for Modifications of Court Order Needed to Protect the Defendant from Additional Harm, docket #211.

33 Report of Ron Nieberding, 13, United States v. Odeh, docket #213.

34 Affidavit of Hawthorne Smith, October 18, 2016, 7; Psychological Addendum of Hawthorne Smith, November 14, 2016.

35 Affidavit of James Jaranson, April 28, 2016.

36 Review of Psychological Assessment of Rasmieh Yousef Odeh by David Benedek, Paul Montalbano, and Roxanna Sheaffer, appended to Response to Government's Opposition to the Admissibility of Defense Expert's PTSD Testimony, November 15, 2016, United States v. Odeh, docket #213–4.

37 Psychological Addendum of Hawthorne Smith, November 14, 2016.

38 United States v. Odeh, Opinion and Order Denying Government's Motion for a Daubert Hearing, to Preclude the Testimony of Mary Fabri, and to Reenter Judgment of Conviction, 11.

39 Yonah Jeremy Bob, "US to Retry Palestinian Convicted of Jerusalem Bombing," *Jerusalem Post*, December 7, 2016.

Chapter 18

1   United States v. Odeh, First Superseding Indictment, docket #222.

2   United States v. Odeh, Motion of the United States to Depose Prospective Witnesses, docket #234.

3   Rule 804(b)(3)(A), Federal Rules of Evidence. United States v. Odeh, Motion in Limine of the United States to Admit Evidence, docket #233, 18–26.

4   Hatem Abudayyeh, "New Indictments against Rasmea," Rasmea Defense Committee, December 13, 2016, http://justice4rasmea.org/news/2016/12/13/new-indictments-against-rasmea/.

5   Charlotte Silver, "US Brings New Charges against Rasmea Odeh," *Electronic Intifada*, December 14, 2016, https://electronicintifada.net/blogs/charlotte-silver/us-brings-new-charges-against-rasmea-odeh.

6   United States v. Odeh, Motion to Dismiss Superseding Indictment, docket #226; Brief in Support of Rasmea Odeh's Motions in Limine, docket #231, 2.

7   United States v. Odeh, Motion to Dismiss Superseding Indictment, docket #226, 3; Brief in Support of Motion to Dismiss, docket #226–1, 8.

8   Brief in Support of Rasmea Odeh's Motions in Limine, docket #231, 8, 12, 13.

9   Dr. Richard McNally, interview by the author, November 30, 2017; Richard McNally, *Remembering Trauma* (Boston, MA: Harvard University Press, 2005).

10 Dr. Elizabeth Loftus, interview by the author, October 30, 2017.

11 Dr. Luan Phan, interview by the author, August 10, 2016. Phan was a professor at the University of Illinois, Chicago, at the time of our interview.

12 Affidavit of Dr. Mary Fabri, July 18, 2014, docket #14, 11, 16.

13 United States v. Odeh, Evidentiary Hearing, October 21, 2014, 11, 16, 43, 53.

14 Affidavit of Dr. Mary Fabri, November 14, 2016, docket #243, 2.

15 Dr. Philip Resnick, interview by the author, July 2, 2018.

16 Dr. Thomas Gutheil, interview by the author, July 3, 2018; Thomas Gutheil, *The Psychiatrist as Expert Witness* (Washington, DC: American Psychiatric Press, 1998).

17 Solomon Fulero and Lawrence Wrightsman, *Forensic Psychology* (Belmont, CA: Wadsworth, 2009), 48.

18 United States v. Odeh, Evidentiary Hearing, October 21, 2014, transcript, 15.

19 Affidavit of Dr. Mary Fabri, November 14, 2016, docket #243, 2.

20 United States v. Odeh, transcript of proceedings, November 6, 2014, 117–18.

21 United States v. Odeh, transcript of proceedings, November 7, 2014, 53.

22 Noura Erakat, "When You Come for Rasmea Odeh, You Come for All of Us," *Jezebel*, March 24, 2017.

23 Linda Martin Alcoff et al., "Women of America: We're Going on Strike. Join Us so Trump Will See Our Power," *Guardian*, February 6, 2017.

24 Kyle Smith, "Meet the Terrorist behind the Next Women's March," *New York Post*, February 25, 2017; Heather Wilhelm, "The Embarrassing Confusion of the 'Women's Strike,'" *Chicago Tribune*, February 23, 2017; "'Illegal Immigrant,' 69, Who Killed Two Young Men by Blowing Up a Supermarket, and Bombed a British Consulate, Wants to Organize the 'Next Women's March' in a Day of 'Anti-Capitalist Feminism' across the US," *Daily Mail*, February 26, 2017; Angelina Newsom, "One of the 'Day Without a Woman' Protest Organizers is a Convicted Terrorist," *Washington Examiner*, February 28, 2017; Stephen Flatow, "Women's 'Resistance' Is Embracing the Wrong Palestinians," *New York Post*, March 5, 2017; William Jacobson, "Convicted Terrorist Rasmea Odeh Co-Organized March 8 #DayWithoutAWoman," *Legal Insurrection*, February 26, 2017.

25 Sofia Arias and Bill Mullen, "On March 8, Stand with Women of Palestine," *Electronic Intifada*, March 6, 2017, https://electronicintifada.net/content/8-march-stand-women-palestine/19766.

26 US Palestinian Community Network, "Rasmea Speech on IWD," US Palestinian Community Network, March 9, 2017, https://uspcn.org/2017/03/09/rasmea-iwd-jvp-tribune/; "Rasmea Speaks on International Women's Day," StopFBI.net, March 11, 2015.

27 Rasmea Defense Committee, "Rasmea Odeh Accepts a Plea Agreement with No Prison Time; Plea Hearing April 25th in Detroit," Rasmea Defense Committee, March 23, 2017, http://justice4rasmea.org/news/2017/03/23/rasmea-accepts-plea-deal/.

28 "Rasmea Odeh Accepts a Plea Agreement with No Prison Time."

29 "Plea Hearing April 25th in Detroit."

30 "Palestinian Activist Rasmea Odeh Accepts Plea Deal with No Jail Time," *Arab American News*, March 23, 2017; "Palestinian Activist Rasmea Odeh, Who Failed to Disclose Israel Terror Convictions, to Leave U.S." Associated Press, March 23,

2017; Niraj Warikoo, "Woman Who Had Terror Conviction in Israel to Be Deported," *Detroit Free Press*, March 24, 2017.

31 Warikoo, "Woman Who Had Terror Conviction."

32 William Jacobson, "Rasmea Odeh Was Offered Similar Plea Deal Three Years Ago—Why Is She Taking It Now?," *Legal Insurrection*, March 26, 2017.

33 Jewish Voice for Peace, "Rasmea Odeh Won't Face Fair Trial in U.S. Court," March 23, 2017, https://jewishvoiceforpeace.org/rasmea-odeh-wont-face-fair-trial-u-s-court/.

34 Jewish Voice for Peace, "Jewish Voice for Peace Is Proud to Host Palestinian Organizer Rasmea Odeh," March 7, 2017, https://jewishvoiceforpeace.org/jewish-voice-peace-proud-host-palestinian-organizer-rasmea-odeh/.

35 Odeh did not wear a hijab at nearly all of her public appearances. In an interview with author Loren Lybarger, Odeh said that "religion gave a false understanding of reality and thereby was an impediment to liberation, especially women's liberation." Loren Lybarger, *Palestinian Chicago: Identity in Exile* (Oakland: University of California Press, 2020), 186–87.

36 Rebecca Vilkomerson, "Letter to the Editor: Why JVP Invited Rasmea Odeh to Speak," *Forward*, March 24, 2017.

37 Alissa Wise, "Why We Invited Rasmea Odeh to Our Conference," *Religion News Service*, March 28, 2017.

38 teleSUR, "Palestinian Revolutionary Rasmea Odeh, Tortured in Israel, To Be Deported from US," April 6, 2017, https://www.telesurenglish.net/news/Palestinian-Revolutionary-Rasmea-Odeh-Tortured-in-Israel-to-Be-Deported-from-US-20170406-0010.html; Steven Emerson, "At JVP Conference, Odeh Claims 'Torturous Ordeal' Led to Guilty Plea," *Algemeiner*, April 3, 2017; "At Jewish Group Event, Palestinian Ex-Terrorist Vows to Fight on for Palestine," *Times of Israel*, April 3, 2017.

39 Jewish Voice for Peace, "Rasmea Odeh 2017 Talk," The True Knowledge, video, 21:54, August 11, 2017, https://www.youtube.com/watch?v=xdsF5-C73HI&feature=youtu.be.

40 "Jewish Voice for Peace Is 'All In' for Palestinian Human Rights," *Palestine in America Blog*, April 7, 2017, https://www.palestineinamerica.com/blog/2017/04/jvp-palestinian-human-rights.

41 United States v. Odeh, Memorandum of the United States in Support of Guilty Plea, docket #243; Motion to Strike Portion of Government's Memorandum in Support of Guilty Plea, docket #244; Response and Brief of the United States in Opposition to Motion to Strike Memorandum in Support of Guilty Plea, docket #247.

42 United States v. Odeh, Rule 11 Plea Agreement, 4.

43 Rule 11, Federal Rules of Criminal Procedure.

44 United States v. Odeh, transcript of proceedings, April 25, 2017, 10–20.

45 United States v. Odeh, transcript of proceedings, April 25, 2017, 17–22.

46 United States v. Odeh, transcript of proceedings, April 25, 2017, 22.

47 Investigative Project on Terrorism, "Rasmiyeh Odeh's Guilty Plea Accepted," *IPT News*, April 25, 2017, https://www.investigativeproject.org/6042/rasmieh-odeh-guilty-plea-accepted/.

48 Investigative Project on Terrorism, "Spinning a Terrorist into a Victim – Part 7 – Justice at Last for Rasmieh Odeh," *IPT News*, video, 12:52, May 12, 2017, https://www.investigativeproject.org/6122/spinning-a-terrorist-into-a-victim-justice/; Palestinian Network, Odeh Rally, April 25, 2017.

49 Investigative Project on Terrorism, "Spinning a Terrorist into a Victim—Part 7."

50 Palestinian Network, Odeh Rally, April 25, 2017.

51 Silver, "Rasmea Odeh Pleads Guilty."

52 Silver, "Rasmea Odeh Pleads Guilty."

53 Investigative Project on Terrorism, "Spinning a Terrorist into a Victim—Part 7."

54 Valerie Richardson, "Convicted Terrorist Odeh Pleads Guilty to Lying about Criminal Record on Visa Application," *Washington Times*, April 25, 2017.

55 Steven Emerson, "Rasmea Odeh's Guilty Plea Accepted," *Algemeiner*, April 26, 2017.

56 Niraj Warikoo, "Guilty Plea, Deportation End Terror Case against Former Michigan Woman," *Detroit Free Press*, April 25, 2017.

57 Investigative Project on Terrorism, "Spinning a Terrorist into a Victim—Part 7."

Afterword

1 Silver, "Rasmea Odeh Pleads Guilty."

2 Loren Lybarger, *Palestinian Chicago: Identity in Exile* (Oakland: University of California Press, 2020), 187.

3 United States v. Odeh, transcript of proceedings, August 17, 2017, 10–19.

4 United States v. Odeh, transcript of proceedings, August 17, 2017, 19–20.

5 United States v. Odeh, transcript of proceedings, August 17, 2017, 7–10.

6 8 U.S.C. § 1451 (2019). For an excellent discussion of the distinctions between civil and criminal denaturalization actions, including the relative disadvantages and problems for defendants, see Cassandra Burke Robertson and Irina Manta, "Litigating Citizenship," *Vanderbilt Law Review* 73, no. 3 (April 2020): 757.

7 There is a ten-year statute of limitations applicable to criminal denaturalization prosecutions, which would have applied in most, if not all, of the Nazi cases.

8 United States Department of Justice, "Justice Department Seeks to Denaturalize Michigan Man Who Was Convicted in Israel," December 18, 2019.

9 United States v. Odeh, Memorandum of United States in Support of Guilty Plea, docket #243.

10 United States v. Odeh, transcript of proceedings, August 17, 2017, 21–22.

11 Brant Rosen, *Wrestling in the Daylight: A Rabbi's Path to Palestinian Solidarity* (Charlottesville, VA: Just World Books, 2012), 275.

12 Investigative Project on Terrorism, "Spinning a Terrorist into a Victim – Part 5."

13 Lisa Hajjar, *Courting Conflict: The Israeli Military Court System in the West Bank and Gaza* (Berkeley: University of California Press, 2005), 203–5.

14 John McCain (with Mark Salter), *Faith of My Fathers* (New York: Random House, 1999), 243.

15 Investigative Project on Terrorism, "Spinning a Terrorist into a Victim—Part 5."

16 For a summary of the many posts on *Legal Insurrection*, see William Jacobson, "2017 Story That Defined My Years, the Conviction and Deportation of Terrorist Rasmea Odeh," *Legal Insurrection*, December 30, 2017.

17 Investigative Project on Terrorism, "Spinning a Terrorist into a Victim – Part 5." All seven parts of "Spinning a Terrorist into a Victim" are linked at https://www.investigativeproject.org/4627/spinning-a-terrorist-into-a-victim.

18 William Jacobson, "Terror Victim's Brother Says Rasmea Odeh Supporters 'Have to Eat Their Words,'" *Legal Insurrection*, April 26, 2017.

19 Investigative Project on Terrorism, "Spinning a Terrorist into a Victim – Part 7."

20 Catherine Kim, "Organizer Rasmea Odeh Speaks at Northwestern for SJP's Israeli Apartheid Week," *Daily Northwestern*, May 16, 2017.

21 William Jacobson, "Can't Make This Up: Soon-to-Be Deported Convicted Terrorist Rasmea Odeh Protests United Airlines," *Legal Insurrection*, April 13, 2017.

22 Diana Block, "Rasmea and Oscar: Resisting the Criminalization of Freedom Fighting," *Counterpunch*, August 29, 2017; "Samidoun Salutes Oscar López Rivera and the Puerto Rican People on the Occasion of His Freedom," *Samidoun*, May 19, 2017; US Palestinian Community Network, "On Rasmea's 70th Birthday, Read Her Speech from Oscar Lopez' Homecoming," US Palestinian Community Network, May 22, 2017, https://uspcn.org/2017/05/22/rasmeas-speech-for-oscar-lopez/.

23 Jonathan Greenberg, "More than 1,000 Leftists Gathered in Chicago to Cheer a Convicted Murderer Who Hates Israel," *The Federalist*, August 17, 2017.

24 William Jacobson, "Chicago Crowd Cheers as Convicted Terrorist Rasmea Odeh Calls for Destruction of Israel," *Legal Insurrection*, August 13, 2017.

25 Tom Burke, "Rasmea Odeh at Detroit Sentencing: 'We Will Continue to Struggle for our Cause! We Will Liberate Our Palestine,'" *Fight Back News*, August 17, 2017, http://www.fightbacknews.org/2017/8/17/rasmea-odeh-detroit-sentencing-we-will-continue-struggle-our-cause-we-will-liberate-our-pa.

26 Maudlyne Iherjirika, "Political Activist Rasmea Odeh a Symbol of Deportation's Many Faces," *Chicago Sun-Times*, September 20, 2017.

27 Teresa Crawford, "Palestinian Activist Deported to Jordan from Chicago," *Chicago Tribune*, September 19, 2017.

28 Niraj Warikoo, "Former Michigan Resident Rasmieh Odeh, Guilty of Immigration Charge, Deported to Jordan," *Detroit Free Press*, September 20, 2017.

29 William Jacobson, "Terrorist Rasmea Odeh Lies One Last Time as She Is Deported," *Legal Insurrection*, September 22, 2017; US Palestinian Community Network, "We Love You Rasmea," US Palestinian Community Network, video, 1:51, September 20, 2017, https://www.facebook.com/USPCN/videos/a-message-from-rasmeaodeh-to-her-supporters-and-we-love-you-rasmea-good-luck-on-/1686434638058038/.

30 "The American Authorities Expel the Struggler Rasmieh Odeh from the USA," *Arab 48*, September 20, 2017; "Rasmieh Odeh, an Icon of the Struggle outside Palestine," Palestine Information Center, September 21, 2017.

Bibliography

"2 Die, 8 Wounded in J'Lem Terror Outrage at Supersol." *Jerusalem Post*, February 23, 1969.

"2 Prominent Terror Suspects Allowed to Go to Jordan." *Jerusalem Post*, April 17, 1969.

"14 East Jerusalem, West Bank Arabs Held by Israel in Supermarket Bombing." *Jewish Telegraphic Service*, February 25, 1969.

"14 Remanded for Fortnight as Blast Suspects." *Jerusalem Post*, February 24, 1969.

Abdo, Nahla. "Palestinian Women Political Prisoners and the Israeli State." In *Threat: Palestinian Political Prisoners in Israel*, edited by Abeer Baker and Anat Matar, 186–87. London: Pluto Press, 2011.

Abdo, Nahla. *Captive Revolution: Palestinian Women's Anti-Colonial Struggle within the Israeli Prison System*. London: Pluto Press, 2014.

Abudayyeh, Hatem. "Judge Paul Borman Recuses Himself from Rasmea's Case." US Palestinian Community Network, August 12, 2014. https://uspcn.org/2014/08/12/breaking-judge-paul-borman-recuses-himself-from-rasmeas-case/.

Abudayyeh, Hatem. "New Indictments against Rasmea." Rasmea Defense Committee, December 13, 2016. http://justice4Rasmea.org/news/2016/12/13/new-indictments-against-rasmea/.

Abudayyeh, Hatem. "Rasmea Odeh NOT Pleading Guilty." US Palestinian Community Network, May 21, 2014. https://uspcn.org/2014/05/21/rasmea-odeh-not-pleading-guilty/.

Abudayyeh, Hatem. "Victory for the Palestinian People." *Fight Back News*, March 9, 2009. http://www.fightbacknews.org/2009/03/gaza-war-victory-for-palestinian-people.htm.

AbuKhalil, As'ad. "George Habash's Contribution to the Palestinian Struggle." *Electronic Intifada*, January 30, 2008. https://electronicintifada.net/content/george-habashs-contribution-palestinian-struggle/7332.

AbuKhalil, As'ad. "Internal Contradictions in the PFLP: Decision Making and Policy Orientation." *Middle East Journal* 11, no. 3 (1987): 361–78.

Abunimah, Ali. "Judge Refuses to Dismiss 'Baseless' Charges against Palestinian-American." *Electronic Intifada*, October 3, 2014. https://electronicintifada.net/blogs/ali-abunimah/judge-refuses-dismiss-baseless-charges-against-palestinian-american.

Abunimah, Ali. "Palestinian Activist Rasmea Odeh Rejects US Plea Deal, Prepares for October Trial." *Electronic Intifada*, May 28, 2014. https://electronicintifada.net/blogs/ali-abunimah/palestinian-activist-rasmea-odeh-rejects-us-plea-deal-prepares-october-trial.

Abunimah, Ali. "Palestinian American Activist Asks Judge to Drop Charges Based on 'Illegal' US Investigation." *Electronic Intifada*, September 3, 2014.

Abunimah, Ali. "Rasmea Odeh in Prolonged Solitary Confinement in Michigan Jail." *Electronic Intifada*, December 5, 2014. https://electronicintifada.net/blogs/ali-abunimah/rasmea-odeh-prolonged-solitary-confinement-michigan-jail.

Abunimah, Ali. "Rasmea Odeh's Day in Court." *Electronic Intifada,* November 14, 2013. https://electronicintifada.net/blogs/ali-abunimah/rasmea-odehs-day-court.

Abunimah, Ali. "Why Is Obama Administration Prosecuting Sexual Torture Victim Rasmea Odeh?" *Electronic Intifada,* June 10, 2014. https://electronicintifada.net/blogs/ali-abunimah/why-obama-administration-prosecuting-sexual-torture-victim-rasmea-odeh.

Alcoff, Linda Martin, Cinzia Arruzza, Tithi Bhattacharya, Nancy Fraser, Barbara Ransby, Keeanga-Yamahtta Taylor, Rasmea Yousef Odeh, and Angela Davis. "Women of America: We're Going on Strike. Join Us so Trump Will See Our Power." *Guardian,* February 6, 2017.

Amar, Delia and Menachem Amir. "The Politics of Prostitution and Trafficking of Women in Israel." In *The Politics of Prostitution: Women's Movements, Democratic States and the Globalisation of Sex Commerce,* edited by Joyce Outshoorn, 144–64. New York: Cambridge University Press, 2004.

"The American Authorities Expel the Struggler Rasmea Odeh from the USA." *Arab 48,* September 20, 2017.

Amnesty International. *Israel and the Occupied Territories: The Military Justice System in the Occupied Territories: Detention, Interrogation and Trial Procedures.* New York: Amnesty International Publications, 1991.

Amnesty International. *Report on Torture.* London: Duckworth in association with Amnesty International Publications, 1973.

Amos, John II. *Palestinian Resistance: Organization of a Nationalist Movement.* New York: Pergamon Press, 1980.

Anderson, Raymond. "Wadi Haddad, Palestinian Hijacking Strategist, Dies." *New York Times,* April 2, 1978.

Antonius, Soraya. "Prisoners for Palestine: A List of Women Political Prisoners." *Journal of Palestine Studies* 9, no. 3 (1980): 29–80.

Arab America, "New Date of October 21st Set for Trial of Rasmea Odeh." Arab America, May 28, 2014. https://www.arabamerica.com/rasmea-yousef-odeh-to-appear-in-detroit-court-on-wednesday-may-28th/.

Arab American Action Network. "Activist Profiles: Rasmea Odeh." Arab American Action Network. Accessed August 4, 2017 (link since removed). http://www.aaan.org/?p=1030.

Arab American Action Network. "ArabAmericanMarkaz." American Arab Action Network. May 7, 2012. Video, 10:15. https://www.youtube.com/watch?v=70bn4VitM_8.

Arab American Action Network. "Press Conference on Palestinian Activist Rasmea Odeh." *CAN TV.* November 18, 2013. Video, 32:57. https://www.youtube.com/watch?v=vVciKRYfKWY&feature=youtu.be.

Arab Information Center (U.S.), "Education in Jordan." In *Education in the Arab States.* New York: Arab Information Center, 1966.

"Arab Students Condemn Terrorist Involvement." *Jerusalem Post,* March 17, 1969.

Arias, Sofia and Bill Mullen. "On March 8, Stand with Women of Palestine." *Electronic Intifada,* March 6, 2017. https://electronicintifada.net/content/8-march-stand-women-palestine/19766.

Associated Press. "US Activist Found Guilty of Not Disclosing Conviction in Fatal Jerusalem Bombing." *Guardian*, November 10, 2014, photograph.

"At Jewish Group Event, Palestinian Ex-Terrorist Vows to Fight on for Palestine." *Times of Israel*, April 3, 2017.

Barakat, Rana. "The Jerusalem Fellah: Popular Politics in Mandate-Era Palestine." *Journal of Palestine Studies* 46, no. 1 (2016): 7–19.

Barrows-Friedman, Nora. "A Political Prosecution: Inside the Trial of Rasmea Odeh." *Electronic Intifada*, November 9, 2014. https://electronicintifada.net/blogs/nora-bar rows-friedman/political-prosecution-inside-trial-rasmea-odeh.

"Beginning of Trial of the Two Women." *Davar*, June 5, 1969.

"Behind the Bars in Israel's Only Female Prison." *Jewish News*, March 21, 2019.

Benaryeh, Terry Joffe. "Rasmieh Yousef Odeh Must Not Be Allowed to Continue the Violence." Associated Press, July 29, 2014.

Benaryeh, Terry. "Bombing Victim's Niece: Rasmea Odeh Is No Hero." *Legal Insurrection*, November 13, 2014.

Bergman-Sapir, Efrat and Rachel Stroumsa. *Public Committee against Torture in Israel: Independent Report to the UN Committee against Torture towards the Review of the Fifth Periodic Report on Israel*. Jerusalem: Public Committee Against Torture in Israel. 2016.

Bergman, Ronen. "Gilad Shalit and the Rising Price of Israeli Life." *New York Times*, November 9, 2011.

Bergman, Ronen. *Rise and Kill First: The Secret History of Israel's Targeted Assassinations*. New York: Random House, 2018.

Black, Ian. *Enemies and Neighbors: Arabs and Jews in Palestine and Israel, 1917–2017*. New York: Atlantic Monthly Press, 2018.

Blitzer, Wolf. "Begin, Sadat Split Differences." *Jerusalem Post*, March 27, 1979.

Block, Diana. "Rasmea and Oscar: Resisting the Criminalization of Freedom Fighting." *Counterpunch*, August 29, 2017.

Blumenthal, Jerry, Gordon Quinn and Fenell Doremus, dir. *Independent Lens: The New Americans*. Episode 1, "Palestinian Bride." Chicago: Kartemquin Films, aired March 29, 2004, on PBS, (link since removed). https://www.pbs.org/independentlens/newamericans/newamericans/palestinian_episode1.html.

Bob, Yonah Jeremy. "US to Retry Palestinian Convicted of Jerusalem Bombing." *Jerusalem Post*, December 7, 2016.

"Bombing Suspects Remanded." *Jerusalem Post*, March 19, 1969.

Bukowski, Diane. "Palestinian Heroine, Torture Victim Rasmea Odeh Convicted, Jailed in Detroit, Appeal Planned." *Voice of Detroit*, November 10, 2014.

Burke, Tom. "Big Detroit Rally for Rasmea Odeh's Day in Court." *Fight Back News*, November 13, 2013. http://www.fightbacknews.org/2013/11/13/big-detroit-rally-rasmea-odeh-s-day-court.

Burke, Tom. "Rasmea Odeh at Detroit Sentencing: 'We Will Continue to Struggle for our Cause! We Will Liberate Our Palestine.'" *Fight Back News*, August 17, 2017. http://www.fightbacknews.org/2017/8/17/rasmea-odeh-detroit-sentencing-we-will-cont inue-struggle-our-cause-we-will-liberate-our-pa.

Burke, Tom. "Rasmea Odeh Court Hearing, Judge Borman Refuses to Step Down." *Fight Back News*, August 1, 2014. http://www.fightbacknews.org/2014/8/1/rasmea-odeh-court-hearing-judge-borman-refuses-to-step-down.

Burns, Gus. "Rasmieh Odeh, Alleged Ex-Terrorist, Takes Stand in Federal Deportation Trial." MLive.com, November 6, 2014, updated April 3, 2019, accessed March 27, 2020. https://www.mlive.com/news/detroit/2014/11/rasmieh_odeh_alleged_ex-terror.html.

Callimachi, Rukmini and Alan Yuhas. "Alabama Woman Who Joined ISIS Can't Return Home, U.S. Says." *New York Times*, February 20, 2019.

Chambers, Bill. "USA vs. Rasmea Odeh: Pro-Israel Judge Refuses to Step Down." *Chicago Monitor*, August 4, 2014.

"Chicago Activist Guilty in Terrorism-Related US Immigration Case." *Chicago Sun-Times*, November 10, 2014.

Chicago Cultural Alliance. "Kerstin Lane: Outstanding Community Leader." Chicago Cultural Alliance. May 13, 2013. Video, 4:35. https://www.youtube.com/watch?v=m-pOwg-IQCy8.

Chicago Cultural Alliance. "Rasmea Yousef Odeh: Outstanding Community Leader." Interview with Odeh, in Arabic with English voiceover, Chicago Cultural Alliance. May 13, 2013. Video, 5:36. https://www.youtube.com/watch?v=7Xxrl8aj8aQ.

Cnaan, Ram. "Notes on Prostitution in Israel." *Sociological Inquiry* 52, no. 2 (1982): 114–21.

Cobban, Helena. *The Palestinian Liberation Organization: People, Power and Politics.* Cambridge: Cambridge University Press. 1984.

Committee to Stop FBI Repression. "Contrary to Erroneous Press Reports, Rasmea Odeh Is Not Pleading Guilty." Committee to Stop FBI Repression, May 21, 2014.

Committee to Stop FBI Repression. "FBI Confirms That They Copied Tens of Thousands of Documents Seized from the Homes of Local Anti-War Activists; Originals Returned, Indictments Still Looming." *4strugglemag*, November 2, 2011. https://4strugglemag.org/2011/11/02/fbi-confirms-that-they-copied-tens-of-thousands-of-documents-seized-from-the-homes-of-local-anti-war-activists-originals-returned-indictments-still-looming/.

Committee to Stop FBI Repression. "FBI Returns Personal Papers to Hatem Abudayyeh." *Fight Back News*, September 17, 2014. http://www.fightbacknews.org/2014/9/17/fbi-returns-personal-papers-hatem-abudayyeh.

Committee to Stop FBI Repression. "One Year Since the September 24 FBI Raids and Grand Jury Subpoenas." *Fight Back News*, September 23, 2011. http://www.fightbacknews.org/2011/9/23/one-year-september-24-fbi-raids-and-grand-jury-subpoenas.

Committee to Stop FBI Repression. "U.S. Attorney Escalates Attacks on Civil Liberties of Anti-War, Palestinian Human Rights Activists." *Fight Back News*, May 8, 2011. http://www.fightbacknews.org/2011/5/8/us-attorney-escalates-attacks-civil-liberties-anti-war-palestinian-human-rights-activists.

Confidential Source A, communication, August 7, 2018.

Confidential Source B, communication, February 14, 2020.

Confidential Source C, communication, March 2, 2020.

Crawford, Teresa. "Palestinian Activist Deported to Jordan from Chicago." *Chicago Tribune*, September 19, 2017.

Dabaie, Marguerite. "Rasmea Odeh: Woman without a Country." *The Nib*, September 28, 2017.

Davis, Angela. "Free Rasmea Odeh, Political Prisoner." *Detroit News*, November 4, 2014.

Davis, Charles. "The FBI's Failed Two-Year Campaign against a Group of Non-Violent Activists in the Midwest." *Vice*, March 31, 2014.

"The Defendants from the Supersol Bombing Accuse the Police of 'Sexual Torture.'" *Maariv*, November 11, 1969.

Dershowitz, Alan. *Why Terrorism Works: Understanding the Threat, Responding to the Challenge*. New Haven, CT: Yale University Press, 2002.

Deutsch, Michael. "Remembering Muhammad Salah." *Electronic Intifada*, April 26, 2016. https://electronicintifada.net/content/remembering-muhammad-salah/16451.

Downton, Eric. "Arabs Plan Push." *Sunday Telegraph*, February 23, 1969.

Downton, Eric. "Guerrillas Hail Teacher as First Heroine." *Sunday Telegraph*, March 16, 1969.

Dupre, Deborah. "Rasmea Odeh on Federal Trial in Detroit: Supporters Pack Court." *Voice of Detroit*, November 7, 2014.

el-Rayes, Riad and Dunia Nahas. *Guerrillas for Palestine*. New York: St. Martin's Press, 1976.

El Reporte, September 10, 2014. https://www.youtube.com/watch?v-nu-e3w1TMQI.

Emerson, Steven. "At JVP Conference, Odeh Claims 'Torturous Ordeal' Led to Guilty Plea." *Algemeiner*, April 3, 2017.

Emerson, Steven. "Rasmea Odeh's Guilty Plea Accepted." *Algemeiner*, April 26, 2017.

"Enforcing Apartheid: An Interview with Michael Deutsch." *Jacobin*, November 7, 2014. https://www.jacobinmag.com/2014/11/enforcing-apartheid/.

Erakat, Noura. "When You Come for Rasmea Odeh, You Come for All of Us." *Jezebel*, March 24, 2017.

"Ernest Goodman, 90, Civil Rights Lawyer." *New York Times*, April 2, 1997.

Fallaci, Oriana. "A Leader of the Fedayeen: 'We Want a War Like the Vietnam War.'" *Life*, June 12, 1970.

Farhat, Hasan. "For Rasmea Odeh: The Dawn-Lit Face." *Al-Hadaf*, April 7, 1979.

Farsoun, Samih and Christina Zacharia. *Palestine and the Palestinians*. Boulder, CO: Oxford Westview Press, 1997.

Fernea, Elizabeth Warnock. *Women and the Family in the Middle East*. Austin: University of Texas Press, 1985.

Feron, James. "Bomb Explosion in Jerusalem's Largest Supermarket Kills 2, Injures 9." *New York Times*, February 2, 1969.

Feron, James. "Israelis Warn Arabs." *New York Times*, February 24, 1969.

Feron, James. "Many Israelis Angry." *New York Times*, February 23, 1969.

Fight Back News. "Attorney: Why Is Rasmea Odeh Targeted Now?" *Fight Back News*, November 12, 2013. http://www.fightbacknews.org/2013/11/12/attorney-why-rasmea-odeh-targeted-now.

Fight Back News. "Fighting Repression 4 Years after FBI Raids on Anti-War, International Solidarity Activists." *Fight Back News*, September 23, 2014. http://www.fightbacknews.org/2014/9/23/fighting-repression-4-years-after-fbi-raids-anti-war-international-solidarity-activists.

Fight Back News. "Israel and U.S. Wage War on Lebanon and Palestine." *Fight Back News*, July 22, 2006. http://www.fightbacknews.org/2006/03/hateminterview.htm.

Fight Back News. "Judge Borman Forced to Step Down in Case of Rasmea Odeh." *Fight Back News*, August 12, 2014. http://www.fightbacknews.org/2014/8/12/judge-bor man-forced-step-down-case-rasmea-odeh.

Fight Back News. "More Victories for the Defense in Rasmea's Case." *Fight Back News*, June 15, 2016. http://www.fightbacknews.org/2016/6/15/more-victories-de fense-rasmea-s-case.

Fight Back News. "On the Anniversary of the FBI Raids on Anti-War and International Solidarity Activists, Contribute to the Defense of Rasmea Odeh." *Fight Back News*, September 24, 2015. http://www.fightbacknews.org/2015/9/24/anniversary-fbi-raids-anti-war-and-international-solitary-activists-contribute-defense-ras.

Fight Back News. "Palestinian Activist Rasmea Odeh Given Nelson Mandela Award." *Fight Back News*, December 10, 2013. http://www.fightbacknews.org/2013/12/10/palestinian-activist-rasmea-odeh-given-nelson-mandela-award.

Fight Back News. "Tell Arab-American Civil Rights League that Rasmea's Prosecutor Deserves No Award!" *Fight Back News*, April 29, 2015. http://www.fightbacknews.org/2015/4/29/tell-arab-american-civil-rights-league-rasmea-s-prosecutor-deserves-no-award.

Fight Back News. "Vicious, Unjust Rulings in Case of Rasmea Odeh – Come to Detroit Nov. 4, Stand up for Justice!" *Fight Back News*, October 28, 2014. http://www.fight backnews.org/2014/10/28/vicious-unjust-rulings-case-rasmea-odeh-come-detroit-nov-4-stand-justice.

"First Sabotage Attempt on Supersol Failed." *Jerusalem Post*, May 14, 1969.

Flatow, Stephen. "Women's 'Resistance' Is Embracing the Wrong Palestinians." *New York Post*, March 5, 2017.

Ford, Matt. "Antonin Scalia's Case for Torture." *Atlantic*, December 13, 2014.

"Forty Members of Terrorist Cells Rounded Up in Supermarket Bombing Case." *Jewish Telegraphic Agency*, March 4, 1969.

Freedom Road Socialist Organization, "Resistance Is the Key: The 2010 FBI Raids on Anti-War and International Solidarity Activists." *Fight Back News*, September 24, 2019. http://www.fightbacknews.org/2019/9/24/resistance-key-2010-fbi-raids-an ti-war-and-international-solidarity-activists.

Fulero, Solomon and Lawrence Wrightsman. *Forensic Psychology*. Belmont, CA: Wadsworth, 2009.

"Funeral Today of Two Victims." *Jerusalem Post*, February 24, 1969.

Gavoor, Aram A. and Daniel Miktus. "Snap: How the Moral Elasticity of the Denaturalization Statute Goes Too Far." *William and Mary Bill of Rights Journal* 23, no. 3 (2015): 637–74. https://scholarship.law.wm.edu/wmborj/vol23/iss3/3.

Gelber, Yoav. "Three Case Studies of the War in Palestine in 1948." *Tel Aviv Review of Books*, Winter 2019. https://www.tarb.co.il/three-case-studies-of-the-war-in-pales tine-in-1948/.

Gerstein, Josh. "Arab Activist Balks at Guilty Plea in Detroit." *Politico*, May 21, 2014.

Gerstein, Josh. "Defense Wants Pro-Israel Federal Judge Off Case." *Politico*, July 15, 2014.

Gerstein, Josh. "Trump Officials Pushing to Strip Convicted Terrorists of Citizenship." *Politico*, June 8, 2019.

"Girl, 19, and 30 Others Held for H.U. Cafeteria Blast." *Jerusalem Post*, March 16, 1969.

Goodman, Hirsh. "Bartering with Terrorists." *Jerusalem Post*, March 23, 1979.

Gosztola, Kevin. "Political Case Brought against Palestinian Organizer in Chicago for Immigration Fraud." *Shadowproof*, October 23, 2013. https://shadowproof.com/2013/10/23/activists-targeted-by-justice-department-suspect-arrest-of-palestinian-organizer-for-immigration-fraud-connected/.

Gramlich, John. "Only 2% of Federal Criminal Defendants go to Trial, and Most Who Do Are Found Guilty." Pew Research Center, June 11, 2019. https://www.pewresearch.org/fact-tank/2019/06/11/only-2-of-federal-criminal-defendants-go-to-trial-and-most-who-do-are-found-guilty/.

Greenberg, Jonathan. "More than 1,000 Leftists Gathered in Chicago to Cheer a Convicted Murderer Who Hates Israel." *Federalist*, August 17, 2017.

Grimm, Andy and Cynthia Dizikes. "FBI Raids Anti-War Activists' Homes." *Chicago Tribune*, September 24, 2010.

Gross, Judah Ari. "When the Prime Ministers Took Down the Hijackers." *Times of Israel*, August 13, 2015.

Gutheil, Thomas. *The Psychiatrist as Expert Witness*. Washington, DC: American Psychiatric Press, 1998.

Gutheil, Thomas. *The Psychiatrist in Court: A Survival Guide*. Washington, DC: American Psychiatric Press, 1998.

Hadawi, Sami. *Village Statistics 1945: A Classification of Land and Area Ownership in Palestine*. Beirut: Palestine Liberation Organization Research Center, 1970.

Hajjar, Lisa. *Courting Conflict: The Israeli Military Court System in the West Bank and Gaza*. Berkeley: University of California Press, 2005.

Hajjar, Lisa. *Torture: A Sociology of Violence and Human Rights*. New York: Routledge, 2013.

Halabi, Rafik. *The West Bank Story*. New York: Harcourt Brace Jovanovich, 1981.

Halasa, Malu. "My Cousin, the Hijacker." *Lenny Letter*, January 5, 2018. https://www.lennyletter.com/story/my-cousin-the-hijacker.

Hanania, Ray. "Rasmea Odeh Sentenced to 18 Months Prison." *Arab Daily News*, November 11, 2014.

Harb, Ali. "ACRL, NAACP Honor U.S. Attorney McQuade and Judge Roberts." *Arab American News*, May 8, 2015.

Harkabi, Yehoshafat. *Fedayeen Action and Arab Strategy*. London: Institute for Strategic Studies, 1968.

Harlow, Barbara. *Barred: Women, Writing, and Political Detention*. Middletown, Connecticut: Wesleyan University Press, 1992.

Harrison, William, Clifford Prator, and G. Richard Tucker, *English-Language Policy Survey of Jordan, A Case Study in Language Planning, Center for Applied Linguistics*. Arlington, VA: Center for Applied Linguistics, 1975.

Hasan, Nesreen. "Arab American Action Network's Long Standing History of Serving Palestinians." *Palestine In America*, August 2016.

Higgins, Michael. "21-Month Sentence for Salah." *Chicago Tribune*, July 12, 2007.

"Hijacking of Air France Airbus by Followers of Popular Front for the Liberation of Palestine – Israeli Action to Liberate Hostages held at Entebbe Airport – Inconclusive Debate at UN security Council – Ugandan Recriminations against Britain and Kenya – Severance of Diplomatic Relations with Uganda by Britain." In *Keesing's Record of World Events* (formerly Keesing's Contemporary Archives), Volume 22, August, 1976.

Hill, Marc Lamont. "Why Every Black Activist Should Stand with Rasmea Odeh." *Huffington Post*, October 13, 2015.

Human Rights Watch. *Prison Conditions in Israel and the Occupied Territories, April 1991: A Middle East Watch Report.* New York: Human Rights Watch, 1991.

IDF declassified document translation Gimel, dated July 8, 2014.

Iherjirika, Maulyne. "Political Activist Rasmea Odeh a Symbol of Deportation's Many Faces." *Chicago Sun-Times*, September 20, 2017.

"'Illegal Immigrant,' 69, Who Killed Two Young Men by Blowing up a Supermarket, and Bombed a British Consulate, Wants to Organize the 'Next Women's March' in a Day of 'Anti-Capitalist Feminism' across the US." *Daily Mail*, February 26, 2017.

"In Travesty of Justice, Rasmea Odeh Found Guilty Despite History of Israeli Torture." *Mondoweiss*, November 10, 2014.

International Commission of Jurists and Law in the Service of Man. *Torture and Intimidation in the West Bank: The Case of Al-Fara'a Prison.* Geneva: International Commission of Jurists and Law in the Service of Man, 1985.

Investigative Project on Terrorism. "Rasmiyeh Odeh's Guilty Plea Accepted." *IPT News,* April 25, 2017. https://www.investigativeproject.org/6042/rasmieh-odeh-guilty-plea-accepted/.

Investigative Project on Terrorism. "Spinning a Terrorist into a Victim – Part 5 – A Spin Strategy Larger Than Rasmieh Odeh Herself." *IPT News*, October 31, 2014. Video, 11:41. https://www.investigativeproject.org/4639/spinning-a-terrorist-into-a-victim-part-5-a-spin/.

Investigative Project on Terrorism. "Spinning a Terrorist into a Victim – Part 7 – Justice at Last for Rasmieh Odeh." *IPT News*, May 12, 2017. Video, 12:52. https://www.investigativeproject.org/6122/spinning-a-terrorist-into-a-victim-justice/.

Irving, Sarah. *Leila Khaled: Icon of Palestinian Liberation.* London: Pluto Press, 2012.

"Israel Exchanges 66 Palestinians for Soldier Captured in Lebanon." *New York Times,* March 15, 1979.

"Israel in First Prisoner Exchange with Arab Terrorist Organization." *Jewish Telegraphic Agency*, March 15, 1979.

"Israel Tortures Arab Prisoners." *Sunday Times,* June 19, 1977.

"Israeli Police Arrest Minister, 2 Professionals, in Market Bombing." *Jewish Telegraphic Agency*, March 5, 1969.

"Israelis Outraged by Bombing of Hebrew U. Cafeteria; 7 Students Injured Seriously." *Jewish Telegraphic Service*, March 7, 1969.

"Israel's Week." *Jerusalem Post*, February 29, 1969.

Iyad, Abu (Salah Khalaf) and Eric Rouleau. *My Home, My Land: A Narrative of the Palestinian Struggle,* New York: Times Books, 1981.

Jacobson, William. "2017 Story That Defined My Years, the Conviction and Deportation of Terrorist Rasmea Odeh." *Legal Insurrection*, December 30, 2017.

Jacobson, William. "Can't Make This Up: Soon-to-Be Deported Convicted Terrorist Rasmea Odeh Protests United Airlines." *Legal Insurrection*, April 13, 2017.

Jacobson, William. "Chicago Crowd Cheers as Convicted Terrorist Rasmea Odeh Calls for Destruction of Israel." *Legal Insurrection*, August 13, 2017.

Jacobson, William. "Convicted Terrorist Rasmea Odeh Co-Organized March 8 #DayWithoutAWoman." *Legal Insurrection*, February 26, 2017.

Jacobson, William. "Rasmea Odeh Conviction: Jury Verdict." *Legal Insurrection*, November 11, 2014.

Jacobson, William. "Rasmea Odeh Prosecutor: Justice Award." *Legal Insurrection*, May 1, 2015.

Jacobson, William. "Rasmea Odeh Was Offered Similar Plea Deal Three Years Ago – Why Is She Taking It Now?" *Legal Insurrection*, March 26, 2017.

Jacobson, William. "Rasmea Odeh: DePaul Fundraiser: Conviction." *Legal Insurrection*, February 1, 2015.

Jacobson, William. "Sisters of Leon Kanner Seek 'Maximal Sentence' for Rasmea Odeh." *Legal Insurrection*, March 2, 2015.

Jacobson, William. "Terror Victim's Brother Says Rasmea Odeh Supporters 'Have to Eat Their Words.'" *Legal Insurrection*, April 26, 2017.

Jacobson, William. "Victim's Brother: Rasmea Odeh Deserves 'Significant Sentence.'" *Legal Insurrection*, February 15, 2015.

Jamail, Dahr. "Tortured and Raped by Israel, Persecuted by the United States." *Truthout*, September 2, 2014.

Jeffries, Stuart. "Four Hijackers and Three Israeli PMs: The Incredible Story of Sabena Flight 571." *Guardian*, November 11, 2015.

"Jerusalem Supersol Re-Opens for Business; 2 Young Bombing Victims Are Buried." *Jewish Telegraphic Agency*, February 24, 1969.

"Jerusalem Terror Suspects for Trial." *Jerusalem Post*, March 21, 1969.

Jewish Voice for Peace. "Rasmea Odeh 2017 Talk." The True Knowledge, August 11, 2017. Video, 21:54. https://www.youtube.com/watch?v=xdsF5-C73HI&feature=youtu.be.

Jordan. Dā'irat al-Iḥṣā'āt al-ʿĀmmah. *The Hashemite Kingdom of Jordan, 1952 Census of Housing: Statistics for Districts, Subdistricts, Nahiyas, and Principal Towns*. Jerusalem: Hashemite Kingdom of Jordan, 1952.

Kan'ane, Sharif and Nihad Zeitawi, *Deir Yassin*. Bir Zeit: Bir Zeit University Press, 1987.

Kattan, Victor. *From Coexistence to Conquest: International Law and the Origins of the Arab-Israeli Conflict, 1891–1949*. New York: Pluto Press, 2009.

Katz, Shmuel. "The Bare Realities." *Jerusalem Post*, March 30, 1979.

Kawar, Amal. *Daughters of Palestine: Leading Women of the Palestinian National Movement*. Albany: State University of New York Press, 1996.

Khader, Nehad. "Rasmea Odeh: The Case of an Indomitable Woman." *Journal of Palestine Studies* 46, no. 4 (2017): 62–74.

Khalidi, Dima. "Odeh's Guilty Verdict Doesn't Mean Her Battle for Justice Is Over." *The Hill*, November 14, 2014.

Khalidi, Rashid. "The Palestinians and 1948: The Underlying Causes of Failure." In *The War for Palestine: Rewriting the History of 1948*, 2nd ed., edited by Eugene Rogan and Avi Shlaim, 12–36. Cambridge: Cambridge University Press, 2007.

Khalidi, Rashid. *The Hundred Years' War on Palestine: A History of Settler Colonialism and Resistance, 1917–2017*. New York: Metropolitan Books, 2020.

Khalidi, Walid. *All That Remains: The Palestinian Villages Occupied and Depopulated by Israel in 1948*. Washington, DC: The Institute for Palestine Studies, 1992.

Kim, Catherine. "Organizer Rasmea Odeh speaks at Northwestern for SJP's Israeli Apartheid Week." *Daily Northwestern*, May 16, 2017.

Kirisci, Kemal. *The PLO and World Politics: A Study of the Mobilization of Support for the Palestinian Cause*. New York: St. Martin's Press, 1986.

Klein, Aaron. *Striking Back: The 1972 Munich Olympics Massacre and Israel's Deadly Response*. New York: Random House, 2005.

Krivine, David. "Flawed Insight on Torture." *Jerusalem Post*, August 5, 1977.

Krivine, David. "More Insight on Torture." *Jerusalem Post*, October 28, 1977.

Landau, Moshe, Yaacov Maltz and Itzhak Hoffi, State of Israel. *Commission of Inquiry into the Methods of Investigation of the General Security Service Regarding Hostile Terrorist Activity Report, Part One*. Jerusalem: State of Israel Government Press, 1987.

Langer, Felicia. *With My Own Eyes: Israel and the Occupied Territories 1967–1973*. London: Ithaca Press, 1975.

Lee, John M. "Hijacking Mastermind Is No. 2 in the Popular Front." *New York Times*, September 14, 1970.

"The Liberated Comrades Meet the Children of Martyrs and School Children." *Al-Hadaf*, April 7, 1979.

"Local Palestinian-American Faces Prison or Deportation." *Worldview*, WBEZ Radio, Chicago: WBEZ, November 20, 2013.

MacDonald, Eileen. *Shoot the Women First*. New York: Random House, 1991.

"Major Terror Gang Seized." *Jerusalem Post*, March 6, 1969.

Manta, Irina and Cassandra Burke Robertson. "(Un)Civil Denaturalizations." *NYU Law Review* 94, no. 3 (2019): 402–71.

"Market Blast Hurts 2 Arabs; Officials Escape Injury in British Consulate Explosion." *Jewish Telegraphic Service*, February 26, 1969.

Marx, Rebecca Flint. "An Arab Bakery in Oakland Full of California Love." *New York Times*, November 11, 2017.

"Massacre of 18 in Kiryat Shemona Continues to Provoke Indignation." *Jewish Telegraphic Agency*, April 18, 1974.

McCain, John (with Mark Salter). *Faith of My Fathers*. New York: Random House, 1999.

McNally, Richard. *Remembering Trauma*. Boston, MA: Harvard University Press, 2005.

Meisner, Jacob. "Feds: Woman Hid Terror Conviction to Get Citizenship." *Chicago Tribune*, October 22, 2013.

Melchior, Jillian Kay. "Death in the Supermarket." *National Review*, May 21, 2014.

Melchior, Jillian Kay. "Rasmieh Gets Justice." *National Review*, November 11, 2014.

Miller, Anna Lekas. "Prominent Palestinian-American Community Activist Arrested." *Daily Beast*, November 1, 2013, updated July 11, 2017. https://www.thedailybeast.com/prominent-palestinian-american-community-activist-arrested.

Mishal, Shaul. *The PLO under Arafat: Between Gun and Olive Branch*. New Haven, CT: Yale University Press, 1986.

Mondalek, Mark. "The Campaign against Rasmea Odeh." *Jacobin*, October 13, 2015. https://www.jacobinmag.com/2015/10/rasmea-odeh-palestine-israel-midwest-23-bds-fbi/.

Morris, Benny. "The Historiography of Deir Yassin." *Journal of Israeli History* 24, no. 1 (2005): 79–107.

Morris, Benny. *1948: A History of the First Arab-Israeli War*. New Haven, CT: Yale University Press, 2008.

Morris, Benny. *Righteous Victims: A History of the Zionist-Arab Conflict, 1881–2001*. New York: Vintage Books, 1999.

Morris, Benny. *The Birth of the Palestinian Refugee Problem Revisited*. London: Cambridge University Press, 2004.

"Mrs. Meir Says Arab Population Loyal." *Jerusalem Post*, March 19, 1969.

Murphy, Maureen Clare. "Palestinian Arrested in Chicago because of her Community Activism, Groups Say." *Electronic Intifada*, October 26, 2013. https://electronicintifada.net/blogs/maureen-clare-murphy/palestinian-arrested-chicago-because-her-community-activism-groups-say.

Murray, Jim. "Blood on Olympus." *Los Angeles Times*, September 7, 1972.

Ñ Don't Stop. "Episode 14, Interview with Hatem Abudayyeh." *Ñ Don't Stop*. September 10, 2014. Video, 10:05. https://www.youtube.com/watch?v=nU-e3w1TMQI.

Naber, Nadine. "Organizing after the Odeh Verdict." *Jacobin*, January 14, 2015. https://www.jacobinmag.com/2015/01/rasmea-odeh-verdict-organizing.

Nassar, Jamal. *The Palestine Liberation Organization: From Armed Struggle to the Declaration of Independence*. New York: Praeger, 1991.

National Lawyers Guild, Middle East Delegation, 1977. *Treatment of Palestinians in Israeli-occupied West Bank and Gaza: Report of the National Lawyers Guild, 1977 Middle East Delegation*. New York: National Lawyers Guild, 1978.

National Lawyers Guild. "NLG Chicago: Jim Fennerty." National Lawyers Guild. Undated video ca. 2016. Accessed February 12, 2020. Video, 16:43. https://vimeo.com/146698892.

Nevins, Sean. "Rasmea Odeh: Raped and Tortured by Israel, Now Being Prosecuted by the U.S." *Mint Press News*, October 28, 2014. https://www.mintpressnews.com/rasmea-odeh-raped-and-tortured-by-israel-now-being-prosecuted-by-the-u-s/198257/.

"A New Column Joins the Troops of the Revolution." *Al-Hadaf*, March 17, 1979.

"New Revelations in the Supersol Trial." *Maariv*, June 6, 1969.

Newsom, Angelina. "One of the 'Day without Women' Protest Organizers is a Convicted Terrorist." *Washington Examiner*, February 28, 2017.

Nowak, Margaret Collingwood. *Two Who Were There: A Biography of Stanley Nowak*. Detroit, MI: Wayne State University Press, 1989.

Nusseibeh, Sari. *Once Upon a Country*. New York: Farrar, Straus and Giroux, 2007.

Odeh, Aisha. *Ahlam Bel-Hurriah (Dreams of Freedom)*. 4th ed. Amman, Jordan: El-Birony Press, 2016, 70.

"Odeh's Conviction a Racist Attack on Arab Americans." *Arab American News*, November 12, 2014.

"On the Anniversary of the FBI Raids on Anti-War and International Solidarity Activists, Contribute to the Defense of Rasmea Odeh." *Fight Back News*, September 24, 2015.

Oren, Michael. *Six Days of War: June 1967 and the Making of the Modern Middle East.* Oxford: Oxford University Press, 2002.

"Palestinian Activist Rasmea Odeh Accepts Plea Deal with No Jail Time." *Arab American News*, March 23, 2017.

"Palestinian Activist Rasmea Odeh, Who Failed to Disclose Israel Terror Convictions, to Leave U.S." Associated Press, March 23, 2017.

"Palestinian Woman Found Guilty of U.S. Citizenship Fraud." *USA Today*, November 10, 2014.

Palumbo, Michael. *The Palestinian Catastrophe: The 1948 Expulsion of a People from Their Homeland.* Boston, MA: Faber and Faber, 1987.

Pappe, Ilan. *The Ethnic Cleansing of Palestine.* Oxford: Oneworld Books, 2006.

PATV. "In a Fighter's Home." PATV, Aisha Odeh interview, August 27, 2013. Video, 3:39. https://www.youtube.com/watch?v=ySFOBuPXaOI&feature=youtu.be.

Pearlman, Wendy. "The Palestinian National Movement." In *The 1967 Arab-Israeli War: Origins and Consequences*, edited by William Roger Louis and Avi Shlaim. 126–148. Cambridge: Cambridge University Press, 2012.

Peled, Miko. "Remembering Theresa Halasa: Revered Veteran of the Palestinian Resistance." *MintPress News*, March 31, 2020. https://www.mintpressnews.com/remembering-theresa-halasa-veteran-palestinian-resistance/266222/.

Posner, Richard. "The Best Offense." *New Republic Online*, September 5, 2002.

"Printer Guilty of Hiding Supersol Bomb Girl." *Jerusalem Post*, June 10, 1969.

Punamaki, Raija-Leena. "Experiences of Torture, Means of Coping, and Level of Symptoms among Palestinian Political Prisoners." *Journal of Palestine Studies* 17, no. 4 (Summer 1988): 81–96.

Prison Conditions in Israel and the Occupied Territories. New York: Human Rights Watch, 1991.

"Questions on Release of Rev. Khoury." *Jerusalem Post*, April 18, 1969.

Qumsiyeh, Mazin. *Popular Resistance in Palestine: A History of Hope and Empowerment.* London: Pluto Press, 2011.

Raab, David. *Terror in Black September: The First Eyewitness Account of the Infamous 1970 Hijackings.* New York: Palgrave Macmillan, 2007.

"Ramallah Girl Being Deported." *Jerusalem Post*, March 23, 1969.

"Rasmea Yousef Odeh Goes to Trial." *Worldview*, WBEZ Radio, Chicago: WBEZ, October 31, 2014.

"Rasmieh Odeh: An Icon of the Struggle outside Palestine." The Palestine Information Center, September 21, 2017.

"Release of Terror Suspect Protested." *Jerusalem Post*, March 30, 1969.

"Reply to Fatah." *Jerusalem Post*, February 29, 1969.

Richardson, Valerie. "Convicted Terrorist Odeh Pleads Guilty to Lying about Criminal Record on Visa Application." *Washington Times*, April 25, 2017.

Robbins, Annie. "New Black-Palestinian Solidarity Video Features Lauryn Hill, Rasmea Odeh, Danny Glover." *Mondoweiss*, October 14, 2015.

Robertson, Cassandra Burke and Irina Manta. "Litigating Citizenship." *Vanderbilt Law Review* 73, no. 3 (2020): 757–810.

Ron, James, Eric Goldstein and Cynthia Brown. *Torture and Ill-Treatment: Israel's Interrogation of Palestinians from the Occupied Territories.* New York: Human Rights Watch, 1994.

Rosen, Brant. *Wrestling in the Daylight: A Rabbi's Path to Palestinian Solidarity.* Charlottesville, VA: Just World Books, 2012.

Saeed, Eid. "Make Zakat-Eligible Donation." US Palestinian Community Network, August 12, 2014. https://uspcn.org/2014/07/28/reminder-rasmeas-status-hearing-in-detroit-july-31-make-zakat-eligible-donation/.

Saleh, Abdul Jawad and Walid Mustafa. *Palestine: The Collective Destruction of Palestinian Villages and Zionist Colonization, 1882–1982.* London: Jerusalem Center for Development Studies, 1987.

"Samidoun Salutes Oscar López Rivera and the Puerto Rican People on the Occasion of His Freedom." *Samidoun*, May 19, 2017.

Sayigh, Rosemary. *Palestinians: From Peasants to Revolutionaries.* London: Zed Books, 1979.

Sayigh, Yezid. "Turning Defeat into Opportunity: The Palestinian Guerrillas after the June 1967 War." *The Middle East Journal* 46, no. 2 (1992): 244–65.

Sayigh, Yezid. *Armed Struggle and the Search for State: The Palestinian Movement 1949–1993.* Oxford: Institute for Palestine Studies, Clarendon Press, 1997.

Schiller, Kay and Christopher Young. *The 1972 Munich Olympics and the Making of Modern Germany.* Berkeley: University of California Press, 2010.

Segal, Mark. "Terrorist-held Israeli Freed for 76 Prisoners." *Jerusalem Post*, March 15, 1979.

Shahshahani, Azadeh. "Demanding Justice from Chicago to Palestine." *Guild Notes* 39, no. 4 (2014): 3.

Shavit, Ari. "Survival of the Fittest? An Interview with Benny Morris." *Haaretz*, January 8, 2004.

Shavit, Ari. *My Promised Land.* New York: Spiegel & Grau, 2013.

Silver, Charlotte. "After Tense Last Day, Jury Begins Deliberations on Rasmea Odeh." *Electronic Intifada*, November 8, 2014. https://electronicintifada.net/blogs/charlotte-silver/after-tense-last-day-jury-begins-deliberations-rasmea-odeh.

Silver, Charlotte. "Court Motion Details Palestinian American Rasmea Odeh's Torture by Israeli Jailers." *Electronic Intifada*, July 31, 2014. https://electronicintifada.net/blogs/charlotte-silver/court-motion-details-palestinian-american-rasmea-odehs-torture-israeli.

Silver, Charlotte. "Defense Promises to Appeal Guilty Verdict against Rasmea Odeh." *Electronic Intifada*, November 10, 2014. https://electronicintifada.net/blogs/charlotte-silver/defense-promises-appeal-guilty-verdict-against-rasmea-odeh.

Silver, Charlotte. "Dozens Travel to Detroit to Support Rasmea Odeh as Trial Begins." *Electronic Intifada*, November 5, 2014. https://electronicintifada.net/blogs/charlotte-silver/dozens-travel-detroit-support-rasmea-odeh-trial-begins.

Silver, Charlotte. "Judge Deals Major Blow to Rasmea Odeh's Defense." *Electronic Intifada*, October 28, 2014. https://electronicintifada.net/blogs/charlotte-silver/judge-deals-major-blow-rasmea-odehs-defense.

Silver, Charlotte. "Judge in Case against Palestinian-American Pulls out Due to Israel Business Ties." *Electronic Intifada*, August 12, 2014. https://electronicintifada.net/blogs/charlotte-silver/judge-case-against-palestinian-american-pulls-out-due-israel-business-ties.

Silver, Charlotte. "Judge with Strong Israel Ties Refuses to Step Down in Case against Palestinian-American." *Electronic Intifada*, August 6, 2014. https://electronicintifada.net/blogs/charlotte-silver/judge-strong-israel-ties-refuses-step-down-case-against-palestinian-american.

Silver, Charlotte. "Rasmea Odeh May Get New Trial, US Appeal Court Rules." *Electronic Intifada*, February 25, 2016. https://electronicintifada.net/blogs/charlotte-silver/rasmea-odeh-may-get-new-trial-us-appeal-court-rules.

Silver, Charlotte. "Rasmea Odeh Takes the Stand in Her Own Defense." *Electronic Intifada*, November 7, 2014. https://electronicintifada.net/blogs/charlotte-silver/rasmea-odeh-takes-stand-her-own-defense.

Silver, Charlotte. "Surrounded by Supporters, Rasmea Odeh Pleads Guilty." *Electronic Intifada*, April 25, 2017. https://electronicintifada.net/blogs/charlotte-silver/surrounded-supporters-rasmea-odeh-pleads-guilty.

Silver, Charlotte. "US Brings New Charges against Rasmea Odeh." *Electronic Intifada*, December 14, 2016. https://electronicintifada.net/blogs/charlotte-silver/us-brings-new-charges-against-rasmea-odeh.

Silver, Charlotte. "US Demands Long Prison Term for Rasmea Odeh, Based on Israeli Accusations." *Electronic Intifada*, February 26, 2015. https://electronicintifada.net/blogs/charlotte-silver/us-demands-long-prison-term-rasmea-odeh-based-israeli-accusations.

Silver, Charlotte. "US Government Focuses on 45-year-old Israeli Military Ruling in Trial of Rasmea Odeh." *Electronic Intifada*, November 6, 2014. https://electronicintifada.net/blogs/charlotte-silver/us-government-focuses-45-year-old-israeli-military-ruling-trial-rasmea-odeh.

Silver, Charlotte. "US Judge's Pro-Israel Activism Challenged in Palestinian Organizer's Deportation Trial." *Electronic Intifada*, July 19, 2014. https://electronicintifada.net/blogs/charlotte-silver/us-judges-pro-israel-activism-challenged-palestinian-organizers-deportation.

Smith, Kyle. "Meet the Terrorist Behind the Next Women's March." *New York Post*, February 25, 2017.

State of Israel Ministry of Defense. *Confidential document Gimmel (undated), declassified and retrieved July 8, 2014.* Transmitted to the U.S. Department of Justice by Apostile, August 28, 2014.

Stein, Rebecca. "Israeli Routes through Nakba Landscapes: An Ethnographic Meditation." *Jerusalem Quarterly* 43, (2010): 6–17.

Strauss, Robin. "Rasmea Odeh Conviction Part of US War on Dissent." *Freedom Socialist*, December 2014. https://socialism.com/fs-article/rasmea-odeh-conviction-part-of-us-war-on-dissent/.

Sundin, Jess. "Rasmea: We Will Be Strong." November 10, 2014. Video, 3:08. https:// www.youtube.com/watch?v=ieFeazVZ78Q.

"Supermarket Blast by Woman Who Wasn't There." *Jerusalem Post*, March 17, 1969.

"Supermarket Outrage." *Jerusalem Post*, February 29, 1969.

"Supersol Accused Turn Backs on Informer." *Jerusalem Post*, June 6, 1969

"Supersol and Cafeteria Indictments Laid." *Jerusalem Post*, May 12, 1969.

"Supersol Blast Suspects Held in Round-Up of 40." *Jerusalem Post*, March 2, 1969.

"Supersol Blast." *Jerusalem Post*, February 23, 1969.

"Supersol Crime Reconstructed." *Jerusalem Post*, March 3, 1969.

"Supersol Reopens; Business as Usual." *Jerusalem Post*, February 24, 1969.

"Supersol Saboteurs Sentenced to Life." *Jerusalem Post*, January 23, 1970.

"Supersol Victims Buried; Allon Promises Vengeance." *Jerusalem Post*, February 24, 1969.

"Suspects Held in Both U.K. Consulate Bombs." *Jerusalem Post*, March 14, 1969.

"Suspects of the Bombing." *Davar*, March 6, 1969.

Szremski, Kristin. "AAAN's Abudayyeh Struggles to Rebuild after Fire Guts Office." Washington Report on Middle East Affairs, January–February, 2002.

"Teenagers Jailed for Attempt on Supersol." *Jerusalem Post*, July 11, 1969.

teleSUR. "Palestinian Revolutionary Rasmea Odeh, Tortured in Israel, To Be Deported from US." teleSUR, April 6, 2017. https://www.telesurenglish.net/news/ Palestinian-Revolutionary-Rasmea-Odeh-Tortured-in-Israel-to-Be-Deported-from-US-20170406-0010.html.

Tell Your Tale, Little Bird. Directed by Arab Loutfi. Cairo: Cinema Maa. 1993. Video, 1:30:32. https://www.youtube.com/watch?v=wdkoxBjKM1Q.

"Terror Chain." *Jerusalem Post*, March 7, 1969.

"Terrorist-Held Israeli Freed for 76 Prisoners." *Jerusalem Post*, March 15, 1979.

Tessler, Mark A. *A History of the Israeli-Palestinian Conflict.* Bloomington: Indiana University Press, 1994.

"Testimony of the Father of the Main Defendant." *Hatzofeh*, June 6, 1969.

"There's Only One Women's Prison in Israel." *Business Insider*, April 12, 2018.

"Torture – Israel Replies." *Sunday Times*, July 3, 1977.

"Trial Begins of Supersol Accused." *Jerusalem Post*, June 5, 1969.

"Trial Due Soon of 143 Jerusalem Terror Suspects." *Jerusalem Post*, May 4, 1969.

"Two Passengers on Hijacked Plane Seriously Wounded; Terrorists Separate Jews and Non-Jews on Plane." *Jewish Telegraphic Agency*, May 11, 1972.

"University Bombing Suspects." *Jerusalem Post*, March 16, 1969.

United Nations General Assembly Special Committee to Investigate Israeli Practices Affecting the Human Rights of the Population of the Occupied Territories. *Report of the Special Committee to Investigate Israeli Practices Affecting the Human Rights of the Population of the Occupied Territories.* New York: United Nations General Assembly, 1977.

United States Department of State. *Country Reports on Human Rights Practices: Report Submitted to the Committee on International Relations, U.S. House of Representatives, and Committee on Foreign Relations, U.S. Senate.* Washington: U.S. Government Printing Office, 1978.

US Palestinian Community Network. "Call for Nakba Commemorations to Highlight Rasmea Odeh's Case." US Palestinian Community Network, May 2, 2014. https://uspcn.org/2014/05/02/call-for-nakba-commemorations-to-highlight-rasmea-odehs-case/.

US Palestinian Community Network. "Critical Ethnic Studies Association Supports Rasmea Odeh." US Palestinian Community Network, May 13, 2014. https://uspcn.org/2014/05/13/critical-ethnic-studies-association-supports-rasmea-odeh/.

US Palestinian Community Network. "Detroit U.S. Attorney Threatens Supporters of Rasmea Odeh." US Palestinian Community Network, October 6, 2016. https://uspcn.org/2014/10/06/detroit-u-s-attorney-threatens-supporters-of-rasmea-odeh/.

US Palestinian Community Network. "November 14, New York City: Emergency Action for Rasmea Odeh." US Palestinian Community Network, November 12, 2014. https://uspcn.org/2014/11/12/november-14-new-york-city-emergency-action-for-rasmea-odeh/.

US Palestinian Community Network. "November 4, San Jose: Justice for Rasmea Odeh." US Palestinian Community Network, November 3, 2014. https://uspcn.org/2014/11/03/november-4-san-jose-justice-for-rasmea-odeh/.

US Palestinian Community Network. Odeh Rally video, 40:26. April 25, 2017. https://www.facebook.com/watch/live/?v=1534229493278554.

US Palestinian Community Network. "On Rasmea's 70th Birthday, Read Her Speech from Oscar Lopez' Homecoming." US Palestinian Community Network, May 22, 2017. https://uspcn.org/2017/05/22/rasmeas-speech-for-oscar-lopez/.

US Palestinian Community Network. "Peace and Justice Committee of Episcopal Diocese of Chicago Stands in Solidarity with Rasmea Odeh." US Palestinian Community Network, March 28, 2014. https://uspcn.org/2014/03/28/peace-and-justice-committee-of-episcopal-diocese-of-chicago-stands-in-solidarity-with-rasmea-odeh/.

US Palestinian Community Network. "Rasmea's Sentencing March 12 – Need Letters for Leniency." US Palestinian Community Network, January 14, 2015. https://uspcn.org/2015/01/14/rasmeas-sentencing-march-12-need-letters-for-leniency/.

US Palestinian Community Network. "Rasmea Speech on IWD." US Palestinian Community Network, March 9, 2017. https://uspcn.org/2017/03/09/rasmea-iwd-jvp-tribune/.

US Palestinian Community Network. "Report: First Day of Rasmea Odeh Trial." US Palestinian Community Network, November 4, 2014. https://uspcn.org/2014/11/04/report-first-day-of-rasmea-odeh-trial/.

US Palestinian Community Network. "Report of Trial Day 3: Rasmea Takes the Stand." US Palestinian Community Network, November 6, 2014. https://uspcn.org/2014/11/06/report-on-trial-day-3-rasmea-takes-the-stand/.

US Palestinian Community Network. "USPCN Joins 50 Organizations to Stand against the Persecution of Palestinian American Activist Rasmea Odeh." US Palestinian Community Network, October 24, 2013. https://uspcn.org/2013/10/24/uspcn-joins-50-organizations-to-stand-against-the-persecution-of-palestinian-american-activist-rasmea-odeh/.

US Palestinian Community Network. "We Love You Rasmea." US Palestinian Community Network. September 20, 2017. Video, 1:51. https://www.facebook.

com/USPCN/videos/a-message-from-rasmeaodeh-to-her-supporters-and-we-love-you-rasmea-good-luck-on-/1686434638058038/.

"Victory: Bank Returns Abudayyeh Family Money, Government Involvement Alleged." *U.S. Palestinian Community News*, May 10, 2011.

Vilkomerson, Rebecca. "Letter to the Editor: Why JVP Invited Rasmea Odeh to Speak." *Forward*, March 24, 2017.

Wallsten, Peter. "Activists Cry Foul over FBI Probe." *Washington Post*, June 13, 2011.

Warikoo, Niraj. "Former Michigan Resident Rasmieh Odeh, Guilty of Immigration Charge, Deported to Jordan." *Detroit Free Press*, September 20, 2017.

Warikoo, Niraj. "Guilty Plea, Deportation End Terror Case against Former Michigan Woman." *Detroit Free Press*, April 25, 2017.

Warikoo, Niraj. "Palestinian Woman Guilty of Lying on Citizenship Papers." *Detroit Free Press*, November 10, 2014.

Warikoo, Niraj. "The Case of Rasmieh Odeh, 68, a Former Resident of Michigan, became a Flashpoint in the Debate over Israel." *Detroit Free Press*, February 25, 2016.

Warikoo, Niraj. "Woman Who Had Terror Conviction in Israel to Be Deported." *Detroit Free Press*, March 24, 2017.

Weil, Patrick. *The Sovereign Citizen: Denaturalization and the Origins of the American Republic.* Philadelphia: University of Pennsylvania Press, 2013.

Wessler, Seth Freed. "Is Denaturalization the Next Front in the Trump Administration's War on Immigration?" *New York Times Magazine*, December 19, 2018.

"When Plane Hijackings Were Palestinian Terrorists' Weapon of Choice." *Haaretz*, March 29, 2016.

White, Ed. "Jury Picked in Detroit Trial of Chicago Activist." *Associated Press*, November 4, 2014.

Wilhelm, Heather. "The Embarrassing Confusion of the 'Women's Strike.'" *Chicago Tribune*, February 23, 2017.

Wise, Alissa. "Why We Invited Rasmea Odeh to Our Conference." *Religion News Service*, March 28, 2017.

"Woman Claims She Led Supersol Explosion." *Jerusalem Post*, June 4, 1969.

"Women Beyond the Walls." *Haaretz*, September 30, 2006.

"Women's Magazine: Labor Day Focus on Immigrant Women (interview with Nadine Naber)." KPFA, September 1, 2014.

Women in Struggle. Directed by Canaan Khoury. Ramallah: Majd Production. 2004. Video, 56:33. https://www.youtube.com/watch?v=v0Va7-cNxf8.

Ya'ari, Ehud. "Israel's Prison Academies." *Atlantic*, October 1989, 22–30.

Ya'ari, Ehud. *Strike Terror: The Story of Fatah.* Translated by Esther Yaari. New York: Sabra Books, 1970.

Yamehi, Nasima. "Teaching and Training Issues in Palestine." *TESOL Quarterly* 40, no. 4 (2006): 861–65.

Zumbach, Lauren. "Lawyer: Palestinian Community Activist Unfairly Targeted." *Chicago Tribune*, November 12, 2013.

Index

8th Day Center 251

A

Abdo, Nahla (Arab feminist academic), 24, 70–71, 75, 225
Abdulmutallab, Umar Farouk ("underwear bomber"), 112
Abu Anni (interrogator), vii, 39, 57
Abudayyeh, Hatem (AAAN, executive director), 94, 102–3, 106, 111, 114–15, 117, 121–23, 127, 158, 161, 169, 193, 196–97, 202, 207
Abu-Hadiga, Khalil (PFLP leader), 56
Abu Tor, 43
activism, political, 21, 95, 108–9, 116, 151
activists, 88, 99, 100, 101, 105, 109, 115, 140, 161–62, 165, 168, 178, 193, 194, 202, 206
African American, 3, 107, 121, 124, 178
Ahituv, Avraham (Director, Shin Bet), 82
Al-Ahliyya University, 88
al-Ahmad, Shaykh Qasim, 12
Air France (Flight 139 hijacking), 19, 79, 81
Al Ismailia Film Festival, 7
Allon, Deputy Premier Yigal, 27–28
American Civil Liberties Union (ACLU), 107
AmeriCorps (Domestic Peace Corps), 94, 95–96
amicus curiae, 180
Amin, Idi (Uganda dictator), 81
Amman, Jordan, 7, 9, 18, 28m 43, 48–50, 59, 87–90, 91, 142, 144, 145, 159, 231, 232
Amnesty International, 35, 45, 125
Amram, Avraham (Israeli soldier), 83, 84
Anglican Bishop of Jerusalem, 43
Anglican Church, 51
anti-Semitism, 16, 66
Antonius, Soraya (Lebanese journalist), 6, 18, 36, 58, 69, 88, 131
Arab American Action Network (AAAN), 94–96, 98, 100, 102–3, 106, 108, 111, 115, 129, 153, 158, 182, 202
Arab Community Center, 94
Arab Nationalist Movement (ANM), 15–16, 18, 31, 91, 99, 115

Arab states, 12, 237
Arab Women's Committee, 95–100, 103, 152, 153, 158
al-Arabia University, 18, 100
Arafat, Yasser (Palestinian National Authority, President), 17, 21, 22
Armed Forces of National Liberation (FALN), 206
assassinations, 62, 66, 215
Associated Press, 116

B

Baader, Andreas (Red Army Faction leader), 80
Balfour Declaration, 11
Barak, Ehud (10th Israeli Prime Minister), 78
Begin, Menachim (cabinet minister), 28, 83, 212
Beit HaKerem, 11
Benedek, David (psychologist), 254
Ben-Gurion Airport, 78
Ben-Gurion, David (1st Israeli Prime Minister), 14
Bergman, Ronen (Israeli journalist), 46
Bernawi, Fatima (activist), 88
Biden, Joe (46th US President), 5
Bir Zeit University, 212
al-Bireh, 7, 14, 16, 29–32, 38, 42, 54, 61, 89, 213–14, 219
Black, Ian (*Guardian* journalist), 212
Black Panthers, 111
Black September, 19, 77–79
Borman, Honorable Paul D. (judge), 110–11, 119–24, 130
British Consulate, 6, 28, 35, 51, 57–58, 61, 131, 186
British Mandate, 11, 14, 53, 115, 210, 233
British Mandatory Palestine, 12
Buraq Revolt, 12

C

Camp David accords, 83
Canaan Khoury, Buthina (film maker), 7

Carlos the Jackal (Ilich Ramirez Sanchez)
(terrorist), 82
central police station, Jerusalem 30, 40; *see also*
Russian Compound, Moskobiya
character witness, 151–52
Chicago Cultural Alliance, 98, 99, 103, 115,
152
Chicago Human Relations Council, 98
civil denaturalization, 196, 201
Clore, Raymond (government witness), 90,
144–45
cognitive filtering, 184, 191
Cohen, Eli (Israeli attorney), 54
Communist Party, 91–92, 137
Congregation Shaarey Zedek, 121
Council on American–Islamic Relations, 109
Cunningham, Dennis (lawyer), 137

D

Damascus, 83, 85
Damascus Gate, 26
Damascus University, 48
Daubert hearing, 182
Davis, Angela (political activist), 140, 206
Dayan, Moshe (Israeli Defense Minister), 26, 51,
78
Deir Yassin, 10, 13, 212–13
Democratic Front for the Liberation of Palestine,
47, 75
denaturalization, 137, 196, 201
Department of Homeland Security, 103, 109, 137,
142, 167, 171, 197
Dershowitz, Alan (professor), 44
Detroit, Michigan, 93, 106, 110–11, 124, 126, 129,
136–37, 163, 170, 192–93, 197
Deutsch, Michael (defense attorney), 111, 113–16,
119–20, 122, 124–27, 129–30, 132–35, 137,
139–45, 147, 149, 151–58, 160, 163, 165–71,
174–75, 179, 181–82, 187–89, 191, 195–201,
203–4
reprimanded, 139
Downton, Eric (foreign correspondent),
48
Drain, Judge Gershwin, 124, 126–28, 132, 134,
136–39, 153, 169–73, 176–77, 179–82,
184–85, 193, 195, 198–200

E

Eban, Abba (Israeli Foreign Minister), 28
El Al airlines, 19, 24, 48, 76,
el-Khairy, Bashir (attorney), 43
Entebbe Airport, 19, 81–82, 187
ethnic cleansing, 174
evidentiary hearing, 133–34

F

Fatah (formerly the Palestinian National
Liberation Movement), 23, 28–29, 31, 75,
82, 88
fedayeen, 23, 32, 77, 79, 80, 82
Fennerty, James (lawyer), 105–6, 108–11, 113–14,
117, 119, 129–30, 137, 147–48, 160, 172,
201, 203–4
"Fernandez, Miss," 76–77
Fifth Amendment, 124, 140
First Intifada, 100, 115
Forces of Colombia (FARC), 101–2
Fred Butzel Award, 119, 121
Freedom Road Socialist Organization (FRSO), 101
Fuerzas Armadas de Liberación Nacional, *see*
Armed Forces of National Liberation,
FALN

G

general intent, 132, 134, 180, 182–83
General Security Service, 45–46, 55; *see also* Shin
Bet, Shabak
Glover, Danny (actor), 179
Goldman, Emma (anarchist), 4
Goodman, Ernest (lawyer), 137
Goodman, William (lawyer), 119, 137, 193
Grand Rapids, Michigan, 101, 106
guerrilla activity, 6–8, 17–19, 22–24, 28, 48, 49,
61, 67, 74, 76–81, 83, 88, 92, 100
Gutheil, Dr. Thomas (Harvard professor of
psychiatry and the law), 190

H

Habash, George (ANM cofounder), 15–16, 18,
22–23

Trump Administration, 2, 5, 192
Trump, Donald (45th US President), 191
Tsemel, Leah (lawyer), 224
Tukel, Jonathan (assistant US attorney), 107, 108, 112, 126–27, 134, 137, 142–43, 145, 151–54, 158–60, 163–66, 168–70, 172, 175, 181, 189, 190, 192, 196–97

U

United Nations, 12, 14
United States Palestinian Community Network (USPCN), 109
U.S. Supreme Court, 4, 182

V

Vesey, Denmark (Black American leader), 174

W

Wailing Wall, 11
Walter Reed National Military Medical Center, 184
Wayne County, Michigan, 136
Webber, Stephen (Special Agent, Department of Homeland Security), 137–38, 142–44, 167
Weizman, Ezer (Defense Minister), 84
West Bank, 14, 16–19, 21, 22, 24, 42, 43, 47–50, 52–53, 56, 59, 83, 85, 87, 89, 99, 100, 115, 118, 121, 126, 198, 213, 214
West Germany, 80, 81
Williams, Jennifer (adjudication officer), 93, 138, 148, 156, 163, 164, 189
Wise, Rabbi Alissa, 194
Works Agency for Palestine (UNRWA), 15
World War I, 4, 11
World War II, 4